THE OXFORD ILLUSTRATED HISTORY OF

SHAKESPEARE

ON STAGE

The Globe

A BOOK IN HONOUR OF

STANLEY WELLS

THE OXFORD
ILLUSTRATED HISTORY OF
SHAKESPEARE
ON STAGE

EDITED BY
JONATHAN BATE
AND
RUSSELL JACKSON

OXFORD
UNIVERSITY PRESS

OXFORD
UNIVERSITY PRESS

Oxford University Press, Walton Street, Oxford ox2 6dp*dp*
Oxford New York
Athens Auckland Bangkok Bombay
Kolhata Cape Town Dar es Salaam Delhi
Florence Hong Kong Istanbul Karachi
Kuala Lumpur Madras Madrid Melbourne
Mexico City Nairobi Paris Shanghai Singapore
Taipei Tokyo Toronto
and associated companies in
Berlin Ibadan

Oxford is a trade mark of Oxford University Press

Published in the United States
by Oxford University Press Inc., New York

First published as Shakespeare: An Illustrated Stage History 1996

First published as an Oxford University Press paperback 2001

British Library Cataloguing in Publication Data
Data available

Library of Congress Cataloging in Publication Data
Shakespeare: an illustrated stage history/edited by Jonathan Bate
and Russell Jackson
Includes bibliographical references and index.
1. Shakespeare, William, 1564-1616—Stage history--England.
2. Shakespeare, William, 1564-1616—Dramatic production.
3. Theater—England—History.
I. Bate, Jonathan.   II. Jackson, Russell, 1949-
PR3106.S48   1996
792.9'5—dc20   95-12059

ISBN 0-19-280213-5

1 3 5 7 9 10 8 6 4 2

Printed in Spain by
Bookprint S. L., Barcelona

Preface & Acknowledgements

THIS book was conceived, and all the chapters in it specially commissioned, in honour of the distinguished Shakespearian scholar, Stanley Wells. All the contributors are colleagues, friends, or former students of Professor Wells. In all his work—as general editor of the Oxford Shakespeare and editor of individual plays, as author of essays, reviews, and books (notably *Royal Shakespeare* and *Shakespeare: A Dramatic Life*), as editor of the journal *Shakespeare Survey*, as Director of the Shakespeare Institute and Professor of Shakespeare Studies at the University of Birmingham, as a governor of the Royal Shakespeare Company—Stanley Wells has been unswerving in his commitment to the distinctively *theatrical* life of Shakespeare's plays and to the interests of playgoers and those whom the editors of the First Folio of Shakespeare's works called 'the great variety of readers'. It therefore seemed to us that the most appropriate tribute was not some dusty academic *Festschrift*, but rather a book written to please and inform all who are interested in Shakespeare on the stage.

But the publication of this book is fitting to its time as well as its origin. The end of the fourth century during which Shakespeare has held the stage is an excellent moment for a retrospective survey, especially since the discipline of theatre history has in recent years been transformed. Older stage histories, such as G. C. D. Odell's once-standard *Shakespeare from Betterton to Irving*, tended to consist of dry catalogues of performance details and snippets from reviews; in contrast, the chapters of this book draw on many kinds of evidence—from archaeology to political polemic to painting—in order to demonstrate how the history of Shakespeare on the stage has always been bound up with wider histories and broader cultural changes. The introduction elaborates upon the range of approaches employed. Our one regret in planning the book was that, in order to keep it within bounds, we have largely had to restrict ourselves to *English* theatre: all the world has become Shakespeare's stage, but it would have been impossible to do justice to the history of his international life in a single book— perhaps one day soon new technologies will allow for the assembly of an archive providing material for this much larger project. It would, however, have been parochial to ignore the international dimension altogether, so one chapter is devoted to some case- studies in the cross-fertilization between various Shakespeares on the English and European stages.

Illustration is essential to a book about the stage, and we have accordingly attempted to integrate visual material closely with discussions in the text; many of the pictures are concentrated on a small number of key plays, in order to illustrate how the same work has been reimagined in different periods and styles. The editors are deeply grateful to the institutions and individuals cited in the List of Illustrations for providing photographs and for permission to reproduce copyright material in their collections. Particular thanks are due to Roger and Marian Pringle of the Shakespeare Birthplace Trust for sharing in the tribute to Stanley Wells by greatly reducing fees for the reproduction of material in the Shakespeare Centre, Stratford-upon-Avon, and to the late Professor Kenneth Muir for facilitating a grant towards the cost of illustrations from the Davenport Fund of the Liverpool University English Department. For various forms of assistance, we would like to thank Ingeborg Boltz, Susan Brock, Cheek by Jowl, Sally Homer, Richard Mangan, Sonia Massai, Niky Rathbone, Christopher Robinson, Linda Rosenberg, Claude Schumacher, Tamar Thomas, and Andrew Lockett, Edwin Pritchard, Vicki Reeve, Kim Scott Walwyn, and Frances Whistler at Oxford University Press.

R.J.

J.B.

Contents

List of Illustrations

Colour Plates

(Between pages 50–51 and 66–67)

For permission to reproduce copyright material, grateful acknowledgement is made to the institutions and individuals cited in parenthesis.

Contributors

JONATHAN BATE, *University of Liverpool*

RUSSELL JACKSON, *The Shakespeare Institute, University of Birmingham*

ANTHONY DAVIES, *Stratford-Upon-Avon*

DAME JUDI DENCH

MICHAEL DOBSON, *University of Surrey Roehampton*

INGA-STINA EWBANK, *University of Leeds*

R. A. FOAKES, *University of California, Los Angeles*

PETER HOLLAND, *The Shakespeare Institute, University of Birmingham*

ROBERT SMALLWOOD, *The Shakespeare Birthplace Trust*

PETER THOMSON, *University of Exeter*

MARTIN WIGGINS, *The Shakespeare Institute, University of Birmingham*

Introduction

JONATHAN BATE

> The Stage is one great source of public amusement, not to say instruction. A good play, well acted, passes away a whole evening delightfully at a certain period of life, agreeably at all times; we read the account of it next morning with pleasure, and it generally furnishes one leading topic of conversation for the afternoon. The disputes on the merits or defects of the last new piece, or of a favourite performer, are as common, as frequently renewed, and carried on with as much eagerness and skill, as those on almost any other subject.

So begins the preface to William Hazlitt's collection of 'dramatic criticisms', *A View of the English Stage*, published in 1818. It is a passage which ought to speak for readers of this book as well as Hazlitt's: in our formative years we may take a particular delight in the theatre; we go to see Shakespeare for pleasure and to be instructed in human behaviour (sometimes also as instruction towards our formal studies); with our friends, we like to compare productions with others we have seen and to discuss the merits and failings of the major players; we read reviews by professional critics in the newspapers as a continuation of that dialogue. A good way of beginning to consider the history of Shakespeare on the English stage is to ask whether Hazlitt's sentiments would have been recognizable to a playgoer in the dramatist's own time, just over two centuries earlier, in the same way that they hold good for playgoers in our time, nearly two centuries later.

In the medieval era, pageants dramatizing biblical stories were performed for the amusement and instruction of citizens at certain festive times of year in many major English cities. In the sixteenth century there emerged for the first time in England a public, secular drama. Travelling players made some of this drama available across the nation, but by the end of Queen Elizabeth's reign Londoners—who formed an increasingly large proportion of the population—had the benefit of something new: purpose-built theatres open daily (save on Sundays) for most of the year (save in times of plague, when they were closed for risk of infection), performing a wide repertory of plays. Once you have a theatre building, you can charge an entrance fee; once you have an established personnel, a name (and a patron) for your company, and a repertoire, you have a theatrical profession. In all these essentials, the English stage emerged in something resembling its modern form during Shakespeare's lifetime. Furthermore, Shakespeare himself was the age's most successful all-round man of the theatre: he was founding shareholder, house dramatist, and actor with the company who in 1603 gained the ultimate accolade of patronage, the title King's Men. He himself, as Martin Wiggins notes in Chapter 2, was a member of the first 'Royal Shakespeare Company'.

Among our earliest images of the Shakespearian

FIG. 1 The City of London, detail from John Norden's panorama, *Civitas Londini* (1600). The two prominent theatres on the south bank of the Thames are the Beargarden to the right and the Swan towards the left; the Rose and the Globe are hidden among the trees to the extreme right.

theatre is that of the newly established playhouses standing on the south bank of the river Thames in John Norden's panoramic representation of 'the moste Famous City LONDON' in 1600 (fig. 1). The Globe (built in 1599) and Rose (1587) nestle in obscurity among trees to the right, but the Swan (1595) and the Beargarden (bought by the actor Edward Alleyn in 1594, rebuilt as the Hope in 1614) stand out clearly as the tallest buildings on Bankside. What is most striking about the location of the theatres is that they are virtually in the country—the densely populated city lies across the river, whilst open fields dominate the foreground of the picture. Another theatre, at Newington Butts, was further out in St George's Fields, while those north of the river, the Theatre (1576) and the Curtain (1577) in Shoreditch, the Fortune (1600) and Red Bull (1604) to the north-west, were some way along the roads leading out of the city in the opposite direction. For anyone living in the city centre, going to the theatre involved a considerable journey—from certain parts of London the walk would take as long as a train or bus ride to Stratford-upon-Avon today.

These locations on the margins of the metropolis, beyond the jurisdiction of the puritanically inclined city fathers who controlled local London politics from the Guildhall, provide striking evidence that Shakespeare's theatre was associated with amusement more than instruction. Defenders of the stage, such as the dramatist Thomas Heywood, argued that by showing the fall of tyrants and usurpers, and the punishment of villains, the drama incited its spectators to obedience, loyalty, and good behaviour. But in practice a steady stream of official complaint suggests that the theatres were associated with licentiousness, absenteeism from work (the arenas being outdoors and without artificial lighting, performances took place in the afternoon), and the danger of discontent or riot which is always attendant upon large crowds in public places. As the name of the Beargarden reminds us, the liberties south of the river were also the place of 'lowbrow' forms of amusement such as bear- and bull-baiting (fig. 2). And some of the buildings near the theatres in the Norden engraving were undoubtedly brothels.

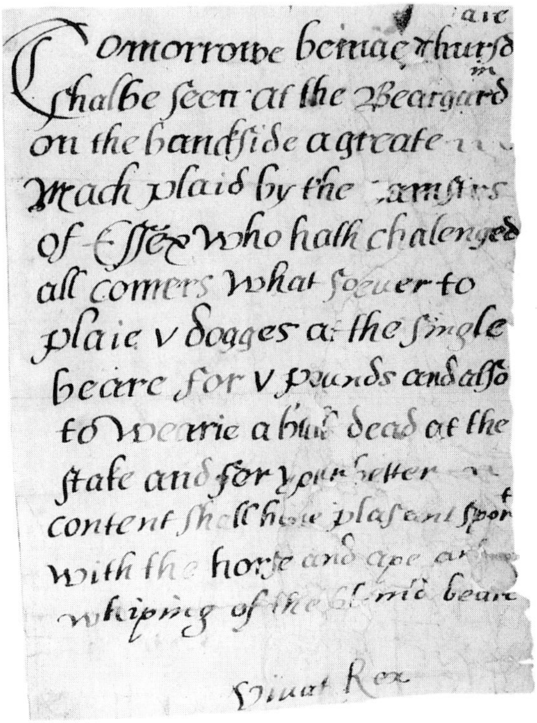

FIG. 2 A bill advertising a bear-baiting: plays would have been announced in similar fashion.

We can certainly assume that 'the merits or defects of the last new piece, or of a favourite performer' would have been a lively topic of conversation on the walk back over London Bridge and in the tavern during the evening after the show. But what the Elizabethan playgoer could not do was 'read the account of [the play] next morning with pleasure': daily newspapers and weekly magazines only emerged in the eighteenth century, so there was no equivalent of the review, that staple resource for the theatre historian. For a time, Hazlitt made his living as primarily a theatre reviewer; he was one of the first so to do. At least until the Restoration, we can only get a sense of the 'buzz' about plays and players by piecing together fragments of evidence—dedicatory poems and epitaphs, prologues and epilogues, allusions in other plays, letters, and pamphlets, a few sparse accounts in commonplace books (notably those of the astrologer Simon Forman). On the basis of this kind of material, parts of Chapter 1 and all of Chapter 2 of this book explore the ongoing life of Shakespeare's plays in the Elizabethan, Jacobean, and Caroline periods, and during the Cromwellian years when the London theatres were closed.

The notion of the drama providing both amusement and instruction has a long history, going back to classical times: the art of poetry, said Horace, is to profit and to please (*aut prodesse, aut delectare*). In his dedicatory poem prefacing the First Folio of Shakespeare's plays (1623), Ben Jonson, who had set himself up as the English Horace, praised the 'Sweet swan of Avon' for elevating the national drama to the extent that it outshone even that of ancient Greece and Rome. The poem ends with an image of Shakespeare living on in the form of a stellar influence who will 'chide or cheer the drooping stage'. The image is prophetic in that ever since the reopening of the theatres at the Restoration of the monarchy in 1660, Shakespeare has been the central figure in the repertory. From the 1660s until the 1830s only two London theatres had the royal patent allowing for the performance of spoken ('legitimate') drama. As Chapters 3 to 5 show, a constant theme during this period was rivalry for possession and novel performance of Shakespeare between figures associated with the two houses—Davenant versus Killigrew, then Garrick versus Barry, then Kemble versus Kean. And when the licensing system collapsed, it was largely because the 'illegitimate' theatres had found ways round it by performing Shakespeare in adapted form, mimed, sung, or danced.

The claim that a new production had greater 'authenticity' than that of a rival company was often a weapon in the wars between the theatres. Charles Macklin in the mid-eighteenth century, John Philip Kemble in the early nineteenth, and William Poel in the late nineteenth all made innovations in the name of a return to historical accuracy. That the proper due to Shakespeare's 'classic' status is a reverence which respects his original language, staging, and costuming is a powerful view, still manifest in the hostility which many playgoers feel towards 'modern-dress' productions and 'tampering with the text'. But a stronger argument is that Shakespeare's 'classic' status

has been created by the very processes of adaptation and mutation. It is these which keep him alive. A so-called 'authentic' production is just another new mutation.

Adaptation is a constant theme in this book. Chapter 1 examines changing acting styles in relation to changing theatrical conditions in Shakespeare's own time; Chapter 2 shows how in *The Woman's Prize, or The Tamer Tamed* John Fletcher initiated the tradition of 'adapting' Shakespearian material in the form of a sequel; Chapters 3 to 6 trace the long history of full-scale adaptation from the late seventeenth century to the early nineteenth (a history exemplified by the long-standing popularity of Nahum Tate's *King Lear* with a happy ending); Chapter 7 broadens the focus to Europe, using Ibsen and Brecht as case-studies of later dramatists who have responded to Shakespeare by adapting aspects of his work in their own. The majority of the productions analysed in the remaining chapters, on the twentieth century, are 'true' to Shakespeare's text, but their innovations of style, design, and directorial vision (the particular focus of Chapter 10) make them adaptations in their way as radically different from their 'originals' as anything produced in the Restoration. It is sometimes said to be deplorable that Jan Kott's *Angst*-ridden critical study *Shakespeare our Contemporary*[1] influenced many of the hard-edged, 'Theatre of Cruelty' productions of the 1960s, but it has always been the case that Shakespeare has amused and instructed on the stage by being made contemporary. As example after example shows, from the constitutional crises of 1678–85 to the Regency to the Thatcher decade, productions have engaged with topical politics and the *mores* of their age.

Furthermore, distinctions between different theatrical traditions are often bound up with wider cultural divisions. Chapters 9 and 12 examine aspects of the postwar Shakespearian stage in this light. The current position is that two major companies, the Royal Shakespeare Company and the National Theatre (now known as the Royal National Theatre), rely on considerable subsidy from the public purse; this, combined with their high ticket prices, means that they cater for a predominantly 'cultured' audience and that the forms of socio-political critique they express remain within the bounds of liberal dissent. They are in this sense comparable to the old patent or 'legitimate' theatres. The smaller touring companies, whose grants are smaller and ticket prices lower, who often perform in sports halls and other venues that have less of a 'middle-class' stamp than the big London and Stratford theatres, are more like the non-patents or 'illegitimates' and they are accordingly more radical in their liberties of both interpretation and critique. In the 1960s, a decade when there was a Labour government, the RSC could produce their highly Brechtian *Wars of the Roses* (for the German influence see Chapter 7), but by the 1980s, their main house shows were all too often bland tourist-pleasers with lavish design (this was the time when the Andrew Lloyd Webber musical was the paradigm of economically successful theatrical production). In the Thatcher years it was left to the touring English Shakespeare Company to produce a modern-dress, politically alert cycle of history plays. Equally, if one is looking for a production which is challenging in its reflection of the sexual and racial politics of late twentieth-century Britain, one would do better to go to Cheek by Jowl than the National Theatre (though in 1995 a woman, Fiona Shaw, played Richard II at the National under the direction of another woman, Deborah Warner).

Our procedure throughout this book will be to prefer case-studies to broad overviews, to examine exemplary productions and key developments in some detail. Thus, for example, Peter Holland in Chapter 4 focuses on five representative Garrick performances (*Hamlet*, *Romeo and Juliet*, *A Midsummer Night's Dream*, *King Lear*, and *Macbeth*) and Tony Davies in Chapter 8 pays special attention to such seminal productions as John Gielgud's 1935 *Romeo and Juliet* and Peter Brook's 1955 *Titus Andronicus*. For my purposes here, Cheek by Jowl's much-praised *As You Like It* (1991–5) provides an excellent test-case in the relationship between authenticity and contemporaneity in Shakespearian production. In many respects it was remarkably authentic to what we know of the Elizabethan theatre. It eschewed those Restoration innovations of proscenium arch and realistic scenery, returning to the open, empty stage that characterized the Globe. The journey to Arden of Rosalind / Ganymede, Celia / Aliena, and Touchstone was simply but most evocatively represented by their walking round and round the bare boards: the language and the action were enough to tell us we were in the forest; we needed no property trees. Roles were doubled economically, as they would have been by Shakespeare's Chamberlain's Men (the same actor played both bad and good Dukes, in vigorously contrasting styles). Dress was modern, but more colourful and larger than life than that of everyday— as it would have been in the 1590s, when costumes included the cast-off robes of courtiers, second-hand wear, but still of a lavishness beyond the purse of most playgoers. Cheek by Jowl's costume designer chose stiff evening dress for the scenes at court, whereas the forest brought out bright primary colours: the use of colour symbolism was widespread in Renaissance drama (Hamlet's inky cloak denoting melancholy, Malvolio's narcissistic yellow stockings). Certain touches of costuming, however, hinted at historical authenticity—Touchstone wore different coloured socks, in allusion to the Fool's motley. In this sense, there was an eclecticism of dress analogous to that suggested by the earliest surviving illustration of Shakespeare, Henry Peacham's drawing of *Titus Andronicus*, in which Titus wears a Roman toga and Tamora a medieval-looking robe, whereas the men-at-arms are 'modern-dress' Elizabethan halberdiers (fig. 3).

The style of performance was pacey and irreverent, with frequent direct addresses to the audience and occasional improvised interjections on the part of Touchstone. It was, in Peter Brook's phrase, Rough Theatre, and in this it was true to the Elizabethan theatre:

It is always the popular theatre that saves the day. Through the ages it has taken many forms, and there is only one factor that they all have in common—a roughness. . . . The arsenal is limitless: the aside, the placard, the topical reference, the local jokes, the exploiting of accidents, the songs, the dances, the tempo, the noise, the relying on contrasts, the shorthand of exaggeration, the false noses, the stock types, the stuffed bellies. The popular theatre, freed of unity of style, actually speaks a very sophisticated and stylish language: a popular audience usually has no difficulty in accepting inconsistencies of accent and dress, or in darting between mime and dialogue, realism and suggestion.[2]

The show was as the audience liked it: an Elizabethan pun one moment, a bunch of flowers used as an interviewer's microphone the next. The authenticity was ultimately in the spirit, not the particulars; there was not a jot of antiquarian 'reconstruction'.

Meanwhile, a lighting design of a technological sophistication only possible in the late twentieth century made a major contribution to the atmospheric effect. Declan Donnellan's directorial conception was deeply and committedly of our time in its unabashed celebration of gay desire (manifested for instance when Le Beau touched up Orlando on the line 'I shall desire more love and knowledge of you') and homosocial bonding (Jaques was persuasively wooed back into the group at the very end). The most original feature of the production was very authentic in one respect but very contemporary in another: the cast was all male but Rosalind was played by a black actor, Adrian Lester. The Peacham drawing includes the figure of Aaron, a reminder that there are black roles in Shakespeare, but these would originally have been played by blacked-up white actors, as Othello has continued to be played for most of his English stage history. The giving of a 'white' Shakespearian lead to a black British actor remains a novelty even in the multiracial 1990s.

The original Rosalind would, like all Shakespeare's female leads, have been a 'boy'—I place the term in inverted commas, since it is slightly misleading when we note that, though boys entered their apprenticeship with the adult companies between the ages of 10 and 13, they might continue playing female roles to the age of 19 or even, in one recorded case, 21. Cheek by Jowl gave modern audiences a very rare opportunity to experience something similar to the Elizabethan convention of watching males play females. The extraordinary thing about Adrian Lester was that, with his beautiful voice and grace of movement, when he played the female Rosalind playing at being the male Ganymede he seemed more like a woman playing a man than a man playing a woman. And when he played at Rosalind playing Ganymede playing Rosalind, one simply gave up trying to work out in one's mind whether one thought he was a woman playing a man playing a woman or a man playing a woman playing a man playing a

FIG. 3 Henry Peacham's sketch of *Titus Andronicus*. Two passages from the text are transcribed below, suggesting that the image is a composite representation of the moment in the first act when Tamora pleads for her son's life and that in the last when Aaron exalts in his own villainy.

woman. When the text drew attention to the idea of the male actor, as in the epilogue, one thought about it, but for much of the time the audience was held so spellbound by the strength and the wit and the pain of Rosalind that the actor's gender was forgotten. Some feminists condemned the production, arguing that by flaunting its drag it reduced the play to a homosexual romp; a campy Celia and an obviously cross-dressed Phebe provided hostages to such an attack, but the androgynous delicacy and subtlety of Lester's Rosalind (together with the affectionate exuberance of Richard Cant's bimboish Audrey) seemed to me to nullify it.

'Seemed to me': there's the rub with theatrical criticism. Critical debate can only operate effectively when the object of knowledge—playtext, poem, painting, novel, musical score—is there in front of us as a constant point of reference. But 'the player's art', as Hazlitt says later in his preface to *A View*, 'is one that perishes with him, and leaves no traces of itself, but in the faint descriptions of the pen or pencil' (p. vii). 'How eagerly', he continues, 'do we stop to look at the prints from Zoffany's pictures of Garrick'—but a picture freezes a moment and can do nothing to summon up the ebb and flow of a performance. As Russell Jackson shows in Chapter 6, it was a feature of many Victorian productions to highlight key moments of spectacle in the form of tableaux which resembled paintings framed by the proscenium arch, but even such moments only have meaning in the wider context of performance. A print after Zoffany or Wilson tells us something about Garrick's Macbeth or Lear (figs. 33, 30), but it is as partial a reproduction as a photograph of the Cheek by Jowl *As You Like It* (fig. 101)—evidence of this kind cannot do enough to convince us of the greatness of a performance we have not seen ourselves. If you did not see Adrian Lester's Rosalind, you are in no position to argue with my assertion of its excellence. A modern production may be transferred to the medium of video, but it is only with those which rely on an enclosed, boxed-in atmosphere—such as Trevor Nunn's *Macbeth* starring Ian McKellen and Judi Dench—that the experience of watching the video can even remotely reproduce the experience of watching the play. And even here

judgements may vary: to my spectator's eyes, the video caught much of the power of Judi Dench's stage performance, but she herself says in Chapter 11, 'I thought that I had given a much better performance of Lady Macbeth on stage than the one I saw'.

The strokes of the pen can perhaps do more than any two-dimensional visual recreation to give imaginative access to theatre at its most riveting. The best drama critics can intuit, and in so doing further, major new developments in acting style and theatrical vision. Hazlitt did so when he hailed the advent of Edmund Kean as an epiphany (see Chapter 5); Kenneth Tynan did so in his review of Peter Brook's Kott-influenced *King Lear* with Paul Scofield:

Lay him to rest, the royal Lear with whom generations of star actors have made us reverently familiar; the majestic ancient, wronged and maddened by his vicious daughters; the felled giant, beside whose bulk the other characters crouch like pygmies. Lay also to rest the archaic notion that Lear is automatically entitled to our sympathy because he is a king who suffers.

A great director (Peter Brook) has scanned the text with fresh eyes and discovered a new protagonist—not the booming, righteously indignant Titan of old, but an edgy, capricious old man, intensely difficult to live with. In short, he has dared to direct *King Lear* from a standpoint of moral neutrality.

The results are revolutionary.[3]

Hazlitt never saw Garrick, but his prose can still give a glimpse of another great Lear:

once, when GARRICK was acting Lear, the spectators in the front row of the pit, not being able to see him well in the kneeling scene, where he utters the curse, rose up, when those behind them, not willing to interrupt the scene by remonstrating, immediately rose up too, and in this manner, the whole pit rose up, without uttering a syllable, and so that you might hear a pin drop. At another time, the crown of straw which he wore in the same character fell off, or was discomposed, which would have produced a burst of laughter at any common actor to whom such an accident had happened; but such was the deep interest in the character, and such the power of rivetting the attention possessed by this actor, that not the slightest notice was taken of the circumstance, but the whole audience remained bathed in silent tears. The knowledge of circumstances like these, serves to keep alive the memory of past excellence, and to stimulate future efforts.   (*View*, p. ix)

(To move the audience to tears was, as Peter Holland points out in Chapter 4, the chief aim of Garrick's performance as Lear.)

Hazlitt's two stories are in the venerable genre of the theatrical anecdote. Usually spoken in a personal voice, sometimes questionable as to their precise veracity, such anecdotes serve, as Hazlitt says, to keep alive the memory of dramatic excellence. Chapter 8 includes a sampling of them from the age of that great trio, Olivier, Gielgud, and Ashcroft; Chapter 11 is a speaking of some of them in the very voice of one of the great actors of our age, Dame Judi Dench. Actors' reminiscences from the past, such as Sarah Siddons's 'Remarks on the Character of Lady Macbeth', have proved to be an invaluable resource for later researchers: we include Dame Judi's account of her career in Shakespeare for this reason and in order to give the reader an insider's view of some part of our history.

Our great difficulty in reanimating the theatre of Shakespeare's own time is that we have very little in the way of either illustration or anecdote and nothing

FIG. 4 Robert Armin, company clown for the Chamberlain's / King's Men in the middle of Shakespeare's career.

at all in the voice of the great actors such as Richard Burbage. The Peacham drawing is the only 'illustration' of Shakespeare from the dramatist's own time, but—though probably influenced by an awareness of theatrical convention—it is almost certainly based on a reading rather than a viewing of *Titus Andronicus*.[4] The nearest we can get to a pictorial representation of a moment in an original Shakespearian staging is probably the figure of Robert Armin engraved on the title-page of the actor's own play, *The History of the Two Maids of Mortlake* (1609, fig. 4). Armin was the original Touchstone, Feste, and Lear's Fool; although his costume here is that of the simpleton or 'natural' fool, not the court jester, his confident pose, hands on hips, head quizzically to one side and feet spread wide, might just be that of Feste baiting Olivia or the Fool telling Lear some hard home truths.

Still, a mass of other evidence survives to tell us about the day-to-day life of the Elizabethan theatre. The first scholarly treatment of it was Edmond Malone's 'Historical Account of the English Stage', included in his 1790 edition of Shakespeare. The principal elements of our perception of the Elizabethan stage are there in Malone: the roots in mystery and morality plays, the construction of permanent playhouses in London during the later sixteenth century, the contribution to the dramatist's art of the university wits, royal patronage, the distinction between public and private theatres (Globe and Blackfriars), the pit and the gallery, the 'above' space, the bare stage, the clown's improvisations, the boy actors for women's roles. Malone also reproduced a line-drawing of the Globe, based on a sketch by one Revd Mr Henley, deriving from J. C. Visscher's 1616 panorama of London. Visscher based his panorama on Norden's, but added some nice embellishments such as smoking chimneys. He was inattentive to accuracy, placing the Globe nearer to the river than it actually was, but his image of the theatres with little figures standing outside them is the most pleasing evocation we have of playgoers in Shakespeare's London (fig. 5).

The surviving documents that are most valuable to the historian of Elizabethan theatre are those relating

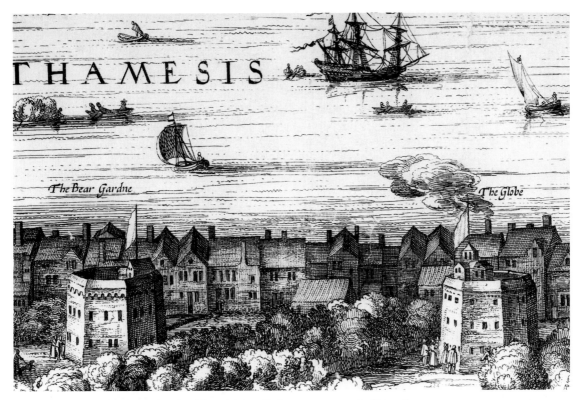

FIG. 5 The Globe and the Beargarden, detail from J. C. Visscher's panorama, engraved in 1616 but adapted from Norden's of 1600.

to Philip Henslowe's Rose Theatre, where some of Shakespeare's early plays were performed. They tell us a great deal about the commercial side of the theatrical profession, about the enormous success of certain works (Kyd's *Spanish Tragedy* and Marlowe's *Jew of Malta* are revived again and again), about the frequency with which new plays were introduced into the repertory, about the purchase of props and costumes, about the instability of the companies in the early 1590s before the reorganization in the summer of 1594 when there emerged for the first time the pattern of the Admiral's Men—with the Marlowe repertory—at the Rose and the Chamberlain's Men—with the Shakespeare repertory—north of the river at the Theatre (until they moved back across London Bridge, timbers and all, to build the Globe in 1599).[5] But an owner-manager's business papers are no substitute for details of stage and performance. As Hazlitt complained in his preface to *A View*, 'How much we are vexed, that so much of Colley Cibber's *Life* is taken up with accounts of his own managership, and so little with those inimitable portraits which he has occasionally given of the actors of his time!' (p. vii). There can be no hope that we will one day discover a sheaf of pen portraits of Elizabethan actors, but the excavation in 1989 of a considerable part of the foundations of Henslowe's Rose has given us a new and unexpected glimpse of the stage trodden by the celebrated Ed Alleyn and perhaps even the youthful Will Shakespeare. It is with this archaeological evidence and the conclusions which may be drawn from it that R. A. Foakes begins our history.

I

Shakespeare's Elizabethan Stages

R. A. FOAKES

The Rose

HAMLET. Speak the speech, I pray you, as I pronounced it to you, trippingly on the tongue, but if you mouth it, as many of our players do, I had as lief the town-crier spoke my lines. Nor do not saw the air too much with your hand, thus, but use all gently, for in the very torrent, tempest, and, as I may say, whirlwind of your passion, you must acquire and beget a temperance that may give it smoothness. O, it offends me to the soul to hear a robustious periwig-pated fellow tear a passion to tatters, to very rags, to split the ears of the groundlings, who for the most part are capable of nothing but inexplicable dumb shows and noise. . . . Be not too tame neither, but let your own discretion be your tutor. Suit the action to the word, the word to the action, with this special observance, that you o'erstep not the modesty of nature . . . O, there be players that I have seen play—and heard others praise, and that highly—not to speak it profanely, that, neither having th'accent of Christians nor the gait of Christian, pagan, nor man, have so strutted and bellowed that I have thought some of Nature's journeymen had made men, and not made them well, they imitated humanity so abominably.   (*Hamlet*, III. ii. 1 ff.)

HAMLET'S advice to the players, spoken by a patrician with a neo-classical training, and patronizing as it is both to the actors and the audience, has so often been taken as Shakespeare's own thoughts on the matter that it is worth setting it in the context of what is known about Shakespeare's early stages. In recent years, and especially since the discovery of the remains of the Rose Theatre in 1989, our concept of what E. K. Chambers called 'The Elizabethan Stage' has been changed out of recognition. The title of his monumental work crushed decades into a single phrase, and seemed to imply that all the public theatres and stages were much alike. When we look back to a distant period it is hard to imagine day-to-day changes and developments, and easy to accept the

convenience of telescoping time, and settling for a unitary 'Elizabethan age' and 'Elizabethan stage'.

For his concept of the theatre, Chambers relied heavily on the well-known drawing of the Swan theatre by Aernout van Buchell, copied from a sketch made by Johannes de Witt about 1596 (fig. 6); 'with all its faults', he wrote, 'the drawing is the inevitable basis of any comprehensive account of the main structural features of a playhouse'.[1] So easily did he slide from the particular, a drawing of one theatre, the Swan, into the general features of 'a playhouse', i.e. every playhouse. Later historians continued to bypass the 'faults' of the drawing and accept the sketch 'without modification, interpolation, or any other unwarranted change' as 'our best guide to the appearance of the interior of an

FIG. 6 Interior of the Swan Theatre, drawn by Johannes de Witt in about 1596 and copied by Aernout van Buchell.

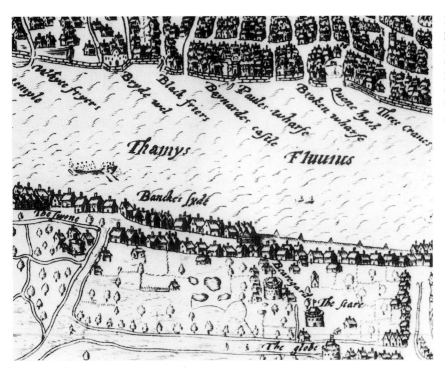

FIG. 7 Location of Bankside playhouses, map inset in Norden's *Civitas Londini* (1600). The Swan is to the left, the Beargarden, Rose (misnamed 'The Stare') and Globe (furthest from the river) clustered in the centre.

Elizabethan public theatre'. The Swan drawing was, in fact, the only extant visual record of the interior of an Elizabethan theatre, so that scholars wanted to be able to relate it to other theatres, especially in order to have some idea of the interior of Shakespeare's Globe. The Swan drawing had to be regarded as 'the best evidence we possess'[2] because it was the only visual evidence.

Quite apart from the matter of the accuracy of the sketch, which, it turns out, may be the copy by a poor draughtsman of a copy of the original, the uniqueness of the drawing distracted attention from the question of the Swan theatre itself, which provided a model for the later multi-purpose Hope theatre, and may have been a multi-purpose arena, unlike the Globe and Fortune.[3] The finding of the remains of the Rose in 1989 revolutionized our perception of Elizabethan theatres by demonstrating that they were not all alike, something it would have been impossible to guess from such evidence as John Norden's panorama of London, valuable as that is in demonstrating the location of the Bankside theatres (fig. 7).

The Rose turned out to be much smaller than anyone imagined, about 72 feet in diameter, with fourteen irregular sides, and a relatively small, tapered stage, very different from that in the Swan drawing (fig. 8). The subsequent discovery of the location of the Globe, and excavation of a small segment of its foundations, created a further flurry of excitement, and prompted urgent debate about the nature of this theatre, especially in relation to the reconstruction then in progress on Bankside. So little of the old Globe has been excavated that interpretation of the remains must remain speculative until further digging is possible, but most of the experts who have studied the evidence argue for a much larger theatre, about 100 feet in diameter, with twenty sides, and a huge rectangular stage.[4]

The small area of the Globe so far revealed consists of fragments of the base of inner and outer gallery walls and a stair-turret, and throws no light on the stage. Our idea of its stage is thus derived from the contract for the Fortune, built in 1600, which specifies that the stage should be 43 feet wide, extend to 'the middle of the yarde', and be 'in all other proporcions' fashioned like the stage at the Globe. This would seem to be conclusive evidence for its size, though not necessarily for its shape; the builder needed to have the placing of the stage 'prefigured in a Plott thereof drawen', possibly because its shape was not rectangular, or possibly to show its orientation, its location on whichever side of the square theatre it was positioned.[5]

Thus, in spite of the discovery that Elizabethan theatres were not all alike, and that the stage at the Rose was of a different shape from that made familiar by the Swan drawing, the exact nature of the stage area at Shakespeare's playhouses remains uncertain. Of his earliest plays, one or two were probably staged at the Rose: *Titus Andronicus* and at least one part of *Henry VI*, a version of *Hamlet* (which may not be his), and *The Taming of a Shrew* (which is related to, but not identical with, *The Taming of the Shrew* published in the First Folio). Others were played at the Theatre, which was larger than the Rose, since its timbers could be used to construct the Globe, and at the Curtain, about which little is known. The first stage at the Rose tapered to 26 feet 10 inches across the front, measured 36 ft. 9 ins. at the rear, and was 16 ft. 5 ins. deep, unless its boards extended over the perimeter support made of wood.

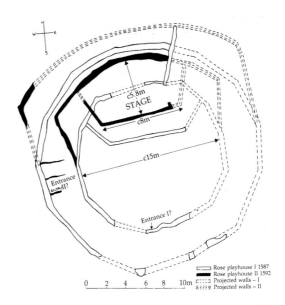

FIG. 9 The Rose Theatre, ground plan outlining both the theatre walls and the stage as originally built in 1587 and following the enlargement of 1592.

When this playhouse was enlarged in 1592, a new, larger stage was constructed, about 18 feet deep, and the brick foundations of the perimeter support for this stage make it more conceivable that the boards extended a foot or two beyond that supporting wall (fig. 9). The piling that may be for a column just inside the perimeter support would be easier to explain if actors could move around it on a stage extending beyond it. The first stage had an area of roughly 490 square feet, the second 533 square feet, or more if the boards were carried beyond the supporting wall.[6] The stage at the Fortune, by contrast, if we assume that it was rectangular, and that it extended literally to the middle of the auditorium, was more than twice as large, with an area of 1,161 square feet. It is possible that this stage, too, and the one at the Globe, were also tapered, in which case the area would have been somewhat reduced.

The stages at the Rose abutted directly on to the inner wall of the theatre, so that the rear of the stage was concave, not flat. Debate still continues about what the Fortune contract means in calling for the stage and tiring house to be set up within the frame of the theatre. Does it mean that a flat *frons scenae*, or

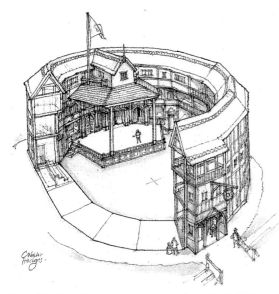

FIG. 8 The Rose Theatre, reconstruction drawn by C. Walter Hodges. The size and shape of both auditorium and stage are based on the archaeological findings, but the details above ground level can only be highly speculative.

stage façade, was constructed across several bays of the inner wall of the theatre, and if so, was the tiring house behind it but separate from the inner frame of the theatre itself? At the Rose, it appears that the tiring house was made out of the space between the inner and outer walls of the theatre behind the stage, for when Henslowe rebuilt this part of the Rose, he paid for putting a ceiling in the room 'over the tyerhowsse', and for making a 'penthowsse shed at the tyeringe howsse dore'. Evidently there was a door to the tiring house in the external wall of the theatre. The Fortune contract also specifies that the stage and tiring house were to be 'erected & settupp within the saide fframe', and that the tiring house was to have 'convenient windowes and lights glazed'.[7] These windows and lights were again presumably in the external walls of the theatre, indicating that the space at the rear of the stage, including that between the inner and outer walls, was used at the Fortune, and presumably at the Globe, as at the Rose.

If a flat *frons scenae* was built across several bays at the Fortune and Globe, with two doors, one on either side, and a curtained opening between, the space between the *frons scenae* and the inner wall of the theatre would have added to the area available to manage entrances and exits, for manipulating properties, and perhaps for the tiring house. So a flat stage façade, if there was one, would have had little effect on the total usable area of the stage, though it would have reduced somewhat the area on which plays were staged and actors performed.

Alleyn and Burbage

We are thus faced with an apparent paradox: on the more cramped stage and in the smaller auditorium of the Rose, Edward Alleyn (fig. 10) made his name in plays like Marlowe's *Tamburlaine*, which became a type

or symbol of noise ('the ordnance playing like so many Tamburlaines'[8]), of a 'stalking' or stamping player,[9] and, for Ben Jonson at any rate, of '*scenicall* strutting, and furious vociferation'.[10] It was on the larger stage of the Globe, however, that Richard Burbage (fig. 11) made a reputation by 1619 as a tragedian whose acting was so natural,

> soe livly, that Spectators, and the rest
> of his sad Crew, whilst he but seem'd to bleed,
> amazed, thought even then hee dyed in deed.[11]

The words which Shakespeare put into the mouth of Burbage's Hamlet sound like a plea for a restrained, 'naturalistic' acting style and a scoff at the grandiose style of Alleyn. The paradox is that we might expect a quieter style of acting on the small stage of the Rose, and a more expansive and fuller style on the large stage, and in the much larger auditorium, of the Globe.

Tamburlaine is of especial interest in this connection for two reasons; it was the only play by Marlowe published (1590) during his lifetime, and during the period when the Rose theatre was active; and it was so sensational that the play and its central character came rapidly to represent a particular style of playing. Already by 1597 the 'stalking steps' of Alleyn, linked with 'furious gesture as if he had beene playing Tamberlane on a stage', could be parodied in the absurd rant of Ancient Pistol, corrupting Tamburlaine's 'Holla, ye pampered jades of Asia' (Part 2, IV. iii. 1) into 'And hollow pampered jades of Asia' (*2 Henry IV*, II. iv. 159).[12] The play was still in the repertory at the Rose in 1595, where both parts were staged on successive days on 12 and 13 November.[13] Here Shakespeare may have been mocking Pistol rather than Marlowe, for the eponymous heroes of *Richard III* and of *Henry V* are capable of high astounding terms; 'Once more into the breach, dear friends' is not so far distant from the style of Tamburlaine. But by 1600 or so, with the move to the Globe, Shakespeare seems to have distanced himself from such rhetoric, most famously in *Hamlet*, where the First Player's speech about Pyrrhus (II. ii. 500) echoes, in stiffer and more turgid terms, the account of the death of Priam by

Aeneas in Marlowe's *Dido Queen of Carthage*, and is followed in III. ii by Hamlet's advice to the players.[14] Hamlet's neo-classicism, seen in his preference for plays on classical themes that are 'caviare to the general' (II. ii. 433), is reflected in his denunciation of the 'groundlings' as 'capable of nothing but inexplicable dumb shows and noise', and in his repetition of commonplaces derived from Cicero via Donatus in his advice to the players to practise 'temperance' and not to overact; but it may well be Shakespeare who speaks through his attack on actors who 'tear a passion to tatters, to very rags, to split the ears of the groundlings', and on those who imitate humanity abominably by strutting and bellowing (III. ii. 9, 32).[15]

It would seem, then, that by 1600 or so Shakespeare had been distancing himself from the kind of play represented by works like *Tamburlaine*, and the kind of acting associated with it in the 1590s. It does not follow, however, that, as is often said, two disparate acting styles can be identified with Alleyn at the Rose and Fortune, and Burbage at the Theatre, the Curtain, and the Globe. After William Armstrong, criticizing a long tradition of associating Alleyn with Hamlet's attack on rant, showed how Alleyn and Burbage were praised by their contemporaries in similar terms, Andrew Gurr reformulated the traditional argument by claiming that two styles of acting were created by the two most famous actors of the age, one, derived from Alleyn, violent in voice and gesture, and given to exaggeration, that led from *Tamburlaine* in the 1580s to the mode of the Fortune and Red Bull; the other, more moderate, refined, and natural, stemming from Burbage, and characterizing the mode of the Globe and Blackfriars.[16] The two actors were credited with creating the 'divergence of style which led the pretensions of the King's Men at the Blackfriars to differ so clearly from those of the Fortune and Red Bull companies through the seventeenth century'.[17] I believe this theory is too neat and simple. *Tamburlaine* was such a sensational play that Alleyn's name was inevitably linked to it. There were four early editions, in 1590, 1593, 1597, and 1605–6. The last may have followed on a revival at the Fortune when Alleyn returned briefly to acting there before he retired about

FIG. 10 Edward Alleyn, leading player at Henslowe's Rose in such roles as Marlowe's Tamburlaine the Great.

1604–5.[18] Alleyn is known to have acted the roles of Doctor Faustus and Barabas (both 1592 or earlier), Orlando in Greene's *Orlando Furioso* (1592), and the eponymous heroes of the lost plays *Cutlack* (in production 1594), and *Tamar Cham* (in production 1592). All of these are early plays, and give little sense of the range of his acting, though they do suggest he had some talent for comedy (Barabas), and for introspection (Dr Faustus).

Burbage, by contrast, tends to be identified with roles he played much later, and although he was almost the same age as Alleyn, being two years younger, he is now regarded primarily through the perspective of the much-quoted anonymous funeral elegy on him in 1619, in which he is praised for 'suiting the person' so well that spectators thought he died indeed when he 'but seem'd to bleed'. Burbage is, of course, reasonably associated with a range of Shakespeare's leading parts, tragic and comic, in a

Fig. 11 Richard Burbage, leading player in Shakespeare's company; believed to be a self-portrait.

large number of plays, many staged long after Alleyn retired. Where Alleyn tends to be identified with roles written for him before 1592, Burbage tends to be conceived in terms of roles written for him after 1600. This makes too simple a picture. So, for instance, in the mildly satirical scene in Act IV, Scene iii of the Cambridge play, *The Return from Parnassus*, Part 2 (?1601), in which 'Burbidge' is brought on stage to advise the scholars on acting, he is identified with speeches from old 'ranting' parts, Hieronimo (*The Spanish Tragedy*) and Richard III, which he recites, and then invites the scholars to imitate. Furthermore, the 1619 elegy on Burbage is matched by the comment of Thomas Nashe on the character Talbot in 1 *Henry VI*, played no doubt by Alleyn as the leading actor of Lord Strange's Men in 1592; he drew 'the teares of ten thousand spectators at least, (at severall times), who, in the Tragedian that represents his person, imagine they behold him fresh bleeding'.[19]

The extent to which Alleyn and Burbage were stars in their time can be gauged by the plays written as vehicles for them, that is to say, plays with unusually long central roles. The list of such plays, with roles of

800 or more lines, is relatively short. It includes, among parts in extant plays Alleyn probably played, those of Sir Thomas More in the collaborative play to which Shakespeare contributed, of Marlowe's Tamburlaine and Barabas, of Hieronimo in Kyd's *Spanish Tragedy* as expanded in 1602, and of Henry VIII in Rowley's *When You See Me You Know Me* (1604); the roles of Richard III, Henry V, Hamlet, Othello or Iago, and the Duke in *Measure for Measure* can confidently be assigned to Burbage. These two actors shared all the known huge roles up to about 1604, when another, probably John Lowin, began to take on some large parts for Shakespeare's company, and evidently they could command the stage and attract audiences.[20] Alleyn was said by Thomas Fuller in his account of the 'worthies' of Britain (1662) to have excelled in majestic parts, but it is notable that many of the great roles of Burbage also were of a majestic kind. If the roles of More and Henry VIII can be attributed to Alleyn, then it helps to explain why Thomas Heywood could describe him in a late prologue written for *The Jew of Malta* as 'Proteus for shapes, and Roscius for a tongue'. It is not known what other roles these star actors may have played, but they must have been able to adapt to the mixed repertories of theatres that offered a different play almost every day, and play a variety of widely differing parts.

A change in acting style is better explained by considering the repertory of the leading companies in the period up to 1604 or so, roughly when Alleyn retired. The swirling relationships of actors to companies, companies to patrons, and playbooks to owners, remains something of a puzzle in the years before the Admiral's Men and the Chamberlain's Men gained their dominance from 1594 onwards; but Alleyn and Burbage played in the same company for a time, and actors seem to have moved from company to company fairly freely.[21] However, if Alleyn's known roles prior to this time are mainly majestic ones of huffing lines, it is probable that Burbage was also playing parallel strong, vigorous parts, as, for example, in 2 and 3 *Henry VI*, *Titus Andronicus*, *Richard III*, and *The Taming of the Shrew*. All of these plays have leading roles that demand exuberant acting. The debt to

Marlowe is often apparent, not only in such deliberate echoes as those in the soliloquy of Aaron the Moor in *Titus Andronicus*, II. i, 'Now climbeth Tamora Olympus' top . . .',[22] but more generally in *Henry VI*, for instance, in the fluid rush of lines with only two or three stressed syllables. A feature of Marlowe's poetic technique in *Tamburlaine*, for example, is his creation of a sense of pace and a soaring quality in lines that establish their effect through counterpointing two or three speech stresses against the five-beat iambic blank verse line, as in

> Is it not passing brave to be a king,
> And ride in triumph through Persepolis.

Shakespeare's mature verse typically offers a weightier musical effect in pitching four speech stresses against the five beats, but in the *Henry VI* plays, the bouncier rhythms of a Marlovian manner are often noticeable, as in Talbot's lines in the first part:

> And that hereafter ages may behold
> What ruin happened in revenge of him,
> Within their chiefest temple I'll erect
> A tomb, wherein his corpse shall be interr'd . . .
>
> (II. ii. 104)

These lines were probably written for Alleyn, but the style can be seen in the other parts of *Henry VI* in lines like

> And prove the period of their tyranny.
>
> (Part 2, III. i. 149)

The cadences continue in Gloucester's role in Part 3:

> But I will sort a pitchy day for thee,
> For I will buzz abroad such prophecies
> As Edmund shall be fearful of his life . . . (V. vi. 85)

They continue also in *Richard III*, in lines like 'I am determined to prove a villain', which is analogous to lines like Marlowe's 'A god is not so glorious as a king' (*1 Tamburlaine*, II. v. 57). Marlowe's mighty line demands a bolder delivery than the more loaded style that Shakespeare developed in the 1590s, one less dependent on prepositions, conjunctions, and the like, a style that makes possible the brooding soliloquies of the tragic heroes of his mature plays, as, for example, in lines like Hamlet's

> For who would bear the whips and scorns of time,
> Th'oppressor's wrong, the proud man's contumely,
> The pangs of despised love, the law's delay,
> The insolence of office, and the spurns
> That patient merit of the unworthy takes,
> When he himself might his quietus make
> With a bare bodkin?
>
> (III. i. 70)

Shakespeare learned his trade in the shadow of Marlowe, and it seems likely that a number of Burbage's early roles, such as that of Gloucester in *3 Henry VI* and *Richard III*, were in some measure designed to match those of Alleyn in *Tamburlaine*, *1 Henry VI*, and *Doctor Faustus*.

Companies and Commerce

A sense of competitiveness between the leading companies is confirmed by recent reassessments of the commercial nature of their operations, and the challenge of the repertory system in attracting audiences from a similar spectrum of society. The neat opposition once proposed between an unscrupulous, bullying Philip Henslowe, cowing actors and hack-playwrights into submission at the Rose and Fortune, and a high-minded group of friends concerned only to create art at the Theatre and Globe, has given way to a better understanding of the theatres as all primarily concerned with making money.[23] Probably 'the men's companies acquired and scheduled their offerings by similar techniques of management year to year';[24] and a comparison between what is known of the repertories of the Admiral's Men and the Chamberlain's Men indicates that they responded to the same changes in taste and fashion, and competed with plays on similar themes, for their share of the available audience.

Tamburlaine seems to have established a fashion for two-part and serial plays, a fashion that persisted for some years according to the entries in Henslowe's Diary, and was matched by the Chamberlain's Men with such offerings as the three parts of *Henry VI*, and the two parts of *Henry IV*. The success of Chapman's *Comedy of Humours* at the Rose in 1597 no doubt prompted Jonson to write his *Every Man in his Humour* for Shakespeare's company. Both companies staged domestic tragedies, such as *Page of Plymouth*, written for the Rose by Ben Jonson and Thomas Dekker in 1599, and *A Warning for Fair Women* (Chamberlain's), published in the same year as recently acted. Much more is known about the repertory of the companies financed by Henslowe than about that of the Chamberlain's Men, who tend to be identified mainly with Shakespeare in the period 1594–1608. However, scrutiny of the non-Shakespearian plays that can be identified from title-pages or other evidence as staged by the Chamberlain's/King's Men confirms the sense that, after moving to the Globe, they continued to present a repertory that in many ways paralleled that of the Fortune.[25] Both companies revived old plays, to judge by reprintings, as well as new ones after they moved respectively to their new theatres. Both put on plays with Jews as central figures (*The Jew of Malta*, *The Merchant of Venice*), citizen romances (*The Shoemakers' Holiday*, *The Freeman's Honour*), plays with magic (*Doctor Faustus*, *The Merry Devil of Edmonton*, the Induction of which in 1603 consciously echoes the end of Marlowe's play), and plays on recent history (*Cardinal Wolsey*, *Thomas Lord Cromwell*). If the companies consciously competed in the kinds of play they staged, it is probable that they both also competed in their range of acting styles.

It should not surprise, then, that the early attacks on the stage, by Puritans like Stephen Gosson, or by satirists like Joseph Hall, are directed generally at the public stages, and their display of

> A goodly *hoch-poch*, when vile *Russettings*
> Are match'd with monarchs, & with mighty kings.[26]

The dramatists who began to write for the new children's theatres (Paul's, Blackfriars) in 1599–1600 distanced themselves and their audience from the public stages by implying that at the arena theatres one

might be 'choakte | With the stench of Garlicke', or 'pasted to the barmy Jacket of a Beer-brewer',[27] and that the adult players merely railed, 'loud and full of players' eloquence'.[28] The Fortune has often been linked rather casually with the Red Bull as a 'citizen' theatre, in contrast to the 'courtier' Blackfriars,[29] and certainly in later years, when the King's Men made this their principal house, they appealed to a more sophisticated and wealthier audience. But the Fortune does not seem to have been linked with the Red Bull before 1615, though by 1612, when 'cutt-purses and other lewde and ill disposed persons' were said to resort there at the end of a play on account of the jigs and dances that followed,[30] it may have acquired the reputation that it had in later years. In the early years of the seventeenth century, however, the patronizing or condescending comments on the 'common'[31] playhouses by writers for the private theatres lumped them together, as if at any of them one would find 'A dull Audience of Stinkards sitting in the penny-galleries of a Theater, and yawning upon the Players';[32] while satirists, perhaps more accurately, noted how after the play and the jig which usually followed,

> at all the playhouse dores,
> When ended is the play, the daunce, and song,
> A thousand townsmen, gentlemen, and whores,
> Porters and serving-men together throng.[33]

The evidence suggests, then, that a vigorous, loud, stalking-stamping style of play and of acting, popular in the 1580s, gave way during the 1590s, with the consolidation of the two leading companies at the Rose and the Theatre or Curtain, to a quieter style more suited to a new range of plays concerned less with battles, conquest, and spectacle than with romance and domesticity. After 1599, the writers for the newly established children's companies at the private theatres, Paul's and Blackfriars, which specialized in satire (the only humour in request there being to 'rail'[34]), attack public theatres indiscriminately, and, as Dekker observed, 'A Gentleman or an honest Cittizen shall not sit in your pennie-bench Theatres, with his Squirell by his side cracking nuttes',[35] without being mocked by the likes of Ben Jonson. Some time after 1604, and more especially after the King's Men took over Blackfriars in 1608, the Fortune and Globe came to be identified with different styles of acting, different repertories, and different classes of audience, even as Burbage gained unchallenged dominance as the leading actor of the age. By 1611 or so Nathan Field, himself a notable actor, who played both with the Lady Elizabeth's Men, one of Henslowe's companies, and with the King's Men, could gibe at the Fortune as a playhouse where one might go to see *Long Meg*, an old play popular in 1594, and where the players were the companions of whores.[36] In *This World's Folly* (1615), I.H. refers to the Curtain and Fortune theatres in attacking players who 'with *Scylla*-barking, *Stentor*-throated bellowings, flash choaking squibbs of absurd vanities into the nosthrils of your spectators'.[37] A clown in Thomas Tomkis's play *Albumazar* (1615) links the Fortune and Red Bull theatres as places where he learns the words he speaks and does not understand.[38] By 1623, Leonard Digges, a not unprejudiced witness, could praise Shakespeare by suggesting that the Red Bull, Cockpit, and Fortune had to put up with the 'lame blancke verse' of inferior dramatists; and by 1632 the 'silkes and plush and all the witts' frequenting the Globe are contrasted with the 'prentizes and apell-wyfes' attending the Fortune.[39]

It seems likely that the differences between the public theatres only became marked after 1604, perhaps later still. If we may take their rival repertories as indicating that the two leading companies competed in other ways until this time, then an explanation of the apparent paradox proposed earlier, namely that we might expect a quieter style of acting on the cramped stage of the small Rose than in 'the vastness of the Globe',[40] may depend upon the answer to another question: why did the 'stalking steps' and 'huf-cap terms'[41] typified by *Tamburlaine* and popular at the Rose and, as far as we know, at other public playhouses, in the period up to about 1594, begin to seem increasingly old-fashioned and available for rejection or parody thereafter?

Developing Theatre Designs

A partial answer may lie buried in the statistics of population growth, for the population of London grew rapidly between 1580 and 1604, and some think may have almost doubled during this period.[42] As theatres competed for a growing potential audience, and became more socially acceptable for women spectators,[43] they refined their techniques of presentation, and extended the range of the kinds of plays they offered, in order to attract a wider and more knowledgeable body of spectators, many of whom were eager for novelty, as exemplified in the popularity of the new comedies of humours from 1597 onwards. Theatres consumed plays then much as the cinema consumes films now, and few lasted long in the repertory. At the same time, the growth of population affected the suburbs more than the city; the wealthy in a modern city often live in suburbs and commute to offices in the otherwise impoverished centre, but in seventeenth-century London the wealthy were concentrated more in the city, while fortune-seekers and the poor flocking in from the country tended to cluster in the impoverished suburbs, perhaps especially in the north, where the Fortune and Red Bull were located, theatres that increasingly catered for a lower-class audience. Shakespeare's company, by contrast, seem to have made the Blackfriars, an indoor playhouse located in a 'liberty' (i.e. an area not under the control of the city authorities)[44] within the wealthier city of London, their main theatre from 1609 onwards.

Another kind of partial answer may lie in the design of the theatres. Here too it would appear that there were significant changes, even if there is no clear line of development. The Red Lion (1567), as far as is now known the earliest purpose-built theatre, had a large rectangular stage, with only a turret or tower at the rear. Nothing is known for certain about the stages at the Theatre (1576) and the Curtain, where Shakespeare and his fellows played between 1594 and 1599, or about the stages at other early theatres, such as that at Newington Butts, or those set up in innyards. As we have seen, the Rose had a relatively small, tapered stage, and the evidence suggests that the later arena playhouses had large platform stages, with a canopy or cover over the stage that developed into the enormous twin-gabled structure drawn by Wenceslaus Hollar in his 'Long View' of London (1640, after drawings made about 1638, fig. 12) as a feature of the second Globe (erected in 1613 after the first burned down). There are many gaps in our knowledge of the way Elizabethan stages developed, but it is reasonable to assume that owners and companies of actors looked for ways to improve their facilities. One feature of special interest in relation to the present discussion is the canopy over the stage: we do not know for sure when or why this was introduced, but it evidently became important.

It is difficult to imagine how plays were staged almost daily in all sorts of weather, with no cover for the groundlings standing in the arena, and with actors working on a stage that lacked a canopy over it. The large fluctuations in Henslowe's receipts in the early 1590s, ranging from 74s. to 5s. for a performance, may have had as much to do with the weather as with interest or lack of it in the play being staged. The contract for the Fortune calls for a 'shadowe or cover' over the stage, without providing details as to how it was to be erected, except that it was to be supported on the 'postes' of the 'Stadge forwarde'.[45] The first Globe presumably had a similar cover, and the second Globe a much more elaborate one. There was no cover at the Red Lion, so far as is known, and the evidence is insufficient to show how stage covers evolved. A trench worn by water dripping around the first stage at the Rose may indicate some kind of canopy there designed to protect the stage area, though no bases for supporting columns have been found. The contract for the Hope, a dual-purpose theatre designed for bear- and bull-baiting as well as plays, patterned on the Swan, and built in 1613, requires that 'the Heavens' shall be built 'all over the saide stage, to be borne or carryed without any postes or supporters to be fixed or sett upon the said stage',[46]

and perhaps the first Rose had some kind of light canopy cantilevered without posts. The base for a column inside the perimeter of the second stage, set up when the Rose was extended in 1592, indicates a more substantial cover, one that could permit the installation of the machinery to work the 'throne in the hevenes' (i.e. heavens) Henslowe paid for in June 1595.[47]

In 1596, Johannes de Witt wrote that the two most splendid theatres in London were the Rose and the Swan, the largest being the Swan, which, in the very unreliable copy van Buchell made of de Witt's sketch of it, shows a simple, shallow, sloping cover of boards or tiles extending no further than the middle of the stage, a cover that in rainy weather would have poured water on to the front area of the stage. What were the functions of the stage cover? Initially it seems to have served, as at the early Rose and the Swan, simply as a means of protecting part or all of the stage in bad weather. It developed into a more elaborate structure that included a space to accommodate machinery and a flat, painted underside, adorned with sun, moon, stars, and signs of the zodiac. This is what Henslowe seems to have introduced at the Rose, and a second function of the stage 'heavens', located directly above the 'hell' beneath the stage, was to make it possible, as suggested in the 1605 Prologue to Chapman's *All Fools* at the Fortune, for properties and actors to descend, and for the elaboration of other kinds of

> strange effects
> That rise from this Hell, or fall from this Heaven.

The satiric sketch of a player in R.M.'s *Micrologia* (1629) points to the presence of a visible stage-hand: 'If his action prefigure passion, he raves, rages, and protests much by his painted heavens, and seems in the height of this fit ready to pull Jove out of the garret where perchance he lies leaning on his elbows, or is employed to make squibs and crackers to grace the play.'[48]

I would suggest that a third, and possibly crucial, function of the more elaborate 'heavens' was to provide a sounding-board for the actors, to enhance the acoustics of the outdoor theatres. As Andrew Gurr observed, 'A large open auditorium with a good proportion of the audience on its feet would certainly generate a level of background noise much greater than the smaller gatherings, all seated, in the hall playhouses'.[49] If we assume that the canopy in the Swan drawing is shown roughly to size, then it covered only part of the stage, and its primary function may have been to provide a sounding-board for actors at the rear, rather than to afford protection from rain. The private or hall playhouses, Blackfriars and Paul's, encouraged a softer delivery and different acting style: so in *Poetaster* (1601), written for a children's company, Ben Jonson introduces a character, Histrio, who, as a walking parody of a public-theatre player, 'stalkes by', a 'two-penny teare-mouth', and is punningly linked both with the Fortune and the Globe theatres; in a later scene, Histrio starts a speech loudly, and is told, 'Speake lower, you are not now in your theater, Stager'.[50]

Jonson mocks here the stalking tragedian who no doubt continued the tradition of the old theatres in revivals of plays like *Doctor Faustus* at the Fortune and *The Spanish Tragedy* at the Globe; and his presentation of Histrio further confirms the change in acting style encouraged by the indoor playhouses. However, the changing repertories of the Admiral's and Chamberlain's companies in the 1590s point to a shift away from stalking and raging tragedies and histories to more emphasis on comedies, on domestic and citizen themes, plays of disguise, of humours, plays on recent political history, and romance, in fact, a great diversity of new drama, with few plays remaining in production for more than a year (though popular old plays continued to be revived from time to time).[51] It may always have been necessary in the arena theatres for actors to speak '*loud and full* of players' eloquence', but by 1600 they had a whole range of plays that demanded a style of acting quite different from that symbolized by *Tamburlaine*. The development of a sounding-board in the 'heavens' may have been the technical advance that made possible a change to a quieter delivery and more restrained style of acting even before the impact of the private stages.

The development of the sounding-board has a bearing on the paradox proposed earlier, but perhaps one other factor deserves to be noted as well. The first Rose had an area of about 1,400 square feet available for the groundlings to stand to see a play, and this was extended to roughly 1,800 square feet when the theatre was enlarged in 1592. This larger area Andrew Gurr thinks would have held 800 people standing,[52] but this is to suppose them packed in tightly, and I suspect rather fewer would have filled the space to a gatherer's eye at the entrance gate. The galleries held a maximum of about 1,650, a figure confirmed both by a calculation of possible seating on benches, and by Henslowe's maximum receipts for a single performance, so that the total audience capacity was in the region of 2,200.[53] When the Admiral's Men moved to the Fortune, their new theatre was constructed on a plan that provided almost the same space for groundlings as at the extended Rose, namely 1,843 square feet. If the Globe was indeed 100 feet in diameter, even allowing for a stage as large as or larger than that at the Fortune, it had an area for a standing audience in excess of 3,000 square feet, perhaps as much as 3,200 square feet, or space for at least 1,000 groundlings, so that the total capacity of this playhouse could have been between 3,500 and 4,000 spectators.

At the public theatres there were lord's rooms close to the stage, and the Fortune contract calls for 'gentlemens roomes and Twoe pennie roomes' to be plastered. Most of the better class of audience, those who paid extra to sit in the galleries, were furthest from the stage, and in the early theatres an actor may have needed to 'split the ears of the groundlings', in Hamlet's phrase, in order to be adequately heard in the galleries. In the later private playhouses, the expensive seats were those closest to the stage, so that the actors would naturally 'speake lower'. It may have been that in a huge theatre like the Globe, the most strident actors' voices, having further to carry than at the Rose or Fortune, sounded softer. Whatever the explanation for the paradox, it would seem that old-style adult playing, as typified by the stalking-stamping, ranting actor in roles such as Tamburlaine, was already old-fashioned by the late 1590s, and that a new style of playing was well established by the companies playing at both the Globe and Fortune when these were built. The scornful comments about tearing a passion to tatters directed by satirists and writers for the private theatres against acting in the public playhouses attack what was obsolescent there. At the Globe and Fortune things were already very different from the time when 'the old theatres cracked and frighted the audience'.[54] Hamlet, who prefers plays that are caviare to the general, and would have been a private theatre patron, to judge by his comments on old styles of acting, is a character in a play that provides Shakespeare's most eloquent testimony to the change I have outlined.

2
The King's Men and After

MARTIN WIGGINS

King and Parliament

THE stage history of Shakespeare's plays during the early seventeenth century is in large measure bound up with the King's Men, the acting company to which the dramatist belonged and which retained control of his work after his death in 1616. It had existed since 1594 under the patronage of Lord Hunsdon, but was officially reborn on 19 May 1603 when, within two weeks of his arrival in London, King James issued its shareholding members, including Shakespeare himself, with a royal patent. They became the king's servants, licensed 'freely to use and exercise the art and faculty of playing comedies, tragedies, histories, . . . as well for the recreation of our loving subjects as for our solace and pleasure when we shall think good to see them'.[1] The company acquired a new, privileged status (at least among those in the kingdom who approved of stage plays) and the expectation of future bookings for court festivities and the entertainment of visiting dignitaries. Much of our direct evidence about its repertory comes from the Chamber Account's records of payments for such royal command performances.

The new king seems to have been a theatre enthusiast, despite his later reputation for impatience at longer shows: in Scotland he had given support, money, and, from 1601, explicit royal patronage to a troupe of English players. It is no surprise that he should have chosen to adopt one of the London companies after coming south, and the selection of Shakespeare and his colleagues for that honour is often read as implied theatre criticism: 'To be able to count the King as one's patron', writes Peter Thomson, 'was, in a fiercely hierarchical society, a proof of quality.'[2] There is a superficial logic to this interpretation: as Queen Elizabeth's Lord Chamberlain, Hunsdon had run the department responsible for (among many other things) providing the sovereign's entertainment, so his players might have seemed the natural choice for the royal livery. The ominous inference is that the king appropriated by fiat one of the dignities of a prominent subject—an early instance of that overdeveloped sense of royal prerogative that would eventually cost his younger son his head. There is, however, another way of understanding the transfer of patronage: it may have been received, as distinct from taken over, by King James. In the Renaissance court culture of gifts and compliments, a company of players might well be proffered as a human 'gift' to the new sovereign, the transaction conferring honour and prestige on both donor and recipient. In other words, the creation of

23

the King's Men may have had more to do with the scramble for royal favour in the reconfiguration of court politics after the queen's death, than with any qualitative assessment of the acting company itself.

This hypothesis begs several questions. The Lord Chamberlain was not the only senior court official to be a patron of players: the two other major London companies owed allegiance to the earls of Nottingham and Worcester respectively, and could also have been advanced as potential King's Men. Moreover, Hunsdon was the least likely of the three to be bidding for power when James arrived in London: by then, ill health had forced him to give up his official duties; he would be dead before the year was out. Paradoxically, it may have been that illness which made the fortunes of his theatrical retainers. The king reappointed Nottingham as Lord Steward and Worcester as Master of the Horse, their former offices, but Hunsdon was obviously incapable of continuing as Lord Chamberlain. Accepting the gift of his acting company would have been one of the few honours that James could bestow on the dead queen's dying servant.

We cannot, then, say with any confidence that the Lord Chamberlain's Men were chosen to be the original 'Royal Shakespeare Company' simply because they were the best actors in London: if, like his Scottish predecessor, James wanted signs of nobleness to shine on all deservers, then to accept either of the other important adult companies would have compromised his even-handedness. Conversely, however, it would not have suited his royal dignity to be the patron to an obviously inferior troupe of players, and what we know of their affairs in the years before 1603—none of it, unfortunately, deriving from contemporary reviews or box-office records—tends to confirm their popularity and commercial success.

The company in general and William Shakespeare in particular were evidently a selling-point for printed editions of their plays: from 1597 onwards they are usually mentioned by name on the title-pages, which served at this time as publishers' advertisements. Even more suggestively, the quartos of four Lord Chamberlain's Men plays—*Romeo and Juliet*, *Henry V*, *The Merry Wives of Windsor*, and *Hamlet*—print what

are obviously unauthorized versions, each stolen surreptitiously by one or more actors reconstructing the text from memory, and then sold, perhaps to other acting companies, perhaps directly to publishers. All this implies the success of the original Lord Chamberlain's productions: with such desirable commodities on their hands, and with Shakespeare writing new plays every year, the conditions were right for prosperity. A series of property transactions made by members of the company during the later 1590s confirms that prosperity: in 1596 James Burbage made the first abortive moves to acquire a new indoor playhouse in the up-market Blackfriars district as a replacement for the Theatre, on which the lease was running out; the following year, Shakespeare bought New Place, an expensive town house in Stratford-upon-Avon, and late in 1598 he entered a partnership with four other actors to help Cuthbert and Richard Burbage finance the erection of the Globe. Unless these men were being irresponsibly Micawberish, business must have been going well for the Lord Chamberlain's Men.

The royal patent came at a crucial moment for company morale. The king's accession coincided with the start of an epidemic outbreak of bubonic plague which kept the London playhouses closed, as a public health measure, until April 1604. With the future uncertain, memories of the recent past were not encouraging: the last great plague ten years earlier had seen Queen Elizabeth's Men, once England's premier acting company, break up their London operation and sell off many of their play books; they struggled on as a provincial touring group, but never again played the capital. The theatre boom could all too easily turn to bust, and this time at least two London companies, no doubt under heavy financial pressure, apparently gave illicit performances in defiance of the restraining order. The King's Men, in contrast, seem to have enjoyed a confidence in their long-term security: their patent explicitly licensed a resumption of playing at the Globe 'when the infection of the plague shall decrease'.[3] An index of that confidence is Shakespeare's own behaviour: deprived of a theatre to write for during the epidemic of 1592–4, he had turned to non-dramatic poetry and sought aristocratic patronage; under similar conditions in 1603–4 he sat down to write *Measure for Measure* and *Othello*.

The company's first recorded performance for their new patron took place at Wilton House about six months later; tradition has it that the play was *As You Like It*. Their contributions to the Christmas revels at Hampton Court not long afterwards included, on New Year's Day 1604, 'a play of Robin Goodfellow', which may have been a revival of *A Midsummer Night's Dream*. By January 1605 they had performed at court nineteen times, including at least five more plays by Shakespeare, and there was no sign of any slackening of demand.[4] On the contrary, the revels were extended: 'It seems we shall have Christmas all the year,' wrote Dudley Carleton ten days after Twelfth Night, the traditional end of the seasonal festivities. The king had left London for hunting at Royston, but Queen Anne's court partied on, and the MP Sir Walter Cope, who evidently had little expertise in such matters, was given the job of finding some professional entertainment for them. Poor Cope spent the best part of a winter morning trudging around London trying to locate the players, and was eventually reduced to 'leaving notes for them to seek me'. This brought him a visit from Burbage, who explained that they had exhausted their current repertory, or at least those parts of it which they were willing to present before a royal audience: 'there is no new play that the Queen hath not seen.' Clearly the court's appetite for plays was beginning to strain the company's resources, and for the next few occasions they were forced to dip into their back catalogue. For the queen they chose to revive what was probably their most feminine comedy, *Love's Labours Lost*, 'which for wit and mirth', Burbage promised Cope, 'will please her exceedingly'.[5] The following month they offered *The Merchant of Venice* for the Shrovetide entertainment of the king and the Florentine ambassador, which evidently did please James enough for him to order a repeat performance of the play two days later.

Not everyone was so fond of plays. The moralistic elements in Elizabethan and Jacobean culture saw in the theatre a public nuisance and a moral danger:

drama was denounced from pulpits and in print. For the best part of a generation, the London civic authorities had petitioned the Privy Council against the playhouses ensconced just beyond their official reach in the suburbs and liberties of the metropolis; and in 1596 the Lord Chamberlain's Men were prevented from occupying their new Blackfriars theatre after a concerted campaign by the district's Puritan residents, worried about the crime and promiscuity, noise and traffic jams that a local playhouse would bring to the neighbourhood. Beneath such pragmatic objections, however, there was usually a more fundamental antitheatricalism. To their opponents, professional players were the profiteers of sin: idleness gave them their market, and filthy lewdness was their stock-in-trade. Lurid tales circulated among the godly about the sex and violence, the swearing and blasphemy to be seen in plays: 'such wanton gestures, such bawdy speeches; such laughing and fleering; such kissing and bussing; such clipping and culling; such winking and casting of wanton eyes.'[6] The arguments against such spectacles have changed little in the intervening four centuries: to portray sexual behaviour, however mildly, was indecent, and to represent immoral or irreligious conduct was to teach by bad example. Reprobate playwrights might protest that when they showed wickedness it was not for imitation but merely for it to be known and hated; but right-thinking people knew better that, for corrupt, fallen mankind, ignorance was eternal bliss.

The new royal family's patronage of the drama— also extended to the King's Men's commercial rivals by the time the plague had subsided and the theatres reopened—would not have seemed a scandalous innovation to the opponents of stage plays: companies of actors had long worn aristocratic and occasionally royal livery, and several Elizabethan controversialists had had to incorporate awkward manœuvres in their arguments to avoid risking *lèse-majesté*. However, the politics of antitheatricalism did not go unaffected by the change of regime. Unlike their Elizabethan predecessors, the Jacobean Lord Mayors of London seem never to have bothered the Privy Council about the playhouses. It is not impossible that this might indicate nothing more than a change of priorities at the Guildhall, but in any case the Privy Council had made its own position clear in April 1604 when it wrote to the local authorities of London, Surrey, and Middlesex giving order that the players should once again be allowed the use of their theatres.

With king and Council both well disposed towards professional drama, the only effectual focus for antitheatrical activity was the third side of the early seventeenth-century triangle of power. The Jacobean Parliament, and the House of Commons in particular, was increasingly taking over some of the functions of the Privy Council as a channel for grievances and the redress of abuses, and it is possible that the enemies of the stage took to lobbying their MPs, the majority of whom held broadly Puritan views and would probably have been sympathetic. In any event, 1606 saw the enactment of a measure prohibiting the profane use of the names of God on stage. Introduced to the House in February, the bill was seen through committee by the Gray's Inn barrister Nicholas Fuller, an experienced parliamentarian who was also a zealous Puritan, and became law on 27 May. It was not repealed until 1844.

At first glance the Act to Restrain Abuses of Players seems itself remarkably restrained in view of the breadth of the case against stage plays. In practice, however, there was little else that the House of Commons could reasonably have enacted against the perceived abuses of players, whatever the personal opinions of its honourable members. Given the king's known tastes, to attempt sweeping antitheatrical legislation based on the presumption that plays were inherently vicious and playhouses an inevitable source of moral corruption would have been a naïve and provocative action. Moreover, generalized systems of censorship and control were already in place: every acting company required an aristocratic patron, and all plays were subject to scrutiny and possible amendment by a court official, the Master of the Revels, before a licence was granted for public performance. Any legislation on the agenda set by the drama's critics would have to concentrate on reforming specific elements of theatrical practice

which were opprobrious in themselves. One obvious possibility was stage transvestism, but to ban that would be tantamount to banning plays altogether by making the entire existing repertory unusable, or else would open the way to the even more objectionable Continental practice of employing actresses to play women's parts. In contrast, there were no such obstacles to the interdiction of theatrical swearing, and the arguments against the practice were unanswerable once it was granted that oaths were an abuse of the holy name of God. Stage profanity was a shrewdly chosen target.

If anything, the Act is notable not for restraint but severity. Whereas the statutory fine for drunkenness was 5s., an oath in a play would cost its perpetrators £10; the right to offer legal excuse was also expressly disallowed. It was an extreme measure, characteristic of the crude moralism that often afflicts English parliaments in times of national emergency: not many months before, the Commons had narrowly escaped a collective death by gunpowder explosion in Guy Fawkes's abortive attempt to assassinate the king, and in the aftermath the House radicals were asserting themselves.

Besides the stringency of the prescribed penalty, moreover, there is arguably a degree of bloody-mindedness in the Act. No theatre company could afford to ignore its demands, for it made provision for its enforcement by offering half the fine as a reward to the informer: reporting an actor's *zounds* was now an easy way to earn £5. Accordingly, the King's Men and their rivals would have been obliged to expurgate their working repertory—perhaps nine or more plays—and to continue the process as new plays came into production and old ones were revived. It must have been an extensive and fiddling operation, and potentially also a costly one if new prompt-books had to be prepared. Parliament could not hope to close the playhouses in 1606, but at least it could put the players to a great deal of trouble.

As an example of the damage wrought by expurgation, we may compare two early versions of a passage from 1 *Henry IV*, a play itself much concerned with the conflict between pious and profane language.

Before the Act, the King's Men would have performed the following:

PRINCE HAL (*playing King Henry*). The complaints I hear of thee are grievous.
FALSTAFF (*playing Prince Hal*). 'Sblood, my lord, they are false. Nay, I'll tickle ye for a young prince, i' faith.
PRINCE HAL. Swearest thou, ungracious boy?   (II. v. 447–50)

This version, printed in the Quarto of 1598, is already one layer of censorship removed from what Shakespeare originally wrote, for in 1596 Falstaff was briefly known as Sir John Oldcastle, the Protestant martyr, before pressure from Oldcastle's powerful descendants forced the company to change the character's name. After 1606, with their abuses restrained, the company had to perform the text as it later appeared in the First Folio:

PRINCE HAL. The complaints I hear of thee are grievous.
FALSTAFF. I'faith, my lord, they are false. Nay, I'll tickle ye for a young prince.
PRINCE HAL. Swearest thou, ungracious boy?

The deletion of the offensive oath ''Sblood' (by Christ's blood) and the transposition of the milder 'i'faith' seems a trivial enough alteration, but its effect is to make even dissolute Falstaff swear, as Hotspur would put it, like a comfit-maker's wife, while the Prince's righteous indignation now appears merely prissy.

Shakespeare, who had probably just finished writing *Macbeth* when the Act was passed, may well have been asked to take part in this necessary task of artistic vandalism. An author who cared as much about language as he evidently did, and who used it so precisely, cannot have done so with any enthusiasm, but equally cannot have wanted the job done by other, less sensitive hands. For the next five years, he determinedly avoided the restrictions that had been imposed by choosing to set his new plays exclusively in antiquity, when Christian oaths would be inappropriate even if permissible. Only in 1611 did he venture back into the Christian epoch with *The Tempest*, and only with his collaborative play about Henry VIII, a monarch notorious for swearing, did the Act's demands significantly limit his options. A

previous stage Henry, in Samuel Rowley's *When You See Me, You Know Me* (1605), had sworn the air blue with everything from 'Mother of God' to 'Holy Saint Peter'; the part contains fifty-one several oaths and would have been a bonanza for post-1606 informers. Shakespeare's version gets away with seven. It was perhaps the first time that a parliament's moral censure had succeeded in restraining an English king.

Going Private: The Blackfriars

In 1608 the King's Men finally acquired the use of the Blackfriars theatre which James Burbage had bought and converted for them twelve years before. His son Richard had inherited the property on his death, but, unable to occupy the theatre himself, had leased it in 1600 to a boy company, the Children of the Chapel Royal. Specializing in satire, the boys were in and out of trouble with the authorities for eight years before they eventually surrendered the lease unexpired. Local opposition notwithstanding, the sharers of the King's Men took control of the playhouse on 9 August, and probably began to perform there the following autumn.

The Blackfriars was the theatre for which the King's Men became best known in their day, but it was not their only London venue: in an arrangement unprecedented in English theatrical history, they retained the Globe for summer performances, and played at the indoor theatre during the winter months. There were probably several reasons for their adopting this dual-playhouse operation, which continued until the company's demise more than thirty years later. One consideration would have been health and comfort. The winter of 1607–8 had been especially severe: Londoners would have been able to reach the Globe on foot across the frozen Thames, though it seems unlikely that, even if the theatres remained open, many would have cared to brave the cold for the sake of a play. For the now middle-aged company principals, outdoor performances in such weather must have entailed the risk of rheumatism and pneumonia; it may have been the cold that killed Shakespeare's younger brother Edmund, also a player, at the end of 1607. Equally, in the height of summer the indoor auditorium of the Blackfriars would have become close, sticky, and airless. The two theatres offered performing conditions which each suited a different half of the year.

However, it would be misleading to present the Blackfriars venture as simply an extravagance undertaken by men who had reached that mid-career point when ambition and providence give way to the desire for an easier life: it was also a shrewd move in terms of company finance. The new theatre is often interpreted as a sign of the growing prosperity of Shakespeare and his colleagues under their royal patron, but the project could equally have been born out of severe cash-flow difficulties. The early years of King James's reign had not been propitious ones for the theatrical profession: there is reason to think that, for the sake of public health or public order, the London playhouses were frequently closed between 1603 and 1608, perhaps more often than they were open. In these circumstances, the King's Men needed to maximize their income during the periods when they were able to perform. The advantage of operating a smaller, 'private' playhouse like the Blackfriars was that the admission prices were traditionally very much higher (starting at 6d., which was also the top price at the Globe); and, given that one cannot expect theatres always to be full, a larger per capita income would make for a lower financial risk, especially during the winter when the Globe audiences would have dwindled. Moreover, the Blackfriars did not demand a major new outlay from the company: already owned by Burbage and already fitted up for use as a theatre, it cost the sharers considerably less than their Southwark amphitheatre had done nine years earlier. In 1608, 'going private' made good financial sense.

The disadvantage was that the 'private' theatre audience tended to be seasonal. The price of seats and

the more central location of the playhouse, within the city walls, meant that the Blackfriars attracted its clientele from the upper social strata of Jacobean England. To cater for such influential playgoers befitted the company's premier status as the King's Men, but many of them would spend their summer months in the country; during that part of the year, to perform at the Globe was the more profitable option. (It may also have been thought difficult to dispose of the property: with the Swan underused and the Rose derelict, there was evidently no great demand for South Bank amphitheatres.) The effective result was that, from 1608 onwards, the King's Men entertained two distinct theatre-going constituencies.

It is not known whether the company operated separate repertories at the two theatres. Obviously it would have been economical to stage the same plays at both, and there was certainly a good deal of overlap between its offerings at the two theatres: Quarto title-pages indicate that *The Moor of Venice* (as *Othello* was generally known in performance) and John Webster's tragedy *The Duchess of Malfi* were staged in both, as were, later on, revivals of *The Taming of the Shrew* and *Love's Labours Lost*, probably in 1631. In so far as one can read anything into what a title-page does *not* say, however, it is possible that *The Two Noble Kinsmen* may have been a Blackfriars-only play; there may also have been Globe-only plays. One reason for such an arrangement would have been differences in taste between the two houses' audiences. Several King's Men plays, including *Richard III* and *Titus Andronicus*, were known for their down-market appeal to relatively unsophisticated playgoers, and *Pericles* in particular was to become the object of a tradition of intellectual snobbery initiated by Ben Jonson in 1629. Though two of these were performed at court (*Pericles* in 1619, *Richard III* in 1633), it is tempting to theorize that they and their like were retained in the repertory primarily for the benefit of the Globe audience.

Another consideration would have been the differences between the Globe and the Blackfriars as performance spaces. The indoor theatre was very much smaller than the amphitheatre: the upstairs auditorium, reached by climbing a large, winding staircase, measured just 66 feet by 46, dimensions which may also have contained the stage and tiring house areas. The intimacy and proximity to the action which this promoted was evidently reckoned to be one of the chief attractions of the house, for the most expensive seats were (unlike at the Globe) those closest to the actors; until the practice was abolished by royal command in 1639, the more fashion-conscious members of the audience (and also late comers) could even hire stools and sit on the stage itself, wrecking the sight-lines for anyone unlucky enough to be sitting behind them. There were also some different facilities to be exploited: there was as yet no elaborate movable scenery, but rudimentary lighting effects would have been possible on the candlelit stage that could not be achieved under the afternoon sun at the Globe. The company may well have needed to re-rehearse plays when they transferred from one theatre to the other; in some cases they may even have needed to perform different versions altogether.

Probably one of the first plays the King's Men performed at the Blackfriars was *Coriolanus*: its composition coincided roughly with the acquisition of the new theatre, and in several respects Shakespeare seems to be testing out the dramatic possibilities of the different space. The play has little of the heroic sweep of the earlier tragedies: with its narrow, geographically restricted setting of early republican Rome, it is his most relentless and gripping portrayal of political debate; even the densely compacted language demands an attention that is more intellectual than emotional. In these respects it can benefit from the lower performance register and more intense audience concentration which the smaller theatre allowed. Whether in 1608 it actually received such concentration is less certain: it is pure speculation to suggest that the play failed, or transferred badly, or simply that fashions changed, but it is notable that Shakespeare never again wrote in this style. Most of his later plays lace their politics with romanticism and spectacle, and insist on close attention only intermittently (which is not to say that they do not always repay it). Their musical content was also

greater than before; between 1609 and 1623, one of the king's musicians, Robert Johnson, provided the company with scores for a number of plays, including *The Winter's Tale*, *Cymbeline*, *The Tempest*, and a revival of *Macbeth*. There seems to have been little place in the repertory for the hard realities of *Coriolanus*.

One lasting innovation was the play's five-act structure, which Shakespeare continued to use for the rest of his working life: even the intricate narrative maze of *Cymbeline* is firmly held within these limits. He had occasionally written five-act plays before (notably *The Comedy of Errors*, *Romeo and Juliet*, and *Henry V*), but this was more for literary than theatrical reasons: editions of Seneca and Terence might contain formal act-divisions, but in the outdoor, 'public' theatres plays were performed continuously from the first scene to the last. One of the long-standing practices of the indoor playhouses, however, was the separation of a play's five acts with musical interludes. This was not simply an affectation: unless trimmed at regular intervals, the candles which lit the stages would smoke and eventually go out. Shakespeare had perforce to write his Blackfriars plays in five acts.

This was a major change of practice because the intervals in a performance are more than just dead time. For the audience they are a pause for reflection, for the play a form of punctuation, separating the story into discrete units of narrative: one of the artistic effects was to impose a regularity of pacing and structure on Shakespeare's late plays. The five acts of *Coriolanus*, for instance, mark out the successive stages of the hero's rise and fall, taking him from battlefield success to the consulship, then to banishment, alliance with the Volsces, and finally to destruction: the audience is repeatedly given a sense of progression, and also some respite for the attention span. In the romantic plays, notably *The Winter's Tale*, the four intervals often work to underline contrasts of setting and tone between the different sections of the narrative: Sicilia and Bohemia, winter and summer, tragedy and comedy. *Coriolanus*, however, uses the divisions to bring out the extent to which, in spite of the developing events, things do not change in Rome: the tortured protraction and repetitiveness of the confrontations, potentially so tedious in continuous performance, is set against the interval-inculcated sense of the story's having got somewhere, with the result that the audience can become intensely aware of both sides' political inflexibility and inertia, which will have such destructive consequences.

When Globe plays were revived at the Blackfriars, they too needed to be given in five acts, but this could only rarely have been a simple matter of tipping in four musical interludes. A strict, classical regularity of form does not suit all plays, particularly if they were written for continuous performance: the unconventional, baroque structures of *Hamlet* and *Antony and Cleopatra* were later badly mangled by the ignorantly learned attempts of Shakespeare's editors to impose act-divisions on them. Unburdened by editorial responsibility, the King's Men probably adapted their old plays for five-act Blackfriars revivals: in particular, to perform the original text of *Love's Labours Lost*, with its disproportionately long final scene, would have left the actors and their audience darkling, and choking, before the end of the play.

Responses

There is relatively little direct evidence about audience reception of Shakespeare's plays during his lifetime: in contrast with the depressing volume of generalized censure from people who had probably never been near a theatre in their lives, few playgoers took the trouble to record their thoughts about their afternoon's entertainment. The bulk of our knowledge must be inferred from allusions and imitations, evidence of what people noticed and remembered, but inevitably at one remove from the audience response to which they bear witness.

Occasionally this material records a specific piece of stage business: Falstaff with his bottle of sack in his pistol-case, Flute as Thisbe trying to kill 'herself' with Pyramus' scabbard, Hamlet's leaping into Ophelia's grave, are all mentioned in minor Jacobean literature. More often, we can identify broader patterns of reception from other authors' attempts to repeat Shakespeare's success: as Virginia Mason Vaughan has said,

> We know from contemporary mass culture that imitation is not just a form of flattery: when a rival company seeks to capitalize on its competitor's success by imitating a product, it often exaggerates the characteristics of the product it believes are the most popular. By examining the imitation, we may learn what was so appealing about the original.[7]

By this principle it is clear that, for example, *Macbeth* was noted particularly for its supernatural elements, though the twisted dynamics of the murders also made an impression. Set-piece comic routines were popular, too: the sequence in *The Comedy of Errors* in which Antipholus of Ephesus is locked out of his own house turns up again in Thomas Dekker and Thomas Middleton's *The Honest Whore, Part 1* (1604), as does *Twelfth Night*'s mock-duel in Ben Jonson's *Epicoene* (1609); Dekker even inserts into his dialogue a wry acknowledgement of the source, testament to the instant recognizability of the material, and so the success of the original play.[8]

Certain characters were also important facets of the plays' appeal. Comic figures like Trinculo in *The Tempest* and Boult in *Pericles* were popular, if only for what moralists regarded as their 'antic and dishonest gestures'; Justice Shallow and Doll Tearsheet also stuck in some memories.[9] Writing about court performances in the 1630s, Leonard Digges pointed to the auditorium-filling power of some of the most popular:

> let but Falstaff come,
> Hal, Poins, and the rest, you scarce shall have a room,
> All is so pestered. Let but Beatrice
> And Benedick be seen, lo, in a trice
> The Cockpit galleries, boxes, all are full
> To hear Malvolio, that cross-gartered gull.[10]

His claim is supported by the changes of title which some plays underwent from the 1610s onwards. In

April 1635, for example, *Sir John Falstaff* was to be seen at the Blackfriars, eponymity finally confirming the centrality of Falstaff rather than Henry IV or the merry wives of Windsor (depending on which play it really was). Abstract, 'literary' titles were especially at risk: *Much Ado about Nothing* was referred to as *Benedick and Beatrice* in 1613; *Twelfth Night* was *Malvolio* in 1623; *All is True* was acted as *King Henry VIII* in 1628; and by the 1640s *All's Well that Ends Well* had probably become *Monsieur Paroles*. It is not certain that these were the 'authorized' titles under which the King's Men performed the plays; but even if they were not, they provide further evidence that the audience's modes of reception tended to be character-centred far more than thematic.

While some characters grew to be coextensive with the plays in which they appeared, others transcended them. It is striking that two of the most popular, Hamlet and Falstaff, were remembered as much for their physical qualities as for their parts in their respective plays: not as persons in a story, or even roles performed by an actor, but as embodied beings. Early allusions to Hamlet emphasize his disordered clothes and his melancholy mannerisms, while Falstaff, of course, became notorious as an exemplar of fatness. They seem almost to have acquired a life independent of their plays, to have been abstracted from their original context and reconfigured in the cultural imagination in a simplified form emphasizing their most popular attributes. This process is apparent in the way such successful characters were exploited by continuation. Hamlet was obviously unavailable for further adventures, but after the *Henry IV* plays Falstaff was given his own vehicle in *The Merry Wives of Windsor*; his dissolute qualities survived the transplantation, but many of his earlier complexities were lost.

Petruccio, who was evidently regarded as the centre of *The Taming of the Shrew*'s appeal, also featured in a sequel, John Fletcher's 'amends for ladies' comedy, *The Woman's Prize; or, The Tamer Tamed*, written for the King's Men probably early in 1610. The play presents Petruccio with his second wife, Maria, who uses Lysistrata's tactics of sexual denial to challenge his hierarchical view of marriage. For a sequel, however, it pays scant regard to the details of the Shakespearian play which it purports to extend: Petruccio is transferred without comment to a London setting, and despite his name he is portrayed as an Englishman rather than an Italian. Significantly, moreover, his married life with Katherina is described in terms which are strikingly discontinuous with what was anticipated at the end of *The Taming of the Shrew*:

> did I want vexation,
> Or any special care to kill my heart?
> Had I not every morning a rare breakfast,
> Mixed with a learned lecture of ill language,
> Louder than Tom o' Lincoln, and at dinner
> A diet of the same dish? Was there evening
> That e'er passed over us without 'Thou knave'
> Or 'Thou whore' for digestion? (III. iii. 155–62)[11]

He is even said to have nightmares about his first marriage: 'the bare remembrance of Katherina', it is said,

> Will make him start in's sleep, and very often
> Cry out for cudgels, cowl-staffs, anything,
> Hiding his breeches, out of fear her ghost
> Should walk and wear 'em yet. (I. i. 31–6)

A cowl-staff, traditionally used both as a weapon and to parade henpecked husbands around the community, makes a neat emblem of this Petruccio's stormy life with an untamed shrew.

All this might make the conclusion seem as 'inescapable' as it did to Baldwin Maxwell in the 1930s that, contrary to scholarly tradition, '*The Woman's Prize* was not originally planned as a sequel, continuation, or adaptation of *The Taming of the Shrew*.'[12] The King's Men seem to have thought differently in 1633, however, when they presented the two plays in consecutive court performances: clearly there was understood to be some significant connection between the two. The fact is that Fletcher's play is inconsistent in its assumptions about Petruccio's past: he may have had an unhappy marriage, but he is also 'famous for a woman-tamer, . . . a brave wife-breaker' (I. iii. 268–9), which accords better with Shakespeare's conclusion. The anomaly is explicable if we consider the play not simply as a sequel to *The Taming of the Shrew*, but also a document in its cultural reception: because Shakespeare's play stages only the early, discordant period of Petruccio's marriage, repeated performances would build up the overall impression given in *The Woman's Prize*, whilst at the same time reinforcing Petruccio's reputation as a tamer.

If that hypothesis is correct, then the way Petruccio is conceived in *The Woman's Prize* may be taken as indirect evidence about the Jacobean understanding of the Shakespearian original. In some respects this was evidently very different from that of *The Taming of the Shrew*'s modern critics. What the sequel makes clear is that Petruccio's access to his independent, semi-legendary existence is a function of his ability to dominate unruly women. In particular, it establishes that he was seen as a wife-beater even during Shakespeare's lifetime, armed not with the whip of later stage tradition but with a cudgel (mentioned several times in *The Woman's Prize* but never in *The Taming of the Shrew*). At one point he exasperatedly threatens his second wife with physical violence:

> If I should beat thee now, as much may be,
> Dost thou not well deserve it, o' thy conscience?
> Dost thou not cry, 'Come beat me'? (IV. ii. 140–2)

Shakespeare's Petruccio, in contrast, will beat his servants, but never his wife: if Fletcher's play is to be understood as a self-consciously 'enlightened' riposte to Shakespeare's, then it achieves this at the expense of misrepresenting *The Taming of the Shrew* as a typical exemplar of the sado-masochistic 'wife-taming' literature from which in fact it deviates.

That some Jacobean audiences interpreted Shakespeare's play in these terms is confirmed by an allusion in a misogynistic pamphlet written by the verse satirist Samuel Rowlands in 1609:

> The chiefest art I have I will bestow
> About a work called taming of the shrew.
> It makes my heart to fret, my looks to frown
> That we should let our wives thus put us down;
> But for mine own part I have now decreed
> To do a good and charitable deed.

> If she begin her former course afresh,
> I have a trick to mortify her flesh:
> Unto you all example I will give,
> Perhaps you'll thank me for it while you live.[13]

This is spoken by one of a gaggle of henpecked husbands, and seems to recall not only the title of Shakespeare's play, but also Petruccio's appeal to the audience to contribute advice on shrew-taming—''Tis charity to show' (IV. i. 197). It is as if Rowlands (or his character) has come away from the theatre feeling, like Christopher Sly in the complete version of the framing story, that he has learned how to deal with his own wife; the reference to mortification (a word which Rowlands used to mean bruising) suggests that, like Sly again, he has not paid very close attention. The original sophistication of the Shakespearian text has been filtered out and, like the dyer's hand, it has come into conformity with the cultural preconceptions which it ostensibly challenges—misogynistic orthodoxies about the proper subordination of women.

We can see something approaching this process in the few surviving eye-witness accounts of Jacobean performances. For several of these we are indebted to the astrologer and society quack-doctor Simon Forman, who made detailed notes about the four plays he saw at the Globe in the spring of 1611.[14] The first, though not the only, imperative in each of these early 'theatre reviews' is simply to get down the plot: the hurried scramble of Forman's syntax shows how exciting he must have found *Cymbeline* in particular. The company's performance of *The Moor of Venice* at Oxford in September 1610 had a similar impact on a junior don, Henry Jackson, who wrote in a Latin letter that 'they acted decorously and aptly' and 'moved tears not only by speaking but also by their actions'. Most of all he was impressed by the final scene: 'indeed that Desdemona, murdered by her husband before our eyes, although she always played very well, yet moved more having been killed, when, lying on the bed, she appealed for the pity of the spectators by her very face.'[15]

The original Latin of this passage is interesting in its consistent use of feminine grammatical forms when referring not only to Desdemona but also the actor playing her: not a naïve man, Jackson is none the less so entirely engaged in the dramatic illusion that the male performer's gender (and so, to a degree, the medium of the performance) is momentarily elided. There is a similar, if cruder, confusion between the facts of the production and of the story in Forman's account of *Macbeth*, which he evidently wrote after supplementing his memory with a look at the standard historical account in Holinshed's *Chronicles*: the play's passing reference to Donalbain's flight to Ireland, for instance, is conflated with Holinshed's allusion to Fleance's escape to Wales; and Forman describes the witches as 'fairies or nymphs', recalling an illustration in the book rather than the midnight hags he must have seen in the theatre. The underlying assumption is that the play is an unmediated transmission of historical events which can also be found in other authors, even if Forman does not seem to have paid them very close attention. Both he and Jackson illustrate, in their different ways, John Webster's praise of the excellent Jacobean actor's power of enchantment: 'what we see him personate, we think truly done before us.'[16] The corollary is that their accounts are of extremely limited utility as evidence of Jacobean staging.

None the less, Forman's notes in particular remain a valuable record of how Shakespeare was seen and used by one member of the Globe clientele. Interestingly, he seems to have had no great interest in the spectacular: he records no parade of kings in *Macbeth*, no descent of Jupiter in *Cymbeline*, no bear in *The Winter's Tale*. He is much more concerned with the exemplary features of the stories: the working-out of nemesis in *Macbeth*, or of Apollo's prophecy in *The Winter's Tale*. On occasion, he will even formulate a nugget of homespun wisdom: 'Beware of trusting feigned beggars and fawning fellows,' he counsels after seeing the cony-catching exploits of Autolycus, 'the rogue that came in all tattered like colt-pixie'. Forman kept his summaries not merely as an *aide-mémoire* of plays he had enjoyed but, as it says at the head of the manuscript, 'for common policy'—in other words, to provide examples and advice on matters of moral and social conduct.

There is some indirect evidence that Forman was not unique in using plays as a source of moralistic instruction. This anecdote about Pompey the Great in an anonymous murder pamphlet of 1614 was presumably culled from a commonplace book entry made after seeing a performance of *Antony and Cleopatra*:

It is reported that Pompey . . . whose valiant deeds had purchased him the name of great, Julius Caesar, Mark Antony, and he contending for the empire and domination of the world, where many bloody battles was fought between them; yet at last there was a truce agreed upon for a certain time, in the which truce these three mighty commanders did feast and were merry together divers times, and being once invited to sup aboard of Pompey's galley, as they were sat, one of Pompey's servants whispered him in the ear, and asked him if he would be master of the whole world. Pompey told him yes, if he knew how. Then said his servant again, 'Let us cut Caesar and Antony's throats, and then all the world is thine.' Pompey made answer, 'Thou shouldst,' quoth he, 'have done it without my knowledge, but now it shall not be done, for in me it is villainy, but in thee it had been good service.' Thus the heathen man may be a pattern to all Christians, that by his example they should abhor and detest murder; for Pompey would not basely take away the lives of his two mighty, mortal, and only enemies, although he knew the doing of it would have gained him the monarchy of the whole world.[17]

This material was indubitably drawn from the play's scene on Sextus Pompey's galley (II. vii. 73–4 is quoted almost verbatim), though the characters of Caesar and Pompey are confused with their more famous forebears. Here it is reapplied for exemplary purposes in an entirely unrelated context, and without reference to its dramatic origins: in this we see the ultimate object of Forman's notes 'for common policy'.

All this evidence stands in powerful contradiction to the argument that the theatre was a school of abuse. Henry Jackson did not learn from *The Moor of Venice* how to commit murder, but experienced humane feelings for the victim, while Simon Forman and the anonymous pamphleteer actively used plays as a storehouse of good example. If anything suffered from this process it was not the morals of the audience but, as in responses to *The Taming of the Shrew*, the sophistication of the plays. Among the most striking features of contemporary accounts of Shakespeare in performance are the simple errors of fact in describing what were not yet the familiar plays they later became: John Manningham thought Olivia was mourning for a dead husband, not a brother, when he saw *Twelfth Night* at the Middle Temple in February 1602, for instance. Dialogue too is often misrepresented. Unlike the pamphleteer, Forman had quite a poor verbal memory: 'Thane of Cawdor' becomes 'King of Codon', and Cymbeline is said to be King of England rather than Britain; the name 'Innogen' which appears in his account of the same play may well have been a mishearing, or misremembering, of the published text's 'Imogen', possibly influenced again by his reading of Holinshed. These Jacobean playgoers did not pay the sort of concentrated, critical attention that modern academic writers give to Shakespeare.

Equally, however, they were not the empty vessels the antitheatrical controversialists supposed, ready to be filled with whatever corrupt ideas and examples might be presented on the stage. Rather they pieced out with their minds not only the imperfections of the medium but also their own inattentive reception of the play itself. For example, *The Winter's Tale* allows its audience to feel liking, sympathy, and even admiration for Autolycus, that tattered victim of court unemployment living by his wits. We don't know how Forman responded to the character as he watched the Globe performance, but what he took away from the play was the standard moralistic message not to trust such rogues: preconceptions about subject matter win out over any perception Forman may have had of the distinctive qualities of the play's own treatment of that material. In the pamphleteer's response to *Antony and Cleopatra*, too, the ethical complexities of the situation, which so ambiguate Sextus Pompey for modern commentators, are flattened out: there is no sense that he is compromised by his willingness to be the unwitting beneficiary of treachery and murder, only that he is an honourable pagan in his rejection of the proposal; the resultant, simplified version of the event is therefore usable in support of orthodox moral attitudes to the wickedness of homicide.

It is worth remembering that this evacuation of the

plays' original sophistication, however distasteful it may be to modern scholarly purists, is an important part of the process by which they became popular and so achieved longevity. It is also something over which playwrights and actors have relatively little control: dramatists like Ben Jonson or John Arden who seek to dictate the reception of their plays have a tendency to end up leaving the 'loathed stage' altogether, to cater instead for the judicious reader.[18] For the King's Men, what mattered, commercially as well as artistically, was to delimit that reception rather than prescribe its nature: like all successful entertainment industries, the company thrived on the management of desire, exploiting its ability not only to retail but to withhold access to their repertory. When plays seldom come, they wished-for come: by keeping supply slightly below the level of demand, a company can expect to keep its titles popular. A corollary of that principle is the need to prevent other organizations from giving unauthorized performances, topping up supply to meet demand and thereby saturating the market.

In seventeenth-century France, the custom was that publication of a play made it legitimately available for performance by any company. Whether England was in a similarly unregulated position in the early years of the century remains unclear. In practice, the commercial threat posed by a script's accessibility in print seems to have been inconsequential. If anything, it was amateur actors who took most advantage of the availability of printed texts of Shakespeare. In 1607, for example, sailors on the East India Company's ship the *Dragon*, then off the coast of West Africa, entertained themselves by performing *Hamlet* and *Richard II*. It was probably in the next decade that the Red Bull, rowdiest and most plebeian of the suburban amphitheatres, was host to a youth production of *Richard III*, in which the 'little Richard' so impressed the theatre's resident playwright, Thomas Heywood, that he wrote a special prologue and epilogue for the 'young, witty lad', which begins, charmingly,

> If any wonder by what magic charm
> Richard the Third is shrunk up like his arm . . .[19]

In 1622 Sir Edward Dering prepared an adapted

conflation of the *Henry IV* plays, apparently for an abortive local production at Surrenden Hall in Kent, and Buckden in Huntingdonshire saw a scandalous, sabbath-breaking performance of *A Midsummer Night's Dream* in about 1631, which earned the actor who played Bottom twelve hours in the stocks, still wearing his ass's head.

In contrast, there is no certain evidence of any professional company in Jacobean London seeking to stage rival productions of Shakespeare. In 1610 *King Lear* and *Pericles* were performed in Yorkshire by a minor troupe of country players (who responded to accusations of interpolating papist propaganda by insisting that they played the Quarto texts as printed). A number of plays—or possibly adaptations of them—were also available in the repertory of English players on the Continent. However, it was not until 1627 that the King's Men had to seek official action to prevent the Red Bull company from giving unauthorized performances in London. By then, Shakespeare was dead and his plays had become established classics.

The Triumph of Time

The touchstone for the development of Shakespearian stage history in the 1610s is *All is True*, later known as *Henry VIII*. Shakespeare wrote the play in collaboration with John Fletcher, with whom he had already produced the lost *Cardenio*, and who was later to succeed him as the principal dramatist for the King's Men. When it opened at the Globe late in June 1613, the leading role of the King was probably taken not by Burbage but by the younger actor John Lowin. After a decade of fraught expansion, the original King's Men and their playwright were coming to the end of their time. There is a melancholy aptness to the events of 29 June, when, after the play had been acted 'not passing

two or three times', the theatre burned down during a performance.[20]

The fire happened when a peal of ordnance was discharged in the first act to salute the King's arrival at Cardinal Wolsey's house, and a piece of smouldering wadding from one of the cannons landed on the amphitheatre's thatched roof. The hot summer afternoon made for easy kindling, but the audience was too busy watching the play to give much attention to the smoking roof until it was too late: the wind blew the fire around the theatre's polygonal frame, and within two hours only the foundations were left. It is said that John Heminges, one of the company's senior members, wept.

Miraculously, the only major loss, human or proprietary, was the building itself. Though the house was nearly full, the actors and audience all escaped safely, if narrowly in a few cases such as the heroic playgoer who rescued a child and got himself scalded, or the man who 'had his breeches set on fire, that would perhaps have broiled him, if he had not by the benefit of a provident wit put it out with bottle ale'; it was, wrote John Chamberlain, 'a great marvel and fair grace of God that the people had so little harm, having but two narrow doors to get out'. As for property, 'nothing did perish but wood and straw, and a few forsaken cloaks', presumably abandoned by members of the audience in their haste to get out.[21] If we take this report literally, then the company's effects—properties, costumes, prompt-books—must have been stored elsewhere, possibly at the Blackfriars. Whereas the actors at the Fortune lost everything and had to start again from scratch when their playhouse burned down in 1621, the King's Men would have been able to continue operations with their repertory intact.

The opening-night prologue to Shakespeare and Fletcher's *The Two Noble Kinsmen*, one of the first new plays staged after the fire, communicates the actors' desolate mood, but exaggerates the seriousness of the crisis:

> If this play do not keep
> A little dull time from us, we perceive
> Our losses fall so thick we needs must leave. (30–2)

Perhaps by now the company's founder members

were feeling the effects of 'dull time', but there was no question of their being forced to leave acting, bankrupted by their losses in the fire. By the time *The Two Noble Kinsmen* opened at the Blackfriars, they would already have laid plans to rebuild the Globe at a cost of about £1,400.

This decision should not be taken for granted. One of the few benefits of large-scale destruction is that, in the immediate aftermath, it allows a serious reconsideration of future policy, free from the limitations which inertia can impose on thought and action. Though the ground lease on the Globe's site still had another sixteen years to run, it would have been easy for the King's Men to cut their losses and transfer all their activities to the Blackfriars. In the event, however, they chose not only to continue their existing arrangement but to consolidate it. Built in the spring of 1614 and open to playgoers by the summer, the new Globe (fig. 12) was described by eye-witnesses as 'a stately theatre', 'the fairest that ever was in England'.[22] Expensively but prudently roofed with tile rather than inflammable thatch, it was a costly, even an extravagant venture: the fact that, eight years later, Edward Alleyn and his partners were able to rebuild the Fortune, a playhouse of similar size, for only £1,000 illustrates the extent of the company's investment in upgrading the Globe. Evidently it was an important part of their operation, not just a cheap, second-string house for use when the rich Blackfriars audiences were out of town.

No doubt there were a variety of commercial, artistic, and sentimental reasons for keeping the Globe. The playhouse seems to have inspired genuine affection in some Londoners, evident in the elegiac regret with which Sir Henry Wotton, once an amateur playwright himself, wrote of its demise: 'This was the fatal period [i.e. full stop] of this virtuous fabric.'[23] Some members of the company may also have felt piqued at the activities of Philip Henslowe, the theatre financier, whose arrangements for the erection of the Hope, a multi-purpose bankside amphitheatre for bear-baiting and plays, followed the fire with unseemly haste and were perhaps an attempt to cut in on the Globe's market. Most fundamentally, however, the effect of the decision was to avoid a disruption of the company's familiar working practices: with the expectation of a difficult, unstable period to come, the opportunity for reconsideration may have been the last thing the King's Men needed.

The fire happened about a week before Richard Burbage's 45th birthday. 'Old stuttering Heminges'— he achieved the first adjective early, and it clung to him

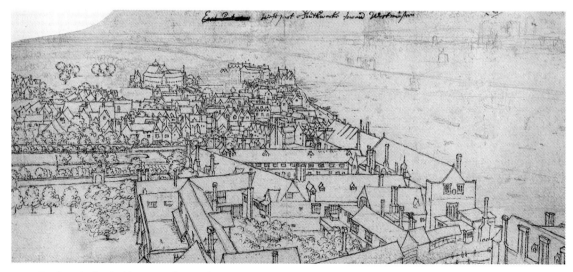

FIG. 12 Southwark, sketched by Wenceslaus Hollar in 1638. The second Globe is the large double-gabled building in the background, towards the left.

for the rest of his life—was 46, and Shakespeare 49; Henry Condell, who had married in 1596, must also have been in his forties. Heminges had already cut down on his acting appearances, probably to concentrate on theatre administration. It is possible that this semi-retirement was an enforced one: the stuttering, unkindly noted in a ballad on the Globe fire, may have been a speech impediment or even a mild aphasia that affected his ability to deliver his lines. (Of course, it may equally have been just a trade-mark of his performances: he is often supposed to have specialized in senile parts, and indeed his only known role is the aged dupe Corbaccio in Jonson's *Volpone*.) In any event, what we know of life expectancy in the period suggests that the King's Men could look forward to losing many of their key personnel within ten years.

The most important loss was, of course, Shakespeare, who must have been considering retirement in 1613. His share of the Globe rebuilding costs was to be his last major financial contribution to the company. He made his last literary contribution, his share of *The Two Noble Kinsmen*, at about the same time. The play does not appear even to have been a true collaboration: an index of the limited communication between the two authors is their failure to agree on how to pronounce the name 'Pirithous'.[24] It is almost as if each contributor was working in isolation from the other; perhaps Shakespeare had by then already retired to Stratford, where he was to die in 1616.

Six years after the Globe fire, only Condell and 'old' Heminges remained from the original King's Men. Heminges's son-in-law William Ostler, who created the role of Antonio in *The Duchess of Malfi*, died prematurely late in 1614. Robert Armin, the company's clown, followed at the end of 1615. Richard Cowley, for whom Shakespeare wrote Verges in *Much Ado about Nothing*, died in March 1619. On the day after the funeral Richard Burbage also died. He was 50 years old.

Burbage's death seems to have been quite sudden: he had evidently made no plans to retire, for the company's new royal patent, issued two weeks afterwards though obviously drafted earlier, still names him among its principal members. Among colleagues and audiences alike, the shock and sense of loss overshadowed the public mourning for Queen Anne, who had also died ten days earlier:

> Burbage the player has vouchsafed to die;
> Therefore in London is not one eye dry.
> The deaths of men who act our queens and kings
> Are now more mourned than are the real things.[25]

There were indeed more elegies composed on Burbage than on the queen, no doubt reflecting a more heartfelt grief: the violation of proper hierarchy, remarked on by this verse satirist, indicates the extent of the actor's public esteem.

The satire is churlishly antitheatrical in its implicit observation that Burbage's kings, unlike Queen Anne, were not real people to be grieved for, but its coldly rational perspective none the less exposes, by indirections, a singular and significant feature of the mourning. For the King's Men, the death of their leading actor, the greatest of his generation, was a real loss, not only of a respected colleague but also of a valuable commercial asset: he was later remembered as 'the flower and life of his company, the lodestone of the auditory, and the Roscius of the stage'.[26] For most playgoers, however, it was the loss not so much of one person as of many parts: as the longest and most famous of the elegies put it,

> He's gone, and with him what a world are dead,
> Which he revived, to be revived so.
> No more young Hamlet, old Hieronimo,
> Kind Lear, the grieved Moor, and more beside
> That lived in him, have now forever died.[27]

Of course, Hamlet, Othello, and the rest didn't truly die with Burbage: they were just recast. However, the hyperbolical exaggeration here should not simply be dismissed as naïve: as the first Hamlet, the first Lear and Othello, Burbage's might legitimately be called the definitive performances; the elegy's conflation of the actor with his roles serves to underline the point. In mourning for Burbage, the Jacobeans were in a sense mourning for the end of authenticity. More than the move to the Blackfriars and consequent adaptation of the plays, more than the burning of the Globe, more even than the death of Shakespeare himself, it was the loss of the original leading actor which marked for contemporaries the end of a theatrical era.

The fame which made Burbage 'the lodestone of the auditory' should not lead us to overestimate his centrality in the operations of the King's Men, however. It is notable that later Jacobean drama, including Shakespeare's, tends less and less to be structured around a towering principal performance like Lear, Othello, or Malevole in John Marston's *The Malcontent*, also a Burbage role. Increasingly the preference, even in tragedy, was for ensemble-orientated plays like *Cymbeline*, often with two shorter, more or less evenly balanced leading parts. Whatever the cultural reasons for this shift of sensibility, the theatrical advantage was to make it possible for an acting company to reduce the pressure and responsibility laid on its star actor—a division of the kingdom, so to speak, with one moiety conferred on younger strengths. When the King's Men produced *The Duchess of Malfi* at the Blackfriars in the winter of 1613–14, it was John Lowin who headed the cast as the truculent assassin Bosola, while Burbage took the secondary lead of Ferdinand, his psychotic master; it was probably the same arrangement that saw Lowin, not Burbage, playing the King in *All is True* earlier that year.

Lowin (fig. 13) was the only person to remain a member of the King's Men throughout the forty-odd years of their existence. Born in 1576 and first hired by the company in 1603, he rose over the next decade to leading man status. As well as Henry VIII he played Falstaff, a part for which he was especially suited not only by his girth but also by the diversity of his talents, evident in the range of his known non-Shakespearian roles: as well as villains like Bosola, he played Jonsonian comic knights such as Sir Epicure Mammon in *The Alchemist* and Sir Politic Would-Be in *Volpone*, and also heroic characters like the honourable soldier Melantius in Beaumont and Fletcher's *The Maid's Tragedy*. Few of the King's Men can have been better qualified to strike the comical-pathetical-sinister balance which Falstaff ideally requires.

Burbage's successor as Hamlet was Joseph Taylor,

FIG. 13 John Lowin, the longest-serving member of the King's Men, whose Shakespearian roles included (unsurprisingly) Falstaff and Henry VIII.

who joined the company in 1619, while Richard III and Othello went to new recruit Ellyaerdt Swanston after 1624. With Lowin, these men were the nucleus of the King's Men's second generation in the 1620s and 1630s. The greatest pressure on this new company must have been the reputation of the old. The careers of Shakespeare and Burbage had coincided with, and to a large extent contributed to, a quarter-century of exceptional creativity in English drama and theatre. Because the artistic energies of such periods are usually too prolific for immediate assimilation, cultural production tends to idle in the aftermath: further consideration of the brilliant recent past takes a high priority, and new work is most acceptable when it attempts to recreate the original experience (actual or presumed) of the old.

'Old plays, you know, are best.'[28] William Heminges, John's playwright son, astutely caught the post-Shakespearian period's theatrical taste in the proverbial-sounding words of the wicked Queen in *The Fatal Contract* (1639). Naturally Shakespeare remained in the repertory of the King's Men: at least seventeen of his plays were revived, some of them several times, during the twenty-five years after his death.[29] We know relatively little about these productions: there are few eye-witness accounts, and allusions and imitations are only intermittently illuminating about the plays' impact on the stage. In the little and often cryptic evidence that survives it is possible none the less to detect a trace of what may be the first stirring of that nostalgic concern for a lost authenticity which has been one of the major conflicting imperatives throughout Shakespearian stage history. Twice during the 1630s the King's Men gave court performances of a play whose title is recorded as *Oldcastle*, and which can scarcely have been anything other than *1 Henry IV*. Shakespeare's enforced renaming of the fat knight was the best-known theatrical anecdote of the mid-seventeenth century; some allusions to the character even call him by his original name. Could it be that, long before the Oxford editors restored Sir John Oldcastle to notoriety in their text of the play, the Caroline King's Men, acknowledging that old was best, had reverted to using the name in some performances?

The World Turned Upside-down

English civil authorities have often responded to the start of a war by closing places of public entertainment; the start of the Civil War in 1642 was no exception. On 31 August, nine days after the king had raised his standard at Nottingham, the House of Commons instructed Francis Rous, the MP for Truro who would later become the Speaker of the Barebones Parliament, to draft 'an order that all stage plays may be put down during this time of distractions and of fasting'. Two days later, Rous presented the bill and it was passed by both houses: London's theatres were officially closed by a Parliament seeking 'all possible

means to appease and avert the wrath of God'.[30] It was the beginning of the end for the King's Men.

The suppression of plays had also been a topic of debate earlier in the year. On 26 January a motion to that effect proposed by Sir Edward Partridge was abandoned after it met with the humane opposition of Edmund Waller and John Pym, who pointed out that such a measure would deprive the players of their trade. This early debate is important because it complicates the notion of a long-standing parliamentary antitheatricalism, which, unfettered once the king had abandoned London, found its ultimate expression in Rous's bill: the unexpected combination of Pym, greatest of parliamentarians, and Waller, the royalist poet, in support of the players makes it clear that attitudes to the theatre did not divide neatly along factional lines. However, when a depleted House of Commons voted the closure bill through on 2 September, with only sixty-nine members present of a possible 507, it seems to have been a routine, uncontroversial measure: the parliamentary diary of Sir Simonds D'Ewes speaks only of 'some motions and orders of little moment'.[31] This was neither the first nor the last time that the capital's theatres were closed during a period of national emergency.

The acting companies had, of course, been technically royalist in their allegiances since 1603, and theatre had been an increasingly important feature of Caroline court culture in the decades leading up to the war: parliamentarian propaganda of the 1640s insistently emphasized the court's extravagant taste for plays and masques. Both the importance and the extravagance (if they are distinct qualities) are apparent in the decision to convert the Whitehall cockpit erected by Henry VIII into a permanent theatre building, the Cockpit-in-Court (fig. 14). Designed by Inigo Jones, the foremost architect of the day, the theatre opened in 1630 and set a new standard of theatrical magnificence with its concave, Palladian stage façade and sumptuous gold and blue décor:

at a play or masque, the darkest night was converted to the brightest day that ever shined, by the lustre of torches, the sparkling of rich jewels, and the variety of those incomparable and excellent faces, from which the other derived their brightness.[32]

Throughout the 1630s this was a regular venue for the professional companies' court performances (although St James's Palace was used when a larger auditorium was required); Shakespeare plays performed there included *Oldcastle*, *Caesar*, and *The Merry Wives of Windsor*.

So how political was the professional theatre, and in particular its Shakespeare productions, in the period leading up to the Civil War? 'The Players' Petition to the Parliament', a verse protest against the closure probably written in the first half of 1643, admits that some plays, including revivals of *Henry VI* and Jonson's Roman tragedies, might be used to glance at current affairs:

> we vow
> Not to act anything you disallow:
> We will not dare at your strange votes to jeer,
> Nor to personate King Pym with his state-fleer;
> Aspiring Catiline shall be forgot,
> Bloody Sejanus, or whoe'er would plot
> Confusion to a state; the wars betwixt
> The Parliament and just Henry the Sixth
> Shall have no thought or motion . . .[33]

The poem tells us nothing about the actual circumstances of the theatre at this time: it was probably not the work of a player, and was certainly never delivered as a petition; and the plays mentioned are unlikely to have been considered for revival despite the apposite political situation. It is revealing in that it explicitly invokes the possibility that old plays might be 'reread' in production with a contemporary, dissentient application.

This was probably not a new phenomenon. Contemporary parallels certainly were drawn after a Globe performance of *King Henry VIII* in August 1628, at the height of Buckingham's unpopularity and mere weeks before his assassination. To stage a play whose first movement presents the fall and execution of a former duke of Buckingham might seem an ill-timed impudence but for the fact that, astonishingly, the play was requested and attended by Buckingham himself, apparently in order to see his counterpart's disgrace,

after which he left. His critics seized their opportunity: 'Some say he should rather have seen the fall of Cardinal Wolsey, who was a more lively type of himself.'[34]

Presumably Buckingham was either insensitive to the possibility of topical application or arrogant enough not to care about it. His behaviour is an extreme illustration of the extent to which the king and his courtiers failed to make (or at least affected to ignore) such connections. A scan of the history of command performances from the death of Burbage to the outbreak of civil war reveals several uncomfortably applicable choices of play. It might seem especially tactless to give the court *Pericles, Prince of Tyre*, its action organized around the systole and diastole of a wife's death and resurrection, a few months after Queen Anne had died, even though the king was not to be present at the performance; but in the event the only person upset by the occasion was the earl of Pembroke, who 'being tender-hearted, could not endure to see [the play] so soon after the loss of my old acquaintance Burbage'.[35] Fifteen years later, *Cymbeline* might not have been the best selection for New Year's Day 1634: with its wicked queen who induces her husband into war with Rome, it could easily have been read as covert criticism of Queen Henrietta Maria's dabblings in aggressive, anti-Spanish foreign policy in the early 1630s. In fact the play was 'well liked by the King' (though the queen herself was not present).[36] The Solicitor-General John Cooke was wrong when he claimed in 1649 that Charles had undone himself by paying more attention to Shakespeare and Jonson than to the Bible. If anything he did not pay enough attention to the implications of Shakespeare. The Second Folio was famously among his reading during his imprisonment in the later 1640s, but then, as before, these old plays served not to confront him with contemporary concerns but to release him from them—part of the retreat into the golden world of neo-classical aesthetics which so characterized that inept monarch's handling of the crisis.

Many of the King's Men left London when the theatres closed. Some of them enlisted in the royalist army, though Lowin and Taylor were by now too old to fight. Swanston remained in the capital, supported

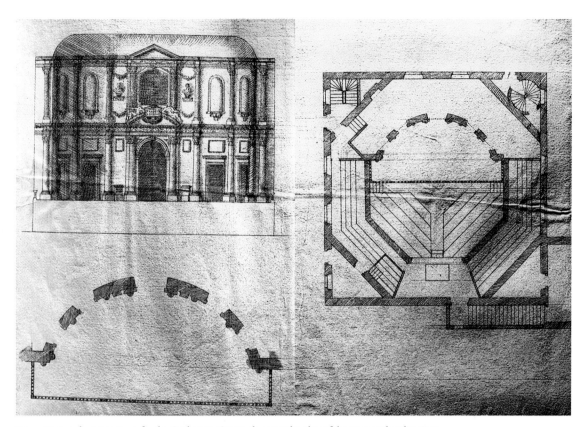

Fig. 14 Designs by Inigo Jones for the Cockpit-in-Court, showing the plan of the stage and auditorium (right), the stage façade (top left), and the plan of the stage area (bottom left) showing the five doors.

Parliament, and became a jeweller: the star of *Richard III*, the play which Milton was later to quote acidly against the king in *Eikonoklastes* (1649), was the only member of the King's Men to side against his former patron. The rump of the company continued occasionally to act before the king at his displaced court in Oxford.

In London, other troupes struggled on, giving illegal performances in defiance of Parliament. Meanwhile the relicts of the King's Men were despoiled. Many of the company's movable effects— costumes, stage drapes, prompt-books—were sold off. The play manuscripts were mostly bought by the crypto-royalist printer Humphrey Moseley: in 1653 he registered his ownership of *Cardenio*, and to his lasting discredit failed to publish an edition. Meanwhile the Blackfriars fell into disrepair, and the Globe, its land lease expired, was demolished in 1644.

The company itself died a protracted death over the next five years. The royalist forces were routed at Naseby in June 1645, and the king faced bankruptcy. Within two months his players had abandoned him and were back in parliamentarian London. Unable to perform, they were said to 'complain very much that their profession is taken from them', but somehow they survived until the following spring; perhaps they were able to live on a share in the proceeds from the sale of their property.[37] At the end of March, however, they were desperate enough to petition the House of Lords for payment of their arrears of salary as royal employees; but though their lordships were sympathetic, they could only pass on the request to the Commons, who controlled public expenditure and who seem to have ignored this claim.

Hope temporarily returned for London's impoverished actors in the spring of 1647. It had been more than four years since Parliament had closed the theatres 'while these sad causes and set times of humiliation shall continue', but at last the war had come to an end.[38] By the summer of 1647 some playing had recommenced; but on 17 July Parliament again ordered it suppressed by the local authorities concerned. Remarkably, the decree was widely flouted by the actors: as summer turned to autumn, more and more of the old playhouses began to reopen, and by October the King's Men had set about refitting the Blackfriars; it was said that they planned to open with, perhaps inevitably, a performance of Beaumont and Fletcher's *A King and No King*. Parliament's response became increasingly irritated as its own ineffectuality grew more apparent: the authorities were instructed 'to be very diligent and strict' in August, and in October to treat players as common rogues, implying their liability to prosecution under the Elizabethan and Jacobean vagrancy laws. Finally, at the end of January 1648, the Commons determined to do away with filthy stage plays for good, and appointed the lawyer John Stephens, MP for Tewkesbury, to draft a bill to that end.

It was with the Stephens Act, passed after some delays on 11 February, that the routine emergency closure of 1642 was finally and explicitly transformed into an ideological exercise in official antitheatricalism:

Whereas the acts of stage plays, interludes, and common plays, condemned by ancient heathens, and much less to be tolerated among professors of the Christian religion, is the occasion of many and sundry great vices and disorders, tending to the high provocation of God's wrath and displeasure, which lies heavy on this kingdom, and to the disturbance of the peace thereof.[39]

The postulates so bluntly stated in the Act's preamble led on to draconian measures. Playgoers were made subject to a fine of 5s. for every performance attended; the takings were to be sequestered as immoral earnings and disposed to charitable uses within the parish. Playhouses were to have their fittings removed to prevent further theatrical use, and players were formally declared to be rogues, to be publicly whipped and then bound over never to perform again; if they did so, they would become liable to the death penalty as incorrigible rogues.

Lowin, Taylor, and their colleagues made written representations against the bill, which were discussed and then disregarded by the Lords. With no prospect of support even in the upper house, the theatre's fortunes had reached their nadir. But surreptitious performances continued even under the newly repressive conditions, and local authorities were still less vigilant than Parliament might have wished: only a few months later, the House of Commons empowered its own Committee of Complaints, chaired by the regicide Thomas Scott, to investigate breaches of the Act; it also appointed one of its members, Major-General Philip Skippon, to supervise the dismantling of the Middlesex playhouses.

The remnants of the King's Men, including Lowin and Taylor, continued to perform intermittently during the late 1640s. Presumably they offered a repertory of pre-war standards: only a few titles (all from the 'Beaumont and Fletcher' canon) are recorded, but it seems likely that some of the plays would have been Shakespeare's. A number of private performances for small groups of noblemen and gentry were given at Holland House in Kensington and other houses of peers; each member of such an audience would customarily give a sovereign for the actors, more than five times the price of the best seats at the Blackfriars. The company was also giving public performances at whatever venues and with whatever co-stars they could find as late as the winter of 1648 (though it is unclear whether this means the beginning or the end of the year). Their final London appearance was in Fletcher and Massinger's tragedy *Rollo, Duke of Normandy* at the Phoenix, the West End playhouse in Drury Lane which had once been home to a rival company. During the performance, the theatre was raided by government troops, an occupational hazard for members of the acting profession in the 1640s, and the players were arrested and taken, still in costume, to prison. Under the government's orders, these thespian 'rogues', some of them in their sixties and seventies, could have been flogged, in the savage

Elizabethan phrase, until their backs were bloody; they were lucky only to be detained and later released without their clothes, which had been confiscated as stage apparel.

If the company performed again, it was discreetly outside London. Taylor died in penury at Richmond late in 1652. Across the river at Brentford, tradition has it, Lowin kept an inn, the Three Pigeons. Later, possibly after his old friend's death, he moved to Westminster, where he in turn died in the summer of 1653; he was 76, and 'his poverty was as great as his age'.[40] Both men had outlived their former colleague, Ellyaerdt Swanston, who died in London in 1651. Only the Blackfriars theatre stood, deserted, as a reminder of the Shakespearian stage, until it too was pulled down to make way for tenements in 1655.

The gradual dissolution of the King's Men during the Civil War and Interregnum turned Caroline stage history into a blind alley. Though later commentators liked to emphasize a continuity of stage tradition, tracing lines of descent from Shakespeare to Lowin and Taylor to Davenant and so to Betterton, most of the period's developments were lost with the company's prompt-books. How *Love's Labours Lost* was revised for the sake of the candles, or whether the name Oldcastle was used in *1 Henry IV*, can never be known for certain because the post-war generation started performances afresh from the texts that were established in print in 1623. Only through the maddening opacity of allusion can we occasionally glimpse what may be distinctive performance practices of the time. In the summer of 1659, for instance, Henry Cromwell, the fourth son of the late Lord Protector who had recently been recalled from the lieutenancy of Ireland, compared his position with that of Christopher Sly, the drunken on-stage audience for *The Taming of the Shrew*:

The players have a play where they bring in a tinker, and make him believe himself a lord, and when they have satisfied their humour, they made him a plain tinker again. Gentlemen, but that this was a great while ago, I should have thought this play had been made of me: for if ever two cases were alike, 'tis the tinker's and mine.[41]

Evidently someone, somewhere, had performed a version of the play with the full frame structure, including the final scenes absent from the Folio text.

It is possible that Cromwell's allusion refers not to a full-scale production but to a 'droll', one of the abbreviated comic adaptations of pre-Civil War plays which were illegally performed during the prohibition years of the Interregnum. Some of these playlets were the work of the actor Robert Cox, who had already achieved some popularity and even fame with them among the dissident underground of Rump-ruled London by the time of Lowin's death. As a discreetly unadvertised second feature to the safely non-dramatic activity of rope-dancing, they were acted at fairs and taverns around England, and also at the Red Bull: ironically, the Clerkenwell playhouse which had been forbidden to produce Shakespeare in 1627 may by the 1650s have been one of the few stages that offered even a glimpse of his plays.

Of the three dozen or so drolls which survive, only three are drawn from Shakespeare. The shortest is *The Grave-Makers*, extracted from a single scene of *Hamlet* and requiring a cast of only four. The other two are more extensive, and so more elaborate in their textual adaptations. Five of Falstaff's scenes in *1 Henry IV* are conflated to produce *The Bouncing Knight; or, The Robbers Robbed*, though curiously the action begins only in the aftermath of the Gadshill episode. *The Merry Conceited Humours of Bottom the Weaver* offers quite a full rendering of the artisans' subplot of *A Midsummer Night's Dream*, retaining (unusually) several lyrical speeches from the fairies. For a presumably small because officially criminalized Interregnum troupe, they are demanding plays to stage: *The Bouncing Knight* calls for eight actors, and *Bottom the Weaver* only achieves its casting requirement of nine by doubling six of the roles (including Oberon / Duke and Titania / Duchess, the first recorded instance of that popular combination), and even then there is a minor role unaccounted for. If these drolls really were performed 'in Oliver's time', as their Restoration publishers averred, then a surprising number of people had risked involvement in the illicit enterprise. But then, when even a Cromwell could cite a filthy stage play with such a wry, matter-of-fact equanimity, one may wonder whether attitudes to the theatre had begun to lighten in the late 1650s. By the end of 1659, full-length productions of Shakespeare were back on the London stage: although players were still being fined for their activities as late as February 1660, and although plays were briefly prohibited again from 23 April, there was, to quote the document which officially reopened the theatres, an 'extraordinary licence . . . used in things of this nature'.[42]

The drolls are not even an attenuated continuation of the Shakespearian stage tradition that was broken with the slow demise of the King's Men: they were clearly compiled from printed quartos of the plays concerned. What is interesting about the published collection, which appeared in 1662, is the way it attests to the severance even as it tries to assert the contrary. The engraved frontispiece (fig. 15), unsigned but probably the work of John Chantry, presents a number of the characters on an out-of-perspective apron stage, including Falstaff and the Hostess in the foreground. This is in no sense a representation of an actual performance: several of the figures, including the Hostess, are based on other, unrelated engravings rather than on the artist's observation. The picture's importance lies rather in what it seeks to imply. It is notable that Falstaff's costume dates from the 1630s: to the book's original purchasers, it would have had distinctly pre-war associations, which must have seemed appropriate for these versions of pre-war plays. In other words, authenticity is presumed to inhere in the figure's being discernibly non-contemporary. But, of course, Falstaff is not a product of the 1630s: rather like the tradition which sought to accreditate Betterton's Hamlet by referring the performance back to the directions which Shakespeare supposedly gave to Joseph Taylor, the actual effect of the illustration is to undermine the claim by failing to go back far enough. It is as if anything snatched from across the abyss of history will now serve to establish a 'Shakespearian' ambience.

It is possible to exaggerate the devastation wrought by the Interregnum on the traditions of the English theatre. At the Restoration, the last legal performances by the King's Men were still within living memory; actors were still alive who had worked with Lowin, Taylor, and Swanston. Even some manuscripts seem to have survived: when William Davenant adapted *Macbeth* in 1664, he was able to include full texts of the two songs, which had been included in performances at least since Middleton adapted the play in the 1610s, but which are represented only by cues in the First Folio. None the less, the frontispiece to *The Wits* stands as testament to the extent to which the line of descent had snapped by the latter half of the century: the period's attempts to talk up or even fabricate a living tradition only call attention to the frustration of its absence, and to the prospect that Restoration Shakespeare would perforce be very different from what had gone before.

Fig. 15 Frontispiece to *The Wits* (1662), probably engraved by John Chantry. The illustration almost certainly does not represent a performance.

3

Improving on the Original: Actresses and Adaptations

MICHAEL DOBSON

Revived, with Alterations

ALTHOUGH in some respects they were the culmination of trends already visible before the Puritans closed down the playhouses in 1642, the conditions under which English drama was revived by the restored Stuart monarchy in 1660 produced a theatre worlds away from that in which Shakespeare had worked fifty years earlier. While a handful of Shakespeare's plays, never wholly forgotten during the Interregnum, were among the first to be revived at the fall of the Commonwealth regime, and several more had by the late 1690s securely established themselves as perennial staples of the theatrical repertory, a transformation of the London theatre, carried out by royal warrant, took place soon after Charles II's return to his capital. This forever altered the relationship between drama and the state, the design and location of playhouses, and the typical composition of theatrical companies, and ensured that Shakespearian productions from 1660 onwards, rather than simply resuming the tradition of performance interrupted by the Commonwealth, would express a distinctively post-Civil War theatrical sensibility. Sumptuously baroque in costume and music, technologically sophisticated in design and elegant in diction, the Shakespeare of the Restoration and early eighteenth-century stage belonged at least as much to the

Enlightenment as to the Renaissance, his plays reimagined by managers and performers with what was in every sense a new perspective on theatrical production.

This new perspective, strikingly, was largely imposed on the theatrical world from above, for the first great novelty of the Restoration theatre, and that which mandated and shaped all the others, was the unprecedented involvement of the Crown in the running of the public playhouses. As early as late 1659, once it became clear that the restoration of the monarchy was likely, groups of players (some of them pre-war veterans who had not acted, legally at least, for seventeen years) had begun to resume scattered public performances in London, and these first glimpses of legal theatre for two decades had included revivals of *1 Henry IV*, *The Merry Wives of Windsor*, *Othello*, and *Pericles* performed on the same largely open stages (at venues such as the Red Bull in Clerkenwell and the Phoenix in Drury Lane) that were used in Shakespeare's time. But this brief, spontaneous revival of an older theatrical tradition was brought to a close on 21 August 1660, when Charles II issued a warrant to Thomas Killigrew and Sir William Davenant appointing them as the respective patentholders of two royal theatrical troupes, the

King's Company and the Duke of York's Company, who would from now onwards enjoy a monopoly on all legitimate theatrical activity in London. Its terms made it perfectly clear that the theatre fostered and supervised by the restored monarchy was to be a very different institution from the diffuse commercial enterprise then reviving at the Red Bull and the Phoenix.

For one thing, its chief executives, although both experienced in the professional theatre (albeit chiefly as gentleman playwrights), were not entrepreneurs but courtiers ('our trusty and well-beloved Thomas Killigrew, Esq., one of the Grooms of our Bedchamber, and Sir William Davenant, Knight'): the new patent companies were designed in the first instance to serve the monarchy rather than the market. While Charles's interest in the theatre was to a large degree personal (he had inherited a genuine love of the drama from his father, and took a close interest in theatrical affairs throughout his reign, adopting several playwrights as drinking companions and regularly offering them suggestions as to plot and character), he also recognized the potential value of the stage as a means of consolidating his precariously restored royal authority through the propagation of a revived royalist culture. The very existence of live theatre in London was already helping to demonstrate that the Commonwealth was definitively over, but under direct court control the playhouses might serve even more emphatically as an arena for the display of the new regime's power. In this respect Charles's choice of Sir William Davenant as one of his two managers makes particular sense: as Poet Laureate under Charles I, Davenant had collaborated with Inigo Jones in devising court masques, and he had continued to experiment with the production of highly visual, semi-operatic entertainments even under the Commonwealth. He and Charles's favourite Killigrew were now to take the perspective scenery and special effects of the masque—a 'virtual reality' technology purposely designed to celebrate the monarchy's power over the physical universe—and adapt it for use in new playhouses designed as public expressions of royal magnificence. This emphasis on opulent spectacle is amply visible in their 1660 warrant: as well as being suitably equipped for the representation of 'tragedies, comedies, plays', the two theatres it calls for are to have 'all necessaries thereto appertaining' for the production of 'operas, and all other entertainments of that nature', and their admission charges are to take into account 'the great expenses of scenes, music, and such new decorations as have not been formerly used'.[1]

The immediate effect of this particular stipulation was the end of the outdoor playhouse. Killigrew's King's Company, recruited mainly from the veterans who had been performing at the old Red Bull, shunned the innyard to begin operations indoors at an elaborately adapted tennis-court in Clare Market ('the finest playhouse, I believe, that ever was in England', recorded the diarist Samuel Pepys on his first visit on 20 November 1660),[2] while Davenant's Duke's Company, recruited from the younger actors who had already been using the roofed Phoenix, began their playing career at the covered Salisbury Court, transferring six months later to a far more sophisticated indoor auditorium (splendidly converted from another tennis-court) in nearby Lincoln's Inn Fields ('very fine and magnificent', reported Pepys, 2 July 1661). This move from the open yard to the more genteel covered theatre continued a trend initiated by Shakespeare's own company when they opened the indoor Blackfriars theatre to supplement the Globe, but the new playhouses went further in adding to the standard equipment of the pre-war private theatres two crucial features hitherto confined to masquing houses, features which would reframe the performance of Shakespeare's plays for the next three centuries: proscenium arches, and 'scenes' (what would now be termed 'flats'). Although it retained an open forestage eminently suitable for soliloquies and asides, extending some twenty feet into the auditorium, the typical Restoration stage was dominated visually by the area behind the proscenium arch, where painted scenery created an in-depth, illusionist 'picture stage' or 'scene'. (At Lincoln's Inn Fields, Davenant developed the technique by which this area could be closed off behind painted shutters so as to permit the dramatic 'discovery' of new sets during performances.) In the age of Newton and Locke, the place of the actor on stage would be defined not in the symbolic, cosmological terms of the Renaissance (between 'the Heavens' and 'Hell'), but in relation to a specific, secular three-dimensional space simulated by the mechanical manipulation of perspective. The consequences of this development for the production of plays written for the open stages of the Elizabethan era, as we shall see, could be drastic.

As the 1660 warrant recognized would be necessary, the cost of these innovations in design was reflected in higher prices for the 500 or so spectators who could be accommodated for each afternoon performance. According to their income and sense of where they fitted into the social hierarchy displayed by the divisions of the auditorium, Restoration playgoers might pay 1s. for a place in the upper gallery, 1s. 6d. in the middle gallery, 2s. 6d. in the pit and the first gallery, or 4s. in the boxes, prices which might be doubled for a première: alternatively, although the practice was never officially sanctioned, they might skip the first four acts and squeeze in wherever there was room to see the last one free. These comparatively high admission charges naturally had consequences for the social dimension of playgoing, which were reaffirmed by the new theatres' location. Both Clare Market and Lincoln's Inn Fields were closer to the royal palace of Whitehall than to the commercial City (a factor appreciated by Charles himself, who made regular visits to the public theatres from 1661 onwards), convenient to the fashionable shops and residential squares of Covent Garden and St James's, and in this respect they would be followed by all successive patent theatres. In 1663 the King's Company moved to a new auditorium in Covent Garden, on a site close to Bridges Street; this theatre would be comprehensively upstaged in 1671 when the Duke's Company relocated to a grandiose new headquarters built by Sir Christopher Wren (capable of seating nearly 1,000 spectators) at Dorset Garden, off Fleet Street. Fighting back after a fire destroyed their Bridges Street theatre in 1672, the King's Company commissioned Wren to design a new playhouse as grand as Dorset Garden, and in 1674 they resumed operations in a building on the same site but with a new name, destined for more lasting renown—the Theatre Royal, Drury Lane. (Wren's longitudinal section of this theatre, fig. 16,

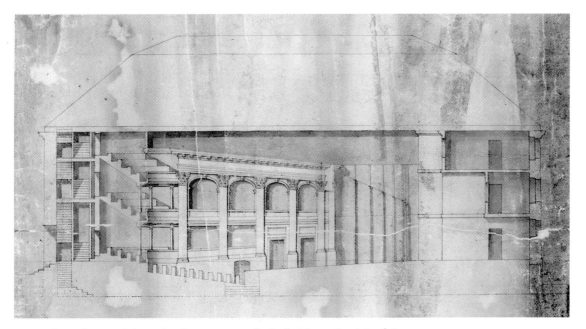

FIG. 16 Christopher Wren's design for a theatre, presumed to be the Theatre Royal, Drury Lane, 1674.

perfectly exemplifies the neo-classical proportions favoured by the new indoor playhouses of the Restoration: the pillars at either side of the proscenium arch are exactly half-way between the front and back walls of the 112-foot long building, and exactly bisect the raked acting area—the curved front of the forestage extends, at its central point, 20 feet into the auditorium, while the 'scene' or picture-stage with its peepshow-like seven sets of flats goes back a corresponding 20 feet behind the proscenium.) With all this elaborate architectural activity in progress north of the river, Bankside, the heterogeneous area directly opposite the City (where the second Globe had been demolished by the Puritan government in 1644) would never again be London's theatre district, and it would be many years before London's playhouses would again cater to so large a percentage of its population as had the Globe, the Rose, and their competitors. However diverse the spectators it still attracted (and we know from Pepys and other sources that the Restoration audience included servants, apprentices, and citizens as well as courtiers and their satellites), from 1660 onwards the theatre would belong to the elegant West End.

Even these innovations, however—direct royal patronage, a two-company monopoly, perspective scenery, West End venues—pale into insignificance beside the one announced before a performance of *Othello* at Clare Market on 8 December 1660:

> I come, unknown to any of the rest,
> To tell you news; I saw the lady dressed!
> The woman plays today, mistake me not,
> No man in gown, or page in petticoat . . .[3]

It is still not known for certain whether this was the first ever public appearance of an English actress on the professional stage (we know, for example, that Killigrew had already compelled his apparently unwilling veterans of the all-male theatre to agree to act with women by mid-October), nor can we even be certain of the identity of this epoch-making Desdemona (although the likeliest candidate seems to be Anne Marshall, destined to give many other notable performances in tragedy over the coming years). What

is certain is that the female roles written for young men before the Civil War would never be the same again: with the advent of the professional actress, the transvestite convention within which Shakespeare had written became as much a thing of the outmoded past as the innyard stage. Although in the early months of the restored theatre some women's roles were still played successfully by men (Pepys, watching Edward Kynaston as Olympia in Fletcher's *The Loyal Subject* on 18 August 1660, declared that he 'made the loveliest lady that ever I saw in my life'), male cross-dressing would hereafter be reserved for broadly comic, travesty parts, ancestresses of the modern pantomime dame (James Nokes, for example, in mid-1660 a player of heroines, would be better known thereafter for his performances as Juliet's Nurse). On a stage now moulded to the illusionist conventions of the proscenium arch, boy players would be confined to playing boys. According to the historic prologue quoted above, the older practice was simply no longer adequately realistic—especially with female roles, after two decades during which no new youths had been recruited, in the hands of players who had not worn dresses since the reign of Charles I:

> Our women are defective, and so sized
> You'd think they were some of the Guard disguised;
> For, to speak truth, men act that are between
> Forty and fifty, wenches of fifteen,
> With bone so large and nerve so incompliant,
> When you call *Desdemona*, enter *Giant*.

This comic complaint, however, cannot entirely account for the newly restored monarchy's willingness to sanction such a controversial innovation. Charles II and his court, spending their exile in Paris, had grown accustomed to the spectacle of handsome female performers as an ordinary part of the pleasure of theatre-going, and thus may have had purely hedonistic motives for introducing two-sex theatre to England, but they may also have seen the introduction of actresses to the London stage as a particularly vivid means of both demonstrating and celebrating the defeat of Puritanism. Certainly, given the virulence with which pre-war antitheatrical campaigners had attacked Charles I for allowing women to take part even in court masques (on the grounds that no virtuous woman could possibly agree to appear on any stage, however privately), it is hard to imagine Charles II signing Thomas Killigrew's patent without an ironic smile at its twisting of another Puritan objection to the stage into a tongue-in-cheek justification for the unprecedented appearance of women in the public theatres:

for as much as . . . women's parts . . . have been acted by men in the habit of women, at which some have taken offence . . . we do likewise permit and give leave that all the women's parts to be acted in either of the said two companies for the time to come may be performed by women.[4]

As it turned out, Puritans would soon be able to point out that the way of life of the typical Restoration actress more than confirmed all their polemics about the moral dangers of acting; subjected to almost continuous sexual harassment off-stage and sometimes on, many actresses were taken into keeping by members of the court (including, most famously, Charles himself, whose numerous mistresses included the gifted comedienne Nell Gwyn), and some may deliberately have entered the theatrical profession with a longer-term future as a courtesan in mind. But for the time being the direct protection of the Crown kept such objections in check, and in the midst of the backstage solicitations and on-stage whistles the first generation of Englishwomen permitted to earn their livings in the theatre began to develop their considerable thespian skills in roles inherited from adolescent boys.

If the factors behind the overnight introduction of actresses are thus more complicated than they might appear, the reason the first one made her début as Desdemona rather than in a tailor-made new role is simple enough: just as there had been no boy actors taken on during the twenty-year hiatus of the Interregnum, so there had been no working dramatists. In the early 1660s, while the first Restoration playwrights were only beginning to learn their trade, the two royal theatres were compelled to rely heavily on the revival of old plays, and thus one of

the first matters requiring adjudication between Killigrew and Davenant was the division between their companies of the usable pre-war repertory. With the exception of a very few well-loved scripts confined to quarto editions (such as Middleton and Rowley's *The Changeling*), this meant, in the status-conscious 1660s, those pre-war plays which had achieved the literary respectability (and sheer survival) guaranteed by publication in large folio volumes, and so it was that the new theatres turned in particular to the 'Comedies, Histories and Tragedies' of the Shakespeare Folio, the works of Ben Jonson, and the plays gathered in 1647 as the work of Beaumont and Fletcher.

Of these three potential sources of material, the Shakespeare Folio was at the time the least valued. Although a small number of his plays had survived in the memories of veteran actors and were already back on the boards (principally *Othello*, *The Merry Wives of Windsor*, and 1 *Henry IV*, which would all remain popular throughout the period), Shakespeare was widely regarded as not only the oldest but the most outdated of the pre-war playwrights, his writing unfashionably prone to elaborate metaphor and his cast lists inelegantly liable to include punning rustics. As even one of his greatest Restoration admirers, John Dryden, put it in 1679, 'the tongue in general is so much refined since Shakespeare's time, that many of his words, and more of his Phrases, are scarce intelligible . . . and his whole style is so pestered with Figurative expressions, that it is as affected as it is obscure'; another, Margaret Cavendish, wrote her most detailed praise of Shakespeare (in a letter of 1662) in response to repeated objections that his plays were 'made up only with Clowns, Fools, Watchmen, and the like'. By contrast Ben Jonson seemed desirably neo-classical (as well as better suited to satisfying the contemporary demand for satirical depictions of London society), and his plays would in consequence exert far more influence than Shakespeare's on the development of Restoration drama: so too would those of Beaumont and Fletcher, which combined Jonson's classicism with an appropriate feeling for the right class of subject-matter—as Dryden observed in

1668, '[t]heir Plots were generally more regular than Shakespeare's . . . and they understood and imitated the conversation of Gentlemen much better'.[5] In the theatre of 1660, witty gentlemen of Westminster were in considerably more demand than untaught swans of Avon, and this preference was made clear when the question of performing rights to the old plays was settled by a series of agreements reached from December 1660 onwards. Killigrew, who as Charles's favourite had already been given the King's Company title and the most experienced actors, was allowed most of the best-known plays of Jonson and Fletcher, along with a smaller share of the Shakespeare canon which none the less included the three plays already re-established as popular favourites: by contrast the younger players of Davenant's second-string Duke's Company were grudgingly allowed to act Davenant's own pre-war plays, and given the rights to the remaining plays of Shakespeare.

It is a tribute to Davenant's sheer resourcefulness that from this inauspicious position at the end of 1660 the Duke's Company had risen by the middle of the decade to being by far the more vigorous and successful of the two companies, their technical and generic innovations rapidly and slavishly imitated by their King's Company rivals. They owed this achievement to a number of intelligent managerial policies—including a superior attention to rehearsal, décor, music, and scenic effects, and a (necessarily) more active programme of commissioning and obtaining new scripts—but the most influential for the history of Shakespearian production was the strategy by which Davenant set about making the most of the apparently unpromising old plays allotted to his actors. Although a lifelong devotee of Shakespeare (he used to boast that the playwright had stayed at his parents' tavern in Oxford on his journeys between Stratford and London, and even hinted that Shakespeare was his natural father), Davenant recognized that, to achieve popularity with Restoration playgoers, Shakespeare had to be made their contemporary. In a token gesture towards placating Puritan opinion (not unlike the clause licensing the introduction of actresses), the patents issued to both Davenant and Killigrew had

specified that any old plays containing 'profane, obscene and scurrilous passages' should be 'reformed and made fit' before being acted, but of the two managers it was Davenant who took the initiative in deciding to subject some of his stock of vintage scripts to aesthetic rather than moral reformation. When he staged *Hamlet* for the first time in August 1661 he not only made various cuts to its text designed in part to accommodate the changeable scenery he had introduced only the previous month (removing, for example, the appearance of Fortinbras and his army in Act IV, which would otherwise have required an additional scene change), but also updated its diction to suit Restoration tastes. In Davenant's revised version of the 'To be, or not to be' soliloquy, for example, 'To grunt and sweat under a weary life' becomes the more delicate 'To groan and sweat under a weary life' (contemporary sensibilities, apparently, did not object to a prince referring to sweat but drew the line at grunting), and the native hue of resolution, instead of being 'sickled o'er with the pale cast of thought', simply 'Shews sick and pale with thought'.[6] This comparatively minor clarification and modernization, however, gave place in succeeding Shakespearian revivals to full-scale adaptation. In February 1662 the successful production of Davenant's *The Law against Lovers*—a devoutly royalist version of *Measure for Measure* which deliberately highlights the parallels between Angelo's short-lived rule and England's recent experiences of Puritan government, while at the same time managing to incorporate the courtship of Beatrice and Benedick from *Much Ado about Nothing*—established an enduring pattern by which hitherto untried or unpopular Shakespeare plays would be placed before the theatre-going public in substantially rewritten form. From the 1660s until the late eighteenth century, many of Shakespeare's plays, as the title-pages of contemporary acting editions put it, would be 'Revived, with Alterations'.

However objectionable the practice may seem today (after two centuries during which his texts have been treated as virtually sacred), the fact that Shakespeare was 'improved' in the 1660s for reasons as much pragmatically economic as literary is sufficiently

PLATE 1 (*above*) *The Wrestling Scene in 'As You Like It'* by Francis Hayman, with Hannah Pritchard as Rosalind and Kitty Clive as Celia.

PLATE 2 (*below*) *Mr Garrick in the Character of Richard III* by William Hogarth: the tent scene on the night before Bosworth, Richard startled by the ghosts—the most celebrated, and frequently engraved, theatrical image of the eighteenth century.

PLATE 3 *John Philip Kemble as Coriolanus* by Sir Francis Bourgeois. Caius Martius broods beneath
a statue of Mars in the house of Aufidius.

confirmed by the comparative unprofitability of unrevised plays. While *Othello*, *1 Henry IV*, and *The Merry Wives of Windsor* remained 'stock' plays for the King's Company, and the only slightly revised *Hamlet* became a similar fixture for the Duke's (along with *Henry VIII*, first revived with much spectacular royal pageantry in 1663), attempts to extend this proven Shakespeare repertoire without recourse to adaptation were in general unsuccessful. At the King's Company, *Richard III*, despite a prologue topically identifying Richard with Oliver Cromwell, failed to catch the public imagination, and would not do so until Colley Cibber rewrote it (as a star vehicle for himself) in 1699 (adding some lines, such as 'Off with his head—so much for Buckingham' and 'Richard's himself again', which would survive in acting texts down to Olivier and beyond). *A Midsummer Night's Dream*, revived in 1662, signally failed to impress Pepys (who called it 'the most insipid ridiculous play that ever I saw in my life', 29 September 1662), and would not reappear until 1692, rewritten as an operatic spectacular called *The Fairy Queen*, with a lavish score by Henry Purcell. It is not surprising that when in 1663 the company decided to try out one last Shakespearian comedy, *The Taming of the Shrew*, they did so only in a heavily adapted version by the actor John Lacy which resituates its plot in contemporary London. (The play was rechristened *Sauny the Scot* after its rewritten Grumio, who became a comically stereotypical Restoration Scotsman.) Meanwhile at the Duke's Company a 1662 revival of the original *Romeo and Juliet* proved no more pleasing to Pepys than *A Midsummer Night's Dream* ('It is a play of itself the worst that ever I heard', he declared, 1 March 1662), and despite a now-lost revision (with a happy ending) by James Howard it would not regain public acceptance until rewritten by Thomas Otway in 1679 as a play about Roman politics, *The History and Fall of Caius Marius* ('O Marius, Marius, wherefore art thou *Marius*?', wonders its heroine, as well she might). *King Lear* reappeared in 1664, but seems to have provided no hint of the immense success it would enjoy in Nahum Tate's version of 1681 (which, famously, supplies a happy ending, keeping Lear and Gloucester alive and marrying Edgar to Cordelia).

Twelfth Night, with Viola's disguise as Cesario transformed overnight into an opportunity to display an actress's legs in close-fitting breeches, managed at least three separate revivals, but Pepys for one remained unconvinced ('but a silly play', 6 January 1663) and the play was laid aside after 1669, not to return until 1703, when William Burnaby would revise it as the equally unsuccessful *Love Betrayed; or, The Agreeable Disappointment*. Pepys's comments on these various revivals seem especially revealing; without rewriting, Shakespeare's plays were liable to seem merely fanciful, 'silly', or 'insipid', especially when placed alongside the biting social comedies and exotically operatic tragedies which were beginning to displace the old plays from the stage.

In marked contrast, two of the most lucrative shows of the 1660s (and indeed of the first eighty years of the reopened theatre) were adapted Shakespearian plays, each carefully redesigned to make the maximum use of the new resources of the Restoration stage and pay maximum court to the monarchy which had provided them. One was the version of *The Tempest* first staged by the Duke's Company in 1667, *The Tempest; or, The Enchanted Island*, prepared by Davenant in collaboration with John Dryden, a lastingly popular adaptation perhaps most conspicuous for its exuberant determination to show off the company's female performers. Ingeniously multiplying the original play's opportunities for actresses, it not only transforms Miranda from a boy's part to a woman's, but adds two wholly new female roles (a younger sister for Miranda, called Dorinda, and a girlfriend for Ariel, called Milcha) and in one instance even reverses the cross-dressing convention within which Shakespeare wrote by adding a youthful male ward to Prospero's extended family ('*Hippolito*, one that never saw Woman, right heir of the Dukedom of *Mantua*') who is played throughout by a woman. The play's sometimes sophisticated, sometimes downright crude games with contemporary ideas about gender are completed by the provision of a sister for Caliban (called Sycorax) who is played by a male actor (and sought in marriage by Stephano and Trinculo alternately). Contemporary in its stage personnel, the play is made equally so in its politics: the drunken rhetorical claims to dominion over the island made by Stephano, Trinculo, Caliban, and Sycorax (along with two new and equally inept colleagues, Mustacho and Ventoso) deliberately parody the notions of contractual sovereignty espoused by republicans during the Interregnum, and the concluding restoration of a triumphant and unforgiving Prospero (who neither makes the 'our revels now are ended' speech nor renounces his magic) is clearly intended to recall the return of another banished prince, Charles II. (Charles's enjoyment of the show is perhaps demonstrated by the fact that the actress who played Hippolito, Mary 'Moll' Davis, became his mistress shortly after he attended its première.) Shakespeare's inclusion of magic, meanwhile, provided an occasion for the grandest scenic and musical effects of which the Restoration theatre was capable, much elaborated after the company transferred to the larger Dorset Garden playhouse in 1671. The opening and closing stage directions to the first scene, as recorded in the 1674 acting edition of the play, provide a good idea of the sort of aural and visual pleasures which could bring contemporary theatre-goers to Shakespeare:

The Front of the Stage is opened, and the Band of 24 Violins, with the Harpsicals [harpsichords] and Theorbos [large bass lutes] which accompany the Voices, are placed between the Pit and the Stage. While the Overture is playing, the Curtain rises . . . the Scene . . . represents a thick Cloudy Sky, a very Rocky Coast, and a Tempestuous Sea in perpetual Agitation. This Tempest (supposed to be raised by Magic) has many dreadful Objects in it, as several Spirits in horrid shapes flying down amongst the Sailors, then rising and crossing in the Air. And when the Ship is sinking, the whole House is darkened, and a shower of Fire falls upon 'em. This is accompanied with Lightning, and several Claps of Thunder, to the end of the Storm. . . . In the midst of the Shower of Fire the Scene changes. The Cloudy Sky, Rocks, and Sea vanish; and when the Lights return, discover that Beautiful part of the Island, which was the habitation of Prospero . . .[7]

This incarnation of the play proved remarkably durable; despite a brief return to Shakespeare's unaltered script in the mid-eighteenth century, Dorinda and Hippolito were still adorning the cast lists of acting versions in the early 1800s—and interpreters

of *The Tempest*'s opening shipwreck to this day, whether on the stage or on the screen, have proved no less willing than Davenant and Dryden to go just as far overboard with the special effects.

No less spectacular, in both scenery and success, was Davenant's version of *Macbeth*, first performed in 1664 (and similarly provided with an even grander *mise-en-scène* after the company moved to Dorset Garden). It is clear both from the acting edition published in 1674 (see fig. 17) and from the 1708 memoirs of the company's prompter John Downes that the play as seen by Restoration audiences was at the very least framed by its opulent costuming, scenic design, special effects, music, and choreography:

The Tragedy of Macbeth, altered by Sir *William Davenant*; being dressed all in its Finery, as new Clothes, new Scenes, Machines, as flyings for the Witches; with all the Singing and Dancing in it: The first Composed by Mr. [Matthew] *Locke*, the other by Mr. [Luke] *Channel* and Mr. [Josias] *Priest*; it being all Excellently performed, being in the nature of an Opera, it Recompensed double the Expense; it proves still a lasting Play.[8]

FIG. 17 Title-page to the printed text of Sir William Davenant's adaptation of *Macbeth* , 1674.

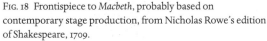

FIG. 18 Frontispiece to *Macbeth*, probably based on contemporary stage production, from Nicholas Rowe's edition of Shakespeare, 1709.

FIG. 19 Frontispiece to *Henry VIII*, from the same edition.

As a subsequent engraving of the apparition scene shows (fig. 18), the 'new Clothes' to which Downes refers, however costly, were contemporary in style; with the exception of his Romans and certain major figures in the histories, Shakespeare's characters still wore modern dress (see, for example, the periwigged Tudor courtiers in fig. 19). This convention was in fact particularly suitable for this *Macbeth*, since in Davenant's version the play (like his *Tempest*) deliberately comments on recent political history, with the usurping general Macbeth becoming a figure analogous to Cromwell and the restored Malcolm to Charles II (although, tactfully, Davenant cuts one rather too pertinent section from Malcolm's feigned warning to Macduff about his fitness for the crown— 'Your wives, your daughters, | Your matrons, and your maids could not fill up | The cistern of my lust', IV. iii. 62–4). The 'Scenes' and 'Machines' also remembered by Downes included not only 'Flyings for the Witches' (who spent much of the play either singing, dancing, or dangling from ropes) but a cloud on which Hecate descended from the sky, a cavern for the apparition scene which disappeared beneath the stage (depicted in fig. 18), and two separate trapdoors for the banquet scene—Banquo's ghost at first '*descends*' through one, to Macbeth's relief, but shortly afterwards '*The Ghost of Banquo rises at his feet.*'[9] It is not surprising that Pepys, who adored this show (seeing it eight times in less than

four years), commented particularly on the range of
entertainment it offered:

> to the Duke's house, and there saw *Macbeth*, which, though I
> saw it lately, yet appears a most excellent play in all respects,
> but especially in divertisement, though it be a deep tragedy;
> which is a strange perfection in a tragedy, it being most
> proper here, and suitable . . . one of the best plays for a stage,
> and variety of dancing and music, that ever I saw. (7 January
> 1667, 19 April 1667)

Pepys, however, commented too that the play was
'most excellently acted' (28 December 1666), for the
production marked one of the greatest early triumphs
of the Restoration's most talented and widely imitated
actor, Thomas Betterton (fig. 20). Betterton
(1635–1710), a highly literate performer who at the time
of the Restoration had recently completed his
apprenticeship to a bookseller, had begun to make his
mark as a young actor even before the formation of the
two patent companies, appearing at the briefly
reopened Phoenix in such challenging roles as
DeFlores (in *The Changeling*) and Pericles (one part he
would never repeat, however, on the less populist
stages of the Theatres Royal). Recruited by the Duke's
Company in mid-1660, he was soon recognized as one
of the troupe's greatest assets, and was from the first
assigned several of the most important Shakespearian
roles in their repertory—Hamlet, in which he
benefited from close tuition by Davenant in the
part's pre-war acting tradition, Henry VIII, Mercutio,
Sir Toby Belch, and, in 1664, Macbeth, a part
completely his own from the beginning (when he
was unable to play the Thane due to illness on 16
October 1667, for example, Pepys's wife Elizabeth
went home in disappointment rather than staying to
watch his understudy). It was a role, like that of
Hamlet, in which Betterton would still be thrilling
audiences during his farewell season some forty-five
years later.

Although none of the surviving contemporary
comments on his Macbeth provide a minutely
detailed, line-by-line description of his interpretation,
numerous accounts of Betterton's style and methods
as an actor enable us to reconstruct the broad outlines
of his performance with some confidence. It is clear,
for example, that the keynote of Betterton's acting in
tragedy was a fierce dignity, which compensated for
what might later have been perceived as a lack of
complexity in characterization or agility in movement.
'His Left Hand frequently lodged in his Breast,
between his Coat and Waistcoat, while, with his Right,
he prepared his Speech', recorded Anthony Aston (cf.
fig. 18). 'His Actions were few, but just . . . his Aspect
was serious, venerable, and majestic.' Betterton's
greatest natural strengths, by all accounts, were vocal
rather than kinetic, and these he cultivated by a close
attention to elocution and poetic diction which invite
comparison, in our own day, with the work of Sir John
Gielgud. 'The Operation of Speech is strong', Charles
Gildon reported him as observing in 1709,

> not only for the Reason or Wit therein contained, but by its
> Sound. For in all good Speech there is a sort of Music, with
> respect to its Measure, Time and Tune . . . Next to the
> Fineness of the Tone, the Variation of it will make the
> Auditors pleased and delighted with what they hear.

FIG. 20 Thomas Betterton, after the portrait by
Sir Godfrey Kneller.

This last observation is reinforced by another remark of Anthony Aston on Betterton's control of his voice—'he could Tune it by an artful *Climax*, which enforced universal Attention, even from the *Fops* and *Orange-Girls*'—and Colley Cibber contributes further to our sense of how Betterton might have treated major speeches by commenting on his understated sensitivity to his audience's attention:

Betterton had so just a sense of what was true or false Applause, that I have heard him say, he never thought any kind of it equal to an attentive Silence; that there were many ways of deceiving an Audience into a loud one; but to keep them hushed and quiet was an Applause which only Truth and Merit could arrive at: Of which Art there never was an equal Master with himself.[10]

All this adds up to a Macbeth who would be particularly strong in the soliloquies, where he would aim less for effects of moment-by-moment psychological realism than for the clear and intense evocation of aspiration and terror.

This is not to say, however, that Betterton was not a gifted ensemble player (colleagues repeatedly praised his self-discipline and immersion in his character when 'off-line'), and, in the crucial scenes between Macbeth and his Lady, Betterton had a worthy foil in his own wife Mary, née Saunderson (*c.*1637–1712). The role of Lady Macbeth clearly elicited an extraordinary performance from its first ever female player (who otherwise tended to specialize in roles of unshakeable virtue, such as Katherine in *Henry VIII*, perhaps as part of a conscious strategy by which she and her husband succeeded in remaining among the few Restoration actors untouched by sexual scandal). The Bettertons were childless (in the later 1660s they adopted the infant Anne Bracegirdle, destined to become one of the most accomplished actresses of the age), and Mary, who always had a reputation for melancholy, was mad for some years before her death: it has often been suggested that Lady Macbeth, by common consent her finest role, struck a particular autobiographical chord. Cibber (a young novice when Mary Betterton left the stage) compared her favourably with her successor in the part, the great tragedienne Elizabeth Barry:

Mrs. *Betterton* . . . was so great a Mistress of Nature, that even Mrs. *Barry*, who acted the Lady *Macbeth* after her, could not in that Part, with all her superior Strength and melody of Voice, throw out those quick and careless Strokes of Terror from the Disorder of a guilty Mind, which the other gave us with a Facility in her Manner that rendered them at once tremendous and delightful.[11]

Given that these words were written more than fifty years after Mary Betterton last played the sleepwalking scene, this is no mean tribute to the haunting intensity of her performance.

Without wishing to belittle her achievement, however, it would be possible to argue that one reason Mary Betterton's performance stood out so vividly in Cibber's memory was that Lady Macbeth's lines were comparatively untouched by the Restoration's revisions to the script. Throughout the remainder of Davenant's *Macbeth*, as in his *Hamlet*, Shakespeare's poetry is considerably diluted for contemporary ears: after the murder of Duncan, for example, Macbeth's

> Will all great Neptune's ocean wash this blood
> Clean from my hand? No, this my hand will rather
> The multitudinous seas incarnadine,
> Making the green one red   (II. ii. 58–61)

becomes the undeniably more lucid

>   can the Sea afford
> Water enough to wash away the stains?
> No, they would sooner add a tincture to
> The Sea, and turn the green into a red.
>   ([Davenant], *Macbeth*, 18–19)

Elsewhere, alterations are dictated by decorums as much social as linguistic: Davenant's Macbeth, for example, never forgets himself in front of the servants, and instead of venting the furious 'The devil damn thee black, thou cream-faced loon!' (v. iii. 11) politely asks, 'Now, Friend, what means thy change of Countenance?' (54). In such a well-spoken Scotland as this there can be no place for the drunken Porter, and his low comic role disappears entirely from the play, deemed inappropriate to tragedy on grounds of both status and genre. (The grave-diggers may have survived in Davenant's *Hamlet* thanks to the popularity they had retained even during the Interregnum in the short fairground sketch *The Grave-Makers*; Falstaff, as well as appearing in a similar 'droll', *The Bouncing Knight*, had his knighthood to protect him.)[12] Perhaps more importantly, though, the moral scheme of the play is as much clarified as its language. In particular the Macduffs explicitly become the Macbeths' virtuous counterparts, supplied with new scenes in which they meet and resist the witches and debate the moral problem of tyrannicide in rhyming couplets. (Along with the expansion of the witches' other appearances, these alterations characteristically increase the prominence of roles for actresses—Lady Macduff not only develops from a one-scene victim into one of the play's leading characters, worthy to be played by the talented Jane Long, but acquires a maid with several lines of her own.) In Davenant's hands the play thus becomes the story of two contrasting couples faced with the political possibilities of evil, one of which chooses Love and Honour and the other Love and Ambition. Within this symmetrical ethical framework and the equally symmetrical framework of the picture-stage, Betterton's Macbeth comes to serve as the principal ampler consciousness in which these abstractions can meet and conflict, his statuesque tragic body and powerfully musical voice dramatizing the doomed struggle of his better impulses with the malign forces displayed more diffusely by the supernatural stage machinery, music, and dance against which his performance competes. With the murder of Lady Macduff and penitent death of Lady Macbeth, the play finally shrinks to his emblematic duel with the loyalist Macduff, and at its close it is this Restoration Macbeth's tragedy to be reduced to a single ethical lesson, as he dies on stage underlining the adaptation's moral—'Farewell vain World, and what's most vain in it, Ambition' (60).

This may be bastardized Shakespeare (perhaps appropriately, given its adaptor's suggestions about his parentage), but both Pepys's responses and contemporary box-office receipts prove that Restoration playgoers found it compelling theatre, and our own reliance on editions of the play which provide explanatory glosses on precisely the sentences which this version paraphrases should make us hesitate before condemning Davenant for giving his audiences a *Macbeth* they could readily understand. (It is possible, indeed, to envy the adaptors of the Restoration for the confidence with which they were able to treat Shakespeare's plays as raw material for their own contemporary work, just as Shakespeare had himself treated earlier scripts, such as the old *Leir* play, in his own lifetime.) In any case this altered, classicized *Macbeth* remained a favourite long after Davenant's death in 1668 (on which the Bettertons took over most of the day-to-day running of his company, closely following the practices he had by then established), and it is a sign of the paramount success of Davenant's policies as both adaptor and manager that in the early 1670s, when *Macbeth* and *The Tempest; or, The Enchanted Island* reappeared in even greater splendour at Dorset Garden, the King's Company were reduced to cashing in on their popularity by staging lewd parodies, an 'Epilogue spoken by the Witches, after the manner of Macbeth' and a full-scale burlesque opera, *The Mock-Tempest* (both by Thomas Duffett). The King's Company may have had the pick of the pre-war star actors and the pre-war theatrical repertory, but it was Davenant who had brought the theatre up to date, and shown how Shakespeare might be brought up to date with it.

Divisions and Unions

No theatrical innovations with such far-reaching consequences for the performance of Shakespeare as those instituted in the 1660s would be carried out over the next seventy years (if ever): what did change more gradually, however, partly thanks to a series of upsets in both theatrical and national politics, was the size and composition of the audience, and with it the composition and emphasis of the Shakespearian repertoire. With the opening of Dorset Garden in 1671 and Drury Lane in 1674, the 1670s saw the number of theatre-goers who might be entertained on any given weekday afternoon between early autumn and early summer more than double, and many commentators have concluded that this change led to a significant expansion of the more middle-class component of the Restoration audience. Whether or not this was the case, it is certainly true that the élite taste for Fletcher was beginning to lose ground, and the batch of revised Shakespeare plays added to the repertory in the late 1670s and early 1680s are far more domestic in emphasis than their precursors, even when one would expect their subject-matter to place them firmly in the aristocratic ethos of high tragedy. John Dryden's *All for Love; or, The World Well Lost* (1677) is a completely new play rather than simply an adaptation of *Antony and Cleopatra*, but in its determination to present Cleopatra as a comparatively docile mistress first and a queen only second it closely foreshadows the next Shakespearian revisions which would follow it ('Nature meant me | A wife, a silly harmless household dove', proclaims its surprisingly stingless serpent of old Nile). Thomas Shadwell's *The History of Timon of Athens, the Man-Hater* (1678), similarly (despite its author's celebrated feud with Dryden), is no less preoccupied with its tragic hero's domestic arrangements, extending Shakespeare's opposition of false friends and true servants by supplying Timon with a mercenary fiancée, Melissa (a wonderfully affected role for Shadwell's wife Anne), and a loyal mistress, Evandra (a piece of heroic virtue in distress for Mary Betterton). In thus extending existing female roles and supplying new ones, these two plays follow the pattern established by Davenant in the 1660s, but they mark a significant departure in that their added material for actresses tends to distract from the political content of their main plots instead of under-lining it—and here they established a precedent which would be especially useful over the next five years.

These were troubled years for the state and the theatres alike. In the autumn of 1678 the revelation of a supposed conspiracy to assassinate Charles II and place his Catholic brother James prematurely on the throne precipitated a series of constitutional crises which would not be fully resolved either by James's accession in 1685 (and the suppression of Monmouth's rebellion which it required) or by the 'Glorious Revolution' three years later (which expelled James in favour of his Protestant daughter Mary and her husband William of Orange). Meanwhile public opinion was bitterly divided between two parties (the high monarchist Tories and more militantly Protestant Whigs), and any new play depicting political issues was liable to be caught in the partisan cross-fire, whether catcalled for inadequate loyalty to the Crown or booed for excessive sympathy with popish absolutism. In this climate several playwrights turned anew to Shakespeare, sometimes in search of material which might be put to obviously topical use, but just as often in quest of a form of serious drama capable of escaping accusations of any such polemical intentions. The most immediately political of the resulting wave of adaptations tended, as would be expected, to be short-lived, sometimes thanks to direct state intervention. The Lord Chamberlain, appointed as chief royal censor of the patent theatres in 1660, was particularly sensitive at this time, and placed actual bans on Nahum Tate's *The History of King Richard the Second* in 1680 (Shakespeare's depiction of an ineffectual monarch's deposition, which had so upset Elizabeth I during Essex's rebellion eighty years earlier, proving as unpopular with the Crown as ever, despite Tate's representation of Richard as a blameless martyr to Whiggish demagoguery) and on John Crowne's *Henry the Sixth, The First Part* in 1681 (Crowne's anti-Catholic additions to *2 Henry VI* having offended James). Several other new revisions, however, politically motivated or not, survived in the repertory for at least forty years, largely through their success in exploiting Shakespeare's tragedies and histories as sources not just of propaganda but of pathos.

These included Thomas Ravenscroft's *Titus Andronicus; or, The Rape of Lavinia* (1678) and John Dryden's *Troilus and Cressida; or, Truth Found Too Late* (1678), the latter simplifying not only Shakespeare's poetry and stagecraft for Restoration use (reducing the twenty-four scenes of the original, for example, to eleven for the convenience of the picture-stage) but his characterization, notably by making Cressida innocent of any sort of infidelity. (In despair of ever convincing Troilus of this, however, she fatally stabs herself, and Troilus is killed soon afterwards by Achilles.) These two plays' newly discovered tragic heroines, Lavinia and Cressida, are not royal by birth, and the more egalitarian possibilities of Shakespearian tragedy and history are developed further in the other successful rewritings of this group. Thomas Otway, as we have seen, dressed *Romeo and Juliet* in togas to produce *The History and Fall of Caius Marius* in 1679, its blameless young lovers made into representative victims of civil discord as a general warning against factional conflict; Thomas Durfey's *The Injured Princess* (1682) adapts *Cymbeline* to make Imogen into an equally passive victim whose innocence is finally rewarded when the rediscovery of her princely brothers relegates her from the line of royal succession into domestic bliss. Most successfully of all, Nahum Tate's *The History of King Lear* (1681) not only adjusts Shakespeare's play in ways which would have been familiar to Davenant (saving and restoring the legitimate monarch, cutting the indecorous Fool, and underlining the parallels between the villainous Edmund and Charles's ambitious illegitimate son the Duke of Monmouth), but greatly enhances its less obviously royalist element of pitiable female suffering. Keeping Cordelia in England throughout, Tate provides a simple explanation for her refusal to humour Lear in the first scene by having her secretly in love with Edgar, and her choice of this comparatively lowly suitor is justified when he thwarts an evil plan by Edmund to rape her in the storm. At the close of the play, the happily betrothed couple are to take over the kingdom as regents for the remainder of Lear's life (an arrangement distinctly Whiggish in tendency), but their priorities sound considerably more private than political—'Divine *Cordelia*, all the Gods can witness | How much thy Love to Empire I prefer!', declares Edgar.[13] Long after Monmouth's rebellion had been defeated and the Stuart dynasty exiled, this story of

domestic virtue rewarded would still be pleasing audiences (Tate's alterations to *Lear* were not wholly removed from acting texts of the play until the 1830s), a sign of the success with which such adaptations as these, whatever their ostensible politics, had fitted Shakespearian tragedy to the comparatively bourgeois tastes and demands of the later Restoration and eighteenth century. It is no accident that the writer commissioned to produce the first 'scholarly' edition of Shakespeare's plays in 1709 should have been one of the leading exponents of the pathos-orientated 'she-tragedy' with which these equally feminocentric, affective adaptations would share the serious repertory for the next hundred years, namely Nicholas Rowe: once more adaptation had successfully rediscovered Shakespeare as an honorary present-day writer.

The most lucrative of these new adaptations— Tate's *Lear* and Otway's *Caius Marius*—were both Duke's Company productions, and with the King's Company's veterans approaching retirement age and both theatres suffering from reduced box-office receipts during the political crises and scares of the time, it is perhaps not surprising that in 1682 the two-company system established in 1660 went into one of its periodic lapses. That summer the King's Company, long ago abandoned by Killigrew, went bankrupt, and for the next thirteen years both Drury Lane and Dorset Garden (now the homes of 'straight' drama and operatic spectacle respectively) would be operated by a single United Company, effectively managed by Betterton under the financial control of Christopher Rich.

The immediate effect of this development for Shakespearian acting, with the withdrawal from the stage of older King's Company stars such as Michael Mohun and Charles Hart, was Betterton's accession to two major roles hitherto the property of his rivals, Othello and Brutus, in both of which he would excel for the remainder of his career. The former suited itself perfectly to the music and intensity of his delivery (Richard Steele, writing elegiacally in the *Tatler* after the actor's funeral in 1710, remembered especially the 'moving and graceful' energy with which Betterton's Othello narrated his wooing of Desdemona), while the latter provided new opportunities for his neo-classical dignity of presence. *Julius Caesar* had first been revived at the end of the 1660s, but with Betterton as Brutus it enjoyed a new lease of life in the 1680s, and after the Glorious Revolution (which had seemed to many to write the libertarian principles espoused by Brutus and Cassius into England's very constitution) it became one of the most important Shakespearian tragedies in the repertory. Provided at some time soon after 1688 with several added lines reinforcing Brutus's unwavering commitment to liberty (in particular a dialogue with Caesar's ghost on the field at Philippi, in which Brutus reiterates his resistance to autocracy, and a new speech by which his suicide becomes an act of defiance rather than of submission), the play in Betterton's hands became the unambiguous tragedy of a man too high-principled for political success, and his stoical Brutus evidently inspired a virtually unqualified admiration in contemporary audiences. Colley Cibber remembered especially the quarrel scene, and his praise of Betterton's self-control as an actor is appropriately inseparable from his positive response to Brutus' self-control as a character:

when the *Betterton Brutus* was provoked in his dispute with *Cassius*, his Spirit flew only to his Eye; his steady Look alone supplied that Terror which he disdained an Intemperance in his Voice should rise to. Thus, with a settled Dignity of Contempt, like an unheeding Rock he repelled upon himself the Foam of *Cassius*.[14]

These two new triumphs on stage, however, were not matched by similar successes behind the scenes, and with the question of who really controlled the United Company increasingly confused by the sale of shares in its patents, Betterton found himself gradually squeezed out of its management, especially after involving the company in some particularly expensive ventures into French-style semi-opera. (One single and characteristic stage effect for Act v of *The Fairy Queen* in 1692, for example, required the construction of a chariot in which Juno could descend from the sky, drawn by immense glittering peacocks whose mechanized tails fanned out to fill most of the proscenium arch.) Christopher Rich, in a bid to save money, began to redistribute certain major roles from older, highly paid actors (such as Betterton) to their lower-paid junior colleagues (such as Cibber), and it was this policy which finally prompted a return to the two-company system in 1695. Betterton, along with several more of the older actors but also some of its younger stars (notably his leading ladies Elizabeth Barry and Anne Bracegirdle), seceded from the company in the feuding which followed this manœuvre, and despite Rich's possession of both royal patents he succeeded in negotiating a special licence from King William to operate a rival troupe. In April 1695 Betterton's new company got off to a flying start with the dazzling première of Congreve's *Love for Love* at a swiftly refitted Lincoln's Inn Fields, and for the next thirteen years cut-throat competition was again the order of the day in the London theatrical world.

It was competition on a different basis from that which had prevailed in the 1660s and 1670s, however, since the old arrangement by which the classic repertory had been divided up between two companies was never resumed, so that either troupe could now stage whichever older plays it wished. One consequence of the actors' rebellion, indeed, was an increase in the proportion of Shakespearian performances given, especially at Lincoln's Inn Fields, where Betterton's particular repute as an interpreter of Shakespeare (coupled with the former tennis-court's inadequacy as a competitive venue for operatic spectaculars) prompted the new company to mount some notable revivals. Some of these are commemorated in the frontispieces to Rowe's 1709 edition of Shakespeare, many of which were clearly inspired by contemporary stage productions: along with the apparition scene from *Macbeth* (fig. 18), for example, the edition preserves glimpses of Betterton's Henry VIII discomfiting John Verbruggen's Wolsey in III. ii (fig. 19) and of his Hamlet knocking over a chair on seeing the Ghost in the closet scene (fig. 21).[15] In addition to such well-established roles as these, Betterton now played Sir John for the first time in all of the Falstaff plays, making his own redactions of both *1 Henry IV* and the hitherto unrevived *2 Henry IV* in addition to staging the unadapted *Merry Wives of Windsor*, and with the support of his protegée Anne

FIG. 21 Frontispiece to *Hamlet*, probably based on contemporary stage production, from Nicholas Rowe's edition of Shakespeare, 1709.

increasingly to other attractions than good acting to swell their audiences. From the 1690s onwards, the theatres started to advertise performances by Italian singers and French dancers in the intervals between the acts of plays, with entertainments such as short farces and harlequinades to conclude the night's fare: 'straight' drama such as Shakespeare became, for the remainder of the eighteenth century and beyond, only one element on the bill of a perpetual variety show (see, for example, fig. 23).

Just as the place of Shakespearian acting was diminishing in importance on playbills, so it was diminishing in size within the physical space of the playhouse. In response to the economic pressures of Betterton's competition, Rich decided in 1696 to increase the potential size of his paying audience for each performance by drastically shortening the Drury Lane forestage and adding new boxes for spectators close to either side of the proscenium, so that actors performing on London's most prestigious boards were henceforward kept much further back from the auditorium, their vocal nuances less readily audible and their gestures and expressions still further subordinated to the rival visual attractions of the picture-stage. (This alteration was eloquently deplored by Colley Cibber, although it is worth noting that as himself a member of the managerial team at Drury Lane from 1710 onwards he never reduced his own box-office income by restoring the apron stage, however much he may have missed it as an actor.[16]) With this further increase in the size of the theatre audience came renewed comments on its changed social composition, which according to some observers helped to explain the increased reliance of the rival managements on variety and music. John Dennis, supplying the 1702 printed edition of his failed adaptation of *The Merry Wives of Windsor* with an embittered preface, 'A large account of the taste in poetry and the causes of the degeneracy of it', lamented that in place of the discriminating educated élite who had devoted their leisure to theatre-going in the early years of the Restoration the theatres were now crowded with uncultured younger brothers and commercially minded *nouveaux riches*, who were

Bracegirdle (fig. 22) in parts such as Mistress Ford, Portia, and Isabella, the turn of the eighteenth century may have seen some of the finest Shakespearian acting of his career.

However, although it is seldom nowadays admitted, the replacement of a benign state monopoly by untrammelled commercial rivalry is rarely an unmixed blessing to the consumer, and this would have been clear to any theatre-goer with a fondness for Shakespearian drama in the late 1690s. For all Betterton's excellence, the rush to mount rival productions of the same play sometimes led to pitiful under-rehearsal at both Lincoln's Inn Fields and Drury Lane, and both managements began to resort unable to appreciate 'any higher entertainment than tumbling and vaulting and ladder dancing' and were thus pleased 'to encourage these noble pastimes still upon the stage'. Dennis places most of the blame for the dwindling pre-eminence of serious drama, however, on the increased presence at the theatre of foreign visitors,

[s]ome of whom, not being acquainted with our language and consequently with the sense of our plays, have been instrumental in introducing sound and show, where the business of the theatre does not require it and particularly a sort of a soft and wanton music, which has used the people to a delight which is independent of reason, a delight that has gone a very great way towards the enervating and dissolving their minds.[17]

Even allowing for Dennis's piqued and xenophobic exaggeration of its decay, it is clear that the last years of the seventeenth century saw a general decline in the standing of the theatre as an institution: after Charles II's death in 1685 England would never again have another monarch with such an informed interest in the drama (or, mercifully, such a lascivious one), and

FIG. 22 Anne Bracegirdle, perhaps the most brilliant of the second generation of Restoration actresses, probably painted by Thomas Bradwell.

deprived of royal patronage and protection the playhouses came under renewed attack from moralists (led by the redoubtable clergyman Jeremy Collier), who wanted the theatre at best stringently reformed and at worst closed down altogether. Not surprisingly, the occasional new adaptations of unfamiliar Shakespeare plays produced in the wake of Collier's *A Short View of the Immorality and Profaneness of the English Stage* (1698)—such as Charles Gildon's *Measure for Measure; or, Beauty the Best Advocate* (1700) and George Granville's *The Jew of Venice* (1701)—are quick to present themselves as impeccably virtuous, and are even more thoroughgoing than their predecessors in excising vulgar low comedy. However irregular the amusements offered between the acts of their incongruously moralized and classicized plays may have been, Pompey Bum, Barnardine, and the Gobbos were all carefully kept off the vulnerable, suspect stages of the 1690s and early 1700s.

In 1705 Betterton's company in turn transferred to a much larger venue, Sir John Vanbrugh's new Queen's Theatre in the Haymarket, but this building, for all its baroque magnificence of design, proved acoustically ill-suited to spoken drama, and after only two seasons it became instead London's sole venue licensed for that allegedly brain-rotting sensation of the early eighteenth-century entertainment industry, Italian opera. Betterton, meanwhile, had at last negotiated a settlement with Rich which enabled his troupe to amalgamate once more with the patent company at Drury Lane in 1708, but the restored monopoly only lasted until 1714, when Rich's son John obtained a licence to set up a second patent company of his own at a once-more rebuilt Lincoln's Inn Fields. Rich junior's company, however, although it continued to offer 'straight' theatre, specialized much more heavily in pantomime, musicals, and spectacle, and for the next two decades the principal home of Shakespearian production in London remained Drury Lane, now under the management of a 'triumvirate' of established actors, Colley Cibber, Barton Booth, and Robert Wilks.

Despite the gifts of these three performers—Cibber excelled as Iago to Booth's solemn Othello, while Wilks was a plaintive and affecting Hamlet—their reign at Drury Lane is not remembered for either distinguished acting or innovative management: when it came to Shakespeare, the company relied on a stable core repertory of proven classics (*Hamlet*, *1 Henry IV*, *Othello*, *Julius Caesar*, Davenant's *Macbeth* and *The Tempest*, Otway's *Caius Marius*, Tate's *Lear*), performed on bills heavily embellished with comical duets and choreographic interludes. A fresh spate of topically rewritten histories and tragedies appeared briefly in response to the Jacobite insurrection of 1715 (such as Dennis's anti-Stuart version of *Coriolanus*, *The Invader of his Country*, 1719), but in general any novelties in the repertoire were confined to the less orthodox troupe at Lincoln's Inn Fields, whose miscellaneous entertainments included a now lost farce after *The Comedy of Errors* (called *Every Body Mistaken*, 1716), a mock-opera version of the mechanicals' play from *A Midsummer Night's Dream* (Richard Leveridge's *Pyramus and Thisbe: A Comic Masque*, 1716), and even an unadapted version of *Measure for Measure* (1720).

Shakespearian acting, meanwhile, in the decades following Betterton's death in 1710, seems to have settled into a grandiloquent vein of static declamation, best exemplified by the stout James Quin (1693–1766). Quin established himself as the principal tragedian at Lincoln's Inn Fields during the 1720s (where he earned the nickname of 'Bellower' Quin), but he came to more prominence after the company moved up-market in 1732, when Rich invested his profits from the sensational success of John Gay's *The Beggar's Opera* in the building of the lavish Theatre Royal, Covent Garden (on the site of the present-day Royal Opera House). Reminiscences of Quin on the Covent Garden stage picture him holding forth as the central, heavily bewigged figure in a deferential semicircle of immobile colleagues, and such accounts of his performances suggest a style that was almost a parody of Betterton's—an impression reinforced by the fact that nearly all Quin's major roles during the first half of his career had been played with far greater distinction by the elder actor. According to contemporaries, the only part in which he may have equalled Betterton was Falstaff, a role in which his ponderous grandeur of delivery was transformed into a triumph of mock-heroic comedy: as Macbeth, by contrast, according to Thomas Davies, Quin 'scarce ever deviated from a dull, heavy monotony'.[18]

Revived, without Alterations

By the 1730s, however, the classical, heroic Shakespeare of Quin's Macbeth was already beginning to look like an anachronism, as a number of cultural and political forces exerted new pressures on the Shakespearian repertory in ways which would transform its profile entirely over the course of the decade. As the example of The Beggar's Opera had shown at Lincoln's Inn Fields in 1728, the theatre in general, no longer an honorary extension of the court, was fast becoming as important a vehicle for the expression of oppositional views as for conservative ones, and the tradition of dramatic political satire was taken up in the 1730s by two new, unlicensed companies, Henry Fielding's players at the Little Theatre in the Haymarket and Henry Giffard's troupe at the Goodman's Fields theatre (just east of the City). On the stages of the two Theatres Royal, meanwhile, a number of high tragedies began to appear which were (implicitly at least) just as critical of Prime Minister Walpole's administration as the more outspoken skits of their 'fringe' colleagues, and Shakespeare soon found himself posthumously recruited to this growing cabal of Opposition playwrights. Celebrated increasingly in print as part of a native pantheon of freeborn English writers (alongside such figures as Milton and Bacon), Shakespeare was in 1738 explicitly claimed as a 'Patriot' (the favourite code-word of the anti-Walpole Opposition) in the prologue to a benefit performance of Julius Caesar at Covent Garden. The performance was staged in order to fund the erection of a memorial to Shakespeare in England's most privileged mausoleum, Westminster Abbey, and, as Julius Caesar had already been demonstrating since the late 1680s, the National Poet whose canonization this statue marked might now belong as importantly to libertarians as he did to the Establishment.

The wave of nationalism on which Shakespeare rose to new prominence in the 1730s, however, was as much social and cultural as narrowly political, in part dramatizing the hostility of an increasingly vocal mercantile class towards the traditionally more cosmopolitan aristocracy. Political nostalgia for an imagined Elizabethan golden age of military glory and commercial expansion went hand in hand with a cultural nostalgia for the native common sense of English Renaissance literature, and both were often accompanied by the Protestant zeal for moral reformation associated in the preceding decades with Jeremy Collier's crusade against the theatre. The convergence of these interconnected movements on Shakespeare was signalled most conspicuously in the mid-1730s by the establishment of the Shakespeare Ladies' Club, an informal pressure group which lobbied theatre managements to revive more Shakespeare, insisting that his patriotic and uplifting drama should drive both the libertine excesses of Restoration comedy and the invading irrationality of Italian opera from the corrupted contemporary stage. Shakespeare's 'small Latin and less Greek' had always made his work attractively accessible to female readers (who were as a rule denied an education in the classics), and he had indeed set a useful example to women writers: as Aphra Behn had observed in 1673, 'Plays have no great room for that which is men's great advantage over women, that is Learning; We all know that the immortal Shakespeare's Plays (who was not guilty of much more of this than often falls to women's share) have better pleased the world than Jonson's works.'[19] It is only fitting that it was an association of women (led by the Whig hostess Susanna Ashley-Cooper, countess of Shaftesbury, and encouraged by writers such as Eliza Haywood and Elizabeth Boyd) who were now most vocal in championing Shakespeare as a vernacular culture hero, an English antidote to the decadence of Continental taste.

The Shakespeare Ladies' Club attracted considerable publicity, and proved remarkably successful in restoring more of Shakespeare's plays to the stage—especially after Walpole, tired of being pilloried in theatres which did not even have a legal right to be operating, finally passed the Stage Licensing Act in 1737. The Act reasserted the two-company monopoly of the Theatres Royal of Drury Lane and Covent Garden (immediately driving Fielding out of business, and temporarily closing down the more tenacious Giffard), and effectively made the censoring Lord Chamberlain a servant of Parliament rather than the Crown, producing a much more rigorous system of state surveillance (which would endure until 1968). In its wake the surviving theatres were understandably chary about staging controversial new plays, and only too delighted to clean up their tarnished reputations by resorting instead to Shakespearian revivals 'At the Particular Request of Several Ladies of Quality' (as playbills proudly described managerial compliance with the Ladies' Club). In 1737, for example, Drury Lane offered an unimpeachably harmless version of *Much Ado about Nothing*, retitled *The Universal Passion*, by the clergyman James Miller ('There's nought but what an *Anchorite* might hear, | No Sentence that can wound the chastest Ear', his prologue promises), and Covent Garden followed suit, not only with a revival of the original *Much Ado* but with a moralized abbreviation of *Pericles* (by George Lillo) which memorably eulogizes Shakespeare's Ladies in its epilogue:

> When worse than barbarism had sunk your taste,
> When nothing pleased but what laid virtue waste,
> A sacred band, determined, wise, and good,
> They jointly rose to stop th'exotic flood,
> And strove to wake, by *Shakespeare*'s nervous lays,
> The manly genius of *Eliza*'s days.[20]

Of these three plays, significantly, it was the unaltered *Much Ado about Nothing* rather than either of the adaptations which would remain in the repertory: as Shakespeare's status as a British hero rose, so the practice of rewriting his plays came to be seen as positively treasonous. 'Where is the Briton so much a

Frenchman to prefer the highest stretch of modern improvement to the meanest spark of Shakespeare's genius?', demanded William Guthrie, to whom this Shakespearian revival signalled little short of a national rebirth:

> Yet to our eternal amazement it is true, that for above half a century the poets and the patrons of poetry, in England, abandoned the sterling merit of Shakespeare for the tinsel ornaments of the French academy. Let us observe, however, to the honour of our country, that neither the practice of her poets, nor the example of her patrons, could extinguish in the minds of the people, the love of their darling writer. His scenes were still admired, his passion was ever felt; his powerful nature knocked at the breast; fashion could not stifle affection; the British spirit at length prevailed; wits with their patrons were forced to give way to genius; and the plays of Shakespeare are now as much crowded as, perhaps, they were in the days of their author.[21]

Although Guthrie's claim that the work of Restoration adaptors had been entirely abandoned was an exaggeration (Davenant and Dryden's *The Tempest*, Tate's *Lear*, and Cibber's *Richard III* in particular still had years of useful life ahead of them), his observation about the relative popularity of Shakespeare in the 1740s and the Renaissance was not; during the 1740–1 theatrical season, for example, performances of Shakespeare's plays (staged not only at the Theatres Royal but at the outlawed Goodman's Fields) accounted for one in four of all theatrical performances given in London, a record which has never been equalled since. Driven by rising nationalism, Bardolatry had become big business at the box-office, and a new generation of actors was emerging who would spend a higher proportion of their time playing Shakespeare than had any of their predecessors, not excluding even Burbage.

One important result was the rapid evolution of an acting style capable of making contemporary sense of some of Shakespeare's hitherto most undervalued plays. Appropriately to Guthrie's Francophobia, the plays restored to the stage during the renaissance of the 1730s included the original *Henry V* (along with two other histories, *Richard II* and the hitherto unrevived *King John*), but the plays which benefited most

FIG. 23 Playbill for the 1740–1 revival of *As You Like It* at Drury Lane.

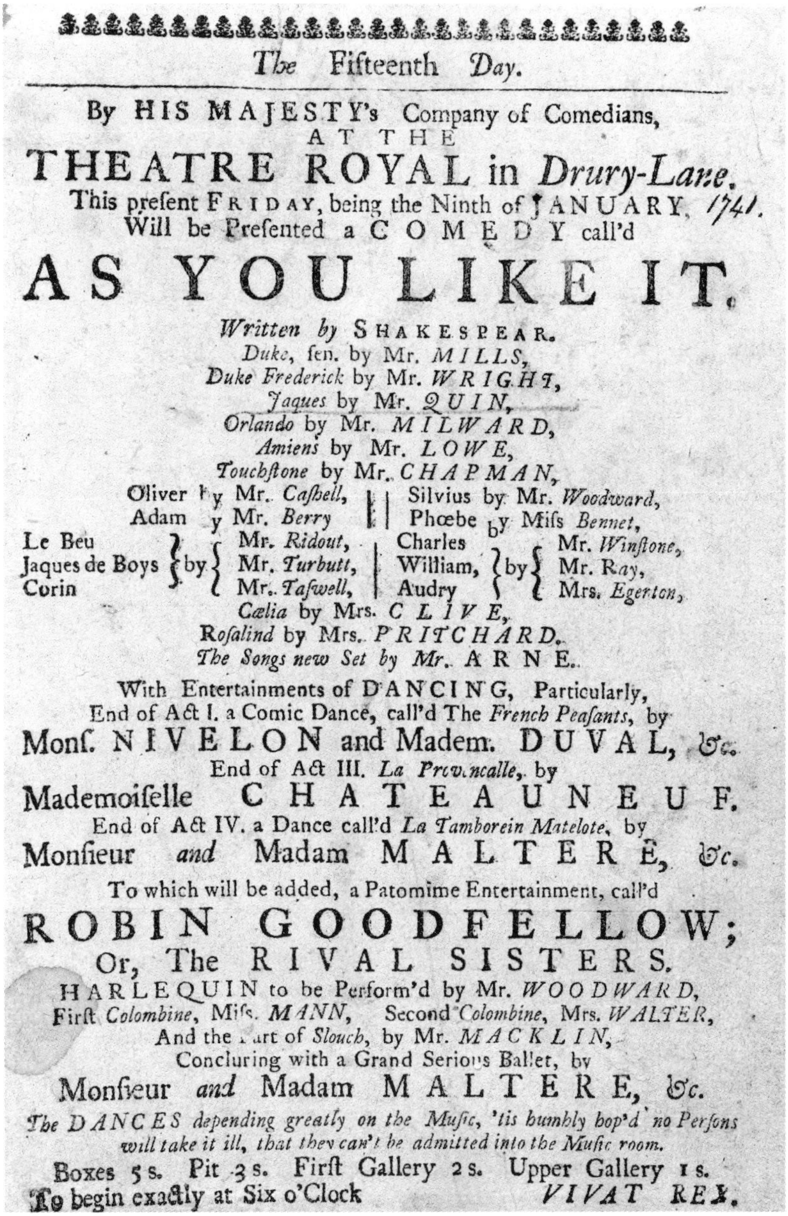

The Fifteenth *Day.*

By HIS MAJESTY's Company of Comedians,
AT THE
THEATRE ROYAL in *Drury-Lane*,
This prefent FRIDAY, being the Ninth of JANUARY, 1741.
Will be Prefented a COMEDY call'd

AS YOU LIKE IT.

Written by SHAKESPEAR.
Duke, fen. by Mr. *MILLS*,
Duke Frederick by Mr. *WRIGHT*,
Jaques by Mr. *QUIN*,
Orlando by Mr. *MILWARD*,
Amiens by Mr. *LOWE*,
Touchftone by Mr. *CHAPMAN*,
Oliver by Mr. *Cafhell*, | Silvius by Mr. *Woodward*,
Adam by Mr. *Berry* | Phœbe by Mifs *Bennet*,
Le Beu, Jaques de Boys, Corin by Mr. *Ridout*, Mr. *Turbutt*, Mr. *Tafwell*, | Charles, William, Audry by Mr. *Winftone*, Mr. *Ray*, Mrs. *Egerton*,
Cœlia by Mrs. *CLIVE*,
Rofalind by Mrs. *PRITCHARD*.
The Songs new Set by Mr. ARNE.
With Entertainments of DANCING, Particularly,
End of Act I. a Comic Dance, call'd The *French Peafants*, by
Monf. NIVELON and Madem. DUVAL, &c.
End of Act III. *La Provincalle*, by
Mademoifelle CHATEAUNEUF.
End of Act IV. a Dance call'd *La Tamborein Matelote*, by
Monfieur *and* Madam MALTERE, &c.
To which will be added, a Patomime Entertainment, call'd
ROBIN GOODFELLOW;
Or, The RIVAL SISTERS.
HARLEQUIN to be Perform'd by Mr. *WOODWARD*,
Firft *Colombine*, Mifs. *MANN*, Second *Colombine*, Mrs. *WALTER*,
And the Part of *Slouch*, by Mr. *MACKLIN*,
Concluding with a Grand Serious Ballet, by
Monfieur *and* Madam MALTERE, &c.
The DANCES depending greatly on the Mufic, 'tis humbly hop'd no Perfons will take it ill, that they can't be admitted into the Mufic room.
Boxes 5 s. Pit 3 s. Firft Gallery 2 s. Upper Gallery 1 s.
To begin exactly at Six o'Clock *VIVAT REX.*

conspicuously from the decade's resurgence of interest in Shakespeare were his comedies. While the scholar Thomas Seward, remembering the phenomenon in 1750, naturally attributed the initial rediscovery of these plays to literary criticism, he gave at least as much of the credit to the performers who brought them to life:

> a very few years since [Shakespeare's] *Comedies* in general were under the highest Contempt. Few durst speak of them with any sort of Regard, till the many excellent *Criticisms* upon that Author made people study him, and some excellent *Actors* revived these Comedies, which completely opened Men's Eyes.[22]

The comedies Seward had in mind included not only *Much Ado about Nothing* but *All's Well that Ends Well*, first revived at Goodman's Fields in March 1741 and subsequently adopted at Drury Lane the following year, and *The Winter's Tale*, similarly pioneered by the innovative Giffard in early 1741 and then taken up at Covent Garden that autumn. But the most dramatic series of such revivals took place in a single season at Drury Lane, where on 20 December 1740 the unadapted *As You Like It* received the first of nineteen consecutive performances (which would be followed by another seven over the remainder of the season: see fig. 23),[23] to be immediately succeeded from 15 January 1741 by nine performances of *Twelfth Night*, and from Valentine's Day by the first six of eighteen performances of the original *The Merchant of Venice*. Giving new life to the roles of Malvolio and Shylock within the space of a few days was Charles Macklin (who would in time also take over the part of

Touchstone); and discovering Rosalind and Viola as pinnacles of the actress's craft was the performer whom this brilliant season would make a household name, Hannah Pritchard.

Just as Guthrie saw the dramatic return of Shakespeare to the boards which these productions exemplify as a reassertion of 'nature', so commentators on the acting of both Macklin and Pritchard in the 1740–1 season continually repeat the terms 'nature' and 'natural', when not being inspired to still higher flights. 'This is the Jew | That Shakespeare drew', jingled one awestruck playgoer after seeing Macklin's Shylock (fig. 24)—a couplet perhaps not breathtaking as either poetry or theatre criticism, but none the less useful as an indication of

FIG. 24 *Charles Macklin as Shylock*, in the trial-scene, by Johann Zoffany. Shylock's face is contorted with rage at being outwitted by Balthazar, the disguised Portia (seen to the right, played by Macklin's daughter Maria).

PLATE 4 Poster for Harley Granville-Barker's production of *A Midsummer Night's Dream*,
Savoy Theatre, London, 1914.

PLATE 5 (*above*) Caliban (Beerbohm Tree) watches Prospero's ship leave the island: the final tableau in
The Tempest, Her Majesty's Theatre (colour illustration after a painting by Charles Buchel, souvenir edition,
1904).
PLATE 6 (*below*) A white box and brilliantly coloured costumes: Peter Brook's production of *A Midsummer
Night's Dream*, designed by Sally Jacobs, Royal Shakespeare Theatre, 1970.

how far not only an actor's level of identification with his role but his fidelity to Shakespeare's inferred intentions had become important criteria by which to judge contemporary performers. To audiences who had hitherto seen only the simplified, caricatured Shylock of Granville's *The Jew of Venice* played for grotesque laughs by comedians such as Thomas Doggett, Macklin's intensely serious portrayal of the role as originally written might have seemed powerfully realistic even had his preparation for it not included many days spent observing the merchants at the Royal Exchange: as it was, his performance was hailed as a triumph of empathy and technique alike, the beginning of a new era of more engaged and naturalistic acting. 'We are at present getting more into nature in playing . . . we have none of the recitative of the old tragedy,' commented John Hill a few seasons later, '. . . It is to the honour of Mr. Macklin that he began this improvement.'[24]

'Nature' and 'natural' are, of course, words regularly applied to the work of younger performers as older styles of acting (and behaviour) go out of fashion, but when applied to the production which outsold even this sensational *Merchant*, the 1740 *As You Like It*, they acquired resonances appropriate not just to its acting but to its entire emphasis. If any single revival marked the rediscovery of a 'natural', pastoral Shakespeare (his rural provincialism revalued as a fitting expression of the England invoked by patriots against court and city alike), it was this one, and the shift in attitudes it embodies—from Shakespeare as ignorant rustic requiring improvement by the educated, to Shakespeare as spontaneous genius of his native soil—becomes especially obvious when one compares the Drury Lane script with the only previous incarnation in which *As You Like It* had been performed since the Restoration. Seventeen years earlier a heavily revised version of the play by Charles Johnson had run for six performances at the same theatre: entitled *Love in a Forest*, it drastically regularized Shakespeare's language and plot, excising almost all its characters beneath the rank of courtier, killing off Oliver in the interests of poetic justice, and marrying Celia to Jaques. Its prologue

characteristically described Johnson's procedure in terms drawn from aristocratic horticulture:

> Forgive our modern Author's Honest Zeal,
> He hath attempted boldly, if not well:
> Believe, he only does with Pain and Care,
> Presume to weed the beautiful Parterre.[25]

By contrast the *As You Like It* revived in 1740 made only a handful of pragmatic abbreviations (losing Jaques's long disquisition on satire in II. vii, for example), refrained from changing the order of any scenes, and interpolated only one new passage (itself drawn from another of Shakespeare's pastoral comedies), the beautiful song 'When daisies pied' (from the close of *Love's Labour's Lost*). In 1740 *As You Like It* was no longer an imperfect formal garden requiring artificial improvement but a dramatic Forest of Arden, to be restored and revelled in. It was in treating the play as precisely this that Hannah Pritchard, the 'natural' Rosalind, came into her own.

Pritchard was 29 when she was cast as Rosalind, and had already been acting for some time, generally in roles of either victimhood (such as Ophelia) or comic affectation (such as Melissa in the Shadwell *Timon*), where she had attracted little attention: the fact that she was given such an important part may suggest that the Drury Lane management were not expecting the experiment of reviving *As You Like It* to be particularly successful. In Rosalind, however, Mrs Pritchard discovered overnight where her true comic forte lay: as Benjamin Victor remembered,

she could not enter into the Characters of Affectation with the same Degree of Excellence, as she did those of genuine, sprightly, unaffected Nature . . . her chief Excellence certainly lay in the natural, sprightly, and what are called the higher Characters in Comedy: Those who have seen her in *Rosalind* . . . will bear Testimony to what I say.[26]

Victor's choice of her Rosalind as his illustration is an especially apt one, since the part not only marked Hannah Pritchard's self-discovery as this kind of comedienne but enacted it. The trajectory of the role itself took Pritchard from the constrained, artificial banter of the opening scenes at Duke Frederick's court, where she appeared an undistinguished, pitiful figure very much in the shadow of Celia, to the wholly different dialogue she enjoyed as Ganymede in Arden, and it was here that the audience of the production's historic first night, who had hitherto reserved judgement, suddenly recognized the extraordinary qualities of both the performer and the play. In this section of her role Pritchard had two tremendous advantages: first a crystal-clear delivery even at passionate speed ('she uttered her words as the great poet advises the actor, smoothly and trippingly from the tongue,' commented one admirer, 'and however voluble in enunciation her part might require her to be, not a syllable of articulation was lost'),[27] and secondly an excellent comic rapport with the actress who played Celia, her close friend 'pretty, witty' Kitty Clive. (This would serve the two equally well in *Twelfth Night*, where Clive played Olivia to Pritchard's Viola, and in *The Merchant of Venice*, where Pritchard played Nerissa to Clive's pert Portia.) The scene which made all the difference was III. ii, in which Rosalind learns from a teasing Celia that Orlando, too, is in the forest: as John Hill recalled,

how were we surprised, when by some good chance [Mrs Pritchard] had got the part of *Rosalind* assigned her in the revived play of *As You Like It*, to hear her speak with a spirit and justice, that none of the then favourites of the stage could come up to, 'Good my complexion, dost thou think that because I am caparison'd like a man, I have a doublet and hose in my disposition? . . .' Every speech after this, convinced us more and more, that we had long been in possession of a jewel that we had scandalously neglected; till toward the end of the play, her raillery to her lover, who had pretended to be dying for her, showed us fully what she was. With what pleasure is it . . . that one remembers the manner in which she said, 'No, faith, die by attorney. . . . Men have died from time to time, and worms have eaten them; but not for love.'[28]

Appropriately, the picture which Francis Hayman based on this much-revived production at some time in the early 1740s (col. pl. 1) depicts precisely the moment at which Pritchard's Rosalind begins her transition from unhappy princess to the ebullient comic heroine applauded by Hill, the point at which she finds herself deeply interested in Orlando's victory over Charles the wrestler. Placed centre stage behind the combatants, she is impetuously beginning to step downstage of Kitty Clive's Celia for the first time in the play. (Although idealized from the stage production, this painting is probably not misleading in representing such a sylvan setting for even this early, court scene, since Hayman was himself employed as the production's scene-painter and is unlikely to have imagined this space in terms fundamentally different from those established by his own flats: not for nothing did this show establish Thomas Arne's new setting of 'Under the Greenwood Tree' as one of the most popular songs of the eighteenth century.)

By a happy stroke of casting, Pritchard's energetic, unaffected Rosalind shared Hayman's leafy Forest of Arden with a Jaques played by James Quin (then nearing his return to Covent Garden after a seven-year sojourn at Drury Lane), and the contrast between Pritchard's volubly playful speaking of prose and his sonorously self-important declamation of verse might serve as an apt image of the changes which had overtaken the Shakespearian theatre over the preceding ten years, if not the preceding fifty. By the end of the 1740–1 season, although Shakespeare had been comprehensively rediscovered as the economic and moral saviour of the two patent theatres, everything about the performance of his plays was in flux. Acting styles were changing at bewildering speed; hitherto unseen plays, especially romantic comedies, were appearing in unadapted form alongside established, heavily rewritten favourites; and with Drury Lane, after the deaths of Wilks and Booth and the withdrawal of Cibber, now in the hands of the unreliable Charles Fleetwood, the principal management involved in the staging of Shakespearian drama was in a highly precarious condition. Although now canonized as England's greatest dramatist, Shakespeare, just as he had been in 1660, was up for grabs—and within a few months the London theatre would see the début of the man who would do most of the grabbing. His name was David Garrick.

4

The Age of Garrick

PETER HOLLAND

ON 15 September 1747 Drury Lane Theatre opened its new season under new management. The play that evening was not a new production: Charles Macklin starred as Shylock, a role he had begun playing in 1740 and would continue playing until his retirement in 1789 (fig. 24). But before the performance David Garrick, now co-manager of the theatre with James Lacy, stepped out to deliver a new prologue written by his friend Samuel Johnson. The prologue is best remembered now for its acknowledgement of the power of the audience to control the theatre's repertory:

> The drama's laws the drama's patrons give,
> For we that live to please must please to live.

But Johnson went on to offer the audience the opportunity of defining a new era for performance:

> 'Tis yours this night to bid the reign commence
> Of rescued nature and reviving sense.

The source of that nature and sense, of 'useful mirth and salutary woe', of 'scenic virtue' and 'truth' was set out at the start of the prologue:

> When learning's triumph o'er her barbarous foes
> First reared the stage, immortal Shakespeare rose.
> Each change of many-coloured life he drew,
> Exhausted worlds and then imagined new.

Having achieved a position of unquestioned pre-eminence in English theatre, Garrick entwined his status with Shakespeare, the figure who had been the source of his fame and with whom his name would stay interlaced. Even on the statue of Garrick in Westminster Abbey the connection was still paramount:

> Though sunk in death the forms the poet drew,
> The actor's genius bade them breathe anew.
> Though, like the bard himself, in night they lay,
> Immortal Garrick called them back to day;
> And, till eternity with power sublime
> Shall mark the mortal hour of hoary time,
> Shakespeare and Garrick like twin stars shall shine
> And earth irradiate with a beam divine.

Historians are reluctant these days to accept the formulation 'the Age of . . .', but for English theatre the mid-eighteenth century cannot be called anything other than the Age of Garrick. No one had ever achieved such dominance over the stage. Rivals at Covent Garden took what chances they could to compete or find out areas of theatre that Garrick ignored. His authority was absolute and, as Dr Johnson said, 'his profession made him rich and he made his profession respectable'. No actor or theatre manager had achieved such status in his lifetime or a grand funeral and burial in Westminster Abbey on his death. No other figure in the century, theatrical or regal, was so often painted. No other actor was so often written about or written to, described, and argued over.

FIG. 25 *Garrick with a Bust of Shakespeare*, engraving after Thomas Gainsborough.

Garrick's acting career began with Shakespeare. At Goodman's Fields in 1741, when an actor fell ill before a performance of a pantomime, *Harlequin Student*, Garrick, then a wine-merchant, stepped in for a few scenes, playing anonymously. At the end of the play mime gave way to scripted language and Jupiter extolled 'immortal Shakespeare's matchless wit' before the scene drew to reveal a reproduction of the Shakespeare monument 'exactly represented as lately erected in Westminster Abbey'.

The coincidence of the début of Garrick and the appearance of Shakespeare in marble is almost too perfect. But Garrick's proper London début was inevitably in Shakespeare—or at least Shakespeare adapted by Colley Cibber—when he played Richard III at Goodman's Fields in October 1741, setting out deliberately to compete with the revival of the play at Covent Garden the week before, the first time the play had been performed in London for six years. His success was immediate and tremendous; the theatre was packed for his subsequent performances and his reputation was quickly assured, especially once his Richard was immortalised on canvas by William Hogarth (col. pl. 2). In the next few years he established his success as King Lear, Hamlet, and Macbeth. By the time he became manager at Drury Lane, his triumph as an actor had been firmly founded on a base of Shakespearian tragic heroes.

It is possible, of course, to see Garrick's use of Shakespeare, his recurrent definition of Shakespeare's centrality in English theatre, culture, society, and, in effect, religion, as a cynical manipulation of a convenient prop. But Garrick was not responsible for the notion of Shakespeare's divinity and immortality, however often he may have emphasized it. If it seems faintly ridiculous of Garrick to erect a temple dedicated to Shakespeare in the gardens of his villa beside the Thames—let alone be painted leaning on the statue (fig. 25)—he did see Shakespeare as at least semi-divine, writing to a friend, 'I will not despair of seeing you in my temple of Shakespeare, confessing your infidelity and bowing your head to the "god of my idolatry", as he himself so well expresses it.'[1] In any case he was well aware that he was more than a little obsessed with Shakespeare: 'I am afraid that my madness about Shakespeare is become very troublesome, for I question whether I have written a single letter without bringing him in.'[2]

Garrick's interest in Shakespeare was not wholly iconic and theatrical. He was endlessly consulted about possible emendations in the text. He lent books from his massive library of Renaissance playtexts to scholars working on new Shakespeare editions and the collection was left by him to the British Museum, the cornerstone of their holdings in the drama of Shakespeare's time. He sought to convince friends in France that their antipathy to Shakespeare was a dreadful mistake. Shakespeare figured in every aspect of his life.

In the theatre his acting and his approach to Shakespeare were equally innovatory. Contemporaries recognized that the energy and theatrical imagination Garrick brought to his acting marked a decisive break with the past. Richard Cumberland described the contrast when, in a play by Rowe, Quin's traditional style of delivery, rolling out 'his heroics with an air of dignified indifference', opened the play but 'when . . . little Garrick, then young and light and alive in every muscle and in every feature, came bounding on the stage . . . heavens, what a transition! It seemed as if a whole century had been stepped over in the transition of a single scene.'[3] As Quin himself muttered, 'If this young fellow is right, I and the rest of the players must have been all wrong.'[4]

Garrick's reign did not increase the number of Shakespeare plays performed in the London theatres. He did, though, establish many as staples of the repertory, stock plays that would be performed a few times every year. More significantly, he began a move to call the texts 'back to day', reversing the movement to adaptation, restoring speeches and scenes, refusing the by then habitual performance of Restoration adaptations. He was limited by his own acute sense of theatrical viability, never demanding more of 'the drama's patrons' than he sensed they might be willing to accept, always acquiescing, even if only temporarily, in 'the drama's laws' they defined. But, while it is often difficult to define easily what is an adapted version and what is not, most plays were increasingly played in relatively unadapted forms.

But Garrick's most decisive innovation was the refusal to fix the text into an unalterable mode. While his performance of the particular Shakespeare roles which he claimed as his territory quickly settled, establishing the approach to character, the reading of the part, early in his confrontation with each one and then continuing to play that same interpretation for the rest of his career, his approach to the playing-text was one of continual reconsideration, re-evaluation, and restoration. While Garrick's first and last performances as Lear, thirty-four years apart, would have been recognizably the same, the Lear of his farewell season spoke far more Shakespeare than would have been conceivable earlier.

In December 1772 Garrick brought on stage an entirely new version of *Hamlet*. His performance was famous, perhaps his greatest Shakespeare role. The most famous moment in it, his shocked reaction to the appearance of his father's ghost, had, over the years, been aided by a remarkable piece of stage machinery, a specially designed wig that used hydraulics to make the hair stand on end in terror at this sight. But, technical help apart, the interpretation, the high points, the authority, and naturalism did not change.

The new acting-text was controversial, not for its restorations but for its cutting. Garrick removed almost all of Act V, managing to get from Ophelia's last exit (Shakespeare's IV. v) to the end of the play in only sixty lines where Shakespeare needed over 800. No grave-diggers, no burial for Ophelia, no formal duel remain. As a piece of brutal cutting it is almost without parallel. Most reviewers praised it: 'The tedious interruptions of this beautiful tale no longer disgrace it; its absurd digressions are no longer disgusting.'[5] But Garrick's treatment of Act v has overshadowed the effect of the cutting on the rest of the play. Adding only eleven lines of his own, he could use the savings at the end as a balance, enabling him to restore over 620 lines of Shakespeare to the earlier acts, putting back on stage characters not seen for a century, building back up roles like Polonius and Laertes and scenes like the players' play and Claudius' prayer. Until

the rapid abbreviation of the end, Garrick's version of *Hamlet* is not unlike the kind of cut versions used in modern productions; indeed it is fuller than most.

The 1772 version was Garrick's last exploration of the text, the final attempt to let Drury Lane audiences hear and see as much of the play as possible. But where previous actors, managers, and adapters had settled a playing version for their careers, Garrick inaugurated a continual revision, a recognition of the fluidity of the text. It is impossible now to document all the changes in his version of *Hamlet* year by year, but three earlier versions survive. Garrick began acting Hamlet in 1742 using the version published in 1718 developed by the actor Robert Wilks in collaboration with the poet John Hughes. He published revised versions in 1751 and 1763, including rather more Shakespeare at each stage.

Hamlet is an epitome of Garrick's Shakespeare productions and I shall go on to look at his responses to four other plays: *Romeo and Juliet*, *A Midsummer Night's Dream*, *King Lear*, and *Macbeth*. But the epitome of his response to Shakespeare was an event that involved no performance of a Shakespeare play at all: the Shakespeare Jubilee of 1769.

The Jubilee

In 1767 the Corporation of Stratford-upon-Avon, having had the Town Hall rebuilt, was looking for some way of being given a bust of Shakespeare to put in an empty niche on the building. Flattery of Garrick seemed a good way of securing a benefaction and they offered to elect him an Honorary Burgess and give him a box made from the mulberry-tree supposedly planted by Shakespeare—though if all the objects made from the wood of Shakespeare's mulberry were authentic, the tree must have been gargantuan. Garrick, flattered, responded as the Corporation hoped, offering a statue and a painting of Shakespeare.

The mulberry box was not ready until May 1769 when the Corporation, flattered in its turn, commissioned Gainsborough to paint a portrait of Garrick and Shakespeare (fig. 25). Together Garrick and the Corporation proposed 'a Jubilee in honour and to the memory of Shakespeare' to be held in September 1769 under the Stewardship of Garrick.[6] Garrick was fired with enthusiasm for the event, announcing it publicly in a new epilogue which closed the theatrical season at Drury Lane:

> My eyes, till then, no sights like these will see,
> Unless we meet at Shakespeare's Jubilee!
> On Avon's banks, where flowers eternal blow,
> Like its full stream, our gratitude shall flow.
> Then let us revel, show our fond regard,
> On that loved spot first breathed our matchless bard.[7]

For the whole of the summer the technical crew of Drury Lane, supervised by Garrick's brother, worked in Stratford, preparing for the great event. On the banks of the Avon they constructed an octagonal wooden amphitheatre, the Rotunda, to hold the main

events. Medals were struck to commemorate the event, ribbons designed to be worn as favours, wooden souvenirs, all carved from the mulberry-tree of course, made to be sold in Stratford.

The events and celebrations were to last three days, a packed programme including a masked ball, fireworks, concerts, processions (fig. 26), and a horse-race for the Jubilee Cup worth £50. No one seems to have considered that a performance of a Shakespeare play might be appropriate; the main performance was of Arne's celebrated sacred oratorio *Judith*, chosen, some said, because of the name of Shakespeare's eldest daughter. The scale grew almost out of control: over 170 performers were to take part in the crowning glory of the whole grand event: the performance of a new ode, written and spoken by Garrick, 'An Ode upon Dedicating a Building and Erecting a Statue to Shakespeare at Stratford-upon-Avon', to the accompaniment of songs, choruses, and other musical interventions.

The Jubilee was certainly going to be the social event of the summer and if the papers were full of

FIG. 26 Caricature of *The Procession from the Jubilee*, which was cancelled due to the bad weather. The bedraggled Shakespearian characters speak parody-quotations which complain of the cold and damp, and mock Garrick for his exploitation of their author.

Fig. 27 *Garrick delivering the*
Ode on the Stage of Drury
Lane, engraving by J. Lodge.

mocking anticipation no one could afford to miss out.
The people of Stratford recognized the right response
to consumer demand and the price of beds and meals
escalated at hyper-inflationary rates. For the first time
Stratford, a provincial backwater that had never traded
on its most commercially viable product, became,
through Garrick and Shakespeare, the centre of
fashionable life.

It was predictable that the events would not go
smoothly. While the first day passed off without
incident, the rain started to pour on the second
morning and pageants were cancelled, firework
displays went off like damp squibs, and the midnight
masquerade was approached through flooded fields.
The racecourse was under water by the third day and
the Rotunda was too flooded for a repeat of the
performance of the Ode. By the time the well-to-do
returned to London, tempers were frayed, not least by
the horrendous costs of attending, and the newspapers
were fuller of letters of complaint than of praise.

One event was, though, an unequivocal success: the
Ode itself. Magnificently staged, complete with a
planted heckler, the actor Thomas King, complaining
that Shakespeare was a provincial low-born nobody,
Garrick's performance spoke of Shakespeare's
immortality, his exploration of nature, and his
significance as the embodiment of everything that

made one proud to be English, with an eloquence and
fervour that even Garrick's greatest admirers had not
previously suspected. 'Mr Garrick', wrote one
reporter, 'distinguished himself equally as a poet, an
actor, and a gentleman.'[8]

However pleased Garrick might have been by the
aesthetic success of the Jubilee, it had been a financial
disaster for him, losing around £2,000. In October 1769,
less than a month after the event, George Colman the
Elder staged an afterpiece on the topic at Covent
Garden, *Man and Wife; or, The Stratford Jubilee*, gently
mocking the pretensions and exploitation of the event
but also finding space for a grand processional
pageant, 'exhibiting the characters of Shakespeare',
organized in four groups (Roman characters, Old
English characters, the Tragic Muse, and the Comic
Muse) and ending with 'The car (drawn by the Muses)
containing the bust of Shakespeare, crowned by Time
and Fame and attended by the three Graces, Cupid,
Satyrs, Bacchanals, &c.' Garrick's response was
startlingly quick: hearing of Colman's plans, 'I set
myself down to work and in a day and a half produced
our Jubilee, which has now had more success than
anything I ever remember; it is crowded in 15 minutes
after the doors are opened and will be played
tomorrow for the 39th time.'[9]

Garrick's afterpiece *The Jubilee* was premièred a

week after Colman's piece and played eighty-eight times that season, a triumph unequalled in the century. As a French character comments in Colman's play *New Brooms* (1776)—and the remarks are not only sour grapes on Colman's part—'Vat signify your *triste* Shakespeare? Begar, dere was more moneys got by de gran spectacle of de Shakespeare Jubilee dan by all de comique and tragique of Shakespeare beside, *ma foi!*'

As well as a grand presentation of the Ode (fig. 27), *The Jubilee* was Garrick's means of turning aristocratic entertainment into popular success. The fashionable world that went to Stratford was exclusive; the far less wealthy theatre-goers who filled Drury Lane night after night were drawn by the same fascination with spectacle. For, while it included metropolitan mockery of the provincial stupidity of Stratford's citizens, the main attraction of Garrick's afterpiece was Garrick's pageant of characters from Shakespeare, a display even more spectacular than Colman's. Nineteen groups depicted characters from nineteen plays, heralded by eighteen dancers and the three Graces, closing with the Tragic Muse drawn in a chariot attended by six Furies and, in the middle of the display, separating the comedies from the tragedies and histories, surrounded by the Graces (again), Apollo, six trumpeters, and a timpanist, came 'the statue of Shakespeare supported by the passions and surrounded by the seven muses with their trophies'. At the end of the play, a grand tableau of the characters surrounds the statue with banners waving, and, as Garrick wrote in his manuscript, 'Every character, tragic and comic, joins in the Chorus and goes back, during which the guns fire, bells ring, etc., etc. and the audience applauds. Bravo Jubilee! Shakespeare forever!'

As a cultural event the Jubilee was unprecedented. Apart from anything else, it transformed the social significance of Stratford. As a theatrical spectacle *The Jubilee* was unequalled, though it quickly vanished from the repertory. As a lesson in the economics of entertainment, the whole business demonstrated Garrick's keen eye for a way to recoup his losses, redefining his audience from participants in Stratford to spectators at Drury Lane. But as an event in the history of Shakespeare production the Jubilee changed

nothing. It did not make productions of the plays more or less popular; it did not make the slightest difference to Garrick's own way of playing and producing the plays. His aims and ambitions in that area were clear long before 1769.

Romeo and Juliet

Nearly twenty years earlier, when Drury Lane reopened for the start of the new theatre season in September 1750, Garrick came onto the stage to deliver a new prologue. The piece epitomizes his recurrent awareness of the tension between commercial necessity and his devotion to Shakespeare:

> Sacred to Shakespeare was this spot designed,
> To pierce the heart and humanize the mind.
> But if an empty house, the actor's curse,
> Shows us our Lears and Hamlets lose their force,
> Unwilling we must change the nobler scene,
> And in our turn present you Harlequin;
> Quit poets and set carpenters to work,
> Show gaudy scenes or mount the vaulting Turk.

In the event he had no need of the 'vaulting Turk'. Instead a production of Shakespeare proved to be both an act of religious homage and hugely profitable. *Romeo and Juliet*, from this season onwards to the end of Garrick's management in 1776, would be the most frequently performed tragedy both at Drury Lane and at Covent Garden and the second most popular of all main-pieces, giving place only to *The Beggar's Opera*. If Garrick needed the aid of carpenters for spectacular, though not gaudy, scenes, he also demonstrated conclusively that the audience wanted its collective heart pierced, though he could hardly guarantee that the play would 'humanize the mind'.

Romeo and Juliet, transformed into Otway's romanized version *The History and Fall of Caius Marius* (1680), had proved enduringly popular. Theophilus

Cibber had revived Shakespeare's title in 1744 at the Little Theatre in the Haymarket with reasonable success but, while his title was Shakespeare's, much of the text was Otway's. Garrick saw the production and loathed it, writing to a friend, 'I never heard so vile and scandalous a performance in my life; and, excepting the speaking of it, and the speaker, nothing could be more contemptible.'[10]

Garrick returned to Shakespeare, rather than Otway, for his own first attempt at adapting the play in 1748, while keeping and expanding Otway's alteration of the death scene so that Juliet wakes before Romeo dies, allowing for a reunion. Recognizing that Romeo was not a natural role for his talents, Garrick chose not to play the character himself but to direct Spranger Barry and Mrs Cibber in the title-roles. But before the 1750 season opened Barry and Mrs Cibber, as well as Macklin, had left Drury Lane for Rich's rival company at Covent Garden, taking Garrick's adaptation with them. The commercial threat of a revitalized Covent Garden company drove Garrick to direct competition and by July he had already resolved on his response, writing to his co-manager Lacy, 'Let them do their worst, we must have the best company, and by a well-laid regular plan, we shall be able to make them as uneasy with Rich, as Rich will be with them.—I shall be soon ready in *Romeo*, which we will bring out early.'[11]

Garrick had already decided on a further change to his text. His preface to the edition of his 1748 version had made clear his recognition of the audience's uneasiness over the rapidity of Romeo's switch from his first love, the unseen Rosaline, to Juliet:

Many people have imagined that the sudden change of Romeo's love from Rosaline to Juliet was a blemish in his character, but an alteration of that kind was thought too bold to be attempted; Shakespeare has dwelt particularly upon it, and so great a judge of human nature knew that to be young and inconstant was extremely natural.

Garrick's hesitancy at this stage is a firm indication both of the popular attitude towards Shakespeare and his own: he does not specify who thought such a change was 'too bold', simply approving the drive towards the acceptance of the Shakespearian text. If Romeo's action is now socially unacceptable, then its justification lies in Shakespeare's unarguable perception of its naturalness.

But by 1750 audience pressure could not be resisted and Romeo's love for Rosaline is neatly excised so that he is already in love with Juliet and it is Benvolio, not Romeo, who at the Capulet ball has to ask the Nurse to identify Juliet.

Elsewhere Garrick's aim in preparing the text for the 1748 production was, as he put in his preface, to 'clear the original, as much as possible, from the jingle and quibble, which were always thought the great objections to reviving it'. Rhyme and puns go—even the lovers' sonnet on meeting at the ball is drastically curtailed; the diction is simplified, the complexity of the imagery reduced, the language made more accessible. Sexual suggestiveness, in the speeches of Mercutio and the Nurse in particular, was left more or less intact. Linguistic orthodoxy, not a narrow morality, was at the heart of his tidying-up.

But the elimination of Rosaline in the new version was hardly going to be crucial in the rivalry with Covent Garden. Instead Garrick chose to play Romeo himself, relying on his own reputation as a draw, and, with Mrs Bellamy as Juliet, to enable the audiences to compare the two productions by the unprecedented step of performing *Romeo* on the same night as Covent Garden. For twelve successive nights from the première on 28 September, both theatres played *Romeo*. If audiences were initially fascinated by the theatrical battle, they were soon irritated; a contemporary squib catches the mood perfectly:

> 'Well, what's today?' says angry Ned,
>   As up from bed he rouses.
> '*Romeo* again!' and shakes his head,
>   'Ah, pox on both your houses.'

Audiences dropped and only Mrs Cibber's illness, forcing Covent Garden to abandon the play, ended the duel, Garrick adding a triumphant thirteenth performance to prove his victory. Mrs Garrick, not surprisingly, was scathing about the Covent Garden performers and relieved the battle was over; in the middle of the run she went to the rival house and wrote to the Countess of Burlington, 'All that I can say of it is that Mr Barry is too young (in his head) for Romeo and Mrs Cibber too old for a girl of 18 [Juliet's age in the adaptation] . . . I wish they would finish both, for it is too much for my little dear spouse to play every day.'[12]

One of Rich's trump cards had been an elaborate funeral procession for Juliet complete with music by Thomas Arne, a spectacular scene that was proudly announced on the playbill for the first performance. Garrick countered quickly, commissioning William Boyce to write the music for a procession at Drury Lane and being able to include his version of the scene by 1 October. Even after the battle of the productions was over the scene was still a high point of the play; a German visitor in 1761 described it at length:

an entire funeral is represented, with bells tolling, and a choir singing. Juliet, feigning death, lies on a state bed with a splendid canopy over her, guarded by girls who strew flowers

and by torch-bearers with flaming torches. The choristers and clergy in their vestments walk in front, and the father and mother and their friends follow. The scene represents the interior of a church. To my feeling this appears rather profane but, putting this aside, nothing could be represented more beautifully or more naturally.[13]

But spectacle had always been a part of Garrick's design for the play. Even in 1748 a playbill made much of 'a new Masquerade Dance, proper to the play' and the elaboration of the scene, with music and dancing and a large cast, while it also necessitated cutting the text, enabled the growing love between Romeo and Juliet to be seen, if not heard, as a counterpoint to the choreography.

Above all, Garrick's production used the carpenters of Drury Lane to create a remarkable atmosphere for the tomb scene (fig. 28). It was not only the elaborate design of the tomb and the suggestions of landscape

FIG. 28 Garrick and Mrs Bellamy in *Romeo and Juliet*: the tomb scene, with elaborate stage-design, by Benjamin Wilson.

and moonlight that engineered the effect. The closed space, claustrophobic and confined, distant from the audience, emphasized the intensity of the scene, allowing Garrick's largest addition to the play its full emotional scope. For the seventy-five lines of the reunion was the emotional high point of the Garrick play. If the language uses every cliché of eighteenth-century tragedy, in the performances by Garrick and Bellamy, Barry and Cibber the effect was immensely powerful:

ROMEO. I thought thee dead. Distracted at the sight—
    Fatal speed!—drank poison, kissed thy cold lips,
    And found within thy arms a precious grave.
    But in that moment—O—
JULIET. And did I wake for this?
ROMEO. My powers are blasted,
    'Twixt death and love I'm torn, I am distracted!
    But death's strongest—and must I leave thee, Juliet?
    O, cruel, cursed fate!

FIG. 29 Barry and Miss Nossiter in *Romeo and Juliet*: the balcony scene, engraving after R. Pyle.

Whatever the work of the set-builders and choreographers, composers and musicians, the nub of the competition was the performances of the stars. Covent Garden's Mercutio was Charles Macklin and was no rival to Woodward at Drury Lane. Mrs Cibber's tragic dignity was balanced by Bellamy's passionate love and effective naturalism. Neither was probably as successful as Miss Nossiter, who played Juliet opposite Barry at Covent Garden in 1753, hugely praised, in an entire pamphlet devoted to her performance, *A Letter to Miss Nossiter* (1753), above all for her naturalness; her sudden start as, on the verge of drinking Friar Laurence's potion, she imagines a new terror, was particularly admired: 'it certainly is the greatest stroke of acting I ever saw, not only as it is a natural Surprise, but as it illustrates the Author's meaning . . . Most of the actions that are commonly called strokes are no more than tricks, but this is nature.'

The critical consensus over the Romeos was that Barry's brilliance in the first half of the play, especially the balcony scene (fig. 29), was outdone by Garrick's triumph at the end of the play so that audiences were reported to watch Barry's Romeo in love in the first three acts at Covent Garden and then take advantage of half-price admission after Act III to watch Garrick's Romeo die at Drury Lane. Yet in spite of the power of the final scenes in Garrick's performance, the mature power of his tragic performance was offset by the difficulty he had in representing the tenderness of the passionate lover. As one woman in the audience was reported to have judged,

Had I been Juliet to Garrick's Romeo, so ardent and impassioned was he, I should have expected he would have *come up* to me in the balcony; but had I been Juliet to Barry's Romeo, so tender, so eloquent and so seductive was he, I should certainly have *gone down* to him![14]

For all the continuing success of the adaptation in performance, Romeo was never one of Garrick's great roles and, after 1760, judging himself too old for the part, he gave it up. The period's orthodox response to Shakespeare's play could not accept what was seen as its unevenness. Francis Gentleman in 1770 complained that the plot 'is romantic and irregular; the characters oddly conceived and strangely jumbled; the scenes very unequal in matter'.[15] If Garrick's version flattens, it also intensifies a narrow range of emotional possibility. Its theatrical viability was unquestioned, its success convincing proof that the stage 'sacred to Shakespeare' could play Garrick's *Romeo* with a clear financial conscience.

A Midsummer Night's Dream

By the time Garrick turned his attention to *A Midsummer Night's Dream*, the play's association with opera seemed indissoluble. *The Fairy Queen* of 1692 provided a dramatic framework for Purcell's brilliant series of musical interventions. The workers' play, 'Pyramus and Thisbe', had twice been used to parody contemporary taste in opera in Leveridge's *Comic Masque of Pyramus and Thisbe* (1716) and Lampe's similar work (1745). It must have seemed logical to take Shakespeare's play and turn it into a fully-fledged opera. The combination of the play's own fascination with song and the earlier attempts at adaptation must have made the task irresistible, especially given the recurrent search by the theatres for English operatic forms to set against the success of Italian opera. Ballad-opera, Gay's brilliant invention in *The Beggar's Opera*, continued to be a staple of the repertory but the putative prestige of combining Shakespeare and opera must have attracted Garrick.

In the event, Garrick seems to have been reluctant to acknowledge *The Fairies*, the operatic version of *A Midsummer Night's Dream* which opened in 1755. The prologue mockingly apologizes for the whole idea of an English opera, 'played by an English band, | Wrote in a language which you understand', and masks *The Fairies'* authorship, into a combination of its source and the normal expectation of Italian origins:

> I dare not say *who* wrote it—I could tell ye,
> To soften matters, Signior Shakespearelli.

But even in private Garrick deflected suggestions of his responsibility for this and for the operatic adaptation of *The Tempest* which appeared a year later, writing to a friend,

if you mean that *I* was the person who altered the *Midsummer Night's Dream* and *The Tempest* into operas, you are much mistaken. However, as old Cibber said in his last epilogue,

> But right or wrong, or true or false—'tis pleasant.[16]

The Fairies was reasonably successful, with nine performances in the 1755–6 season and two more the following year, but Garrick's embarrassment over the work seems undeniable.

The Fairies was innovatory: a new all-sung opera had not been performed at either of the main theatres for many years. In the search for new styles of performance to please audience curiosity, the transformation was an effective choice. The title-page of the published text is explicit about the source, seeing the result as 'an opera taken from *A Midsummer Night's Dream* written by Shakespeare'; Shakespeare is now a guarantee of quality, a culturally respectable seal of approval for the endeavour. But in taking from the Shakespeare play, opera cannot accommodate much and a preface apologizes for the extent of the cutting: 'Many passages of the first merit and some whole scenes . . . are necessarily omitted in this opera to reduce the performance to a proper length; it was feared that even the best poetry would appear tedious when only supported by recitative.'

An opera libretto cannot be more than a fragment of a full-length play: the play's 2,100 lines are reduced to less than 500. But opera's pretensions to dignity provided one obvious clue to how to abbreviate: there can be no room now for Bottom and the workers and, with 'Pyramus and Thisbe' cut completely, the whole of Act v can be reduced to two and a half lines.

The Fairies has room only for fairies and lovers, characters who might reasonably appear in a high-cultural art-form like opera. But it also has to make room for more arias than Shakespeare's play. As well as turning speeches from the play into the words for songs, Garrick drew on Milton, Waller, Dryden, and others to help make up a total of twenty-three songs, all set by John Smith, Handel's pupil. The result is efficient, with characters moving from recitative to aria at regular intervals. In the first scene, for instance, Theseus describes his future wedding, 'With pomp, with triumph and with revelling' and instantly bursts into song ('Pierce the air with sounds of joy, | Come Hymen with the winged boy'); Hermia refuses to marry Demetrius and then sings that 'I scorn the cheat of reason's foolish pride, | And boast the graceful weakness of my heart'; Theseus and Hippolyta leave the stage to the sound of an aria and chorus ('Joy alone shall employ us, | No griefs shall annoy us').

For one disgruntled member of the audience, Horace Walpole, the audience's approval of English opera stemmed from patriotism but, for him at least, the libretto and its source are 'forty times more nonsensical than the worst translation of any Italian opera-books'.[17]

The Fairies did not last and neither did the subsequent operatic version of *The Tempest*. Garrick tried two other experiments in adapting Shakespearian comedy to the forms of his theatre. In 1754 he turned *The Taming of the Shrew* into a three-act farce, an afterpiece called *Catherine and Petruchio*. Stripping away the induction and anything else extraneous to the central line of action, Garrick keeps the pace moving by abbreviating or redistributing any long speeches, as well as ensuring the acceptability of language. Garrick's own comedies are frequently three-act afterpieces—only once, in *The Clandestine Marriage* written with George Colman the Elder, did he write a full-length comedy—and the dramaturgical skills needed to convert *Shrew* are ones he was expert in. The primary theatrical emphasis in such an adaptation is the creation of a stage-worthy vehicle for star performers through the preservation of as much of the Shakespeare text as Garrick could reconcile with both his own commercial instinct and his admiration for the source. In the case of *Shrew*, Shakespeare's play was not widely admired and Garrick's biographer, Thomas Davies, could state that 'the loppings from the luxuriant tree of the old poet were not only judicious,

but necessary to preserve the pristine trunk'.[18] The result certainly was theatrically viable, *Catherine and Petruchio* being played until late in the nineteenth century.

Yet the transformation was also an act of cultural appropriation, ensuring that the play's social awkwardnesses and ambivalences, the difficulties about its attitude towards marriage, were resolved into an acceptable form. Once Catherine has capitulated—but only once she has—Petruchio can reveal his behaviour as a mask and Catherine can respond with similarly appropriate sentiments of orthodox marital subservience:

PETRUCHIO. Kiss me, my Kate; and since thou art become
    So prudent, kind and dutiful a wife,
    Petruchio here shall doff the lordly husband,
    An honest mask, which I throw off with pleasure.
    Far hence all rudeness, wilfulness and noise,
    And be our future lives one gentle stream
    Of mutual love, compliance and regard.
CATHERINE. Nay, then I'm all unworthy of thy love,
    And look with blushes on my former self.

Shakespeare's Kate could never have blushed; Garrick's could hardly be expected to do other.[19]

Two seasons later, in 1756, Garrick used *Catherine and Petruchio* as an afterpiece to his adaptation of *The Winter's Tale* into a three-act dramatic pastoral, *Florizel and Perdita*; characteristically, when the double bill was revived in 1762, the two plays were separated in performance by yet another attraction, 'A New Comic Interlude of Singing and Dancing, called *Hearts of Oak*'. Garrick's prologue to *Florizel and Perdita*, running the image of Shakespeare as a source of wine, sees the adaptation as a rescue:

    The five long acts from which our three are taken,
    Stretched out to sixteen years, lay by, forsaken.
    Lest then this precious liquor run to waste,
    'Tis now confined and bottled for your taste.
    'Tis my chief wish, my joy, my only plan,
    To lose no drop of that immortal man.

Though *The Winter's Tale* had been performed at Goodman's Fields and Covent Garden in 1740–1, it had been dropped from the repertory. Garrick's version, though it has to lose much more than a drop of the original, beginning only in Bohemia with Shakespeare's Act IV, at least brought part of the play back into the stock. But Garrick's adaptation was also a response to the success at Covent Garden of MacNamara Morgan's *Florizel and Perdita* (1754), an afterpiece with the emphasis on the sheep-shearing complete with additional songs. Garrick's play is unquestionably focused on the resurrection of Hermione and, in particular, on Leontes, Garrick's own role in the play, who turns up shipwrecked on the Bohemian coast, a man now overwhelmed by the loss of that conventional domestic bliss which families alone could provide.

The success of these two three-act pieces and the relative failure of the operas must have led Garrick to think again, to find some way of presenting two plays he admired in versions which would work on stage. The return to the play, the insistent need to make something essentially Shakespearian rather than adapted prove a staple of the repertory, was for him a necessary manœuvre; Shakespeare could not be proved unsuccessful. In the case of *The Tempest*, the solution arrived at quite quickly was to produce the play with minimal alteration, cutting some 400 lines but adding little. The new version, as Shakespearian a text as was ever produced of any play in the century, was performed in October 1757 and revived in virtually every season of Garrick's management thereafter.

In the case of *A Midsummer Night's Dream*, Garrick waited longer, turning back to the play in 1763, this time in collaboration with Colman. He began a careful preparation of the play as a full-length comedy, the only Shakespeare comedy, rather than romance, he ever tried to produce in a five-act version. But in September 1763 he left England for a prolonged grand tour of Europe and, though reluctant to be away from the production, left the final adapting to Colman, writing to him from Paris, 'as for *Midsummer Nights*, etc., I think my presence will be necessary to get it up as it ought—however if you want to, do for the best—and I'll ensure its success'.[20] He was right to be anxious and wrong to trust to the play's success. The single performance of Colman's version in November 1763

was catastrophic: William Hopkins, the Drury Lane prompter, noted in his diary,

Upon the whole, never was anything so murdered in the speaking . . . Next day it was reported 'The performers first sung the audience to sleep, and then went to sleep themselves'. Fairies pleased—serious parts displeased—comic between both.[21]

Colman clearly took the hint: three days after the disaster he had produced a two-act afterpiece called *A Fairy Tale*, omitting the 'serious parts'—the lovers—completely, emphasizing the fairies, and including as much of the workers, the 'comic', as was viable in such a version. It ends with Titania reunited with Oberon, and Puck hauling Bottom off-stage still asleep, never, apparently, to awake. The rehearsal of 'Pyramus and Thisbe' survives but the performance itself never takes place. After earlier versions centred on Bottom and the 'Pyramus' play, after Garrick's *The Fairies* centred on the lovers, Colman took the only other option.

Garrick's full-length version, which survives in manuscript, had built on the foundation of *The Fairies*, keeping songs (in all there were to have been twenty-nine) and cutting the last act substantially. Garrick had cut the final reappearance of the fairies in Theseus' palace but Colman tried to persuade him to keep it for sound entertainment reasons: 'I think it very ill-judged to cut out the concluding Fairy scene—restore it with songs, dances, etc., at all events. On the whole I think it may with care and attention be made a most *nouvelle* and elegant entertainment.'[22] Colman did not take his own advice in the printed version of his last act, cutting the 'Pyramus and Thisbe' material completely as well as the final reappearance of the fairies, ending the play after the opening eighteen lines. The rhythm and structure of the play were simply confusing, the demands it made too great for easy assimilation.

Yet it is striking that in his treatment of the play, though not in Colman's, Garrick wanted to leave both the imaginative scale, the sheer opulence of the play's language, and its rhyme-forms intact. For one of the rare occasions in the period, preserving rhyme was a clear intention. Colman not only abbreviated the whole text, cutting 500 lines from Garrick's version, but also turned rhyme into blank verse at nearly every opportunity. Colman's reason is not only an aversion to rhyme; as he suggested to Garrick, who ignored this piece of advice, 'all the other [scenes] except those between the fairies should be thrown out of rhyme. It will also make the fairy-scenes appear more characteristically distinguished'. But in Shakespeare, as Garrick appreciated, rhyme also distinguishes the lovers. Neither version worked on stage but Garrick's aim here, to keep much, much more of the original than Colman could tolerate, is revealing.

Hardly a success as opera or afterpiece, phenomenally unsuccessful as five-act comedy, *A Midsummer Night's Dream* posed a problem for Garrick's theatre; a play he admired and believed in proved simply too complex and various, too disparate in its constituent elements for the canons of eighteenth-century theatre. The play would not fit the available genres of theatrical comedy; its imaginative range was beyond the perspectives of Garrick's theatre. It is as an insoluble problem, not as a manageable solution, that *A Midsummer Night's Dream* indicates the nature of Garrick's response to the tension between Shakespeare and his theatre.

King Lear

If the problem *A Midsummer Night's Dream* posed was where to place it in the genres of performance, the problem *King Lear* posed would appear to have been simpler. There was no question of turning the play into afterpiece or opera; *King Lear* could only be played as a five-act tragedy. Yet throughout his career Garrick kept returning to the text, trying to find ways of bringing the playing-text, the play in the theatre, closer and closer to the Shakespearian play he so much admired.

Garrick played Lear for the first time in March 1742 at the age of 25, improbably young to tackle the part;

he was still playing the role thirty-four years later in his retirement season in June 1776. If the broad outline of his view of the character remained constant throughout this long and continuous encounter with the demands of the massive role, the performance changed and developed as Garrick altered his text again and again. An approach that had started with Tate's adaptation would end with a play which, if not yet by any means free of Tate, restored more of Shakespeare to the theatre than would have been possible in the 1740s.

Two aspects of Tate's text were never dispensed with: the cutting of the Fool and the 'happy' ending with Lear restored to the throne. Yet even over these areas of the text Garrick tried cautiously to find ways of returning to Shakespeare. As early as 1745, Garrick, writing to Francis Hayman, who was considering altering the engravings of scenes from Shakespeare he had produced for Hanmer's edition of the plays, recommended that Hayman work on Lear in the storm:

Suppose Lear mad upon the ground with Edgar by him; his attitude should be leaning upon one hand and pointing wildly towards the heavens with his other, Kent and Fool attend him and Gloucester comes to him with a torch. The real madness of Lear, the frantic affectation of Edgar and the different looks of concern in the three other characters will have a fine effect.[23]

Hayman's engraving, with or without the Fool, was never printed. An illustration for an edition of Shakespeare is not the same as an illustration of a performance and Benjamin Wilson's superb painting of Garrick as Lear on the heath (fig. 30) does not include the Fool. In 1747 Samuel Foote encouraged Garrick to return to 'the original, Fool and all'.[24] Thomas Davies reported that

It was once in contemplation with Mr Garrick to restore the part of the Fool, which he designed for Woodward, who promised to be very chaste in his colouring, and not to counteract the agonies of Lear. But the manager would not hazard so bold an attempt; he feared, with Mr Colman, that the feelings of Lear would derive no advantage from the buffooneries of the parti-coloured jester.[25]

FIG. 30 Garrick as King Lear, mezzotint after Benjamin Wilson.

Garrick as manager was reluctant to follow the instincts of Garrick as actor, taking wise advice from Colman.

Davies does not date this discussion over the Fool but Garrick's thinking about restoring the tragic ending was part of a prolonged reconsideration of the play in 1756, fourteen years after he had first played the role. Garrick's performance of Lear had always provoked critical debate and analysis but in 1753–4 there had been a flurry of published consideration of Shakespeare's play, influenced, in part at least, by Garrick's own performance. Warton, for instance, in an essay in the periodical *Adventurer*, wrote of how 'moved and delighted' he was by Garrick's delivery of 'O me, my heart! my rising heart—but down', a Shakespeare line that was not in Tate's version and which Garrick must already have put back in, 'spoken by the only actor of the age who understands and relishes these little touches of nature, and therefore the only one qualified to personate this most difficult character of Lear'.[26] Arthur Murphy, in a series of

articles on the play, wondered whether the audience could cope with Shakespeare's tragic ending:

But perhaps after all the heart piercing sensations which we have before endured through the whole piece it would be too much to see this actually performed on the stage; . . . from [Garrick] I am sure it would, though I should be glad to see the experiment made, convinced at the same time that the play, as it is altered, will always be most agreeable to an audience.[27]

Garrick did not respond to the suggestion at once, but in February 1756 Covent Garden put on *King Lear* for the first time in ten years, having before abandoned the competition with Garrick. Now, with Spranger Barry in the title-role in Tate's version, and with strong support from Mrs Cibber (fig. 31), it posed a threat to Garrick's dominance. The day after the first performance of *Lear* at Covent Garden, Garrick performed John Brown's *Athelstan*, another play about a king of ancient Britain who dies broken-hearted over his daughter's body. If this was an attempt to see whether the audience might tolerate Garrick as a

FIG. 31 Mrs Cibber as Cordelia, mezzotint after Peter van Bleeck. This production was based on Nahum Tate's text: Cordelia is accompanied by her maid, Arante, as she is assaulted by two of Edmund's ruffians (right), while the disguised Edgar (left) comes to her assistance.

tragic Lear, the critical response warned him off restoring Shakespeare's ending.²⁸ Instead, in October 1756, Garrick performed *King Lear*, advertising the production's 'restorations from Shakespeare'. Advertising hype is prone to exaggerate: Garrick cut nearly 200 lines by Tate but restored only ten by Shakespeare.

As with the battle of the Romeos six years earlier, Garrick again found himself in direct competition with Barry and again won. A contemporary rhyme sums it up:

> The town has found out different ways
>   To praise the different Lears.
> To Barry they give loud huzzas,
>   To Garrick—only tears.
> 'A King? Nay, every inch a king'
>   Such Barry doth appear,
> But Garrick's quite a different thing:
>   He's every inch King Lear.²⁹

Garrick went on performing his version, less Tate but hardly more Shakespearian, for the next decade, but in 1768 George Colman the Elder tried out at

Covent Garden his own new version of the play, aiming, as he announced in his preface, 'to reconcile the catastrophe of Tate to the story of Shakespeare'. For the first four acts, Colman put back in much of Shakespeare, though not the Fool, and stripped out much of Tate. Where Tate believed he was improving Shakespeare, Colman now saw his attempt as a means of purifying the theatre, bringing it closer to the ideal, the performance of Shakespeare's play:

if every director of the theatre will endeavour to do a little, the stage will every day be improved and become more worthy attention and encouragement. *Romeo, Cymbeline, Every Man in his Humour* have long been refined from the current dross that hindered them from being current with the public and I have now endeavoured to purge the tragedy of Lear of the alloy of Tate which has so long been suffered to debase it.

But Colman knew that performance and reading are two widely differing experiences of the tragedy: he did not hesitate to cut Gloucester's attempted suicide at

'Dover cliff' and even wanted to cut Gloucester's blinding, though its necessity for the plot meant that he restricted himself to moving it off-stage, where servants, not Cornwall, are responsible.

Colman's version was not a success, managing thirteen performances over five seasons, so that when Spranger Barry moved from Drury Lane to Covent Garden again in 1773 he took Garrick's version with him. But Garrick's version by this time was again not what it had been. Probably provoked by rivalry with Colman, Garrick rewrote his performing version twice more, cutting back more and more of Tate's lines and restoring hundreds of lines of Shakespeare that he had not felt able to put back in 1756.

By the end of his career Garrick was performing a text recognizably Shakespearian, though still with a happy ending, remnants of Tate's love scenes between Edgar and Cordelia, and the presence of a confidante for Cordelia, Arante. He was also performing a text more unequivocally centred on Lear himself than Tate had provided. The subplots of Tate must have taken attention away from the star's performance and Garrick ensured that, wherever possible, scenes started and finished with Lear.

Garrick described his own view of Lear at length in 1770 in answer to a correspondent:

Lear is certainly a weak man—it is part of his character: violent, old and weakly fond of his daughters . . . His weakness proceeds from his age ('fourscore and upwards') and such an old man, full of affection, generosity, passion and what-not, meeting with what he thought an ungrateful return from his best beloved Cordelia and afterwards real ingratitude from his other daughters, an audience must feel his distress and madness which is the consequence of them.[30]

The primary aim of Garrick's performance was unquestionably arousing the audience's pity. Tears, the visible sign of the effect of the pathos of the performance, were the measure of his success. The primary techniques in the performance were Lear's own distress and his madness. He was particularly concerned to document the slow onset of madness and his researches for the role led him to Bedlam, sharing with his contemporaries the fascinated

observation of the insane, but less as a means of reassuring himself of his own sanity than as a resource to be copied. Above all, Garrick was intrigued by a man who had let his baby daughter fall from an upstairs window and who endlessly repeated the action and his appalled response.

In article after article, pamphlet after pamphlet, critics minutely examined Garrick's Lear throughout his career, praising, blaming, advising, admiring the tiny details out of which his performance was constructed. No other performance in the century can be so completely reconstructed. Often, of course, it is impossible to know whether Garrick responded to the advice. Samuel Foote, describing in 1747 Garrick's Lear in floods of tears at the end of the play, complained, 'You need not make use of your handkerchief; your change of voice sufficiently marketh your distress and your application to your handkerchief is, perhaps, too minute a circumstance and maketh you more present to things than you ought to be at that time'.[31] But Garrick probably went on weeping into his handkerchief.

Garrick used hand-props to focus attention. Foote praised such details in the mad scenes, while getting in a dig at Garrick's height, a feature strikingly apparent in Wilson's painting of the storm:

You enter with all the dignity your insignificant, trifling person is capable of. You throw yourself into many various attitudes of command and, though you have straw in your hand, yet we plainly see that you take it for a sceptre, bow, gauntlet, etc. as the different ideas rise in your imagination.[32]

But Garrick's Lear was not a monochrome portrait of an old man deserving pity. In cursing Goneril, above all, there was a rage and violence that could modulate startlingly. Foote again describes the effect in superbly evocative detail, though he does not mention, as others did, that Garrick's first action was to throw away a crutch on which Lear was leaning:

You fall precipitately upon your knees, extend your arms, clench your hands, set your teeth and, with a savage distraction in your look, trembling in all your limbs and your eyes pointed to heaven (the whole expressing a fullness of rage and revenge), you begin 'Hear, Nature, dear goddess!'

with a broken, inward, eager utterance. From thence, rising every line in loudness and rapidity of voice until you come to 'and feel | How sharper than a serpent's tooth it is, | To have a thankless child'. Then you are struck at once with your daughter's ingratitude and, bursting into tears, with a most sorrowful heart-breaking tone of voice, you say, 'go, go, my people'.[33]

The effect was still there nearly thirty years later in his final performance of the role when the power of the curse, a reviewer noted, 'caused a momentary petrification through the house, which he soon dissolved universally into tears'.[34] The rapidity of the character's change to tears and its consequence for the audience, the sudden switch of emotional effect, were beyond the range of eighteenth-century tragedy's contemplation and something that Shakespeare was much praised for: 'In these mixed passions, . . . the superior abilities of Shakespeare appear.'[35] Throughout his performance Garrick explored this multiplicity of emotions:

Garrick had displayed all the force of quick transition from one passion to another. He had, from the most violent rage, descended to sedate calmness, had seized, with unutterable sensibility, the various impressions of terror and faithfully represented all the turbid passions of the soul.[36]

But the purpose of this exploration was always brought back towards the central attempt: to register the maximum pathos through harmonizing the range of feeling. As one awestruck audience-member wrote to Garrick in 1763,

But what struck me most was the sustaining with full powers, to the last, a character marked with the most diversified and vehement sensations, without ever departing once, . . . even in the quickest transitions and fiercest paroxysms, from the simplicity of nature, the grace of attitude or the beauty of expression.[37]

Garrick's re-explorations of the text of the play, his continual attempts to return closer and closer to Shakespeare, were of a piece with that aim, finding in *King Lear* not the 'heap of jewels, unstrung and unpolished' which Tate described but instead a coherent work of art, demanding the utmost intelligence from its star to encompass its range.

Macbeth

In January 1744 Garrick appeared as Macbeth. He had already played Richard III, Lear, and Hamlet. Now he chose to add another major Shakespearian tragic hero to his repertory. To a modern actor the role might seem a logical continuation of the exploration of the central classical repertory. But *Macbeth* was not a play particularly admired in the 1740s. The performance text was still Davenant's version, with its spectacular scenes for the witches and careful balancing of the Macduffs against the Macbeths. Actors assumed, quite reasonably, that the role quickly tailed off in significance and effect, for in Davenant's version that is indeed the result of the adaptation. Even the appearance of Banquo's ghost was not highly rated:

Before Mr Garrick displayed the terrible graces of action from the impression of visionary appearance, the comedians were strangers to the effects which this scene could produce. Macbeth, they constantly exclaimed, was not a character of the first rate; all the pith of it was exhausted, they said, in the first and second acts of the play.[38]

The play was certainly still popular but the Davenant text, while theatrically and commercially effective, satisfied neither Garrick's interest in the role nor his adulation of Shakespeare. In preparing to play Macbeth, Garrick, for the first time in his career, transformed the traditional text, preparing *Macbeth* as well as his role.

When the production opened, billed as being 'as Shakespeare wrote it', Quin, who had played Macbeth successfully for years, was justifiably confused. 'What does he mean? Don't I play *Macbeth* as written by Shakespeare?'[39] As Stephen Orgel comments,

Twenty years earlier a producer could have expected to attract audiences by advertising a wholly new *Macbeth*, bigger and better; Garrick's assertion, the invocation of the author to confer authority on the production, marks a significant moment in both theatrical and textual history.[40]

In a way that marked an unprecedented collaboration between the theatre and the new traditions of Shakespearian textual scholarship, Garrick paid minute attention to the opportunities offered by the latest scholarly research as he 'broke through the fetters of foolish custom and arbitrary imposition'.[41] His primary text was that prepared by Lewis Theobald in 1740, the most recent edition available to him. But Garrick also consulted Warburton, whose edition was finished, though not published until 1747, and, of course, his friend Samuel Johnson, using some, though by no means all, of the suggestions for emendation and restoration, even for repunctuation, that Johnson had made in his pamphlet *Miscellaneous Observations on the Tragedy of Macbeth*, written but also not yet published by the time of Garrick's performance. In the banquet scene, Theobald's Macbeth says, 'It will have blood, they say; blood will have blood'; but Garrick spoke, 'It will have blood—they say blood will have blood', following Johnson's suggestion that

The line loses much of its force by the present punctuation. Macbeth, having considered the prodigy which has just appeared, infers justly from it, that the death of Duncan cannot pass unpunished, 'It will have blood—'. Then, after a short pause, declares it as a general observation of mankind that murderers cannot escape: 'They say blood will have blood'.[42]

The resulting playing-text is not Shakespeare purified. Some lines are still as rewritten by Davenant. Davenant's recognition of the potential for theatrical display offered by the witches was one Garrick could hardly have resisted and, while there was less flying than in Davenant, there was still plenty of song and dance in these scenes. Some parts of the original were still effectively unplayable: there could be no Porter, only a brief appearance by a polite servant; Macduff's son becomes a silent presence so that the scene concentrates on the pathos of Lady Macduff and the on-stage child-murder is cut too; nor can Malcolm be allowed most of his self-accusations in the scene in England.

Garrick's text is over 250 lines shorter than Shakespeare's but he found space to write in a few

necessary linking speeches, to cover cut material, and, inevitably, a proper dying speech for Macbeth. After an on-stage duel, Macduff, as in Davenant, left the stage, holding Macbeth's sword as a trophy—no decapitation for this tragic hero. On an empty stage, Garrick's Macbeth can draw the moral and contemplate eternal damnation:

> 'Tis done! The scene of life will quickly close.
> Ambition's vain, delusive dreams are fled,
> And now I wake to darkness, guilt and horror.
> I cannot bear it! Let me shake it off.—
> 'Twa' not be; my soul is clogged with blood.
> I cannot rise! I dare not ask for mercy.
> It is too late, hell drags me down. I sink,
> I sink—Oh!—my soul is lost forever!
> Oh! [*Dies.*]

In a production so unequivocally centred on Macbeth, Garrick needed some properly dramatic death speech. Davies, while admitting that Garrick's style, 'though suitable perhaps to the character, was unlike Shakespeare's manner, who was not prodigal of bestowing abundance of matter on characters in that situation', also understands the actor's sense of the way to show himself to his best: 'But Garrick excelled in the expression of convulsive throes and dying agonies, and would not lose any opportunity that offered to show his skill in that part of his profession.'[43] Garrick's professional pride certainly impressed one visitor, Noverre, a French choreographer, who carefully described this moment in Garrick's performance when he saw it in the 1750s:

The approach of death showed each instant on his face; his eyes became dim, his voice could not support the efforts he made to speak his thoughts . . . his legs gave way under him, his face lengthened, his pale and livid features bore the signs of suffering and repentance. At last, he fell; . . . His plight made the audience shudder, he clawed the ground and seemed to be digging his own grave, but the dread moment was nigh, one saw death in reality, everything expressed that instant which makes all equal. In the end he expired. The death rattle and the convulsive movement of the features, arms and breasts gave the final touch to this terrible picture.[44]

Davenant's single line for the dying Macbeth

('Farewell, vain world, and what's most vain in it, Ambition.') draws the same moral as Garrick's but the extent of the horror and the minute depiction of the processes of death were wholly new.

Recognizing how unconventional his performance would be, Garrick took the extraordinary step of defusing potential criticism by publishing an anonymous pamphlet, in advance of the first night, mocking his own performance. *An Essay on Acting, in which will be considered the mimical behaviour of a certain fashionable faulty actor*, to give only part of its title, purports to praise Quin's established performance as against Garrick's own. When confronting the imaginary dagger, for instance,

he should not rivet his eyes to an *imaginary* object as if it *really* was there but should show an unsettled motion in his eye . . . 'Come, let me clutch thee' is not to be done by *one* motion only but by several successive catches at it, first with one hand

and then with the other, preserving the same motion at the same time with his feet, like a man who, out of his depth and half-drowned in his struggles, catches at air for substance.

(p. 17)

Garrick's stillness at such moments, as in his keeping 'a fixed eye' on Banquo's ghost, was in strong contrast to Quin's restless style.

A performance as carefully prepared as this one deserves careful response. Garrick continually found himself dealing with correspondents who picked up on line-readings, pauses, and punctuation with minute attention. In 1762, for instance, Hall Hartson complained of three pauses and one false emphasis which broke the sense of a speech. Garrick apologized for one pause ('when the mind's agitated, it is impossible to guard against these slips'), denied another ('I certainly never *stop* there, that is, close the sense, but I as certainly *suspend* my voice'), and

FIG. 32 Garrick and Mrs Pritchard in *Macbeth*, by Henry Fuseli, painting now in the Kunsthaus, Zürich.

FIG. 33 Garrick and Mrs Pritchard in *Macbeth*, mezzotint after Johann Zoffany.

vigorously defended the other two. In doing so, he described the actor's thinking-through from a conception of the character to the delivery of a line:

[Before the murder of Duncan] Macbeth is absorbed in thought and struck with the horror of the murder, though but an idea ('fantastical') and it naturally gives him a slow, tremulous undertone of voice, and, though it might appear that I stopped at every word in the line more than usual, yet my intention was far from dividing the substantive from its adjective, but to paint the horror of Macbeth's mind and keep the voice suspended a little—which it will naturally be in such a situation.[45]

Superbly supported by Hannah Pritchard's brilliant performance as Lady Macbeth, Garrick's Macbeth embodies his care to marry text and conception, to

return to Shakespeare, and to show off his own talents. Above all the aim was to develop the detailed representation of naturalistically conceived character: as the politician William Pitt the Elder commented, 'Inimitable Shakespeare! But more matchless Garrick! Always as deep in Nature as the poet, but never (what the poet is too often) out of it.'[46]

Though Covent Garden offered other Macbeths, Garrick's pre-eminence as actor in the role went unchallenged long after he gave up the role in 1768. But in October 1773 Charles Macklin put on a production at Covent Garden that did challenge the Garrick tradition. Macklin's own performance as Macbeth was much mocked: 'Shakespeare has made Macbeth murder Duncan; now Mr Macklin, being determined to copy from no man, reversed this incident, and . . . murdered Macbeth.'[47] Originality was objectionable but it is difficult to think of Macklin as a theatrical revolutionary: he was still giving the same performance of Shylock that he had created over thirty years earlier. Driven perhaps by the intensity of his dislike of Garrick, Macklin saw in his new contract with Covent Garden an opportunity to challenge Garrick, now at the end of his career, in his most famous Shakespearian roles.

But it was not the central performance that makes Macklin's *Macbeth* so significant. The bills advertised the production as having 'new dresses and decorations'. It was the design that made the largest statement. Macklin had always researched his own performances with a remarkable attention to historical and realist materials. To play Shylock, he read and reread Josephus' *History of the Jews*, jotting details in his commonplace book, he went every day to observe Jewish businessmen in London coffee-houses, copying manners, gesture, and accent, and he chose to wear a red three-cornered hat because he had discovered that Venetian Jews usually wore them.

For *Macbeth*, Macklin was determined to follow a sense of history. As Cooke, Macklin's biographer, noted,

Macbeth used to be dressed in a suit of scarlet and gold, a tail wig, etc., in every respect like a modern military officer. Garrick always played it in this manner. Macklin, however, . . . saw the absurdity of exhibiting a Scotch character, existing many years before the Norman Conquest, in this manner, and therefore very properly abandoned it for the old Caledonian habit.[48]

While Fuseli's image of the passionate intensity of Garrick as Macbeth (fig. 32) gives no reliable clue to his costume, Zoffany's painting shows the formal and contemporary costume in which Macbeth was usually played (fig. 33). This court version of military uniform was not Garrick's only costume for the role: for his second encounter with the witches, as one reviewer noted, he wore the outfit of 'a modern fine gentleman so that . . . you looked like a beau who had unfortunately slipped his foot and tumbled into a night-cellar, where a parcel of old women were boiling

FIG. 34 Macklin caricatured as *Shylock Turn'd Macbeth*.

tripe for their supper'.[49]

A few months before Macklin's production Garrick too was considering reviving *Macbeth* 'in the old dress'.[50] Throughout his career Garrick explored the possibility of playing Shakespeare roles costumed in the period of the play. The movement towards historicism in costume design was hardly new but Garrick was the first to explore it substantially for Shakespeare. For *Richard III* and *2 Henry IV*, for instance, he made the switch to the 'old English habits' in the 1760s. As Lear, Garrick only changed in his final season in 1776. But in any case the costumes were often a mixture; as early as 1750 Garrick was planning a production of *King John* in which he would 'dress the characters half old English, half modern'.[51]

But Macklin's aim was a significantly new quest for consistency, a coherent approach to costume and set design that would establish an attitude to the play's period. Unlike Garrick, Macklin 'showed the same attention to the subordinate characters as well as to the scenes, decorations, music and other incidental parts of the performance'.[52] His own costume as

Macbeth, mocked in caricature (fig. 34), drapes the plaid over his back, uses the traditional belted tunic and a bonnet, and rightly avoids the kilt, an eighteenth-century innovation in Scottish dress. Other costumes were to be similar: Macbeth's first entrance, Macklin noted, 'should be preceded by fife, drum, bagpipe (query) and a bodyguard in highland dress'.[53] Even the set was to depict the world of the historical Macbeth as Macklin perceived it: for the interior of Macbeth's castle, 'every room should be full of bad pictures of warriors, sword, helmet, target and dirk, escutcheons—and the Hall, boars stuffed, wolves, and full of pikes and broadswords'.[54]

There were anachronisms in the production: the Scottish troops carried pistols, the castle battlements had cannon. But Macklin's vision of the play was by far the fullest attempt to create a design for a Shakespeare play, historical and imaginative, so far seen on the London stage. Where Garrick had wanted to restore the Shakespeare text and set off the brilliance of his own performance, Macklin was concerned only with historical authenticity, a unified production style, and detailed realism. Where Garrick was triumphant, Macklin's *Macbeth* was ridiculed. But it is Macklin's style of production that seems now to prefigure modern approaches to Shakespeare in the theatre.

5

The Romantic Stage

JONATHAN BATE

> An old, mad, blind, despised, and dying King;
> Princes, the dregs of their dull race, who flow
> Through public scorn,—mud from a muddy spring;
> Rulers who neither see nor feel nor know,
> But leechlike to their fainting country cling
> Till they drop, blind in blood, without a blow.
> A people starved and stabbed in th'untilled field;
> An army, who liberticide and prey
> Makes as a two-edged sword to all who wield;
> Golden and sanguine laws which tempt and slay;
> Religion Christless, Godless—a book sealed;
> A senate, Time's worst statute, unrepealed—
> Are graves from which a glorious Phantom may
> Burst, to illumine our tempestuous day.

From his self-imposed exile in Italy, Percy Bysshe Shelley included this sonnet in a letter of 23 December 1819 to his friend, the liberal editor, poet, essayist, and theatre-reviewer Leigh Hunt. King George III was mad; his sons, notably the Prince Regent, were adept in the princely arts of marital infidelity, fathering illegitimate children, gambling, drunkenness, gluttony, and the bestowing of patronage upon favourites; harvests had been bad and poverty was widespread; the church was but an instrument of the state; Parliament was sclerotic and unrepresentative; in St Peter's Field in Manchester that August the militia had ridden into an unarmed crowd who were protesting peacefully for parliamentary reform,

causing death or injury to nearly a hundred. Censorship of the press, already tight, was further strengthened at this time, so there was no prospect of Hunt publishing Shelley's sonnet in his *Examiner*. It did not appear in print until the posthumous *Poetical Works* edited by Mary Shelley in 1839.

Shelley offers us a vivid snapshot of England in one of its few eras of genuinely deep social unrest. The act of writing a political sonnet of this sort is a Miltonic, not a Shakespearian gesture, but there is a dramatic quality to the imagery which makes one think of the structure of Shakespearian tragedy. At the beginning, bad rulers and bad times; in the middle, a language of violence ('blood', 'blow', 'stabbed'), a 'fainting country' like the 'poor country' which 'bleeds' in *Macbeth*; then suddenly at the end, a bursting through of light and hope. The final note is similar to that sounded by the new men who take control in the dying minutes of the play—Fortinbras, Malcolm, Octavius Caesar—though with the difference that for Shelley what will arise is true Liberty, not just another prince.

If Shelley's poem *had* been published in December 1819, might the readers of the *Examiner* (the paper for which William Hazlitt wrote some of the most penetrating theatre reviews in the language) have been put in mind not only of contemporary politics but also of the drama? What would they have conjured up in response to the opening line, 'An old, mad, blind, despised, and dying King'? Surely this king is Lear as well as George III. But subscribers to the *Examiner* would not have had a contemporary staging against which to read Shelley's image, for the correspondence between Lear and George was so close that, out of a combination of deference and fear of censorship, in 1811 the theatre managers had agreed to suspend the play from the repertoire. That *Lear* was not staged in the legitimate theatre during the next ten years provides vivid evidence of how Shakespearian drama is always open to topical interpretation—and, indeed, during that decade productions of plays as varied as *Antony and Cleopatra*, *Cymbeline*, and *Henry VIII* contained recognizable allusions to the 'delicate investigation' into the conduct of the Princess Caroline (an attempt by the heir to the throne to get rid of his wife).

1811 was the year in which the king's insanity was finally acknowledged to be permanent and incurable, with the effect that the Regency was established. That same year, Charles Lamb published in the *Reflector* an essay arguing that *King Lear* should not be staged: partly because of the self-promotion of actors like David Garrick, partly because of the textual butcherings of adaptors like Nahum Tate, but principally because

On the stage we see nothing but corporal infirmities and weakness, the impotence of rage; while we read it, we see not Lear, but we are Lear,—we are in his mind, we are sustained by a grandeur which baffles the malice of daughters and storms; in the aberrations of his reason, we discover a mighty irregular power of reasoning, immethodized from the ordinary purposes of life, but exerting its powers, as the wind blows where it listeth, at will upon the corruptions and abuses of mankind.[1]

It is possible that here Lamb is recognizing that a stage Lear would inevitably be associated with the old, mad, blind, despised, and dying king, and that this would distract from what he took to be the true import of the play, its assault upon 'the corruptions and abuses of mankind'. More generally, however, Lamb's essay 'On the Tragedies of Shakspeare, considered with reference to their fitness for stage representation' is the product of a certain discontent about performance

that was shared by the major Romantic poets and Bardolaters. For them, the imagination was the highest mark of poetry and so Lear and Hamlet were most powerful on the page, when recreated in the individual reader's imagination, not on the stage, when impersonated by an actor. The Romantic ideal was an empathetic feeling with another being, another state: in the theatre one merely saw Lear, whereas alone in the study one could *be* Lear.

When Lamb wrote his essay, the leading actors on the London stage were John Philip Kemble and his sister, Sarah Siddons. For Lamb, the charisma of their performances detracted from the audience's empathy with the characters: 'It is difficult for a frequent playgoer to disembarrass the idea of Hamlet from the person and voice of Mr K. We speak of Lady Macbeth, while we are in reality thinking of Mrs S.' (p. 112). The key word here is 'idea'. Although Lamb's criticism never approaches the philosophical self-consciousness of Coleridge's, this conception of an *idea* of Hamlet, a thing-in-itself independent of its phenomenal manifestations in the particulars of individual performances, is influenced by the German Idealist philosophy which Coleridge brought to England. When Coleridge said that watching Edmund Kean act was 'like reading Shakspeare by flashes of lightning',[2] he meant that Kean could only illuminate certain striking moments in a play—an understanding of the overall *idea* of it was dependent on the insights of the critic in his study or lecture-room.

William Hazlitt was close to Coleridge and Lamb, but in his attitude to Shakespeare in the theatre he stood apart from them. He was frequently incensed by bad productions, butchered texts, vulgar claptraps, and the inferior acting of supporting players, but he remained convinced that at its best the stage 'at once gives a body to our thoughts, and refinement and expansion to our sensible impressions'. By identifying with what we see on stage, we can be taken out of ourselves, redeemed from 'the petty egotism of vulgar life' and brought to an imaginative empathy with humanity that 'has not the pride and remoteness of abstract [philosophical] science'.[3] Furthermore, the actor's identification with the role could become a model for, not a distraction from, the audience's. Hazlitt believed that only three actors in his age lived up to this high ideal: Sarah Siddons, Eliza O'Neill, and Edmund Kean.[4] They may be described as 'Romantic' players.

Sarah Siddons and Eliza O'Neill

Hazlitt had immense respect for the technical accomplishment of John Kemble, but thought that his style came from art not nature, that it was classically polished not romantically empathetic. Kemble prepared his roles through meticulous study. He worked in detail on the texts of the plays, often developing new versions which came closer to the Shakespearian originals than did the Restoration and eighteenth-century acting versions which still held the stage. He was learned in classical rhetoric, able to draw from a long tradition of formality in posture and gesture. He was not only actor but also orchestrator of the company in rehearsal (a role anticipating that of the modern director), especially during the years when he doubled as both theatre manager and leading player; the elaborate spectacle of the whole play was as important to him as the absorbing detail of his own role.

   Siddons's preparation was very different. It looks forward to the Method of Stanislavsky rather than backward to the rhetoric of Quintilian. To the consternation of manager Sheridan, she changed the business in the sleep-walking scene in *Macbeth*. Instead of imitating her renowned predecessor in the role, Garrick's Mrs Pritchard, she imitated a somnambulist she had observed in real life. She tried to get inside her character. As one commentator put it, 'from the moment she assumed the dress she became the character: she never chatted or coquetted by the Green Room fire but placed herself where no word of

the play could escape her, or the illusion for a moment be destroyed.'[5] In the age of Garrick, Macbeth had become a character for whom audiences could find a considerable degree of sympathy, whereas Lady Macbeth remained, in the words of Dr Johnson's general observation on the play, 'merely detested'. Siddons realized that you can't get inside a character unless you sympathize with her; she therefore developed a conception of Lady Macbeth as no innate fiend but rather a woman who undergoes an inner struggle between ambition and feminine virtue. In her invocation to the spirits of night, the character is willing herself to be evil and this proves that she is not naturally evil; the very lines which commentators had adduced as the ultimate marks of her fiendishness, in which she speaks of dashing out her baby's brains, are in fact evidence that 'persuades one unequivocally that she has really felt the maternal yearnings of a mother towards her babe, and that she considered this action the most enormous that ever required the strength of

Fig. 35 Mrs Siddons as Lady Macbeth in the sleep-walking scene, mezzotint after Henry Fuseli.

human nerves for its perpetration'.[6] Her capacity for moments of tenderness, as in the scene when she tries to cheer up her husband before the banquet,[7] heightened by force of contrast those of power and domination.

To playgoers, the most memorable moments were the terrifying, not the tender ones. Siddons's performance of the role was described by almost all commentators in terms of sublimity, the dark underside of Romantic empathy in which the mind goes outside itself and becomes one not with humanity but with darkness, vastness, vacancy, or evil. This Lady Macbeth elicits the language of Gothic: 'It was something above nature . . . Power was seated on her brow, passion emanated from her breast . . . She glided on and off the stage like an apparition'.[8] That last sentence makes her sound like something in a novel by Mrs Radcliffe or 'Monk' Lewis. The startling effect may be glimpsed in Henry Fuseli's wide-eyed painting of the sleep-walking scene (fig. 35).

Following Edmund Burke's well-known distinction between different kinds of aesthetic effect, it may be said that Eliza O'Neill offered the beautiful to Sarah Siddons's sublime. A pair of images will suggest the difference between the two actresses. A moment of awe-inspiring authority, of control over the action, is caught in George Henry Harlow's representation of Siddons as Lady Macbeth in the letter scene (fig. 36). O'Neill, whose most celebrated role was Juliet (fig. 37), is passive rather than active: where Siddons confronts the spectator head on, the younger actress half turns her head away, gazing into the middle distance and holding a hand to her breast, suggesting depths of intense feeling within. Her face, said Hazlitt, reviewing her debut in 1814, 'has that mixture of beauty and passion which we admire so much in some of the antique statues'; on hearing of Romeo's death, 'in the silent expression of feeling, we have seldom witnessed any thing finer'.[9] O'Neill's Juliet answered perfectly to Hazlitt's ideal of sympathy; her acting, he argued, seemed to come not from art but from 'instinctive sympathy', 'a conformity of mind and disposition to the character she was playing, as if she had unconsciously become the very person'. The passion

FIG. 36 Mrs Siddons as Lady Macbeth in the letter scene, engraving after George Henry Harlow, frontispiece to the *Literary Souvenir*, 1830.

that engulfed her spilled over into the audience: 'she yielded to calamity, she gave herself up entire, and with entire devotion, to her unconquerable despair:— it was the tide of anguish swelling in her own breast, that overflowed to the breasts of the audience, and filled their eyes with tears.'[10] Where the sudden, explosive hand gesture is the key to Siddons's style, the rising breast is the key to O'Neill's; if Siddons comes out of Gothic, O'Neill is like the heroine of a novel of extreme sensibility.

It was with O'Neill in mind that Shelley wrote the role of Beatrice Cenci, in what is the most powerful of the many neo-Shakespearian plays of the Romantic age. *The Cenci* provides an excellent illustration of the

FIG. 37 Eliza O'Neill as Juliet,
engraving after P. Henderson.

difference between the drama of Shakespeare's time and that of the late eighteenth and early nineteenth centuries. Whilst many scenes and moments are manifestly imitations of Shakespeare—the disrupted banquet and the jumpy murder-night out of *Macbeth*, the father denouncing his daughter out of *Lear*—the construction of the play is fundamentally different because its main focus is on reaction, not action. Shelley is interested not so much in the fact of Count Cenci's incestuous desire for his daughter as in the effect upon her of its discovery. Where in the Renaissance dramatic 'character' is created through action, in the Romantic period it emerges in reflection upon the effects of action or inaction.[11] The Renaissance soliloquy is a construction of selfhood, made from rhetorical building-blocks; the Romantic reading of Renaissance soliloquy is as the expression (literally, the pressing out) of a sacrosanct interiority. Of all Renaissance plays, *Hamlet* is the one most amenable to such a reading, and that is why the Romantics felt closer to that play than any other.

We think of the 'character' of Lear or Macbeth or Othello as what is always there within him, but Shakespeare would not have thought of it thus. Our conception only became possible with the twin emergence in the eighteenth century of the novel and a recognizably modern theory of human psychology; it was first formally articulated in the 'character criticism' which emerged in the latter part of the century, but it took root because of the acting of Garrick and his successors. For all their differences, Garrick, Kemble, Siddons, and Kean held in common the view that the essence of human nature is to be found in reaction, not action,[12] and so it was that their performances were most intense at certain moments of reflection. As both a creative practice and a theory of human identity, this way of proceeding is essentially 'Romantic': Wordsworth's poetry of the self in *The Prelude* is also most intense at certain moments of reaction and reflection. O'Neill perfected the art of 'reactive' acting and for this she could be claimed as the greatest English Romantic actor.

Shelley's hope of getting *The Cenci* staged in 1819 could never have been realized. The particular theme of incest, and the general denunciation of figures and institutions of authority (father, ruler, court, church), would have ruled it out on grounds of censorship. But it would also have been impossible to cast it as he wanted, with Kean as Cenci and O'Neill as Beatrice. This would have been precluded by the structure of licensed ('legitimate') theatre in London. One hundred and sixty years after the Restoration, the situation established by Charles II's granting of theatrical 'patents' to Davenant and Killigrew still obtained. In London, only the Theatres Royal of Drury Lane and Covent Garden were allowed to stage legitimate—

spoken—drama during the main theatre season which ran from autumn to spring. A third, much smaller, theatre in the Haymarket was licensed for a short summer season, and there were an increasing number of Theatres Royal in the provinces, that in the fashionable watering-hole of Bath being the most prestigious (all the leading actors of the period cut their teeth in the provinces: Mrs Siddons was discovered at Cheltenham, O'Neill was announced as 'Of the *Theatre Royal, Dublin*', Kean toured widely in England, Wales, Ireland, and even the Channel Islands before appearing in London fresh from the Theatre Royal, Exeter). The effective duopoly in London meant that the respective managements of Drury Lane and Covent Garden guarded their assets jealously. Kean's advent in 1814 was widely viewed as the financial salvation of Drury Lane; O'Neill was brought forward later that year as Covent Garden's reply, a female wonder who would take over the mantle of Siddons as Kean had stolen that of Kemble. She left the stage to get married at the end of 1819, having remained at Covent Garden throughout her short career, so she and Kean never acted together and could not have been brought together even supposing Shelley's play had got as far as casting.

A summary of the Shakespearian repertoire of the two theatres in the 1818–19 season gives a clear sense of the importance of the star system.[13] Drury Lane staged the following plays: *Romeo and Juliet, Othello, Richard III, Macbeth, Hamlet, 1 Henry IV*. All these were vehicles for Kean. By 1818–19 the leads in all but one of them were among his best-established roles; the new one that season was *1 Henry IV*, in which he played Hotspur for the first time. The production also featured yet another member of the age's great theatrical dynasty, Stephen Kemble, who played Falstaff (for which he didn't need padding). Covent Garden's problem after John Kemble's retirement was finding someone to rival Kean. In 1818–19 Charles Mayne Young was featured as Macbeth and Othello, and played Brutus in *Julius Caesar* for his benefit. But he was not a sufficiently charismatic male lead to hold an entire season together; halfway through, William Charles Macready was introduced as Hotspur for the first time, in a clear attempt to rival Kean's new role. Next season, Macready took on Richard III; gradually through the 1820s he established himself as the new dominant presence on the London stage. In 1818–19, though, Covent Garden's principal asset was still O'Neill; she played Juliet, Desdemona, Ophelia, and the Queen in *Henry VIII* (for the first time and as her benefit—here she was stepping into one of Siddons's most renowned roles). Since Covent Garden did not have a male lead who could match Kean in the great tragedies, the management also tried another tack: the introduction of several Shakespearian comedies—in 1818–19 *Twelfth Night* and *The Winter's Tale* were revived after long absence from the stage. Towards the end of the season, *The Merchant of Venice* was played for the benefit of the comic actor Frederick Yates; he would have been an utterly different Shylock from Kean, who had first established himself at Drury Lane by playing the Jew with demonic force and high seriousness.

The main attraction of Yates's benefit was not, however, the Shakespearian play which began the evening. It lay in the various afterpieces which were performed subsequently, during which Yates 'introduce[d] the following Imitations—Young in Cassius . . . Kemble, Munden, Kean, Blanchard, Betty, and Matthews, in the opening soliloquy, in Richard the 3d'. This reliance on parody suggests that Regency acting was not a homogeneous phenomenon. More specifically, it provides an indication that the legitimate theatres were becoming contaminated with practices associated more with the non-patents. Kemble and Siddons had done much to advance the respectability of the theatre, but three developments during the Regency temporarily undid their work. I want now to turn to the politics of the London theatre at this time. Having examined the position of Kemble, demonstrable from his *Coriolanus*, his *Macbeth*, and his intentions for the rebuilt Covent Garden, I shall show how the norms which he established were destabilized by the controversy surrounding the rebuilding of Drury Lane, the image and style of Kean, and the increasing strength of the illegitimate theatres.

Kemble and Legitimacy

In February 1789, during Kemble's first season as acting manager at Drury Lane, he introduced *Coriolanus* into his repertoire. It would eventually become his most celebrated role. Its initial success was, however, limited. Siddons was absent that first season, so it was not possible to establish a double act like that of Macbeth and Lady Macbeth; the production was only staged seven times in eight years. According to Mrs Inchbald, it was then withdrawn 'for some reasons of state'. The late 1790s were marked by social unrest in the wake of the French Revolution; there was economic depression and, in particular, shortage of corn. The government of William Pitt the Younger had responded with a series of repressive measures, banning public assemblies and so forth. A play which began with an assemblage of citizens—the word resonant of the French revolutionary 'citoyens'—complaining about shortage of corn was potentially explosive. Mrs Inchbald's view was that in the circumstances a popular audience would not tolerate the lofty disdain with which Coriolanus/Kemble treated those citizens: 'When the lower orders are in good plight they will bear contempt with cheerfulness, and even with mirth; but poverty puts them out of humour at the slightest disrespect. Certain sentences in this play are, therefore, of dangerous tendency at certain times.'[14] After Nelson's victory at Trafalgar, internal politics became more settled and the production was revived at Covent Garden, where Kemble had moved, in 1806. Siddons was introduced as Volumnia to vast acclaim, and the production remained in the repertoire, frequently repeated, until Covent Garden was burnt down in the autumn of 1808. As we will see, the reopening of the theatre was marked by a period of confrontation between manager Kemble and the *populus* in the auditorium which would have made it inadvisable to restage the confrontation between actor Kemble and the citizens in the opening scene of *Coriolanus*, but by 1811 theatrical politics at Covent Garden were calmer and Kemble returned to the role. It remained his most admired role through to his retirement in 1817, when he played it for his farewell performance. It was during these years that Hazlitt began reviewing, and for him Coriolanus was synonymous with Kemble.

For Hazlitt, Shakespeare's imagination was marked above all by its disinterestedness, its capacity to inhabit every variety of being, to treat all viewpoints with equal sympathy. Yet his essay on *Coriolanus*, published in *Characters of Shakespear's Plays* in 1817, made an exception of this play: the aristocratic Coriolanus is invested with dramatic and poetic force, whereas the citizens are prosaic and easily swayed. Hazlitt proceeds from this observation to a conclusion that was anathema to his own liberal politics: 'the language of poetry naturally falls in with the language of power'.[15] The full text of Shakespeare's play is not, however, as simple as this; the citizens are given a surprising amount of space and it is made quite clear that necessary as Coriolanus is as a wartime leader he is a walking disaster area in time of peace. At one level, Hazlitt's reading is a response to current affairs: after the Napoleonic wars finally ended at Waterloo in 1815, there was another government crackdown at home. Shelley's sonnet is a reminder that the four years after Waterloo saw a reversion to authoritarian measures characteristic of the mid-1790s. The massacre at St Peter's Field was popularly known as Peterloo to highlight the irony that the powers who four years earlier had smashed Napoleon at Waterloo were now being turned on the nation's own people. Hazlitt's reading belongs squarely in these turbulent years. It is a reading which is prophetic of Peterloo: you need Coriolanus at Waterloo, but if you give him free rein after the war is over you are asking for trouble.

But at another level, Hazlitt read the play in a way which went against the grain of both his own politics and his sense of Shakespeare's disinterestedness because his sense of Coriolanus was shaped wholly by Kemble's compelling performance. The essay on the play in *Characters* was originally published the previous year in the form of a review of Kemble. And if one examines the text of Kemble's production, one sees that it was subtly altered in ways which made the language of poetry fall in with the language of power, ways which tipped the balance of power firmly towards Coriolanus and away from the citizens.

Kemble's version consisted of a fairly heavily cut text of Shakespeare's first three acts, then two final acts which mingled Shakespeare with James Thomson's 1749 adaptation, *Coriolanus; or, The Roman Matron*. The main reason for the adoption of Thomson in the latter part of the play was that it gave Kemble a Volumnia who persuades less by rhetoric than by action. In Shakespeare, it is a single very long speech which turns Coriolanus around, leading him not to march against Rome but to return to Antium and inevitable death. In Thomson, Volumnia makes a series of briefer and more direct thrusts: she dares her son to 'Tread on the bleeding breast of her, to whom | Thou ow'st thy life!' and threatens to stab herself while Rome is still free.[16] Kemble's adoption of this is a sign of the nineteenth-century theatre's growing impatience with formal Renaissance rhetoric. Where Shakespeare achieved a classical effect in his Roman plays through an elaborate rhetoric which would have had his more educated audience members thinking of Cicero, Kemble relied instead on a visual rhetoric. The vast size of the theatre and the resources of elaborate set design meant that Kemble's audience could see something resembling ancient Rome where Shakespeare's had to rely on hearing it. The Regency Coriolanus returned from his victories via a triumphal Roman arch through which over 150 extras processed. In Aufidius' house, the exiled Kemble brooded beneath a statue of Mars. Martius stood in the pose of Mars, making explicit the link between character and divine archetype (col. pl. 3). Moments like this, together with the strength of Kemble and Siddons (and, one may assume, the weakness of the actors playing the Tribunes), in conjunction with the preference for military processions over disordered crowds, meant that the production read the play as strongly pro-Coriolanus and anti-populus.

Certain cuts also tilted the politics of the play. Kemble removed the whole of a speech in the first scene in which the First Citizen argues that the control of food distribution is a means of propping up the class structure: 'The leanness that afflicts us, the object of our misery, is as an inventory to particularize their abundance; our sufferance is a gain to them . . .' (I. i. 15–25). Again, when Menenius claims that the patricians care for the plebeians, the citizen replies, 'Care for us? True indeed! They ne'er cared for us yet. Suffer us to famish, and their store-houses crammed with grain; make edicts for usury, to support usurers; repeal daily any wholesome act established against the rich, and provide more piercing statutes daily to chain up and restrain the poor. If the wars eat us not up, they will; and there's all the love they bear us' (I. i. 79–86). Kemble cuts. Again, Sicinius' speech in the fourth Act on the peace and prosperity of the Roman polity after Coriolanus has been exiled is cut down to 'We hear not of him, neither need we fear him; | His remedies are tame'—one thus loses 'the present peace | And quietness of the people, which before | Were in wild hurry', together with 'Our tradesmen singing in their shops, and going | About their functions friendly' (IV. vi. 1–8). This cut becomes particularly striking after 1815: when there is a threat of invasion, as there was in England for the majority of the time Kemble's production was in the repertoire, the tribunes are useless and Coriolanus is needed; but when peace finally comes, as it did in 1815, the state is better off without its killing machine.

Players, said Hamlet, show the very age and body of the time his form and pressure. The patrician Kemble, with his patriotic virtue and regulated troupes of extras, throve in the London theatre during the twenty years of war with France. He hitched the national poet to the wagon of traditional values. His first great role, Macbeth, was a potential problem in this. As far as traditional values were concerned, the most heinous crime was regicide (as committed by Robespierre & Co. in France). How to reconcile this with a compelling and sympathetic portrayal of Shakespeare's king-killing hero? What I have described as the 'reactive' tendency of eighteenth-century dramatic poetics came to Kemble's rescue here. He retained in his text the dying words of Garrick's

Macbeth. In accordance with the Renaissance idea of character being forged through action, Shakespeare's Macbeth charges to his end with the challenge 'Lay on, Macduff!' and then a mortal hand-to-hand combat. In accordance with the later idea of character being forged through reflection upon action, Garrick, expanding on the one-line farewell to ambition in Davenant's adaptation, had written a speech to be delivered after Macbeth had fallen (see Chapter 4, above). Kemble spoke a slightly compressed version of it:

> 'Tis done! the scene of life will quickly close.
> Ambition's vain delusive dreams are fled,
> And now I wake to darkness, guilt, and horror.—
> I cannot rise:—I dare not ask for mercy—
> It is too late;—hell drags me down;—I sink,
> I sink;—my soul is lost for ever!—Oh!—Oh!—[17]

For Garrick, this would have been both a fine histrionic moment and a demonstration of the kind of poetic justice—the good end happily, the bad unhappily—on the importance of which his friend Dr Johnson insisted. For Kemble, it could be turned to political account. His reading of Macbeth was that we can sympathize with the man, but not the regicide.

In 1785, Thomas Whately had argued in his *Remarks on some of the Characters of Shakespeare* (a book which partook of the new vogue for character-analysis) that Richard III was more courageous than Macbeth, who showed no more than 'resolution'. Kemble came to the defence of his role in a pamphlet called *Macbeth Reconsidered* (1786), which he revised and greatly extended in a second edition published in 1817, his retirement year. Kemble's argument is that Macbeth is driven into guilt by the instigation of others and that his early principles of virtue never become extinct. The conclusion of the revised version of the essay is in effect a justification for the retention of Garrick's conscience-stricken closing speech:

It is now shown, that Macbeth has a just right to the reputation of intrepidity; that he feels no personal fear of Banquo and Macduff; and that he meets equal, if not superior, trials of fortitude, as calmly as Richard: It may, therefore, be presumed, that no future Critic or Commentator in his observations on Shakspeare, will ascribe either the virtuous scruples of Macbeth, or his remorseful agonies, to so mean a cause as constitutional timidity. If so mistaken a persuasion could prevail, it would entirely counteract the salutary effect of the finest tragedy that has ever been written, and defeat the moral purpose to which, in every age, the Stage has been indebted for the favour and the works of wise and virtuous men, and the protection and support of all good governments.[18]

If Macbeth's scruples are not due to constitutional timidity, to what are they due? Moral and political guilt at the act of regicide—so it is that the essay ends by asserting the play's moral and political orthodoxy. The closing turn from the specific play to 'the Stage' in general and from moral edification to support for the government reveal exactly where Kemble's loyalties lay.

This defence of the stage was written just before Kemble's retirement. Behind it may be a worry about the theatre's future once he was gone and Kean had a clear run. Strikingly, Kean had retained Garrick's dying speech, but not fully submitted to it, suggesting rather a continued defiance on Macbeth's part: 'His death was admirable; full of that fine contrast of fierceness and feebleness, the spirit fighting, while the body was perishing under mortal faintness, which first attracted public fame to his *Richard*.'[19] Here the soul is not going down to hell; rather, the rebellious spirit is fighting even as the body is oppressed. In order to represent Macbeth sympathetically while retaining a notion of the sacredness of kingship, Kemble differentiated sharply between the man and the regicide. Kean led Hazlitt to dissolve that distinction, to deny the importance of kings and king-killing, to read Macbeth instead in terms of a 'common'—a shared, a democratic—humanity:

The two finest things that Mr Kean has ever done, are his recitation of the passage in Othello, 'Then, oh, farewell, the tranquil mind,' and the scene in Macbeth after the murder. The former was the highest and most perfect effort of his art. To enquire whether his manner in the latter scene was that of a king who commits a murder, or of a man who commits a murder to become a king, would be 'to consider too curiously.' But, as a lesson of common humanity, it was heart-rending. The hesitation, the bewildered look, the

coming to himself when he sees his hands bloody; the manner in which his voice clung to his throat, and choaked his utterance; his agony and tears, the force of nature overcome by passion—beggared description. It was a scene, which no one who saw it can ever efface from his recollection.[20]

Hazlitt's description of Kean suggests an acting style that to us will seem melodramatic. But it must be remembered that the theatres of the period were huge buildings and that such histrionics were necessary in order to hold the attention of audience members sitting at a great distance from the stage. The rebuilding of Covent Garden in 1782 gave it a capacity of 2,000; a refurbishment ten years later increased that to 3,000; when Drury Lane was in turn rebuilt in 1794, it housed over 3,500. By coincidence, both playhouses were destroyed by fire in 1808–9, allowing for rebuilding on a potentially even grander scale. But the histories surrounding the reopening of the two theatres were very different.

At Covent Garden Kemble raised the necessary capital with extraordinary speed and his new theatre (fig. 38) opened in September 1809, exactly a year after the fire. Built in high neo-classical style by Robert Smirke, the new theatre was marbled and plushly fitted, adorned with bas-relief depicting the classical muses, Athena, Dionysus, Sophocles, Shakespeare, and the Macbeths. It was intended by Kemble as a shrine to the national drama, a properly elevated home for his renditions of Shakespeare. The play for the first night was, needless to say, *Macbeth*. But the cost of rebuilding had been such that admissions prices were raised and the number of lucrative private boxes increased. So it was that when Kemble stepped forward to deliver a prologue, wearing the 'authentic' Scottish costume that was his hallmark (fig. 39), he was shouted down by shouts of 'Old Prices' and 'No Private Boxes'. The performance of *Macbeth* was continually interrupted and at the end of the evening magistrates were called in to read the Riot Act and disperse the audience. Their presence exacerbated the situation, and to cries of 'No police in the theatre' and renditions of 'God save the King' the crowd remained till two in the morning.[21] The rioters kept

FIG. 38 Auditorium of the rebuilt Theatre Royal, Covent Garden, in 1810.

up their clamour through sixty-seven successive performances until Kemble capitulated to virtually all their demands. Marc Baer describes a typical evening near the end of the great 'OP War':

The playbill for 15 December included an apology and the promise to end legal proceedings against OPs. Kemble acted that evening for the first time since the opening night and came forward to announce the dismissal of Brandon [the doorkeeper who had had Henry Clifford, leader of the OPs, arrested]. Discontented OPs in the pit now demanded an apology from management for having employed boxers [to quell the crowd] back in October; Kemble responded with a humble admission of his errors. This produced applause, and a placard was unfurled which read 'We are satisfied.' Suddenly, however, several OPs complained about the spikes put up in September to prevent movement back and forth

from the front of boxes to the pit. Kemble again came forward, promising the spikes would be removed. The play then continued, but so did the disturbance.

(Baer, *Theatre and Disorder*, 35)

Only with the complete triumph of the rioters did peace return to the theatre. That peace was marked with a dinner at which there were toasts to 'the ancient and unalienable judicature of the pit' and 'the immortal memory of Shakespeare'. The lowering of prices and reduction of the number of boxes were thus associated with the ancient constitutional rights of the English people; the OPs identified themselves with a patriotic and populist image of John Bull, whilst Kemble they identified with King John (one of his leading Shakespearian roles). They saw Kemble's capitulation as analogous to that of John when he

FIG. 39 Caricature by Charles Williams of John Kemble facing the O.P. Rioters.

finally agreed to sign Magna Carta. The issue of private boxes was the key one: even many of those who defended the right of the theatre management in a free market to fix their prices argued that 'that cannot be a *national* theatre, in which a portion is set apart for the exclusive accommodation of a few families'.[22] The affair, then, amounted to a contest for the universal right of access to Shakespeare, a struggle for possession of the national Bard. The claim of the OPs was that Shakespeare belonged to the whole nation, not the aristocracy. The point was made in one of the many scathing satirical poems directed at Kemble:

> Old Shakespear, John, whose brains had furnish'd thine
> With wit to speechify so very fine,
> Both men and manners studied well no doubt,
> Yet he was modest, John, he made no rout—
> He brought no engines 'gainst his Audience, no
> He set no traps to catch his friend or foe;
> He vow'd submission to the public voice
> And deem'd that best which seem'd the people's choice.[23]

The OP Riots were the most widely reported and contentious event of 1809. In the words of the *Monthly Magazine* of that November,

Never did the violence or ebullitions of party rage in the political world—never did the contest between Whigs and Tories—ministerialists—Foxites or Pittites—high church or low-Jacobins—excite more popular clamour, or more cordial enmity against each other, than John Bull (as the OPs are

designated) and John Kemble. The ministerial duel, the chasm in the administration, and the contentions and mortalities on the continent, have all been superseded by the more important subject of OPs and private boxes.

(Baer, *Theatre and Disorder*, 42)

The social composition of the rioters was mixed— among those arrested were labourers and artisans, but also a stockbroker—but to some commentators, the whole affair had the air of class war being conducted by theatrical means. The OP Committee, who pressed home their demands so adeptly, included several former members of the radical pro-Jacobin London Corresponding Society. Prominent among them was Francis Place, a key figure in the turbulent politics of the Westminster constituency. He and his circle had been particularly offended by the 1806 Westminster by-election, occasioned by the death of Charles James Fox, the age's leading opposition politician, at which the duke of Northumberland had put forward his own son as a candidate and then blatantly attempted to buy votes with food and beer. It was this same Northumberland who then put up £10,000, which went a long way towards enabling Kemble to rebuild Covent Garden with such speed. James Gillray's caricature, *Theatrical Mendicants Relieved* (fig. 40), shows 'King John', his younger brother Charles (who would carry on the Kemble theatrical dynasty after John's death), and Sarah Siddons going cap in hand to Northumberland.

The composition of this caricature tells us much about the social ambiguity of the theatre and the concomitant tensions which were brought into the open by the riots. Northumberland's placing of a £10,000 draft in Kemble's hat implies that Kemble is placing himself in the aristocracy's pocket. The actors' ragged clothes and the top caption, 'a Begging we will go!', are reminders of the distance between this alliance and the traditional association of actors with mendicants. Kemble's élitism is also mocked in the bottom caption: 'have Pity upon all our Aches & Wantes!' This is an allusion to the eccentric pronunciations he introduced on stage, in the name of classical scansion and historical authenticity (cf. his kilted Macbeth). 'For this tonight,' says Prospero to

Caliban, 'thou shalt have aches'—but in Kemble's mouth it was 'aitches'. Kemble's insistence on retaining this pronunciation, despite the hostility of the pit, becomes a synecdoche for his refusal to bow to the popular will. Meanwhile in the engraving itself, a Fool and a Harlequin behind Siddons' back are seen jeering at the 'legitimate' actors and celebrating the Covent Garden fire. For the forces of 'popular' theatre, the demise of one of the patents provided an opportunity to capture more of the market. It was exactly because of the spread of the 'illegitimates' that Kemble wanted to make his new Covent Garden bigger and better than ever, but in the long run he could do nothing to prevent the encroachment of illegitimacy upon the patent houses, and indeed upon Shakespeare.

Illegitimacy and Kean

On 30 August 1809, less than three weeks before Kemble reopened Covent Garden with his most celebrated role, a very different *Macbeth* was played at the non-patent Royal Circus (otherwise known as the Surrey) in St George's Fields: *The History, Murders, Life, and Death of Macbeth*. Since by law the words of Shakespeare could not be spoken in a non-patent, the manager Elliston staged it as a 'burletta', which is to say a series of song and dance routines. As Elliston put it in the prologue which he spoke himself,

FIG. 40 *Theatrical Mendicants Relieved*, caricature by James Gillray of the Kemble family going cap-in-hand to the Duke of Northumberland as Covent Garden burns in the background.

Though not indulg'd with fullest pow'rs of speech
The poet's object we aspire to reach;
The emphatic gesture, eloquence of eye,
Scenes, music, every energy we try,
To make your hearts for murder'd Banquo melt;
And feel for Duncan as brave Malcolm felt;
To prove we keep our duties full in view,
And what we must not *say*, resolve to *do*;
Convinc'd that you will deem our zeal sincere,
Since more by *deeds* than *words* it will appear.[24]

This prologue suggests an intention to work upon the audience the same kind of emotional effects that could be achieved in a conventional performance. Though denied the right to play Shakespeare's *words*, the non-patent houses increasingly took the opportunity to present what audiences went to the theatre for—what they could not get from a reading of the plays, the *actions*. Elliston's ingenious project ('*performed with enthusiastic Applause, to overflowing Houses, a Number of Nights*') amounted to a serious challenge to the two-and-a-half-(if we include the Haymarket)-theatre stranglehold upon Shakespeare in early nineteenth-century London.

A typical example of illegitimate Shakespeare is John Poole's *Hamlet Travestie*, which played at the New Theatre in Tottenham Street in January 1811. Two and a half years later, it could be seen at Covent Garden, a sure sign of how the patent houses were being contaminated by 'illegitimate' material. There was a long tradition of musical adaptations of Shakespeare, stretching from the Davenant *Macbeth* and the Purcell *Fairy Queen* (based on *A Midsummer Night's Dream*) in the late seventeenth century to Frederick Reynolds's critically panned but commercially successful musicals based on the comedies, such as *A Midsummer Night's Dream* (1816—a show which made Hazlitt wonder whether he would ever go to the theatre again) and *The Comedy of Errors* (1819—a show so popular that it ran for twenty-seven nights). But full-scale 'travesty' was something new.

Poole's play follows the plot of the original, but with a simplified *dramatis personae* and the language reduced to comic couplets. Laertes' elaborate request to leave the court becomes 'I have a mighty

wish to learn to dance, | And crave your royal leave to go to France.'[25] The soliloquies are turned into songs: where Romantic readers reflected upon the inner life (Lamb said that nine-tenths of the character of Hamlet was to be found in the soliloquies), the illegitimate theatre provided entertaining spectacle. Imagine 'To be or not to be' sung to the tune of 'Here we go up, up, up':

> When a man becomes tired of his life,
>> The question is 'to be or not to be?'
> For before he dare finish the strife,
>> His reflections most serious ought to be.
> *chorus* Ri tol de rol, &c.

Other moments of high drama, such as the appearances of the Ghost, are also cast into the form of song. Hamlet, the Ghost, and the Queen sing a trio to the tune of 'O lady Fair'. And the dialogue is made risible: Hamlet says to Gertrude of the Ghost, 'this once was your hubby'. The play within the play was presented as a pantomimic dumb show, thus providing the opportunity to incorporate a form of drama that was a favourite in the non-patents. More thoughtfully, song is made the medium for retrospection: Ophelia's account of Hamlet's visit to her chamber is sung to the tune of 'Mrs Clarke',

> My lord, you must know,
> A few minutes ago,
> In my room I was darning a stocking:
>> Now conceive my alarm,
>> When (not dreaming of harm),
> I was rous'd by a violent knocking.

The domestication of the scene here is characteristic of a tendency in illegitimate Shakespeare to familiarize elevated material, to bring high tragedy down to the level of the audience. When the old, mad king finally died in 1820, the two patent houses were quick to stage revivals of *King Lear*, but within days a third rival version could be seen at the Coburg: a melodrama by W. T. Moncrieff called *The Lear of Private Life! or, Father and Daughter*.[26]

The climax of Poole's *Hamlet Travestie* is also in the style of another popular form, comic melodrama:

QUEEN. Hamlet, your health. (*Drinks.*) Ha! this is famous stingo!

KING. Don't drink.

QUEEN.   I have.

KING.   The poison'd cup, by jingo!

Melodrama was invented in the 1790s to serve the needs of the non-patent houses. Its first exponent was Thomas Holcroft, a leading radical activist and pro-Jacobin. It was above all a demotic form, a democratization of tragedy. Like its sister form, Gothic, it throws extremes of emotion and reaction together, breaching the social decorum which proclaims tragedy high and comedy low. In this, it draws from the irreverent, indecorous mingling of kings and clowns, of high pathos and low comedy, in Shakespeare himself.

The most telling of the songs in the *Hamlet* burlesque is one preceding the play scene, which provides an opportunity to mock the characteristics of the leading actors in the patent houses. It suggests that the object of travesty in the illegitimate versions is not so much Shakespeare as the presumptuous claim of the legitimate houses to exclusive possession of Shakespeare.

1811 was an opportune moment for the staging of an illegitimate *Hamlet*, since the amount of legitimate Shakespeare available that season was limited, due to the closure of Drury Lane. That theatre was burnt to the ground on 24 February 1809. In contrast to Kemble's experience at Covent Garden, the management had great difficulty raising the capital for rebuilding. Sheridan was ruined by the fire and was eventually eased out. A new committee took over the theatre. It was headed by Samuel Whitbread, who argued, just as Kemble had done, for the 'national' worth of the rebuilding project—the new Drury Lane would be a national theatre for the national drama. But where Kemble looked for support to Tory grandees, Whitbread was a leading figure in the Whig Opposition. This was a chance to take the national cultural high ground; by arguing that his theatre would be devoted to the canon of British drama, Shakespeare pre-eminently (there would be an end to German imports such as the sentimental plays of Kotzebue), Whitbread could demonstrate the impeccable patriotism of the Opposition, thus alleviating the problem which Foxites had always faced that their sympathy for the democratic impulses of the French Revolution had made them seem like appeasers of the enemy. Whitbread co-opted the Prince Regent, who had been long associated with opposition to the Pittites. The Committee began using a rhetoric of public virtue and self-sacrifice which made them sound like the artist-ideologues of the French Revolution.[27] Inevitably this led to the accusation that they were misappropriating Shakespeare for political purposes. The Tory press used the familiar strategy of saying that the Bard was above politics—which was a way of tacitly saying that he must have been a supporter of Tory politics.

On 27 August 1812, the leading Whig paper, the *Morning Chronicle*, published a letter headed 'The Politics of Wm. Shakspeare'. It stated that innumerable aspects of Shakespeare had long been written about, but 'it remained for me to investigate his *politics*, to estimate his party-bias, to inquire whether he was Whig or Tory, constitutional or household, the king's friend or the people's, whether he ever ratted or acknowledged himself incapable—in short, whether he was the advocate of public liberty or its adversary?' The correspondent, who seems to have been a member of the Drury Lane Committee, concluded that Shakespeare was 'a free, noble, and an independent creature, always advocating the right cause, and scorning to lend his power to tyranny, or barter away, like a German princeling, the army of his mind to serve as mercenaries in the attack upon the fortress of public liberty'. The letter concluded by saying that its author would subsequently bring forward a '*Shaksperian Code*', which would demonstrate the Bard's liberal politics.

This Code duly appeared in the same paper on 14 September. Here Shakespeare was shown to stand for 'Integrity of Justice' and 'Liberty of the Press', values which were much needed 'In these sad days of *seat-selling* and *German incorporation*' (the latter phrase suggests that the Drury Lane Committee's professed hostility to imported German drama served as a coded attack on the old, mad, blind, despised, and German king). A passage in *Lear* was quoted and read as 'highly illustrative of that detestation of cruelty which is one of Shakspeare's striking characteristics, and which applies forcibly to 1812, when Authority seems to have put on her sternest aspect, and penal laws rise as fast as mushrooms upon the dunghill of erroneous policy'. That Shakespeare abhorred 'sanguinary penal laws' was argued from the mercy he showed to Barnardine in *Measure for Measure*. Barnardine, it is wittily claimed, was obviously a stocking-weaver; the Bernards or Barnyards were a Nottinghamshire family, so 'this unhappy individual was in all probability condemned for *frame-breaking*'.[28]

This allusion to one of the most contentious political and legal issues of 1812, together with the fact that the first of the two articles was immediately followed by a piece which began, 'Symptoms of riot, owing to the high price of provisions, have appeared in Edinburgh', demonstrate how vigorously Shakespeare was being contested and made contemporary at this time. But this particular argument over the political pedigree of the national Bard took place specifically in the context of the rebuilding of Drury Lane. The second of the two articles was immediately followed by a piece on the near-completion of the new theatre. Meanwhile the Tory *Morning Post* was quick to respond that the *Chronicle*'s reading of Shakespeare's politics was but a mask for 'Drury-Lane Politics'.

The early nineteenth-century Shakespearian theatre was simultaneously upwardly and downwardly mobile. During the Regency, the two patent theatres had very different socio-political identities. Kemble's Covent Garden meant Toryism, the aristocracy, and the anti-populism of boxes and high prices. The rebuilt Drury Lane meant Whitbread, Opposition politics, and a reading of Shakespeare as friend of the people against the autocracy of government. At the same time, both managements were bowing to commercial pressures and in particular the realization that to fill their enormous auditoriums they would have to bring in the 'lower' audience who were packing the burgeoning number of non-patent theatres. This meant that, for all their pieties about only playing the classical repertoire—no burlettas or performing dogs—they relied more and more on 'low' spectacle. It is in these contexts that one must place the dazzling career of Edmund Kean.

Like all the major actors of the period, Kean made his initial reputation in the provinces. In 1814, he negotiated to move to London, and was on the point of committing himself to Elliston at the Surrey when he changed course and signed for Drury Lane. This is a mark of the distance between him and the theatrical dynasty of the Kemble family—none of them would have conceived of the possibility of playing in a non-patent house. Five years later, in 1819, Elliston began a period of seven years as lessee of Drury Lane. For a time, then, one of the patents was dominated by a manager who had begun his career in a non-patent and an actor who could easily have gone to a non-patent. In 1827, Elliston returned to the Surrey and in 1831 Kean played Othello at the Coburg. Such traffic between the legitimate and illegitimate theatres spelt the beginning of the end of the patent and the idea of an exclusive right to the staging of Shakespeare.

It was widely known that Kean himself was an illegitimate child. This, together with his undisciplined, 'natural' acting style, accounted for his reputation as a transgressor. The first we hear of him is as an impish boy getting sacked for messing around and scene-stealing when he played a child's role in Kemble's *Macbeth* of 1794. The careers of Kemble and Siddons were devoted to the legitimation of the actor's profession, symbolized by their acceptance into the best society. Kean reversed the actor's path towards respectability: instead of joining an exclusive gentleman's club (as the theatrical élite of modern times become members of the Garrick), he formed his own rowdy club, the Wolves, who got drunk together and disrupted the performances of his rivals, such as Junius Brutus Booth (fig. 41). In the Green Room, Kean did not focus himself on his role in the manner of Mrs Siddons—what he did instead is suggested by the diary of James Winston, Elliston's deputy manager in charge of day-to-day affairs at Drury Lane:

FIG. 41 Caricature by George Cruikshank of Kean's supporters (The Wolf Club) hounding a rival Richard III, Junius Brutus Booth, from the stage. Booth is on the ground, Henry Harris the manager of Covent Garden beside him, and Kean, in his celebrated posture as Richard, behind the tent. The inscription on the tent, 'Dieu et mon Droit', suggests the association of Covent Garden with the Establishment, while that on the jackets of the Wolves indicates the association of Kean with Opposition politics.

Kean requested the rehearsal might not be till twelve as he should get drunk that night—said he had frequently three women to stroke during performances and that two waited while the other was served. Penley said he had [formerly] seen Storace waiting for her turn. This night he had one woman (Smith) though he was much infected [drunk].[29]

This is an actor dedicated to the disreputable, transgressive origins of his profession.

In London literary circles, there was much talk of Kean and his low company. Keats wished that he could have been in that company instead of among respectable bores. Indeed, Kean's performances were especially praised by the unrespectable young literary radicals of the Regency whom the Tory press loftily dismissed as Cockneys—Keats, Leigh Hunt, and

Hazlitt. It was above all Hazlitt's reviews which precipitated Kean to fame. The Shylock with which the diminutive actor made his début did not especially impress the reviewer for the Tory Morning Post, but in the pro-Opposition Morning Chronicle Hazlitt viewed it as the dawn of a new age in the theatre, just as he had viewed the advent on the literary scene of Wordsworth and Coleridge in 1798 as a revolution.

Kean, who may himself have been Jewish (his probable father had brothers called Aaron and Moses), was especially successful in the roles of outsiders. He was a sympathetic Shylock and at his very best as the disruptive loner, Iago. Coleridge considered he was not enough of a gentleman to play Othello, though the raw passion of his performance in that role was widely

FIG. 42 *The Theatrical Atlas* by George Cruikshank: Edmund Kean props up the finances of Samuel Whitbread's ailing Drury Lane Theatre.

admired by others. He was notably bad as Coriolanus, partly due to his small stature, but also because he was the antithesis of the dignified and authoritative Kemble. Hazlitt said that he should not have attempted Coriolanus, on the grounds that he was a 'radical' performer. This is only one of many occasions on which Hazlitt's reviews of Kean rely on a notably political lexicon: 'In a word, Mr Kean's acting is like an anarchy of the passions, in which each upstart humour, or phrensy of the moment, is struggling to get violent possession of some bit or corner of his fiery and pigmy body—to jostle out, and lord it over, the rest of the rabble of short-lived, and furious purposes.'[30] 'Anarchy', 'upstart', 'violent possession', 'rabble': such a description makes Kean sound like an embodiment of the rioting crowds who had triumphed over Kemble during the OP affair.

In the short term, Kean was the saviour of Drury Lane. In his first couple of seasons, takings on the

FIG. 44 Kean as Richard III: a moment of melodramatic posturing, engraving after Cruikshank.

nights when he played were more than double those of nights on which he did not. George Cruikshank's caricature, *The Theatrical Atlas* (fig. 42) aptly shows him in a famous pose from his celebrated Richard III, raising his stature by standing on the book of Shakespeare and propping Whitbread's theatre on his hunchback. In the medium term, the frenzy and 'illegitimacy' he represented were instrumental in bringing the century-and-a-half-long duopoly on Shakespeare to an end. The melodramatic, pantomimic elements in his Richard III contributed to encourage the non-patent Coburg to put on that play in melodramatic style but using Shakespeare's words in 1820. This led to a prosecution for breach of the patent, but over the next decade the tide of illegitimate Shakespeare became so overwhelming that suppression of further such productions became impossible.[31]

FIG. 43 Kean as Richard III: a moment of still intensity, engraving after J. J. Halls.

Kean's explosive style was innovative, fracturing, radical—it constituted a theatrical revolution. For the high Romantics, Kean's flashes of lightning were those moments when he stood with a still intensity which thrilled the imagination (fig. 43); what discomposed Coleridge was the actor's way of descending the next moment to what he called 'the infra-colloquial' (fig. 44). Such vulgar crowd-pleasing smacked of illegitimacy and marked the decisive incursion into the respectable West End patent houses of the energies and excesses of the East End and South Bank non-patents. But in the long term, it was the legitimation of Shakespeare which triumphed. William Charles Macready, the leading actor of the next generation, took over some of Kean's Romantic and 'radical' techniques—the contrasting tones and tempos, the dramatic pauses—but combined them with a Kemblian respectability. He thus contrived to domesticate Kean's wildness. This was in keeping with a notably 'Victorian' emphasis on the domestic and the paternal in many of his productions. As Brutus in *Julius Caesar*, Macready was noted for his fatherly tenderness towards the boy Lucius; as Lear, he established a similar relationship with the Fool. It was Macready's 1838 production which finally reintroduced the Fool into *Lear*, over 150 years after Nahum Tate

had banished him. But it was a very different Fool from the one who stood jeering behind Mrs Siddons and in front of the burning Covent Garden in Gillray's caricature: a domesticated Fool, bonded to Lear by sentiment, was not a dangerous, topsy-turvy figure showing up the 'corruptions and abuses' of power.

Kean might have marked the advent of 'radical Shakespeare' into the realm of 'legitimate Shakespeare', but Macready contained the threat. Various underground Shakespeares survived throughout the nineteenth century, for instance in provincial Chartist circles,[32] but in the London theatre Shakespearian acting became more and more respectable. By the end of the century, that legitimation meant a knighthood for Henry Irving, while 'popular' theatre was transformed into kinds of vaudeville, music hall, and circus which drew less and less on Shakespeare. The split is nicely dramatized in Angela Carter's Shakespearian fantasy-novel, *Wise Children*. In the words of its narrator, Dora Chance, vaudeville actress and illegitimate daughter of Sir Melchior Hazard, 'prince of players', chief ornament of a Shakespearian acting dynasty: 'our father was a pillar of the legit. theatre and we girls are illegitimate in every way—not only born out of wedlock, but we went on the halls, didn't we! Romantic illegitimacy, always a seller.'[33]

6

Actor-Managers and the Spectacular

RUSSELL JACKSON

Signs of the Times

BETWEEN the 1830s and the First World War the British theatre was dominated by actor-managers. In the best-equipped theatres the plays of Shakespeare were usually presented in elaborate scenic productions, with the texts tailored to meet the demands of the new staging techniques and to feature the leading actors as strongly as possible. By and large the 'problem' plays were excluded from the repertoire, and the plays performed were purged of any avoidable indecency in language and action. The distinctive theatrical quality of the most successful productions was their ability to 'illustrate' the plays, and it is on this pictorial realism and its cultural significance that the present chapter focuses.

Contemporary critics saw the history of the British theatre in the nineteenth century in terms of a gradual improvement in staging techniques, the achievement of a higher degree of artistic unity, and the advancement of the theatre's social status. The Theatres Act of 1843, by effectively repealing the absurdly restrictive legislation which had been inherited from the granting of patents at the Restoration, enabled such managers as Samuel Phelps to present the 'legitimate' repertoire of spoken drama without recourse to subterfuge. This in itself was regarded as a sign of progress. The censorship of new

plays by the Lord Chamberlain's office persisted until 1968, that particular restriction on theatrical freedom not yet being perceived to have outlasted the purpose it had been created to serve, keeping the stage chaste and (more important) politically neutral.

The rise of the actor-manager in his (rarely, her) Victorian incarnation was that of an artist increasingly able to co-ordinate the forces available in the service of his own artistic vision. It was as though the John Philip Kemble version of the leading actor (diligent, learned, earnest) had prevailed over the wayward and less respectable model exemplified by Edmund Kean. Sir Henry Irving's knighthood, bestowed in 1895, gave some countenance to the theatre's insistence that it was 'the Profession', comparable in dignity with learning, medicine, and law. In Victorian accounts of the history of actor-managerial regimes, envisaged at one and the same time as evolutionary development and quasi-royal succession (a line from Garrick to Irving), it was customary to emphasize the struggles of Macready and his successors to wrest artistic control from the hands of mere entrepreneurs. Macready and others were represented (with some justice) as having rendered the theatre more respectable, a fitting pastime for the middle classes and their families. The theatre, now in the hands of artists and able to express the author's vision more fully through their interpretative skills, would also reflect the preoccupations of poets and painters. The theatre also embodied in an actor-managerial version the favourite Victorian biographical theme of the heroic achievement of self-definition in the face of adversity, exemplified in the yearning of Tennyson's Ulysses 'To strive, to seek, to find, and not to yield'. It would be an emblem of change as betterment and enabling, rather than decay.

In *Signs of the Times* (1829) Thomas Carlyle had observed 'a deep-lying struggle in the whole fabric of society; a boundless grinding collision of the Old and the New'.[1] A primary task of the arts was to ensure that change was indeed progress rather than meaningless alteration. An increasingly secular state looked to artists for definition of the purposes that might complement if not replace those attributed to God. Situating the present by evoking the past and invoking its values was a special responsibility of graphic and architectural art. The art and values of the medieval past were considered particularly important, representing a wholeness and community of purpose in spiritual and material life. Its monuments should at all costs be preserved. 'A fair building is necessarily worth the ground it stands upon,' wrote Ruskin, adding that whenever the time might come when such monuments might be destroyed, it was certainly not now, 'when the place of both the past and the future is too much usurped in our minds by the restless and discontented present'.[2] William Morris argued for Gothic as the style best fitted to express the 'New Birth' of society, a mode of building which 'will remember the history of the past, make history in the present, and teach history in the future'.[3] For this socialist thinker, recreating and preserving an 'organic' architecture from the Middle Ages was a means of expressing true progress. Typically, Victorian theorists rejected formalism (and specifically, neo-classicism) and proclaimed the ethical content of works of art and the seriousness of their social purpose. Paintings should imply and illustrate narratives, and there should be clarity and seriousness in pointing the lessons of the stories told. Pictorial realism was a

means to this end, showing how the very fabric of social life had meaning—or, in the case of historical subjects, how the life of the past was picturesquely different from that of the present but enacted the same human impulses and moral dilemmas. In an important study of the visual and literary narrative arts of the period Martin Meisel describes their techniques as 'not just a common style, but a popular style', and identifies a 'persistent pressure towards uniting a concrete particularity with inward signification, the materiality of things with moral and emotional force, historical fact with figural truth, the mimetic with the ideal'.[4] Victorian paintings on historical subjects characteristically identified and enacted human crises in the past as domestic and personal, eliciting pathos from recognizable predicaments. Richness of historical detail in furnishings, architecture, and artefacts loaded the picture with additional signifiers, so that the 'reading' of a successful Victorian painting (for example, in reviews of the annual Royal Academy exhibition) usually retold and commented on the anecdote and its setting at length. The artist devised paintings to challenge and elicit such commentary, and the exhibition and circulation of them was accompanied by reviews, tracts, expository poems, and a body of commentary and celebration.[5]

These attitudes to graphic art and narrative, and in particular to representations of the past, have a direct bearing on the Victorians' treatment of Shakespeare in the theatre. The progress of the theatre itself was located in the achievement of greater historical accuracy in scenery and costumes, fuller attention to *ensemble* in acting and improved techniques of presentation. The plays in the Shakespeare canon, now staged with greater fidelity to the original texts than had been usual in the preceding two centuries, offered stage representations of historical periods and geographical locations central to the Victorians' construction of their cultural heritage: the histories and mythology of Ancient Greece and Rome, Renaissance Italy, and selected scenes from the British past. (Biblical subject-matter, much favoured by painters, was still prohibited on stage.) The all-important task of the theatre, lending legitimacy to a medium which many still considered suspect, was to convey the *ethos* of these scenes with the added advantage of imparting life and movement to them. In this way the theatre could be said to take its part in the assertion of a national cultural identity. Such stirring tableaux as the storming of Harfleur in Charles Kean's 1859 *Henry V* were effectively animated history paintings on themes from English history, and were applauded as such by audiences and critics.

By the end of the century it could be claimed that on a strictly economic level the theatre had changed along with the times, its organization as a labour-intensive capitalist enterprise by now comparable with industry and commerce. Railways made the itineraries of touring companies wider-reaching if no less arduous than in the earlier days of provincial circuits travelled by coach and on foot. London successes were reproduced in the provinces with a considerable degree of faithfulness to the original, but at the expense of variety in the careers of the actors whose work now consisted in playing the same London hit night after night around the country. The actors' working life was still precarious, and as the entertainment business became more thoroughly industrialized it came to need the same regulation of contract terms and working conditions that would eventually protect other work-forces. But, for all the changes in organization, technique, and distribution of the finished product, the aims of theatrical performance, for the serious drama at least, were still those of the 1830s: the achievement of pictorial realism in staging, and of psychological verisimilitude in acting. Allowing for a greater or lesser degree of permissible stylization in the range between domestic comedy and poetic tragedy—modern prose and antique verse—the commercial theatre seemed to have achieved ever greater perfection of technique.

A Shakespearian drama, seen at one of the premier theatres of the capital or the great provincial cities between the 1830s and the first years of the twentieth century, would offer a series of convincing and romantic pictures, within which the characters would move in picturesque and appropriate costumes. The events of the play would unfold in a harmonious and well-planned succession, each movement of the plot climaxing in a striking tableau and the whole welded together with orchestral music. The scenery would be elaborate and might require long intervals, and in the case of Shakespearian plays the texts, although 'faithful' to the original in excluding non-Shakespearian material, were abbreviated and rearranged to answer the demands of what was effectively a different medium from the open stages and continuous action of the theatres for which they had been written. The play's action was 'realized' as fully as possible, framed behind a proscenium arch which corresponded to a picture-frame in its effect, and moved typically from one grand tableau to another. Within the picture was a world which spectators could contemplate but with which they could not communicate directly. The Victorian theatre's conventions for serious drama excluded any open acknowledgement of the audience's presence by the characters, although in practice it was not unusual for actors to acknowledge the applause elicited by a particular effect.

Actor-managers anxious for social and artistic respectability sought to achieve harmonious and convincingly realistic stage-pictures. William Charles Macready, who enjoyed only brief periods of management at Covent Garden and Drury Lane in the 1830s and 1840s, provided a model for personal dignity, the elimination of the theatre's low-life associations, and effective stage-management—what would nowadays be thought of as 'direction'. Macready retired early from a profession whose day-to-day life he found irksome and inartistic. Copies of his prompt-books were used by Charles Kean, whose 'revivals' at the Princess's between 1851 and 1859 brought a new degree of elaboration to scenic spectacle in Shakespeare. The influence of Macready's practice is evident in the work of his former colleague Samuel Phelps, whose management of Sadler's Wells between 1843 and 1862 converted it from a melodrama house of dubious reputation to a dramatic temple for those bent on self-improvement. All three actor-managers presented their aims in terms of social improvement, a wider repertoire of better plays, and a striving for appropriate pictorial effect. Kean was less careful than Phelps about subordinating the pictures to the text, and was more anxious to bring the middle and upper classes back to the theatre. During Phelps's regime at Sadler's Wells it appears that the 'earnest artisan' element predominated in the cheaper seats. The progress of contemporary dramatic literature was thought of in a similar way: there the emblematic success story was the Bancrofts' conversion of the 'Dust-Hole' in Tottenham Street into the Prince of Wales's, home to Tom Robertson's gentle (and genteel) comedies. Irving's achievements at the Lyceum during the last two decades of the century were construed as further evidence (after a period of some uncertainty in the late 1860s and 1870s) of the upward tendency of the legitimate theatre. For these managements and their imitators the creation of comfort and decency in the auditorium was accompanied by a striving for subtlety and period accuracy in what was presented behind the footlights.

Plays and Pageantry

In adapting the Shakespearian plays to suit this kind of theatre it was usually necessary to make considerable cuts and rearrangements. The assumption was that such tampering did not amount to 'a critical liberty, or an ambitious experiment to improve Shakespeare as he wrote', but—in the words of Charles Kean's biographer—'as a zealous effort to place the poet on the stage for which he composed, to the best advantage, and with the reality which he conceived and intended, though without a hope of seeing the accomplishment with his own eyes'.[6] Shakespeare's own theatre was conceived of as a primitive version of that available by the 1850s, rather than a distinct medium with its own capabilities. The Victorian theatre could offer a direct access, not hitherto

available, to the 'reality' which Shakespeare 'conceived and intended'. It was of course axiomatic that a supreme artist, of whom Shakespeare must be the exemplar, must be above all the creator of realistic illusions.

Simply the setting and striking of the elaborate scenery required for such productions would call for radical cutting of the text, but the distinctive character of Victorian Shakespeare performance is to be found not so much in this kind of cutting (or even the removal of indecent scenes, speeches, and words), as in the adjustment of act-endings and reshaping of the plays' momentum to facilitate the 'pictures' or 'tableaux' in which a crisis of the play's story was expressed. These often enlisted all the theatre's resources of staging and acting in order to make good omissions on the part of Shakespeare or the theatre of his day. An outstanding example was the 'episode' that Charles Kean inserted into his *Richard II*, 'wisely' (thought one reviewer) going 'beyond the drama to the Chronicles' (fig. 45). The theatre could now show what in Shakespeare's time had to remain a reported scene, put into the mouth of the Duke of York in v. ii. Richard was shown following Bolingbroke through the streets of London:

This is one of the most gorgeous and effective scenes that we ever witnessed on the stage. Commencing with the Dance of the Itinerant Fools as described in *Strutt's Sports and Pastimes of the English*, we are presented with the multitudes that crowd the streets, the balconies, and the housetops, and witness numerous little episodes, skilfully acted out by competent performers, preparatory to the main event of the scene.

The pathos of Richard as he 'passes over in melancholy and heart-broken silence' is impressive, and the critic is confident in affirming that 'such an interlude as this Shakespeare himself would have doubtless approved of, as a fitting illustration of historic fact'.[7] The scene's 'tendency . . . to realize the whole of the action', praised by the reviewer, makes York's description of it redundant: what in Shakespeare is seen through the eyes of a partial (and not insignificant) observer, and given a specifically 'theatrical' frame ('As in a theatre the eyes of men . . .'), is exhibited by Kean as a

FIG. 45 Charles Kean's *Richard II*, Princess's Theatre, 1857, the 'episode' inserted to show the entry of Bolingbroke into London. Engraving in the *Illustrated London News*.

fulfilment of the theatre's mission to show everything. Kean even added the incident (from 'The Chronicles' of course) in which at the close of this sad spectacle a veteran of Crécy tries to pay homage to the rightful king but is pushed back by the crowd: a small 'history painting' tacked on as a coda. By the same token, productions of *Henry V* which, like Charles Kean's, changed the Chorus into Clio, the Muse of History, and 'illustrated' her descriptions with tableaux vivants behind a gauze, effectively removed from that play one of its principal expressions of the problems of recalling and interpreting historical events. Clio is, after all, an ideal personification of a dignified discipline: 'Chorus' is a representative of the theatre, with all its anxieties and ambitions.[8]

The interpolation in *Richard II* is typical of such additional 'illustrations' added to the history plays: others included the signing of Magna Carta in Herbert

Beerbohm Tree's production of *King John* (how remiss of Shakespeare to omit King John's significance in the establishment of the 'English constitution'!). The list of 'supers' (the 'extras' of the Victorian theatre) in a prompt-book for Kean's *Richard II* shows how labour intensive the theatre had become, and how cheap that work-force could be. The weekly bill for supers came to £76. 7s. for 139 supers, 32 'extra ballet', 13 'extra ballet girls', 40 children, and 3 'men/bells' (presumably to ring the church bells behind the scenes).[9] Production documents regularly indicate the large numbers of supers used in public scenes: the senates of Rome and Venice, the thanes and retainers who throng the courtyard to hear of King Duncan's murder, the crowds who witness the funeral of Julius Caesar, Coriolanus' return to Rome (the 'Ovation' scene, fig. 46), the vanquishing of Shylock, the trial of Hermione, and (in *Henry VIII*) the christening of the infant Elizabeth. The nationalistic significance of the crowd scenes in English history plays is clear from Kean's stage directions for the 'episode' in *Richard II*, which features a procession of city guilds resembling that in the last scene of Wagner's *Meistersinger*. Occasionally the numbers reflect the diminished forces needed to populate smaller stages: Macready's *Julius Caesar* at Drury Lane in 1843 offered a senate scene with twenty-four senators, twelve lictors, sixteen guards, and twenty-four citizens in addition to the speaking roles, but Phelps, at Sadler's Wells in the 1840s, used only twenty-four senators as 'extras' for this sequence.[10] The orchestration of the crowd's responses in this play, and the effect of their numbers, were singled out for praise by reviewers of the Meiningen Court Theatre Company when they visited London in 1881. In fact the aims and techniques had been learned from the practice of Macready and his followers: like Macready, Charles Kean and Samuel Phelps provided detailed business and lines for the citizens during the funeral orations of Brutus and Mark Antony.[11] Revivals of Verdi's Shakespearian operas often replicate these crowd effects now lost to most productions of the plays themselves: the singing and dancing witches and the grand choral response to

Duncan's death reflect the dramaturgy common to opera and spoken theatre in the period. The spoken theatre's use of music and marshalling of stage crowds only needed the addition of singing to make its productions operatic in a literal sense (fig. 47).

This 'sense of arrival'—the use of 'pictures' to mark narrative progression and to encapsulate its various dimensions—was sometimes incorporated in episodes of literal travel. 'Dioramas' (in fact, moving panoramas) showed the journey from the Woods back to Athens in more than one *Midsummer Night's Dream* and even the rarely performed *Timon of Athens* earned its place on Phelps's stage with a panoramic representation of the journey from Timon's refuge back to the city.[12] The techniques were common to pantomime and other theatrical forms, as well as to the shows which were simply geographical panoramas or dioramas.[13] Like the historically accurate period detail, the use of these devices helped to satisfy the prevailing appetite for information, the provision of which formed a major element in the appeal of such managers as Charles Kean to their public. They also reinforced a sense of the stage-picture's ability to show anything and everything. Painters whose own work combined historical (or 'archaeological') accuracy and

FIG. 46 Macready's *Coriolanus*, Covent Garden, 1838, II. ii. 'Authentic' Roman ritual and setting. Engraving by George Scharf.

strong narrative situations were often engaged to advise theatrical managements on the production of historical plays. The appeal of spectacle combined with and legitimized by historical information and edifying morality was inherited by the early cinema, especially in such 'epic' films as D. W. Griffith's *Intolerance* (1915).

The High Victorian insistence on ethical significance in stage-pictures can be found in two reviews of productions of *Coriolanus*. Describing Samuel Phelps's production at Sadler's Wells in 1860, Henry Morley praises 'the scenic effect of the view of Antium by the light of the rising moon, when the banished Coriolanus haunts the door of Aufidius' and finds it admirably 'contrived to give colour to the poetry'. This was excelled by what followed: 'there is no scene in the play more impressive to the eye than

the succeeding picture of the muffled figure of Coriolanus, seated by the glowing embers of the brazier that represents his enemy's hearth.'[14] In his staging of this play, as so often, Phelps was harking back to the work of Macready. A review of Macready's 1838 production of the same play praises the restoration to the British theatre of a true and vivid image of Rome, and describes a view of the port and mole of Antium and its pharos with 'its deadliest enemy . . . gliding into it, like a lone spectre'. The next scene showed 'the *aula* of Tullus' mansion, lit by the glimmering brazier on the hearth', with Coriolanus 'sitting, shrouded in his mantle on the sacred spot, which is flanked on the one side by a lofty trophy, on the other by the ancestral image; the solemn beauty of the whole picture carrying us back to the most touching of all classical associations—the inviolability of the hearth'.[15]

FIG. 47 A quasi-operatic finale: the conclusion of II.ii in Charles Kean's *Macbeth*, Princess's Theatre, 1853. Water-colour after a scene design by Frederick Lloyd.

This reading of Macready's staging suggests another dimension that is more obviously 'Victorian': the affecting image of the domestic ideal as expressed in Roman culture. It is as though both productions of the play have devised a narrative painting, 'Caius Martius at the hearth of Tullus Aufidius', expressive of the ethical significance and humane dimensions of a given historical situation. To achieve the effect, both productions dispensed with most of the dialogue between the disguised Martius and the servants: Martius' relationship with the ideas of the classical world is emphasized, his isolation is unqualified, and his dealings with yet another set of common people are played down. His historical circumstances, in the Victorian construction of them, are more 'ideal' than 'real'.

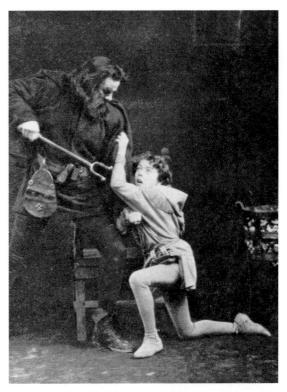

FIG. 48 Hubert and Arthur in Beerbohm Tree's production of *King John*, Her Majesty's Theatre, 1899.

Character in Action

Such pictures, however, were only the more elaborate products of a stagecraft whose principal appeal was visual, and which worked by establishing and 'marking' the stages of emotional progress in individuals and groups of characters. In criticism and in the choice of subjects for paintings, the expression of individual human character was a dominant factor. One of Shakespeare's skills, in his Victorian guise as exemplary author, was his excellence in the creation of 'real' and multi-faceted individuals as the persons of the play. Like the most popular literary criticism on the plays, the paintings of such scenes as Arthur and Hubert (in *King John* figs. 48, 49) or Richard of Gloucester wooing Lady Anne were considered as tributes to this aspect of Shakespeare's own genius . The re-creative talents of critics, painters, and the theatre were directed towards celebrating and imitating Shakespeare's realization of history as character in action.

Actors tended to conceive of their performances as a series of 'points', in which bits of business, physical attitudes, or facial expressions marked the fullest expression of a particular response or emotional state in a character. This was the actor as character-painter. In some cases the descriptions of these moments suggest a degree of stylization not unlike the *mie* in kabuki: attitudes and grimaces which mark an emotional climax or turning-point. Towards the end of the century there was an increasing tendency on the part of critics to value the skill with which the 'points' were subsumed within an impression of continuous emotional life, but they remained to be appreciated and, most important, acknowledged by the audience. Performers would take pride in the establishment of their own distinctive 'points' in a given role. The Victorian performer expected an audience to acknowledge each 'point'. To receive one or more distinct rounds of applause for an effect would be

unheard of in the late twentieth century, when even an 'exit round' (let alone an 'entrance round') for a favourite actor is considered old-fashioned and disruptive. Such customs only survive in a somewhat diminished form in classical ballet and opera—or in popular music and theatre.

Many of these 'points' became customary, so that actors were praised according to their ability to fulfil expectations in some, and surprise in others. Such traditional stage business is described engagingly in Arthur Colby Sprague's survey *Shakespeare and the Actors*, written in the 1940s when it seemed as though the ghosts of these customary pieces of business had finally been laid: exorcizing them had been a primary task of the reformers of Shakespearian production in the first decades of the twentieth century. Audiences no longer expected to see—and to greet as familiar friends—such moments as Hamlet's use of a handkerchief to wipe his hands after holding the skull, the grave-digger's removal of successive layers of waistcoats, Othello's attitude in collaring Iago and (in some cases) grasping his throat in III. iii ('Villain, be sure thou prove my love . . .': fig. 50), or the various elaborations of comic business with pipes and candles in the 'kitchen' scene in *Twelfth Night*.[16] The element of familiarity, the expectation that audiences would applaud during the progress of a scene, and the acceptance that the actor is never wholly sunk in the character are aspects of Victorian Shakespeare production that suggest its inclusion in a popular entertainment medium. Even in the more fashionable West End theatres, audiences were 'mixed', and the gallery-goers prided themselves on their ability to discriminate good acting from bad—and to make their feelings heard. At its best, Shakespeare was still (in John McGrath's term) 'a good night out'. The success of numerous burlesques and travesties, most of them relying on intimate knowledge of the plays and their performers, testifies to this.[17] But many pieces of business that function in the same way as the 'point' were indicative less of variations on custom than of a carefully planned interpretative composition.

One of the most famous of these moments, which used the full resources of the stage rather than simply the individual actor, was Henry Irving's depiction of Shylock's return to his house after the elopement of Jessica. After Jessica, Lorenzo, and the other Christians had left the stage in a carnival crowd there was a 'Very Quick' curtain. The curtain rose almost immediately: 'the stage was empty, desolate, with no light but the pale moon, and all sounds of life at a great distance— and then over the bridge came the wearied figure of the Jew.' As Shylock was about to enter the house, the act drop fell.[18] The isolation of Shylock as a lonely figure in a romantic picture was consistent with the painterly way in which Irving portrayed him throughout. A reviewer in the *Spectator* (8 November 1879) described his 'cold, slow smile, just parting the lips and touching their curves as light touches polished metal' which passed over the lower part of his face but did not 'touch the eyes or lift the brow'. This was 'one

FIG. 50 A famous 'point' in *Othello*: Gustavus Vaughan Brooke as Othello 'collaring' Iago (James Bennett). Engraving after a daguerreotype.

FIG. 49 A pathetic moment realized for the art-gallery: J. C. Northcote, *Hubert and Arthur* (*King John*, IV. i).

of Mr Irving's most remarkable facial effects' and he
could 'pass it through all the phases of a smile, up to
surpassing sweetness' (fig. 51). The same observer
found a suggestion of 'a Spanish painter's *Ecce Homo*' in
the final scene 'as he stood . . . with folded arms and
bent head, the very image of his exhaustion, a victim,
entirely convicted of the justice of his crime'. Under
Irving's management in the subsequent two decades,
the Lyceum was pre-eminently a theatre of romantic
images and his own figure not quite of this world and
not altogether on the side of the angels. Arthur
Symons, writing in the first decade of the new century,
placed Irving firmly among the symbolists rather than
realists: 'He has observed life in order to make his own
version of life, using the stage as his medium, and
accepting the traditional aids and limitations of the
stage.' Irving's Shylock, wrote Symons, was 'noble and
sordid, pathetic and terrifying . . . one of his great
parts, made up of pride, stealth, anger, minute and
varied picturesqueness, and a diabolical subtlety'.[19]

FIG. 52 Ellen Terry as Lady Macbeth, portrait by John Singer
Sargent.

FIG. 51 Henry Irving as Shylock, engraving after a line drawing
by Bernard Partridge.

Irving's temperament produced spectacle in which
his own figure was invariably a disturbing element. He
excelled in the uncanny. Macbeth, Mephistopheles (in
a version of Goethe's *Faust*), Iago, Iachimo, and other
haunted villains were his strongest parts; his Hamlet
and Romeo were touched with the quality, and in the
comic roles of Shakespeare he lacked the 'geniality'
which Victorian criticism associated with them. But
the primacy of pictorial effect in his theatre is entirely
consonant with the aesthetic of less complex actor-

managers of an earlier generation. The essential criteria, apart from skill in execution, were the extent to which the pictures realized were able to express a particular aspect of the play itself, and the harmony achieved between them and the production as a whole. In the former category, the depiction of character traits and of situations expressive of them was accorded a high priority. The Victorian sense of history, however, usually required that such moments should express the ethos of the historical circumstances as well as the predicament and character of the characters. One suspects that Irving created the wildness of Macbeth's Scotland as a context for his own Macbeth rather than—in the more conventional manner—a lesson in the history of those barbaric times.

Irving's 1888–9 production of the play at the Lyceum (he had appeared in the title-role there in 1875, but this was his first production under his own management) epitomizes *fin de siècle* Shakespeare. The settings were predominantly gloomy, illuminated by torches, flickering lightning, and lowering skies, amid which Macbeth and his wife appeared as vivid, tortured beings. Irving explained that Macbeth was 'a poet with his brain and a villain with his heart', a reading which prompted one reviewer to perceive his characterization as 'a more resolute and unscrupulous Hamlet'.[20] Ellen Terry's Lady Macbeth, thought by most critics to be too sensitive and 'womanly' for the evil she connives at, was first seen reading her husband's letter by the light of a blazing fire, a moment which clearly had the style of a Pre-Raphaelite painting. Her most impressive costume was a gown woven from a fine yarn obtained in Bohemia, 'a twist

FIG. 53 Irving's production of *Macbeth*, Lyceum Theatre, 1888–9.

of soft green silk and blue tinsel', decorated with 'real green beetle wings' and a 'narrow border in celtic designs, worked out in rubies and diamonds', and worn under 'a cloak of shot velvet in heather tones, upon which great griffins were embroidered in fine coloured tinsel'. A vivid red wig, with long plaits, was worn under a veil held in place by a circlet of rubies (fig. 52). Oscar Wilde observed that Lady Macbeth 'evidently patronises local industries for her husband's clothes and the servants' liveries, but she takes care to do all her own shopping in Byzantium'.[21]

The staging was organized round a series of emotional and pictorial climaxes, each showing the emotional and spiritual progress of the central couple. At the end of the banquet scene, as the dawn light crept into the hall 'Macbeth [took] a torch from behind a pillar, but suddenly, in a paroxysm, hurl[ed] it blazing to the ground,' and, throwing his cloak over his face, leaned against a pillar. Lady Macbeth fell at his feet and clung to him, 'sobbing, catching at his garment' (fig. 53). It was 'a picture of absolute despair', wrote one reviewer, 'that almost moves to pity for the blood-stained actors in it'.[22] It was characteristic of Irving that this agony, rather than any renewal of spirit in Macbeth (such as Macready had shown in his performances), should be the keynote of the scene, but the subsequent careers of the husband and wife diverged, he becoming hardened, she sinking into remorseful melancholy.

Productions like Irving's treated the plays of Shakespeare as a window onto the romantic past, valued for their poetry and character-drawing. The common assumption was that the dramatic construction of the texts was for the most part a consequence of the inadequate theatrical facilities available to Shakespeare, and that the vision which he sought to express could now be arrived at with an efficacy (and efficiency) he could not have envisaged. The actor-managers' scenography and their work in adapting the texts of the plays offered audiences yet another glimpse of the past, as reassurance that certain human and, specifically, national values could still be cultivated and recalled amidst so much rapid change.

Old Stages Revived

For many critics at the end of the century this was the 'modern' way of staging Shakespeare, a sign of the gradual perfection of a medium which Shakespeare's own age scarcely envisaged. But there was by now a movement of opposition to this theatre of progress, grounded in a desire to revive not merely the vision expressed by the plays, but the techniques themselves, refusing to treat them as a dispensable adjunct of the artistic effect. For these critics, the Elizabethan medium was the message, or at least a part of it. This was the spirit that William Morris had brought to arguing for a reversion to handcraft and the revival of half-forgotten ways of defining the act of making. Minutely detailed pictorial realism was no longer the goal of the *avant-garde* as it had been in the days of the Pre-Raphaelites and their followers. Artists in other media were increasingly absorbed by the opportunities offered for new kinds of expression, drawing on the stylization and symbolism of other artistic traditions.

The vehemence of the opposition to the imposition of scenic realism on Shakespeare was often considerable. In May 1893 William Poel set out his view of 'The Functions of a National Theatre' in the *Theatre*, a magazine directed to playgoers rather than the trade itself:

The extravagance of realism, so often thought healthy and natural, is with scarcely any exception only perverse sentimentality, only the expression, inartistic at best, of an enervated and distorted feeling, an extravagant and debased sentiment in comparison with which the sentiment of Shakespeare is truly refreshing and inspiring. Realism is exhausting and enervating in its effect, while idealism frequently avails to stimulate and fertilize.

This shows clearly the 'High Victorian' terms of the debate, with Poel attacking realism as inimical to plain living and high thinking. (Paradoxically these are the terms in which the magazine's editor Clement Scott, an arch-conservative and defender of Irving's methods, attacked the 'new drama' of Ibsen and his followers.)

There had been a remarkable experiment in the 1840s, when Benjamin Webster presented a virtually uncut text of *The Taming of the Shrew* in what were then thought to be 'Elizabethan' conditions, but the activities of Poel's Elizabethan Stage Society, beginning with his 1881 production of the First Quarto *Hamlet*, gave such ideas greater currency than they had hitherto enjoyed.[23] It would be many years before British audiences became accustomed to the reorganization of the auditorium so as to reproduce the effect of an acting platform surrounded by an audience: many of Poel's Shakespeare productions effectively showed a facsimile of the Elizabethan theatre to audiences seated in rows facing a scenic stage behind a proscenium arch. Poel's costuming was eclectic—faithful to the Elizabethan theatre's principles in this respect rather than straining for

absolute 'authenticity' in dress. He undertook to instruct his actors in a method of speaking Shakespeare's texts which would be musical without being orotund. In this, and in his use of an open, non-scenic stage, Poel was trying to recover lost techniques, and his collaboration with Arnold Dolmetsch indicates parallels with the growth of interest in what is now called 'Early Music' (fig. 54).

The influence of all this was evident in the less austere productions of Shakespeare staged by Harley Granville-Barker between 1911 and 1914. By building a forestage over the Savoy Theatre's orchestra pit, using stylized curtains and simple architectural structures as scenery, and insisting on brisker, less operatic speech and acting, Granville-Barker provided a stylish, brightly decorated Shakespeare.[24] In *A Midsummer Night's Dream* (1914) his fairies were gilded figures moving stiffly in hieratic patterns more reminiscent of oriental sculpture and dance than of the airborne, gauzy, chorines familiar from Victorian productions

FIG. 54 William Poel's First Quarto *Hamlet*, St George's Hall, 1881: 'Ofelia' in black, with a lute, on a reconstructed Elizabethan stage.

FIG. 55 *A Midsummer Night's Dream*, staged by Granville-Barker at the Savoy Theatre, 1914, with designs by Norman Wilkinson. A bare stage and decorated curtains represent Athens (top) and the wood (bottom).

(fig. 55 and col. pl. 4). The text was almost complete, and there was no rearrangement of the sequence of scenes: the direction and setting permitted the flow of action demanded by the open, unlocalized stages of the Elizabethan theatre. Unlike Poel's, these were Shakespearian productions in and of the fashionable theatre. Granville-Barker placed well-known and accomplished actors in central roles, but the texts were not rewritten to favour them, and the designs were fresh and colourful without the pictorial realism that would shackle the plays to a realistic style of acting.

Granville-Barker's Shakespeare, dubbed 'Post-Impressionist' by some critics, responded to a general movement in the visual arts towards stylization, abstract values of colour and space, and the rediscovery of 'primitive' forms and methods. The 'folk' element was there in the music and the dances (on which Cecil Sharp collaborated). The redefinition of Bohemia, Illyria, and the Wood near Athens is comparable to the exoticism and clarity of line and colour found in contemporary painting. To find analogies for a comparison of Granville-Barker with Poel, one might turn to the architecture and interior design of Charles Rennie Mackintosh or the Austrian and German Secessionists on one hand, and the Arts and Crafts historicism of William Morris and such architects as Philip Webb on the other. But both kinds of 'new' Shakespearian production moved decisively away from the elaborate pictorial realism of the mid-century, refusing to provide history lessons and point morals through elaborate pictorial tableaux. Shakespeare productions at the new repertory theatres, established to free the drama from the tyranny of the box-office, reflected this change in approach, and aesthetic preference was supported by the economic convenience of simplified staging.

Nevertheless, the old order survived in the popular theatre. Sir Frank Benson's touring company, bringing economically staged but recognizably 'traditional' Shakespeare to audiences throughout Britain and the Empire, is as representative of Edwardian Shakespeare as the more revolutionary work of Granville-Barker. Benson's vigorous personal performances, his indefatigable touring, and his part in establishing the annual seasons at the Memorial Theatre in Stratford-upon-Avon were of great importance in asserting theatrical production as a vital element in the appreciation of Shakespeare's work. Meanwhile, Sir Herbert Beerbohm Tree's lavishly pictorial and heavily cut productions and others like them continued to define Shakespeare for most theatre-goers. The conclusion of Tree's *Tempest* in 1904, spectacular, sentimental, and unashamedly actor-centred, was representative of his 'modern' method of staging Shakespeare. Prospero's ship is seen drawing away towards the horizon while Caliban watches from the island (col. pl. 5). Ariel's voice is heard, getting higher and higher, 'and gradually is transformed into a lark'.

At this moment, Caliban, who has been watching the departing ship, hearing the voice of the Lark, points in the direction from which the sound is coming, thus forming picture at which the curtain descends.[25]

Tree, of course, played Caliban.

7

European Cross-Currents: Ibsen and Brecht

INGA-STINA EWBANK

WHEN, in the year that saw the 400th anniversary of the birth of Shakespeare, the Royal Shakespeare Company staged the version of the first tetralogy which they called *The Wars of the Roses*, the 'thematic thinking' of the directors was English, if with a Polish undertow;[1] the design owed a great deal to Germany; and some of the most outstanding acting could historically have been seen to be indebted to a Norwegian whose plays helped to revolutionize English acting. That is, the Cambridge-educated directors carved a kind of unity out of Shakespeare's texts, to demonstrate the painful bringing to order of the disordered body politic, the pain in the process partly referred from Jan Kott's *Shakespeare our Contemporary*. Visually the production was the closest the Royal Shakespeare Company had yet come in Shakespeare to the 'epic' theatre of Brecht: the ubiquitous cart (fig. 56) seemed to come straight out of the production of *Mother Courage* with which the Berliner Ensemble had opened their visit to London in August 1956. And in the intense inwardness of Peggy Ashcroft's Queen Margaret, combined with an ability to show the weight of the past on the present as she grew from young bride to embittered ex-queen, there was more of Helena Alving (a part she was soon to add to her Ibsen repertoire) than of Helene Weigel.

Not that the total effect of *The Wars of the Roses* was the gallimaufrey—a kind of theatrical United Nations—which this may suggest. Since World War II

the English theatre has become adept at absorbing what it needs, and discarding what it does not want, from continental Europe. But thus anatomized, *The Wars of the Roses* may serve a twofold function. If, first, the production is a reminder of how much, if eclectically, Shakespeare in the modern English theatre reflects developments in European theatre, it may also, secondly, remind us that Shakespeare has played a major part in those developments. Allowing for exaggeration, there is an important core of truth in the statement that 'if Brecht is probably the most important playwright in the British Theatre since the war, Shakespeare is certainly the most important playwright in the German theatre since the Renaissance'.[2] And, ironically, although Brecht defined his theory and practice of theatre in reaction against the bourgeois, illusionist, 'emotion-addicted' theatre that he saw epitomized in Ibsen, and although Ibsen in his turn had come to shape his mature art in reaction against the Shakespearian tradition of nineteenth-century Germanic drama and theatre, there is little doubt that the experience of seeing and reading Shakespeare remained formative throughout the careers of both. Two apparently antithetical European influences on English Shakespeare may in the end be traceable back to Shakespeare himself.

The swirling of cross-currents does not, of course, allow itself to be reduced to as neat a pattern as the above paragraph may indicate. Many tomes would be

FIG. 56 The Royal Shakespeare Company in Brechtian mode: scene from *The Wars of the Roses* (1964), with battle-worn soldiers pulling a cart in the manner of Mother Courage.

needed to record the full history of Shakespeare in European theatre, from the days of the strolling English players in the sixteenth and seventeenth centuries to our own time. They would have to draw on the many excellent national or regional studies which already exist.[3] They would also have to attempt the almost impossible task of disentangling performed Shakespeare from the whole phenomenon of Shakespeare as a literary and cultural force in Europe from the second half of the eighteenth century onwards. In his massive study of the life and works of Shakespeare (which was widely read across Europe,

including the British Isles), the Danish critic Georg Brandes looked back over the nineteenth century and saw Shakespeare everywhere:

Modern German intellectual life is based, through Lessing, upon him. Goethe and Schiller are unimaginable without him. His influence is felt in France through Voltaire, Victor Hugo, and Alfred de Vigny. Ludovic Vitet and Alfred de Musset were from the very first inspired by him. Not only the drama in Russia and Poland felt his influence, but the inmost spiritual life of the Slavonic story-tellers and brooders is fashioned after the pattern of his imperishable creations. From the moment of the regeneration of poetry in the

North, he was reverenced by Ewald, Oehlenschläger, Bredahl and Hauch, and he is not without his influence upon Björnson and Ibsen.[4]

Before the almost paralysing effect of such a catalogue of names, nations, and genres—or of briefer, though no less expansive, assertions such as Oswald LeWinter's: 'The history of Shakespeare criticism on the Continent is the history of the development of European consciousness since the sixteenth century'[5]—the instinct is to seize the general through minute particulars. This chapter is an attempt merely to point to a general but shifting presence of Shakespeare in European theatre by concentrating on the theatrical context of two encounters with Shakespeare, almost exactly one hundred years apart, each involving one of the two dramatists who may well be said to have exerted the greatest influence on twentieth-century English theatre: Henrik Ibsen and Bertolt Brecht.

Ibsen and the German Shakespeare

In 1852 Ibsen, then aged 24, first saw Shakespeare on stage. His acquaintance with the plays was at that point much the same as that of thousands of young men in northern Europe: through translations in the vernacular which themselves were based as much on the great German Schlegel–Tieck translations as on the texts in English. His own first play, *Catiline*, written in the winter of 1848–9, shows that, like so many young authors across Europe, he had absorbed Shakespeare as mediated by German *Sturm und Drang*. Both thematically and formally the play—the product, as he was later to describe it, of being 'at war with the small community where I was desperately cramped by my own position and circumstances'[6]—owes more to Schiller's *The Robbers* than to any direct influence from Shakespeare. But as a Scandinavian he also knew that

Oehlenschläger had pronounced Shakespeare 'the colossus who should be the model for every modern dramatist';[7] and indeed the fellow student who reviewed *Catiline* on its publication in 1850 thought it 'Shakespearian' because of its 'strength and seriousness' and because 'just as much as . . . Shakespeare's *Coriolanus*' it opposed tyranny and repression.[8] A year as a student and *littérateur* in Christiania (Oslo), 1850–1, had brought no opportunity of seeing Shakespeare: the Christiania Theatre's repertoire (which he often reviewed) was dominated by Danish comedies and vaudevilles, with Scribe as the leading foreign author. In the autumn of 1851 Ibsen was appointed as 'dramatic author' and soon thereafter as 'stage instructor' at the newly founded Norwegian Theatre in Bergen (Norway's first National Theatre); and in the spring and summer of 1852 the theatre gave him a parsimonious stipend 'to take training abroad as a stage instructor'. In Copenhagen, at the Royal Theatre, which was more capable than the Christiania Theatre, let alone the still struggling Bergen Theatre, of maintaining a repertoire of 'classics' as well as vaudevilles, he saw a performance of *Hamlet* and probably also of a version of *As You Like It* (of which more later) as well as *Romeo and Juliet* and *King Lear*. From there he went via Hamburg to Dresden, which is where he enters a context of European Shakespeare.

Unfortunately Ibsen left no record of his experience of the Dresden Court Theatre—perhaps because he had little to gauge it against, no language for what he must surely have seen, nor anyone to tell it to. His letter to the management of the Norwegian Theatre merely complains of having to pay for admission to the theatre which 'it is obvious that I must visit regularly'.[9] If he did visit it regularly, he would have seen performances of three Shakespeare plays—*A Midsummer Night's Dream*, *Hamlet*, and *Richard III*—during the weeks in June and July of 1852 which he spent in Dresden.[10] What would he have seen?

By the 1850s the Dresden Court Theatre, though less famous than some of its counterparts in other German states and cities—Hamburg, Berlin, or Weimar, and later Meiningen—had a well-established Shakespeare tradition.[11] The appointment of Ludwig

Tieck as *Dramaturg* in 1824 had in some measure served to bring together Shakespeare as literature and Shakespeare as theatre—a dichotomy that had prevailed since Lessing's essays and Wieland's prose translations in the 1760s began the naturalization of Shakespeare in Germany and which was strengthened by Goethe's ambivalence about the performability of Shakespeare, in *Wilhelm Meister's Apprenticeship* (1796). When Friedrich Gundolf, in *Shakespeare und der deutsche Geist* (*Shakespeare and the German Spirit*, 1911), writes of August Wilhelm Schlegel's translations, the first of which appeared in 1797, as 'the re-birth of Shakespeare as a German language phenomenon', then the 'world-historical' impact he defines is general-cultural and literary rather than theatrical. But Tieck was interested both in text and stage. His Dresden years coincide with his completion of the Schlegel translation—in fact largely executed by Graf Boudessin and Tieck's daughter Dorothea—as well as with what he describes as a growing urge 'to discover a medium, to set up a theatre that architecturally approximates to the older English one, without entirely banishing painting and decoration'.[12] He left Dresden for Berlin in 1842, where he staged a fairly revolutionary production of *A Midsummer Night's Dream* (the first performance of this play in Germany), with an 'Elizabethan' upper level and inner stage combined with nineteenth-century 'painting and decoration' (fig. 57). This transferred to Dresden the following year and, hugely successful but without any lasting influence on the staging of Shakespeare, was still playing, in Schlegel's translation and with Mendelssohn's music, on 21 June 1852, when Ibsen would have seen it.

Tieck was less interested in the directorial side of the work, which had left the field open for the development of virtuoso playing by a few leading actors, notably Emil Devrient, nephew of the great Romantic actor Ludwig Devrient. For a short period in the 1840s (1844–6) Emil's brother Eduard served the Dresden Court Theatre as *Oberregisseur* (principal director). Unlike Tieck he combined the qualities of a dramaturge with the practical theatre sense of an actor-director; and unlike his egomaniacal brother—

who is said to have insisted that at no moment in a play was any other actor to come within less than three steps' distance of himself[13]—he attempted to educate the company in ensemble playing. Defeated directorially, he stayed on as literary adviser and actor until 1852, but the virtuoso system flourished; and Ibsen would have seen it at work in *Hamlet* and *Richard III*. He would have heard a fairly full text of each play, in the Schlegel translation—not the popular Schröder adaptation of *Hamlet*, a much abbreviated version with a happy ending for the Prince, which was used at the Court Theatre earlier in the century. Even so, the cast list for the *Hamlet* production described as 'neu einstudiert' (newly rehearsed) in January 1852 is not as full as that for Tieck's 1832 production: unlike Tieck's list this one has no Osric, no Reynaldo, and no Voltimand or Cornelius. Emil Devrient, we know, also wanted to cut the lines of Polonius as far as possible, to avoid distractions from his performance as the Prince.[14]

Emil Devrient played 550 different roles in Dresden, including most of the lead roles in the classical and contemporary repertoire. His Hamlet was known as a 'Mondscheinprinz', sweet, dreamy, leaning towards the sentimental. According to a contemporary, his delivery of 'To be or not to be' was like 'laying a bonbon on a plate before the audience'.[15] But here the cross-currents of Shakespeare in the theatre force us to make a detour, for Ibsen would not have seen Emil Devrient, who was at this very time in London, leading a troupe of German players in a guest season at St James's Theatre. They opened with Goethe's *Egmont* on 2 June, and with the queen and Prince Albert (who were to return for four more performances) in the audience. Henry Morley, who was also there, saw Emil Devrient's acting as 'the great triumph of the evening . . . [which] established thoroughly in London his title to the honours accorded him on the German stage'.[16] They went on to present a range of plays, including a compressed version of Goethe's *Faust*, Schiller's *The Robbers*, and *Hamlet* in Schlegel's translation.

Morley, interestingly, seems to have seen quite a different Hamlet figure from the one perceived by

FIG. 57 Ludwig Tieck's design for *A Midsummer Night's Dream*, Berlin, 1843.

Dresden audiences. No doubt this is because he was experiencing *Hamlet* through a foreign language—'The "Hamlet" of A. W. Schlegel is a wonderful translation', he writes, 'but the terse philosophy of Shakespeare is not to be fully translated'—and at the same time measuring it against Victorian expectations of how the title role should be acted. He missed the 'points of stage business familiar to the English, handed down by tradition from actor to actor, which the Germans have not been able to discover for themselves' (p. 49). Hence—ironically, in view of Emil Devrient's reputation in his own country—the production impressed him as an example of ensemble playing:

German acting does not rely at all upon 'points', and many passages which on our own stage are especially made to stand out of course fall back into the ranks. . . . Every line by every actor is studied with an equal care. This conscientious rendering makes it almost as difficult to extract from the actor as from the author any one-sided theory of Hamlet's character.

Even more ironically, while Morley admired Devrient's emotionalism, especially the way he 'marked very strongly Hamlet's natural affection for his mother', he quotes with approbation an overheard tribute to the unselfconsciousness of this most self-conscious actor: ' "The man is in his part" . . . "I do not believe he knows that he is acting" '. Emil Devrient was certainly conscious of success when he returned to Dresden, 'full of England', as Eduard somewhat wryly remarks in his diary, and of the opinion that he had 'created a space for ever, there, for German art'.[17]

The 'space' created was not as large as Emil Devrient liked to think: the effect of foreign visitors to the English stage in the nineteenth century seems on the whole to have been more inspirational than developmental. Clement Scott, the *Daily Telegraph* critic and Ibsen-hater, looks back over a row of such visitors; and, though he admits to having 'used Goethe's *Wilhelm Meister* as a textbook on Hamlet' and remembers having seen 'the celebrated Emil Devrient, supposed to be the greatest Hamlet who ever lived', he prefers the Hamlet of Sarah Bernhardt (who starred at the Adelphi in 1899) and turns his summary verdict into a list of national stereotypes:

So I begin to think, on the whole, that the French temperament is better for the play of *Hamlet* as acted before an audience than the philosophical German, the passionate Italian, the alert American, or the phlegmatic Englishman.[18]

Meanwhile, in Emil Devrient's absence from Dresden, the Hamlet and Richard III whom Ibsen would have seen were those of a no less striking—but strikingly different—actor, Bogumil Dawison. A Pole who had made his acting début in Warsaw in 1837 (at the age of 19), Dawison had decided to become a

German actor; he arrived in Dresden after successful engagements at the Hamburg Thaliatheater and the Vienna Burgtheater. He was formally appointed to the Court Theatre in 1854 (where after a few weeks Emil Devrient pulled out of every production in which Dawison was playing), but was a guest player there during the weeks of Ibsen's stay. Over the years he was to play a range of Shakespearian leads in the German theatre, not only the tragic heroes—Hamlet, Othello, Macbeth, Lear, Richard III—but also Shylock, Falstaff, and Benedick.[19] He came to Dresden at the peak of his early reputation, and as something of a shock, his Hamlet an amazing contrast to the Emil Devrient's idealist and dreamer. Eduard Devrient, who played Polonius to his Hamlet and Clarence to his Richard of Gloucester, noted in his diary how Dawison as Hamlet accentuated his own ugliness and how he played against his audience's expectations: 'his acting full of invention and variety, a talented eclecticism of styles, now truly natural, modest, sincerely emotional, now

FIG. 58 Bogumil Dawison as Richard III.

outrageous, coldly rhetorical, indifferent, colourless and wildly artificial'. Devrient was again bemused by the sheer range of Dawison's acting in the part of Richard III, from the 'frivolous, conversational' way in which he spoke 'I am determined to prove a villain', to the 'demonic energy' he displayed at the end of Act IV (fig. 58). Devrient has to admit that all this adds up to a remarkable whole ('eine bedeutende Totalität'), but he finds such variety in the role of Hamlet too disturbingly untraditional, simply modern eclecticism ('Sammelkunst'): 'He plays as Meyerbeer composes'. What disturbs Devrient most of all is the ironizing effect of Dawison's Hamlet: 'It is a mode of representation that plays with the role.' Contrasting Dawison's acting with the consistency and clarity of that of Seydelmann, the great virtuoso of the previous post-Romantic generation of German actors, Devrient fears that a state of decay is setting in: 'Dawison takes us straight into the modern English manner. Kean must have played like that.'[20]

Ibsen, of course, would have had little to compare Dawison with and, without Devrient's bias, is more likely to have reacted like Ludwig Speidel, the Viennese drama critic, who, writing in 1865, cannot forget how 'shattered' he was by Dawison's Richard III and how 'most profoundly moved' by his Hamlet. Especially arresting, he writes, were Dawison's handling of language and his sheer technical command of his art:

In his mouth, language which had been made stiff and numb by being declaimed was again made to flow and recovered the ability to bend and adapt to every movement of the mind, every turn of the intellect. . . . Never has an actor taken his art more seriously; no one has worked harder than he. He could give an account of each of his roles as detailed as a mechanic can give of a machine that he is building.[21]

Given the technical inexperience of his largely unsophisticated actors at the Norwegian Theatre in Bergen, Ibsen was not likely to return home with the intention to stage either Hamlet or Richard III. In the event, the only Shakespeare play with which he was ever involved in his capacity of stage instructor was the version of As You Like It which he had seen in

Copenhagen and which the Norwegian Theatre put on in September 1855. This was a radical rewriting, by the Danish dramatic translator Sille Beyer, of Shakespeare's original, turning it into a Scribean comédie-vaudeville along lines very similar to those with which George Sand was soon thereafter (1856) to adapt the same play in an attempt to introduce Shakespearian comedy to the Comédie-Française.[22] Independently conceived, both adaptations are a reminder of how Shakespeare's festive comedies were seen in mid-nineteenth-century Europe as—in the words of a Danish critic—'written for a bold Anglo-Saxon public' and 'not accessible to the modern dramatic or theatrical consciousness'.[23] Both adaptations minimize the part of Rosalind and maximize that of Celia, who in the end marries a Jaques whose role in the play has been much enlarged (and merged in Sille Beyer's version with Oliver, whom George Sand, who sees Jaques as a Molièran misanthropist, 'cet Alceste de la renaissance', writes off as a villain). Both therefore also virtually discard the cross-dressing and role-playing which is at the heart of Shakespeare's play. Charles Dickens, who saw George Sand's Comme il vous plaira in April 1856, found it like something got up 'by the Patients in an Asylum for Idiots': 'Nobody has anything to do but sit upon as many grey stones as he can. When Jaques had sat upon seventy-seven stones and forty-two roots of trees (which was at the end of the second act) we came away.'[24]

To their credit, though not for reasons of resenting what had been done to the original, Bergen audiences do not seem to have reacted much more favourably to Sille Beyer's Life in the Forest. Ibsen himself was developing a scorn for a 'Shakespeare' adapted to the tastes and the dramatic conventions of a different culture. The 1850s and early 1860s were for him a period of stock-taking vis-à-vis national culture and national consciousness, marked both by his own attempts at a national drama and by a series of combative articles. In both kinds of writing, there is a kind of undertow of concern for and with Shakespeare; his works are intertextually present in a play like Pretenders (1863) and act as a point of reference when Ibsen wrote on the state of the theatre in the Norwegian capital where, according to him, 'Shakespeare' had become a cultural status symbol. In an underdeveloped society like his own, he writes, 'the consciousness of being semi-educated produces a nightmarish fear of betraying one's lack of sophistication', and so critics and audiences have entered into a conspiracy to 'applaud and admire a bad production of a so-called Shakespeare play, although they only partly understand it. . . . That it is a perverse Shakespeare that is being offered, makes no difference, since they don't know the genuine one.' It is a statement that has often been made in other tongues and in less underdeveloped societies across Europe: the history of Shakespeare on stage has so much been one of adaptations that it is not always easy to distinguish genuine inspiration to creativity from 'perverse' appropriation.

In the voluntary exile during which he wrote most of the plays by which he is now known outside Norway, Ibsen clearly went on reading the 'genuine' Shakespeare, though always in translation (Danish or German) and never with any explicit interest in seeing the plays performed. As he found his own voice and dramatic form, he tended to articulate his position as a rejection of a Shakespearian tradition. When Edmund Gosse criticized him for not writing *Emperor and Galilean* in verse and 'not support[ing] the heroic dignity of the principal character', he replied: 'My new play is no tragedy in the old style' and 'We no longer live in Shakespeare's time'. In so far as 'Shakespeare' meant blank verse and historical subject-matter and great heroic individuals, he had to go; but it seems that Ibsen never lost interest in Shakespeare as a dramatist forever seeing two sides of the plight of human beings in society. Whether or not Ibsen had seen Bogumil Dawison's Hamlet and Richard III and grasped from him the possibility of 'playing with the role', he built just that kind of ironic awareness into the dramaturgy of his mature plays—not only into *Peer Gynt* (1867) but also into the 'realistic' prose plays firmly set in his own time. What is not always clear when Ibsen, in his turn, is appropriated through translations and reinterpretations, is that his famous 'realism' is in

crucial ways dialectical. We are not asked to lose ourselves in the emotional experience of his protagonist: however intense its inwardness and however strenuous his or her will to self-fulfilment, the play as a whole knows and sees more than the protagonist, from Nora in *A Doll's House* to Rubek in *When We Dead Awaken*. There is more 'genuine' *Coriolanus* in *An Enemy of the People* (1882) than in the *Catiline* that his young contemporary found so 'Shakespearian'. Sentimentalized versions of *An Enemy*—like Arthur Miller's, with its up-beat ending— obscure the hard-hitting irony of Ibsen's conception of a hero who is objectively justified in his action over the polluted bath-water but self-preoccupied and subjectively excessive in his veering towards a near-fascist belief in the élitist individual. The final stance of this 'enemy to the people' (*Coriolanus*, III. ii. 119) is both an echo of Coriolanus's 'Alone I did it' and a Brechtian 'gest', as—far from alone, as the stage directions insist on him being surrounded by his wife and children, who will obviously have to carry the burden of his stance— he exclaims 'The strongest is he who stands alone'.

Brecht and Coriolanus

Bertolt Brecht also thought about Shakespeare through most of his career—and, of course, left far more evidence of his thinking. Shakespeare figures in his earliest statements about theatre and, later, is prominent in the 'Messingkauf' dialogue (1937–40) and in the *Short Organum for the Theatre* (1948). Exactly a hundred years after Ibsen's visit to Dresden, Brecht was working on a production of *Coriolanus* and intending to put it in the repertoire at the Theater am Schiffbauerdamm in East Berlin.[25] Other work—such as the production of an eighteenth-century play (Lenz's *Der Hofmeister*)—was seen as merely preparatory, 'so as to cut a path through to

Shakespeare (without whom a national theatre is almost impossible)'.[26] But the intention was not realized, and in the end it was only in 1964 that the Berliner Ensemble staged an adapted version of Brecht's adaptation of *Coriolanus*. So ironically, in view of his impact on English Shakespeare, he never directed a stage production of a Shakespeare play (though in 1927 he adapted *Macbeth* for radio, and in 1930–1 *Hamlet*).

The reason why Brecht could see the staging of Shakespeare as both necessary and impossible is in many ways the same as that behind Ibsen's apparent rejection of Shakespeare: each found Shakespeare identified with a tradition inimical to his ideas of what drama and theatre should be and do. To neither was it a matter merely of style or form; but Brecht in Germany, far more than Ibsen in (and out of) Norway, was dealing with 'Shakespeare' as a national phenomenon in which political ideology and cultural and theatrical aspects were inseparably intertwined. Shakespeare was 'the basis of our great drama',[27] but 'the Shakespearean tradition common to German

FIG. 59 The Berliner Ensemble production of Brecht's *Coriolan*, 1964: the hero's triumphant return to Rome (Shakespeare's II.i). Helene Weigel as Volumnia and Ekkehard Schall as Caius Martius.

Facing: FIG. 60 Laurence Olivier as a heroic Coriolanus in Peter Hall's production, Shakespeare Memorial Theatre, 1959.

theatres [was] that lumpy, monumental style beloved of middle-class Philistines'.[28] Style, that is, was part of a political ideology that celebrated the potential of the individual, regardless of his social context, and that identified Shakespearian drama with the struggle of a single hero.

Brecht's work on *Coriolanus* has been much written about;[29] here we need only note how it focused on making the conflict between the hero and the Roman people meaningful in modern and Marxist terms. Brecht shifted what he saw as Shakespeare's tragedy of the individual to 'the tragedy of the individual's indispensability'.[30] Hence he reduced Coriolanus' motivations to strictly social ones, minimizing any inner conflicts and the complexities of the hero's relationship with his mother, his wife and his antagonist Aufidius. His Coriolanus abandons his attack on Rome because Volumnia informs him that Rome is united and prepared to defend itself.

Brecht's leading idea, which he discusses in journals and notes—that the play must be prevented from becoming the tragedy of the 'unersätzlich' (indispensable) individual—led him not only to make cuts and alterations to Shakespeare's text but also to add a final scene in which the Roman senate learns of Coriolanus' death but, after a brief silence, carries on with its daily business, which includes rejecting a

request from the Martius family to be allowed to wear mourning. His text ends on the one ruthless word, 'Abgeschlagen' ('Rejected') and the stage direction 'The Senate continues its normal business'.

Though his text was completed, Brecht broke off his work on the theatrical adaptation of *Coriolanus* in 1953, unable to feel satisfied that he had the cast and the mode of staging that would make it effective.[31] When the Berliner Ensemble, eight years after Brecht's death, finally put on *Coriolanus* (fig. 59), both the text and the underlying conception had been modified— in a sense readapted, as the Berliner Ensemble, in for example restoring much of Shakespeare's persuasion scene, attempted to combine psychological complexities of characterization with the style of the 'epic' theatre. After the première, a reviewer found that 'Brecht's departures from Shakespeare's text are not more numerous than the departures (often leading back to Shakespeare again) of the Brecht adaptors from the Brecht-text'.[32] So the pendulum swings, and who is in the end to say which is the more 'genuine' Shakespeare, and the more 'European': Laurence Olivier's 1957 heroic Stratford Coriolanus (fig. 60), with his emotion-provoking 'points', such as the death fall, backwards off the battlements, or Ian McKellen's at the National Theatre in 1984 (fig. 84), in which 'irony [was] the keynote of the performance'?[33]

8

From the Old Vic to Gielgud and Olivier

The Repertory Idea

THE rise of the repertory theatre in Britain is no less interesting for its heroism than for its achievement. Implied in the 'Repertory Idea' for the critic P. P. Howe, writing in 1910, was

a secession from the conventional theatre of those dramatic authors whose interest is in extending the scope of their art, in trying experiments and in satisfying their own sense of beauty and fitness ... rather than in ensuring the highest commercial return by subscribing to the conventional ideal of the longest possible run for the safest possible play.[1]

The first endeavour to put some features of the repertory idea into practice was initiated by Harley Granville-Barker, George Bernard Shaw, and J. E. Vedrenne, who opened a season at the Court Theatre in Sloane Square on 18 October 1904 with what Granville-Barker termed 'a stock season of the uncommercial Drama ... [which would] stake everything upon plays and acting—and not attempt "productions" '. Though the venture continued for only three seasons, Granville-Barker considered it a success, short runs keeping the plays 'more alive ... both from a business and an artistic point of view' than if they had been 'run callously to the fullest limit of their popularity'.[2]

Three decades had still to pass before state subsidy

for the arts was established, and the question of financial security for 'uncommercial Drama' remained paramount. Granville-Barker had secured the astute business acumen of Vedrenne for the three seasons at the Court, but sustaining repertory theatre in the early decades of the century would have to depend either upon subscription (as in the case of the Liverpool Repertory Theatre, backed by 900 shareholders when it opened on 20 February 1911) or upon a single patron, as in the cases of Manchester and Birmingham.

Annie Horniman came from a family of tea-merchants. Having inherited a substantial legacy in 1893 she first became involved as a patron of the Abbey Theatre in Dublin, her generosity spurred by her admiration for W. B. Yeats, who described the theatre's aims as being 'remote, spiritual and ideal'.[3] However, Miss Horniman was not accepted as being sufficiently identified with the cause of Irish nationalism, and so she transferred her patronage to Manchester where, with Ben Iden Payne as her artistic director, she set up her repertory company at the Gaiety Theatre opening on 7 September 1908, so giving British repertory theatre its true beginning. 'Miss Horniman's work', wrote St John Ervine, 'is widely known, but the woman herself remains almost unknown, not even, like Lilian Baylis of the Old Vic, a romantic legend, or, like Lady Gregory of the Abbey Theatre, Dublin, a romantic myth.'[4]

Alongside the growth of repertory theatre there developed a campaign for a National Theatre. As early as 1878 Henry Irving—though unashamedly opposed to the New Drama movement—had supported the National Theatre concept in a speech to the Social Science Congress. A year later, the Shakespeare Memorial Theatre opened at Stratford-upon-Avon, and it, too, was seen as part of the National Theatre plans. By the 1920s, then, the impulses behind the growth of British theatre were moving in two directions; one towards small decentralized repertory companies whose audiences were being exposed to the idea of plays as entertainment through the development of the cinema and, later, the accessibility of radio drama, and another towards centralization of a national repertory theatre, financed by national and municipal subsidy.

The Old Vic and Birmingham Rep

But with subsidy still no more than a vision, the evolution of the theatrical presentation of Shakespeare's plays in Britain during the first half of the twentieth century was essentially furthered by the dedication and energy of two remarkable and very different personalities, Lilian Baylis and Barry Jackson. In April 1914 the Old Vic (fig. 61) embarked upon the staging of Shakespeare with *The Merchant of Venice* (in which the 16-year-old Hermione Gingold appeared as Jessica) and *Romeo and Juliet*. The plays were directed by Rosina Filippi, a fiery and temperamental lady, whose tempestuous relationship with Lilian Baylis was not calmed by the poor resources with which she had to work. She complained after her final Old Vic Shakespearian production that she had had to stage

the plays 'with art muslin, two changes of scenery and two hired orange trees!'[5]

Lilian Baylis was not one to step back from a challenge, and there followed further Shakespeare productions on a precarious basis until the arrival of Ben Greet, who offered his services to Baylis as director. If his approach was somewhat rough and ready, there was certainly no lack of energy, and the most valuable quality that Greet possessed was something of a seaman's resourcefulness. 'He had', observed Margaret Webster, 'done the plays so often, in so many extraordinary ways and places . . . In the face of some particularly fearful or ludicrous happening, his eyes would twinkle with enjoyment' (Rowell, *The Old Vic*, 98), and by the time Greet relinquished his directorship in 1918, the Old Vic had established itself as a theatre giving regular seasons of Shakespeare to its audiences.

On 15 February 1913 Barry Jackson's Birmingham Repertory Theatre opened with a production of *Twelfth Night*. Having embarked upon a career as an architect, Jackson inherited his father's wealth at the age of 27 and devoted the rest of his life to the theatre. With his architectural training he personally supervised the design of the building, insisting on an intimate auditorium seating 464, with no seat more than 70 feet from the stage.

With Jackson's vision, enthusiasm, and secure financial backing, the Birmingham Repertory Company was able to be daring and experimental in its productions. He subsidized both revivals of the standard classics and works of new and controversial playwrights. His stated aim was 'to enlarge and increase the aesthetic sense of the public . . . to give living authors an opportunity of seeing their works performed, and to learn something from the revival of the classics; in short, to serve art instead of making that art serve a commercial purpose'. Shaw (whose *Back to Methuselah* had its première there, stretching its five parts over an entire week!) called the Birmingham Rep a place where 'all genuine artists have found themselves genuinely at home'.[6] Actors who made their mark there included Felix Aylmer, Leslie Banks, Cedric Hardwicke, Gwen ffrangçon-Davies,

FIG. 61 The view from the pit at the Old Vic, 1914: Matheson Lang and company in *The Merchant of Venice*.

and Noël Coward; Jackson also drew to his company Peggy Ashcroft, Edith Evans, and Laurence Olivier.

Robert Atkins had succeeded Ben Greet at the Old Vic, and advanced that theatre's standing as London's Shakespeare theatre by producing all the plays in the First Folio, concluding with *Troilus and Cressida* in November 1923. Atkins moved forward from the work of his predecessors by staging each play with a setting suited to its particular dramatic substance. He used curtains as part of the set, created imaginative lighting, and brought the action much closer to the audience by thrusting the acting area out in front of the proscenium. His use of a false proscenium covered in black velvet provided a 'neutral framework for non-representational settings' (Rowell, *The Old Vic*, 105). Doris Westwood has testified to his energy, describing his appearance in the crowd scenes on the first night of a production of *Coriolanus*, cueing in the musical effects as well as pushing the soldiers into correct stage positions. Together with the hectic directorial responsibilities he assumed for this production, he found the stamina to play Cardinal Wolsey, Sir Toby Belch, and Caliban, in the 1923–4 Shakespeare season.

In Birmingham the 1923–4 season was notable for the Repertory Theatre's production of *Cymbeline*. While the staging of the play was not particularly innovative (using upstage curtains, steps, and a proscenium in a well-tried three-space division), the characters wore modern dress. The reviewer for *The Times* wrote (with, one imagines, a slightly raised eyebrow) that Hardwicke's Iachimo was 'vital, subtle and never for an instant ridiculous',[7] and Crompton Rhodes writing in the *Birmingham Daily Post* felt that the modern costuming brought the audience 'closer to Shakespeare's mind than ever before'.[8]

Despite these mildly favourable responses, Jackson's experiments with new plays and new stagings of the classics did not readily win him substantial audiences, and at the end of the 1923–4 season, in a moment of bitterness, he transferred his company's work to the Kingsway Theatre in London. But a year later, as a result of public outcry, he reopened the Birmingham Repertory Theatre, and in 1925 he did what had not been dared before. He staged a modern-dress *Hamlet*, known to theatrical history as 'the plus-fours *Hamlet*'. It was a remarkably audacious move when one considers that Lilian Baylis had not yet secured reliable audience support for her Shakespeare seasons at the Old Vic and that William Bridges-Adams's Stratford company (founded in the same year as Jackson's Birmingham company), although led by Baliol Holloway and Randle Ayrton, whose work was far from consistently uninspired, was saddled with a somewhat tried and traditional style in the work of actors like Eric Maxon, C. Rivers Gadsby, Kenneth Wicksteed, and Stanley Lathbury, who 'had had years of playing Shakespeare—some of them rarely acted in anything else'. Sally Beauman cites a comment made to the influential reviewer, W. A. Darlington: 'Whenever I look back at Stratford, the stage seems to be occupied by Baliol Holloway making a speech, and somehow, whatever the play, the same speech.'[9]

In a newsletter circulated before the first performance of his modern-dress *Hamlet*, Jackson wrote of 'the essential modernity of Shakespeare's characters' and of the problems of ' "the man in the street" who comes to see a traditional production'.

The sublime unnaturalness of the blank verse, the strangeness of the costumes and the conventions of Shakespearean acting interpose a veil between him and the author's intention, and the man in the street comes away with an increased feeling of almost superstitious awe but with no understanding that he has been witnessing a real conflict of real human beings. It is with this end in view that we are producing *Hamlet* just as if it happened today.

(Cochrane, *Shakespeare at the Birmingham Repertory Theatre*, 129)

Jackson's subsequent modern dress productions included a 1927 *All's Well*, a *Macbeth* which opened on 6 February 1928, and *The Taming of the Shrew*, which opened on 30 April 1928 (fig. 62). In all of these later productions, Laurence Olivier appeared in relatively small parts. His Parolles in the *All's Well* (his first Shakespearian role for Jackson—and he was not yet 20) was remembered by some of his Birmingham colleagues as capturing 'both the grim humour of the role and the sympathy Parolles must evoke from the audience' (Spoto, *Olivier*, 55).

The Taming of the Shrew was generally considered especially successful because of the play's suitability for updating. As well as a Ford motor car (whose unpredictable behaviour might have been imported from a circus clown act) there were press photographers and a movie camera in the wedding scene. And despite a dashing Petruchio and a vigorously stubborn Kate, it was apparently 'Ralph Richardson who stole the show as Tranio, a cheeky cockney chauffeur in morning coat and silk hat'.[10] Norman Marshall, however, attributed the success of the *Shrew* experiment to the fact that the play was tedious and crude, so that 'it does not much matter what liberties the producer takes with it'![11]

Macbeth was altogether more difficult to stage in modern dress, and even Jackson had to admit to the first-night audience that 'experiments do have their failures'. Jessica Tandy recalled the production as being

FIG. 62 *The Taming of the Shrew* in modern dress, Birmingham Repertory Company, 1928. The aftermath of the wedding, with Scott Sunderland and Eileen Beldon as Katharine and Petruchio. Ralph Richardson (Tranio) is fifth from the left, with top-hat and cane.

'pretty dire', but that 'whenever [Olivier] came on as Malcolm the whole stage came to light' (Holden, *Olivier*, 52). Norman Marshall ascribed the failure of the *Macbeth* less to the production than to the intractability of the play's 'primitive barbarous setting' and the incongruity of its poetry in a modern ambience (Marshall, *The Producer*, 175–6). There is, however, evidence to suggest that the production was not considered on all counts a failure. The *New Statesman* reviewer considered it 'on the whole, the best production of *Macbeth* I have ever known' and he judged the modern dress and setting as revealing to the audience 'a living drama of extraordinary beauty and power'.[12] Jackson's programme note announced the intention behind the production as being to 'give to the tale of old unhappy far-off things the vividness and actuality of present day happenings' (Cochrane, *Shakespeare at the Birmingham Repertory Theatre*, 171).

Othello, which opened on 23 February 1929, was the last of the Birmingham Rep's series of modern-dress stagings. Crompton Rhodes in the *Birmingham Daily Post* acknowledged that Othello's psychological disintegration gained in authenticity from the updated costuming, but found the setting to be restrictive,[13] and if the *Shrew* was perhaps the most vigorously successful of Jackson's modern-dress productions with local audiences, it was the 'plus-fours' *Hamlet* that brought international renown to Jackson and his director, H. K. Ayliff, with Ayliff being invited to direct a Vienna production soon after.

Ayliff, who directed the modern-dress Shakespeares between 1925 and 1928, deserves wider recognition. James Bridie wrote of his impact on the British theatre: 'Actor after actor leapt to the top of his profession under his command, or as a result of his command. Their illustrious names are as bright as any in our theatrical history . . . and the debt they owe him has not yet been paid.' Paul Scofield remembered his 'terrifying warning signal for the unwary and inept— he sat at rehearsal with legs crossed at the knee and when displeased would swing the upper leg and foot like a pendulum of doom. We all recognised the signal and trembled.' Ayliff worked with Jackson's resident set designer, Paul Shelving, but clearly he did not find

delegation of responsibilities easy. Setting his own lighting and plotting actors' moves well before rehearsals, he gave productions a stamp of 'careful and unobtrusive quality'.[14]

1929 saw the appointment of Harcourt Williams as theatrical director at the Old Vic. The particular qualities which Williams brought to the Shakespeare productions were 'vitality and attack matched by swiftness in scene-changing' (Rowell, *The Old Vic*, 115). But he also chose his leading actors with a view to breaking a tradition of type-casting. Edith Evans played eleven leading parts in nine months, bringing considerable financial success to the company, and John Gielgud was the company's male lead.

The rapid pace of his first two productions (*Romeo and Juliet* and *The Merchant of Venice*) drew the complaint that they were gabbled. Williams, a reticent and serious-minded man, promptly offered his resignation, which Lilian Baylis characteristically—and rightly—refused to accept. Williams's reputation grew steadily with Gielgud's Richard II and Macbeth, and was finally and firmly established with Gielgud's 1929 Hamlet, the first Old Vic Shakespeare production to be transferred to the West End.

Harcourt Williams's last two seasons as Lilian Baylis's director brought Gielgud and Richardson together in a run of strongly played partnerships— Hotspur and Hal, Richard and Bolingbroke, Prospero and Caliban, Antony and Enobarbus, Malvolio and Toby Belch, Lear and Kent. Ralph Richardson won success as Bottom, the Bastard Faulconbridge, and— more surprisingly—as Henry V. Audiences were treated to more of the astounding versatility of Edith Evans, who in the 1930–1 season played both Emilia to Richardson's Iago, and Viola. The 1932–3 season saw Peggy Ashcroft as Imogen, Rosalind, Portia (in a production designed for the Old Vic by Gielgud and Motley), Perdita, Juliet, and Miranda.

The career of Peggy Ashcroft as a Shakespearian actress gathers its momentum in the last three decades of our period, being launched in Maurice Browne's 1930 production of *Othello* at the Savoy. Paul Robeson, it seems, was underdirected as Othello, but the 23-year-old Peggy Ashcroft was identified as one of the bright lights in the production. The *Observer* reviewer, Ivor Brown, described her Desdemona in the purple prose characteristic of much reviewing at this time as 'a true woman opening the petals of her wonder and her love to the African sunlight of her hero's triumph'.[15] There followed her Juliet in Gielgud's 1932 production of *Romeo and Juliet* for the Oxford University Dramatic Society. The production was significant above all for its aggregation of names that were later to become central in the British theatrical establishment. With Gielgud and Peggy Ashcroft, there were George Devine, Edith Evans, Hugh Hunt, and William Devlin. The designs were by the Motley team, whose reputation was growing. The set was 'a triple arched affair backed with drapes and a central raised doorway . . . economical but effective' in affording 'fluency of action' and dynamic pace. Among the London critics who acclaimed the production was Darlington, who wrote of the quality of verse speaking by the student actors, who had obviously learned it from Gielgud, and of the genuineness of Peggy Ashcroft's Juliet as being 'passionately in love' (Billington, *Peggy Ashcroft*, 49–50).

The cast included Terence Rattigan, one of the musicians with the single line, 'Faith, we may put up our pipes and be gone.' To Rattigan's dismay, the line coming soon after Juliet's supposed death attracted a prolonged and—as he rightly felt—an entirely inappropriate laugh no matter how he tried to vary its emphasis. He ended up with an inaudible muttering of the line, but later incorporated it, with obvious feeling, in his own play, *Harlequinade*.

In bringing Gielgud, Richardson, and Peggy Ashcroft into the company relatively early in their careers, Harcourt Williams had no doubt done as much for them as for the stature of the Old Vic. The company's next director was to be distinct from his predecessors in his not being an actor. He was Tyrone Guthrie.

Gielgud's Romeo and Juliet

Gielgud's 1935 revival of *Romeo and Juliet* at the New Theatre (fig. 63) was highly significant for two reasons. While much contemporary critical interest centred on the very different approaches of the two leading actors, Gielgud himself, and Olivier, to the speaking and projection of Shakespeare's verse, the interest for modern theatre historians lies in Gielgud's meticulous integration of all aspects of the staging with the textual and subtextual rhythms in the play.

By 1935 Gielgud had a wealth of experience and acclaimed performances behind him. He had played Hamlet in 1929 (at the Old Vic and then in transfer at the Queen's Theatre) and again in 1934 (fig. 64), at the New Theatre (now the Albery). James Agate found his first Hamlet 'noble in conception . . . thought out in the study and . . . lived upon the stage, with the result that these things are happening to Hamlet for the first time and that he is here and now creating words to express new-felt emotion'.[16] The critics were less impressed with the 1934 revival, judging it, in Agate's phrase, as 'Everest half-scaled'.[17] The queues outside the New Theatre proclaimed a different verdict, articulated in J. C. Trewin's judgement of the production (directed by Gielgud) as 'the key Shakespearean revival of its period'.[18]

Thus at 31 Gielgud had established himself not only as the outstanding Shakespearian actor on the English stage, but also as a theatrical director and as a performer whose range of interpretative brilliance embraced a broad spectrum of classical as well as modern roles. His two Hamlets, together with acclaimed successes as Romeo, Richard II, and Macbeth, seemed to invest him with the mantle of a definitive Shakespearian style. But he retained a shrewd eye for talented style different from his own, and having seen Olivier on stage and having directed him in Gordon Daviot's *Queen of Scots* the previous year, Gielgud offered Olivier the chance to play opposite him, he and Olivier alternating the roles of Romeo and Mercutio. And so was launched a production in which the theatrical priorities of the two leading actors were so different that some have chosen to consider the clashes inherent in the play eclipsed by a clash of cultures in the approach to Shakespeare on the English stage.

Whatever artistic intuition had its part to play in the development of Olivier's iconoclastic characterization of Romeo, there was, as Olivier himself later admitted, a rebelliousness '[against] John's power and gifts'.[19] Olivier, it seems, was not merely bringing a new and vigorous naturalism to a Shakespearian role; he was making an immense statement about the social status of the actor in classic roles on the English stage. Critical reaction to the opening performance of the production at the New Theatre on 17 October, while generally approving of Gielgud's traditional Mercutio, displayed a predictable distaste for Olivier's failure to project the poetic potential in the lines. James Agate, while conceding that Olivier's Romeo was 'the most moving I have ever seen,' went on to complain at some length about his delivery of the lines.

The spoken part of the poetry eluded him. . . . He brought off a twofold inexpertness which approached virtuosity— that of gabbling all the words in a line and uttering each line

FIG. 63 John Gielgud's production of *Romeo and Juliet*, New Theatre, 1935: Laurence Olivier and Peggy Ashcroft in the balcony scene. Designs by Motley.

as a staccato whole cut off from its fellows. In his early scenes this Romeo appeared to have no apprehension of, let alone joy in, the words he was speaking.

At a deeper level than that of technique, however, there emerges from Agate's response a question about just what the ontology of a play—or a dramatic character—is. Olivier would no doubt have answered that a play exists essentially in performance and that a dramatic character exists in the opportunities which the text allows for the actor to create the role along the lines of a particular authenticity. Agate, on the other hand, would seem to suggest that there is a textual authority and there is a legitimate authorial intention:

Throughout one wanted over and over again to stop the performance and tell the actor that he couldn't, just couldn't, rush this or that passage . . . what is the use of Shakespeare's writing such an image as 'The white wonder of dear Juliet's hand' if Romeo is not himself blasted with the beauty of it?[20]

But while Olivier chose to see his Romeo as universally 'hammered', St John Ervine was moved by 'Mr Olivier's Romeo . . . [an] impetuous boy, struggling to be articulate . . . I think [Shakespeare's] eyes would have shone had he seen this Romeo, young, and ardent and full of clumsy grace.'[21] Trewin found a compelling exotic energy in the characterization of Olivier's Romeo, who 'olive-skinned, impetuous, adolescent, entered straight from Renaissance Italy, a world of hot sun, sharp swords and brief lives'. Jessica Tandy spoke later of the work the actor put into the details necessary for attaining momentary visual effects, bending his fingers back 'so that in the balcony scene the visual line from fingertips to neck would be pure. Already', she observed, 'he understood style in a way few actors do.'

Standing to one side of those opinions which lamented the scant regard for spoken poetry on the one hand, and those which found compensation in the power and the emotional accessibility of Olivier's portrayal on the other, was the uneasiness of W. A. Darlington about whether Olivier's characterization could at all points find an accommodation within the poetic conventions of Shakespearian drama: 'One felt sure that this Romeo would never have consented to

stay down in the garden [in the balcony scene] speaking blank verse; he would have swarmed up a pillar and taken Juliet in his arms, and where would your Willie Shakespeare have been then?'[22] Overall critical response, as was understandable, considered Olivier's energetic characterization much more convincing in his Mercutio. On his line 'A sail, a sail . . .' he raised the Nurse's skirt with the point of his sword, a piece of business (taken up and expanded upon in Zeffirelli's 1967 film) which apparently dumbfounded Edith Evans.

Inevitable comparisons emerged. Agate felt the production suffered from the 'almost embarrassing clash of magnanimities', Gielgud deliberately trying to conceal his estimate of 'Mr Olivier's diction in the Queen Mab speech', and Olivier playing down Mercutio's death throes 'to permit us a glimpse of Romeo's contrition'. Of the two Romeos he wrote,

Mr Olivier's Romeo showed himself very much in love but rather butchered the poetry, whereas Mr Gielgud carves the verse so exquisitely that you would say the shop he kept was a *bonne-boucherie*. Yet is this Romeo ever really in love with anyone but himself? . . . I have a feeling that this Romeo never warms up to Juliet until she is cold.[23]

Peggy Ashcroft, playing Juliet, had seemed (understandably) to prefer Olivier's more robust attack on the role in the love scenes, though she felt that Gielgud retained a readier flow of support from the audience. Gielgud, always gracious and generous, wrote in his memoirs in 1947 with wonderful objectivity:

Larry had the advantage over me in his vitality, looks, humour and directness. . . . As Romeo, his love scenes were intensely real and tender, and his tragic grief profoundly touching. I had an advantage over him in my familiarity with the verse, and in the fact that the production was of my own devising, so that all the scenes were arranged just as I had imagined I could play them best. I enjoyed the lightness and gaiety of [Mercutio] . . . But I was again disappointed with my performance as Romeo.[24]

And in 1967 Olivier, speaking to Kenneth Tynan, referred specifically to the 1935 *Romeo and Juliet* with a hint of lingering rebelliousness in his words: 'When I

FIG. 64 John Gielgud as Hamlet, Laura Cowie as Gertrude: New Theatre, 1934.

was playing Romeo I was carrying a torch, I was trying to sell realism in Shakespeare.' He thought that Gielgud 'was paying attention—to the exclusion of the earth—to all that music, all that lyricism . . .'.[25]

Engaging though the issue of Olivier's challenging characterization of Romeo in this production remains, the essential significance of the 1935 *Romeo and Juliet* emerges from research which has pieced together

Gielgud's priorities in production. In the incredibly short rehearsal period of three weeks, Gielgud had the advantage of being able to draw on his earlier successful production for the Oxford University Dramatic Society. Edith Evans and Peggy Ashcroft played the Nurse and Juliet respectively. For the set, Gielgud again relied on the Motley team who had costumed the play for OUDS. As at Oxford, he

presented an almost uncut text in order to 'convey
the poetry of the play's design and language'.[26] In
designing a permanent set which allowed the action
to flow continuously and to develop both pace and
contrasting rhythms for the 'rapid alternation of
tragic action between public and private, large and
small spaces', Motley concentrated primarily on the
placing of the balcony. The central structure of the
set was a tower, angle-on to the audience so that with
platforms its two walls could support action on
different levels, and so allowing fluency of action as
the Elizabethan stage would have afforded, but at the
same time giving a modern audience a sense of place
for the action. What Gielgud strove to do was to
make the text work palpably on the stage, to project
the intricate relationship of language with mood and
action, so that the complexities 'became audible,
visible and even physical as they must have been on
Shakespeare's stage' (Levenson, *Romeo and Juliet*, 60).

In their costume designs, too, Motley strove to be
both clear and subtly articulate. Gielgud's choice of
the Italian Renaissance afforded Botticelli and
Carpaccio as pictorial models. Colour was used to
distinguish the two families, the Montagues being
given an aristocratic assertion while the bourgeois
Capulets were more sombrely dressed. To highlight
the contrast between youth and age which runs
through the play, the younger generation were given
'light, fresh, clear colours . . . shades of spring rather
than summer', while the changing fortunes and
psychological states of the lovers were suggested by
changes of costume, 'Romeo's appearance [in Mantua
becoming] emblematic of his desperation and exile: a
blood-red tunic . . . with dark blackberry-coloured
tights and boots for travel' (Levenson, *Romeo and Juliet*,
60–1).

Of this production, historically significant both for
its two distinctively characterized Romeos and for the
meticulous detail of its staging, there remains one
memorable comment which stands out like a jewel.
It comes again from Darlington, who found Edith
Evans's Nurse 'as earthy as a potato, as slow as a cart
horse and as cunning as a badger' (Holden, *Olivier*, 113).

Guthrie and Wolfit

One of those who saw and complimented Olivier's
Romeo with fulsome praise was Tyrone Guthrie, in
the year after his first brief appointment as director of
the Old Vic Company. It appears that his work during
the 1933–4 season was blighted by uncertainties of trust
between himself and Lilian Baylis. Guthrie brought
into the company Charles Laughton and his wife, Elsa
Lanchester, and Flora Robson. Laughton's Angelo to
Robson's Isabella made *Measure for Measure* the most
successful of the three Old Vic Shakespeare productions
of the season. Laughton's Macbeth was so disappointing
that Lilian Baylis made the devastating comment (for
which the actor never forgave her), 'I'm sure you did
your best. And I'm sure that one day you may be quite
a good Macbeth' (Rowell, *The Old Vic*, 122).

Neither Guthrie nor Lilian Baylis being small-
minded, he accepted reappointment as director of the
Old Vic in the autumn of 1936, and she welcomed him
back. Indeed, after her death in 1937 it was effectively
Guthrie who guided the fortunes of the Old Vic for the
next ten years. To relieve pressure on the company's
leading actors, he advanced the practice of special
engagements, making it possible to attract a range of
established big names. Edith Evans, Laurence Olivier,
Emlyn Williams, and Ralph Richardson played leading
roles for Guthrie, and the supporting roles were cast
with actors of appropriate calibre. In consolidating the
schedules of drama at the Old Vic, Guthrie prolonged
the runs to a maximum of six weeks, and he was able
to mount more extravagant productions. His
Christmas 1937 *A Midsummer Night's Dream* (fig. 65) not
only employed the full acting company, but also the
orchestral and ballet resources of the theatre. Robert
Helpmann played Oberon, with Vivien Leigh as
Titania and Ralph Richardson as Bottom. 'The
wood,' wrote the reviewer for *New Statesman
and Nation*, 'is convincingly romantic, the palace

FIG. 65 Tyrone Guthrie's 'twopence coloured' production of *A Midsummer Night's Dream*, Old Vic,
1937, with Robert Helpmann as Oberon.

is worthy of the Bibienas, and Quince's house is
equally delightful. The finale, with fairies flying with
lighted tapers, is triumphant. Altogether this is the
prettiest as well as the most amusing of Christmas
entertainments.'[27] Darlington judged Richardson's
Bottom as 'never pushful and eager, thrusting his
mates out of the way. He is impelled in front of them
by his own quiet certainty, which they [share] as often
as not, that he is right.'[28] It was of all Guthrie's Old Vic
productions the one which commanded the greatest
popular appeal.

In 1930 Harley Granville-Barker had produced a
small publication, *A National Theatre*. In it, he
envisaged a three-auditorium theatre situated on the
South Bank, its separate audience capacities being
remarkably close to those of the present Royal
National Theatre. Olivier's Hamlet early in 1937, his

Macbeth in the same year, his Iago to Richardson's
Othello, and his Coriolanus to Sybil Thorndike's
Volumnia, all brought to the company's Shakespeare
productions a level of vigorous critical response and a
standing which no doubt established it as the
foundation for the realization of Granville-Barker's
vision, for on 10 March 1939 a meeting between the
Old Vic governors and the Shakespeare Memorial
National Theatre Committee minuted a conditional
proposal that the Old Vic Company offer its planning
expertise in return for its being ultimately housed in
the National Theatre building.

If the decade of the 1930s was one during which the
performance of Shakespeare's plays became a firmly
established feature on London's theatrical landscape, it
was also a fertile period for British Shakespearian
activity in two other respects. One was the energetic

touring commitment embarked upon by Donald Wolfit's company, founded on 11 October 1937.

'There has never been', wrote Kenneth Tynan, 'an actor of greater gusto than Wolfit.'[29] Both gusto and indomitability are enshrined in the bill which announced 'Donald Wolfit with his Shakespearean Company and Phyllis Neilsen-Terry' and then confronted its prospective public with a first weekly schedule:

Monday evg.	*HAMLET*
Tuesday evg.	*THE MERCHANT OF VENICE*
Wednesday evg.	*MACBETH*
Thursday evg.	*THE MERCHANT OF VENICE*
Friday evg.	*MACBETH*
Saturday mat.	*HAMLET*
Saturday evg.	*THE TAMING OF THE SHREW*

Plays directed by Andrew Leigh.[30]

During his first five years as an actor-manager, Wolfit's roles included Macbeth, Hamlet, Othello, Shylock, Petruchio, Benedick, Richard III, Falstaff (in *The Merry Wives*), Malvolio, and Touchstone. Of his comedy roles, Tynan distinguished his *Merry Wives* Falstaff as 'easily the best low performance I have seen him give' (Tynan, *He that Plays the King*, 41). His first attempt at Lear, in August 1942, disappointed Wolfit but he felt sufficiently assured in the spring of 1944 to tackle the role again (fig. 66). It was James Agate who led the critical acclaim. 'I say deliberately that his performance on Wednesday was the greatest piece of Shakespeare acting I have seen since I have been privileged to write for the *Sunday Times*' (Harwood, *Wolfit*, 166). Tynan, writing in retrospect, remembered the special poignancy of the end of Act I. After cursing Goneril, Wolfit's Lear exits

with a dogwhip in his left hand and his right resting for comfort on the Fool's shoulder . . . an irresistible tug to the tears he has so carefully delayed in us throughout the scene; we are prepared for the hurricane in his lungs which later, on the heath, threatens to scorch the stage.

(Tynan, *He that Plays the King*, 41)

Facing: FIG. 66 Donald Wolfit as King Lear.

If Wolfit managed to accomplish the agenda set by Agate for the actor playing Lear, who 'must make us feel in the heath and hovel scenes, that we are in the presence of a flaming torch beside which Michaelangelo and Bach are but tapers' (Harwood, *Wolfit*, 153), his Macbeth drew less concerted praise. While Tynan remembered it as displaying 'overwhelmingly and consistently the effect of a tenebrous obsession eating away the heart of a warrior' (Tynan, *He that Plays the King*, 41), Agate concluded that 'Mr Wolfit's Macbeth fails because the character does not lie in the actor's personality. Because no actor can be Macbeth who deprives him of his poetry, introspection, vacillation and remorse' (Harwood, *Wolfit*, 153). Perhaps it is as much for broadening the spectrum of acting on the English stage as for his individual performances that Wolfit's contribution to staged Shakespeare is significant. 'Wolfit and Gielgud', Ronald Harwood maintains,

represented the two extremes of the wide spectrum of styles . . . Wolfit embodied the heroic, earthy force; Gielgud the lyrical and aesthetic. Between these two extremes existed a whole range of performers embracing styles that, to a lesser or greater extent, combined the two. (Harwood, *Wolfit*, 95)

The Shakespeare Memorial Theatre

The other significant event which illuminated Shakespearian activity in the 1930s was the reopening of the Shakespeare Memorial Theatre, in the new building which replaced that destroyed by fire in 1926, and which Sir Edward Elgar, after being given a special introductory tour, dismissed with the hope that he might never see it again.

The Shakespeare Memorial Theatre had first opened in Stratford-upon-Avon in the spring of 1879. It functioned during its first forty years as a venue for touring companies and as the home for a summer

FIG. 67 Cinematic realism for the new theatre at Stratford-upon-Avon, 1932: a London street in *2 Henry IV*, built on the 'rolling stage' and moved past the proscenium opening.

festival. In 1918 the New Shakespeare Company was established at the Stratford theatre with William Bridges-Adams as its first director. The theatre's destruction by fire on 6 March 1926 has been considered by some 'a lucky accident for Stratford' in bringing the summer Shakespeare festivals to the attention of the world, and so making it possible to raise international funds for the rebuilding of the theatre.[31] The new building opened on 23 April 1932 with a production of the two parts of *Henry IV* (fig. 67). By all accounts it was not an energetic start. Darlington complained of a 'dull and spiritless production' with actors who 'were tired out', and A. E. Baughan reviewing the production for the *Era* faulted the management on not allowing sufficient rehearsal time for the production of seven plays in a season of five weeks.[32]

The lingering fashion 'for melodious periods and graceful cadences, rather than the more rugged manner of speaking verse' was no doubt part of a general expectation that Stratford Shakespeare should be, in some sense, 'classic' Shakespeare. It is not surprising, therefore, that the Russian *emigré* director Theodore Komisarjevsky's productions of *The Merchant of Venice* and *Macbeth* for Bridges-Adams

failed in the 1930s to earn the recognition they deserved. Komisarjevsky was an important innovator at Stratford by virtue of his giving his set designs a thematic articulation. The set for his *Merchant* included 'gaily painted, frankly artificial scenes of Venice [which] at the end of the first scene . . . split down the middle' to reveal Belmont and Portia's garden. For *Macbeth* the set design was expressionistic, a jagged texture created by angular and twisted pieces of aluminium with atmospheric lighting. The *Telegraph* reviewer wrote of 'a baleful atmosphere in which murders and horrors seem to have their natural habitation', but several critics focused their dislike on the aluminium, Ivor Brown 'because no temple-haunting martlet would nest in it' (Beauman, *The Royal Shakespeare Company*, 126, 131–2).

The simmering acrimony between Bridges-Adams and the chairman of the theatre's governors, Archie Flower, culminated on 15 April 1934 with Bridges-Adams's resignation. Ben Iden Payne succeeded as director of the SMT and during his eight-year tenure Komisarjevsky directed a *Merry Wives* which caused predictable outrage and a *King Lear* with Randle Ayrton as Lear on a virtually bare set which relied on variation of lighting for mood effects (fig. 68). Perhaps

Iden Payne's bravest decision was to cast Wolfit as the Prince in his 1936 *Hamlet*. The critics who praised Wolfit's Hamlet did so more with acknowledgement than with enthusiasm. 'What it lacked in grace,' wrote Robert Speaight, 'it made up in guts' (Brock and Pringle, *The Shakespeare Memorial Theatre*, 62). The incongruity of Wolfit in the role did not escape James Agate, who found this Hamlet's reluctance to settle accounts with his uncle 'almost as inexplicable as it would be in the case of a heavy-weight boxer or a Woolwich Arsenal centre forward' (Beauman, *The Royal Shakespeare Company*, 151), and Tynan, perceptive as always, looked back on Wolfit's 1944 revival of the role as 'a fascinating but fruitless adventure into realms where he may not tread' (Tynan, *He that Plays the King*, 41).

At the end of the 1937 season, the public disquiet which had been prompted by the resignation of

Bridges-Adams found a voice in Darlington, who complained that the new theatre was being run on the same basis as the old one, the authorities having failed to adjust themselves to new conditions and to the possibility of running longer, steadily profitable seasons. The management strategies continued to be governed by Archie Flower's stubborn insistence on a low-risk financial policy, with the inevitable consequence that imaginative directors laboured under what they felt were constantly frustrated artistic ambitions. There is evidence, too, to suggest that, in avoiding experimentation, the theatre was failing to find for Shakespeare's plays a modern social and political relevance. An instance was Payne's 1939 *Coriolanus*, which revealed no awareness of the play's potential for reflecting European politics of the late 1930s (fig. 69). Political argument was cut and the

Fig. 68 Expressionist stylization at Stratford: *King Lear* designed and directed by Theodore Komisarjevsky (1936), with Randle Ayrton as the King.

FIG. 69 Stratford Elizabethanism, 1939: *Coriolanus*, directed by William Bridges-Adams with designs by J. Gower Parks. Alec Clunes as Caius Martius, with Dorothy Green (Volumnia) and Lesley Brook (Virgilia).

costuming was, where period could be identified, Elizabethan.

Iden Payne was succeeded at the end of the 1942 season by Milton Rosmer, who was followed after one unpropitious season by Robert Atkins. But the much sought and longed-for shift in the Stratford theatre's priorities came on 12 April 1944, with the replacement of Archie Flower by his son Fordham as chairman of the governors, and it was in the post-war years with Barry Jackson as its artistic director that Stratford swung its bows to the sea and began to assert itself as having a distinctively innovative approach. A turning-point in the theatre's artistic priorities was signalled with the young Peter Brook's 1946 production of *Love's Labour's Lost* (fig. 70). Jackson's invaluable legacy to the theatre was his opening doors to young energetic talent, and there began to emerge, under his post-war leadership, a balance of young actors (Paul Scofield, and Albert Finney among them) with established names (Michael Redgrave, John Gielgud, and Peggy Ashcroft). His resignation at the end of the 1948

season, though clouded with some acrimony, was part of a logical process, allowing one of those he had nurtured in the Stratford company, Anthony Quayle, to come forward as his successor.

The working relationship between Quayle and Fordham Flower was constructive from the start, and Quayle lost little time in persuading the governors to appoint Glen Byam Shaw as co-director. In his autobiography, Quayle suggests that, with the exception of 'Fordie' Flower, the governors were extremely cautious in the trust they reposed in the new directors' judgements. The cycle of histories planned for the Festival of Britain, it was thought, would be too unrelieved to satisfy the celebrative expectations of the time and needed to be spiced with something comic. Against Quayle's sense of congruity, *The Tempest* was yoked in to compensate for what the governors felt to be an inappropriate grimness of blood-letting, war, usurpation, child-murder, severed heads, dungeons, deceit, and deformity. Quayle too, it seems, found a difficulty at this time in his relations with Jackson, sensing a resentment in the older man and describing him as 'an enormously esteemed old bird with a rather academic turn of mind, but immensely distinguished'.[33] Writing of Quayle's early work in Stratford, Kenneth Tynan describes him as

the robust and tireless director . . . [who] seems unable to stand apart from his actors or be ruthlessly impersonal in perfecting a production. Comedy is his forte, and the very greatest directors are never quite at home in comedy: such is Quayle's temperament that good humour keeps flooding in.
(Tynan, *He that Plays the King*, 146)

Arguably the most important idea which began to take shape under Quayle's tenure in Stratford was that of linking the theatre with London, of somehow breaking the provincial isolation of the Stratford activities. With the demise of the Old Vic Centre, a combination of the Old Vic Theatre and the Old Vic School, in 1953, Quayle sought to establish a connection between Stratford and the Old Vic. The attempt was before its time, however, and it might well have run into moves that were already afoot to use the Old Vic as the foundation for a National Theatre.

Among the great names attracted to Stratford during Quayle's tenure were John Gielgud, Peggy Ashcroft, Gwen ffrangçon-Davies, Michael Redgrave, Ralph Richardson, Margaret Leighton, and Harry Andrews. And there also came two of the most remarkable non-acting directors of the century, Peter Brook (who had first directed Shakespeare at Stratford for Barry Jackson) and Tyrone Guthrie. Peter Brook's 1948 *Measure for Measure* is recalled by Tynan as 'a perfect marriage of shrill imagination and sober experience', Brook's triumph being his timing of the fifth act where, unlike most directors of the period, who accelerated the pace to bounce over the 'coincidences and lengthy impossibilities, [the] forced reconciliations and incredible cruelties', he inserted half a dozen long pauses, working up a new miracle of tension which Shakespeare knew nothing about. The thirty-five seconds of dead silence which elapse before Isabella decides to make her plea for Angelo's life were a long, prickly moment of doubt which had every heart in the theatre thudding.

(Tynan, *He that Plays the King*, 151)

Guthrie had come in 1948 to direct *Henry VIII*, and to Quayle's invitation to consider a co-directorship at Stratford, he responded with a condition that he be built a 'tin Globe':

I want to build a theatre with a permanent set surrounded on two sides by the audience in order to bring the people nearer to the actors and so communicate far more in the way that Shakespeare himself did. All this proscenium-arch acting is merely a version of opera. Rubbish!

(Quayle, *A Time to Speak*, 327)

It is difficult to visualize precisely what Guthrie had in mind. In wanting to free Shakespeare's drama from the proscenium frontality, he was looking both back and forward in time, for modern audiences have

FIG. 70 Peter Brook's 'Watteauesque' *Love's Labour's Lost*, Shakespeare Memorial Theatre, 1946, designs by Reginald Leefe.

become much more accustomed to spatial intimacy in dramatic presentation. This is partly because the fixed position of the conventional two-dimensional cinema screen and its capacity to make variable the illusion of space has prompted theatre to exploit its potential in varying the actuality of space in the relation of auditorium to stage, of actor to audience. Modern Stratford audiences will certainly testify to the intense impact of Shakespeare productions staged in the two smaller Stratford theatres in which the acting areas are closely surrounded on three sides by the audience.

By 1955 the Stratford company had established a reputation for being pre-eminently innovative in its Shakespearian productions. In that year Peter Brook directed Laurence Olivier at Stratford in *Titus Andronicus* (fig. 71). Quayle (who played Aaron) considers the production to have been 'one of the notable theatrical achievements for a decade or more in its stunning originality'. It was the integrated totality of effects—intensity of performance, visual effects, and sound—that made the production so striking. Richard David described the set (designed by Brook himself) as 'powerfully simple: three great squared pillars, set angle-on to the audience, fluted, and bronzy-grey in colour'.[34] The object was to dwarf the actors and, by moving the pillars, to provide cavernous spaces, a recessed stage on two levels which might serve as the tomb, or 'festooned with lianas it became the murder pit with the forest floor above it'.

Lighting and colour were carefully calculated to dramatize the play's ritual procession of horror. Flames enclosed within 'strange distorted cages' produced 'a shadowy, smokey effect'. The colours were intensely visceral, 'bile green, blacks, reds and browns, and the liverish colour of dried blood', and the dominant colour shifted from 'an unearthly greenish darkness' at the beginning, to a pervasive blood-red light, 'as if the whole universe on the stage had been drenched with blood' (Beauman, *The Royal Shakespeare*

Facing: FIG. 71 Laurence Olivier as Titus, Vivien Leigh as Lavinia, and Alan Webb as Marcus in Peter Brook's production of *Titus Andronicus*, Shakespeare Memorial Theatre, 1955.

Company, 225). The sound effects, too, were integrated with meticulous care and imaginative genius. For Lavinia's entrance, with red velvet ribbons streaming from her mouth and severed wrists, there was an accompaniment of harp strings being slowly plucked 'like drops of blood falling into a pool' (David, 'Drams of Eale', 127).

Olivier's performance was acclaimed as having 'brought the part of Titus back into the classical repertoire'.[35] For J. C. Trewin, Olivier's cry 'I am the sea!' caused 'its surge to beat on the world's far shore'.[36] Quayle reveals an aspect of this magnificent Titus (played at a time when Olivier's marriage to Vivien Leigh was at the most vicious stage of its disintegration) of which the audience would mercifully have been unaware:

Larry's Titus ranks with all the finest performances I ever saw him give. . . . [Vivien Leigh] standing there beside him while he was speaking words of love and comfort to poor mutilated Lavinia, would be cursing him with the most extreme obscenities imaginable, with a piece of bloody gauze tied over her mouth. (Quayle, *A Time to Speak*, 335)

In identifying historically important productions and portrayals in this period, comedy tends to be a secondary consideration, though it not infrequently brought forth profoundly memorable individual performances. Of Cedric Hardwicke's Sir Toby Belch, for instance, in the 1948 *Twelfth Night* staged at the New Theatre, Tynan wrote:

He preserved an impressive, resigned visage, broken only by the occasional eyebrow movement, of mild contempt, accompanied by the faintest of shrugs. . . . He never roars with laughter, belches, spits or raises his voice, yet an impression of extreme, almost disintegrating alcoholism was perfectly conveyed. He lets rip only once, in the carousing scene, when the catch is being sung. Slowly, with tatterdemalion dignity, he rises and climbs on to the barrel on which he has been sitting, and, with pursed lips, devout nose and only slightly roguish eyes, he executes a stately stomach-dance, his hands gently resting behind his ears. The grave, unself-conscious concentration of this had the genuine world-blindness of all great comic characters.

(Tynan, *He that Plays the King*, 104)

Towards a National Theatre

There arose, now as a major issue, the need to establish a new home for the Old Vic Company. Oliver Lyttleton proposed the purchase of the South Bank site and the naming of the new building as 'The National Theatre, incorporating The Shakespeare National Memorial Theatre and The Old Vic'. Within the Old Vic, too, there emerged the sense of a change in its internal politics. Guthrie found increasing difficulty in working with what he called 'the triumvirate' of Olivier, Richardson, and John Burrell, and ultimately resigned over Olivier's insistence that *Oedipus Rex* be double-billed with Sheridan's *The Critic*. Notable productions at the Old Vic between 1944 and 1947 included *Richard III*, both parts of *Henry IV*, *King Lear*, and *Richard II*.

The Old Vic under the 'triumvirate' was distinguished more by individual performances than by the productions themselves. Ralph Richardson was a memorable Falstaff, Alec Guinness a notable if less assured Richard II, and Olivier's feats of virtuosity included a Richard III which epitomized a particular view of the character (fig. 72). W. A. Darlington caught the articulateness of the detail in his opening entrance:

As he made his way downstage very slowly and with odd interruptions in his progress, he seemed malignity incarnate. All the complication of Richard's character—its cruelty, its ambition, its sardonic humour seemed implicit in his expression and his walk, so that when at last he reached the front of the stage and began his speech, all that he had to say of his evil purpose seemed to us in the audience less like a revelation than a confirmation of something we had already been told.[37]

Under Michael Benthall's directorship, the Old Vic moved towards becoming an exclusively Shakespearian company, stretching its repertoire to include *Troilus and Cressida*, *Titus Andronicus*, and *Henry VI*. But the 1950s saw the Old Vic facing increasingly vigorous competition from the formidable array of names playing at Stratford. Under Barry Jackson and his successors Anthony Quayle and Glen Byam Shaw, a group of, by now, internationally established players—Gielgud, Olivier, Vivien Leigh, Richardson, Redgrave, Paul Robeson, Peggy Ashcroft, and Margaret Leighton—took the leads, and by the end of the 1950s, with Peter Hall as Stratford's director, the Old Vic governors sensed a very real threat to their National Theatre aspirations.

The process whereby those aspirations were transformed from visions, suggestions, proposals, and resolutions to an actuality is discussed in later chapters. What can be said here is that the period embracing the 1920s to the 1950s brought an important substructure of dedication to the production in Britain of Shakespeare's plays, and cultivated audiences hitherto unaware of the riches to be found on the English stage. Not only that. Olivier's films of *Henry V*, *Hamlet*, and *Richard III* brought Shakespeare to audiences very different from those who frequented the theatre and made the English sense of Shakespearian drama known beyond Britain and beyond the borders of the English-speaking world. These films expanded the cinematographic potential to present poetic drama and so were topics for discussion at many levels—both where cinema had cultivated a sophisticated viewing public and in places where theatrical performances and printed texts were, in one way or another, inaccessible.

Tempting as it might be, however, to regard Olivier as the pre-eminent theatrical figure of these decades, the glamour, energy, and brilliant virtuosity of his Shakespearian portrayals is balanced by the profound subtlety, intricate distinctness, and poetic insight brought to the Shakespearian stage by John Gielgud. Moreover, Gielgud, as he had shown in his OUDS *Romeo and Juliet*, was a maker of companies. He understood the importance of forming long-standing associations with those with whom he worked, and ensuring that the players he drew around him were sufficiently strong to ensure the development of a company ensemble. Unselfish both as an actor and as a director, he was able to recognize and work in partnership with other established directors. His

FIG. 72 Laurence Olivier as Gloucester and Ralph Richardson as Richmond in John Burrell's
production of *Richard III*, New Theatre, 1944.

venture into commercial theatre management at the
Queen's Theatre in the autumn of 1937 brought
together, in one company, the directors Tyrone
Guthrie and Michel Saint-Denis as well as such strong
players as Michael Redgrave, Leon Quartermaine,
Harcourt Williams, Harry Andrews, Anthony
Quayle, Alec Guinness, George Devine, Glen Byam
Shaw, George Howe, Dennis Price, Rachel Kempson,
and Peggy Ashcroft, an astonishing concentration of
established theatrical talent. Alec Guinness saw

Tyrone Guthrie and Gielgud as the great liberators
of the English theatre, 'and John in particular paved
the way for what is best in London today'.[38] And
Billington has written of Gielgud's 1937 season, which
included *Richard II* and *The Merchant of Venice*, as laying

the foundations of the work to be done at Stratford-on-Avon
in the 1950s . . . and thereby sowed the seeds that were to
grow into the Royal Shakespeare Company and the National
Theatre. If anyone can claim to be the architect of post-war
British theatre, it is John Gielgud.[39]

9

Shakespeare and the Public Purse

PETER THOMSON

Enter the Arts Council

BROADCASTING to the nation in 1945, the then chairman of a CEMA that was evolving into the Arts Council of Great Britain, John Maynard Keynes, confided: 'I do not believe it is yet realised what an important thing has happened. State patronage of the arts has crept in. It has happened in a very English, informal, unostentatious way—half-baked if you like.' CEMA (the Council for the Encouragement of Music and the Arts) had been founded in 1940 to help boost the wartime morale of the nation. Until then, European examples of state subsidy had been ignored in a 'very English' way, and the actual contribution remained niggardly even after the incorporation of the Arts Council in 1946. The immediate effect was to highlight a distinction between the commercial theatre and the non-profit-distributing companies from which alone the beneficiaries of state subsidy can be drawn. Although elected by the government, the dozen or so members of the Arts Council were encouraged to operate independently, with the government keeping 'at arm's length'. How long, though, is an arm? The question did not seem of much significance in the early years, nor even after Harold Wilson's Labour government raised the status and increased the funding of the Arts Council in 1965. By then, the National Theatre had been in existence,

without premises of its own, for two years, and Peter Hall had been reshaping the Shakespeare seasons at Stratford for five years. The appointment of the vigorous Jenny Lee as Britain's first Minister for the Arts signalled the declared commitment of the Wilson government to include 'quality-of-life' considerations in its policies. It did not, however, simplify or clarify the purposes of the Arts Council and its specialist panels. The Theatre Panel found itself called upon to reconcile demands from at least three distinct interest groups: the two 'national' companies (the National Theatre's South Bank stages were opened piecemeal in 1976–7 under the directorship of the same Peter Hall who had converted the Stratford Memorial Theatre into the Royal Shakespeare Company in 1960), the regional repertory theatres, and the small-scale 'fringe' companies whose forays into politics and international experimentalism gave to the late 1960s and early 1970s a new theatrical excitement.

It was the election of Mrs Thatcher's Conservative government in 1979 that exposed the flimsiness of the ground on which the Arts Council stood. The new Prime Minister could not be relied on to distinguish the arm's-length principle from the short-arm jab, and the Council was harassed into producing a succession of sometimes contradictory policy statements. The insistence on accountability and market values had the effect of emasculating the radical companies without enhancing the potency of the 'established' theatre. The case for state subsidy of a professional theatre is based on an approximate syllogism: 'good' theatre will not be sustained without disinterested financial support and, since the electorate ('society') benefits from 'good' theatre, the government should provide such financial support. For a Prime Minister ethically nurtured on the principles of Samuel Smiles, such an obligation was not to be accepted without question. The case against subsidy for the arts was not fully articulated by Mrs Thatcher or by any of her Conservative cabinet. There was no need. Innuendo and the propaganda of accountability were sufficient to undermine confidence and deter experiment— because a threat to subsidy was always implicit. By 1993, when the government called for further cuts, the Arts Council had lost, or been systematically deprived of, its direction, and the Regional Arts Associations, indistinctly emulating each other, had accepted the blistering demands of self-help, which they imposed in turn on their 'clients'.

Reservations about state subsidy of the arts were not confined to the Conservative party. Part of the original charter of the Arts Council committed it 'to increase the accessibility of the fine arts to the public throughout Our Realm'. In the new charter of 1967, the qualifying 'fine' was dropped, but even when the Council was floating comparatively free of government intervention, its committee discriminations, at least until the rise of the community arts lobby, were normally between 'high' and 'higher' art. The dominant attitude, liberally embodied by the Arts Council, was the attitude of the cultural dominators. And there remained, and remains, the vexed question of the relationship between subsidy and 'society'. In the age of accountability, the efficacy of the Arts Council's attempt to involve more people in the arts is numerically judged. Confident in earthy cliché, the local councillor reminds the theatre board of management that 'when you get down to the nitty gritty, what we need is bums on seats'. Even

Shakespeare, and even Shakespeare at Stratford, is subject increasingly to the archly expressed 'bums-on-seats' test. The temptation to stage *Timon of Athens* precisely because it is so rarely seen, a respectable enough reason, is set aside, and yet another *Midsummer Night's Dream* is put into rehearsal. A moderately talented director thinks up a newish approach, a designer embellishes it, and another subsidized Shakespeare achieves a decent 75 per cent box-office in Newchester's 450-seat playhouse. This, or something very like it, is the routine of unremembered Shakespearian productions throughout the United Kingdom. In the early years of subsidy, regional repertory theatres quite often presented two or more Shakespeares per year. Now, balancing actors' wages in an enlarged company against on the one hand box-office income, and on the other cultural prestige, a single production is more common. Directors relish the challenge, and it is rare to encounter a performance that contains nothing of interest. In general, though, Shakespearian productions are heavy going for audiences. My greater interest, in this chapter, will be in positive achievement; but such achievements need to be seen against a background of flawed versions of what might have been. The theatre's propensity for congratulating itself camouflages the important fact that it is very difficult to present Shakespeare's plays adequately, let alone well. The English theatre allows too little rehearsal time to build individual performances into the ensemble, inadequate actors cannot be replaced, and decisions taken in haste are defended at leisure. Anticipating weaknesses, directors collaborate with designers to cover them over. It is a technique which Peter Ustinov has called 'veneer disease'.

Run-of-the-mill productions of Shakespeare, spuriously decorated school texts, are products of an industry under threat. In a healthier theatre, Shakespeare's plays would hold their place alongside other plays of the classic repertory, distinct among the distinguished. Singled out, as they generally are outside the national companies, they are occasions for resentment, disappointment, and admiration in approximately equal measure. But it has, without doubt, been the achievement of the subsidized sector to preserve them as part of the living theatre. We should expect a living theatre to record movements in the society that contextualizes it, sometimes even to initiate them. I shall take as an example the passage of *The Taming of the Shrew*, a play that has been problematized as perceptions have shifted, through the subsidized theatre.

Shrews

There was, in the early twentieth century, a broad agreement that *The Taming of the Shrew* played (as farce) better than it read (as comedy). Mother-in-law jokes and whimsical references to 'my better half' were still accepted currency in 1960, when Peggy Ashcroft and Peter O'Toole joined battle in John Barton's first Stratford production (fig. 73). I took with me to Stratford a boyhood memory of Patrick McGoohan's piratical Petruchio (Sheffield, 1952) and very little else. To me, it was a revelation that Kate could be so dignified in defeat. Ashcroft may have been the first shrew to enact a recognition of her own mirror image in Petruchio's misbehaviour and, through that recognition, to fall in love with her persecutor. Her submissive finale was an act of collusion rather than self-annihilation. Even so, Kenneth Tynan could get away with an *Observer* review which concluded: 'Dame Peggy plays the last scene . . . with an eager, sensible radiance that almost prompts one to regret the triumph of the suffragette movement.'[1]

A worthy but slightly harassed production at the Little Theatre in Bristol in 1967 exposed the vulnerability of the Bianca plot. This is where repertory companies are likely to place their weaker actors—in roles that demand the physical precision of *commedia dell'arte* players—but there was some

compensation in the unexpected richness of the Pedant, an over-enthusiastic amateur actor as Polonius probably was. This was the last occasion on which I was part of an audience that readily accepted a *happy* ending. The director, Christopher Denys, had cut the Induction. The next month, I saw a production in Weimar by the Nationaltheater of Halle, in which Christopher Sly was the dominant figure. Subsidized theatre in East Germany reached sections of the population that the members of the Arts Council of Great Britain might have glimpsed in the public bar of the Rover's Return. My impression is that a theatre ticket in Weimar cost less than a bar of chocolate; and this was a regular audience that clapped not only the cast at their interval bow, but also any 'point' effectively made by an individual actor. The director was more concerned with the class struggle than with the battle of the sexes, in which Kate was an easy winner. It is a fundamentally optimistic proposal of Shakespeare's play that people can change. No one changed in the Halle production, which ended with Sly humiliatingly discarded by a carousing gang of landowners and bourgeois capitalists.

In the 1970s, subsidized Shakespeare frequently made a virtue of irreverence. Charles Marowitz's collage versions at the Open Space in London were avowed attempts to wrench new meanings from familiar texts. Marowitz was a ferociously articulate spokesman for a new theatre, who, after working with Peter Brook through the early 1960s until the 'Theatre of Cruelty' season of 1964, seemed in danger of taking on the self-appointed task of translating Brook's English into English. But the two men were temperamentally dissimilar. Brook sought to gather apparent disparities into unpredictable coalescence, Marowitz to dissect or separate and only then to reassemble. The reassembled *Hamlet* was controversial in 1965. I saw it in Parma, where a demonstrative international audience seemed to suspect that a joke was being played on it. *The Shrew* (1973), Marowitz's fourth Shakespeare collage, was certainly not a joke. It was, on the contrary, a provocative contribution to the feminist debate. It sought to inspire women into fury

FIG. 73 Harmony achieved in a festive setting: the final scene in *The Taming of the Shrew*, directed by John Barton, Royal Shakespeare Theatre, 1960, with Peter O'Toole as Petruchio and Peggy Ashcroft as Kate.

against Petruchio at a time when the patriarchy was beginning to notice itself. In his 'head-on confrontation with the intellectual sub-structure'[2] of Shakespeare's play, Marowitz found, not love, but an endorsement of systematic male oppression. He unfolds the story of the taming entirely in Shakespeare's words and sequence, but the male bonding of Petruchio, Hortensio, and Grumio in the humiliation of Kate is his significant addition, and the potentially fond moment at the end of v. i, when Kate kisses Petruchio, is absent. In its place, wittily and deceptively transposed from the Induction, are the promises of future kindness there made to Sly. Kate receives them in wide-eyed wonder, until Petruchio instructs her gently, in Sly's words: 'Madam, undress you and come now to bed.' Her answer is that of Sly's Page / Wife:

> Let me entreat of you
> To pardon me yet for a night or two,
> Or, if not so, until the sun be set.
> My physicians have expressly charged
> In peril to incur a former malady,
> That I should yet absent me from your bed.
> I hope this reason stands for my excuse.

FIG. 74 Thelma Holt as Katherine and Malcolm Tierney as Petruchio in *The Shrew*, by Charles Marowitz, Open Space Theatre, London, 1973.

For this dereliction, her punishment is immediate. Held down on the table by her father and her servants, she is buggered by Petruchio (fig. 74). The final speech is recited against 'a surreal tribunal-setting' by a Kate who, taking the lunar references of Shakespeare's play to a savage extreme, is clearly a drugged lunatic, destroyed by the 'overtly psychopathic' Petruchio, who has to prompt her when she forgets her lines. Intercut with the Kate/Petruchio scenes is a modern story of a love affair between a young man and a young woman of a higher class. It taps into both Christopher Sly and Bianca, but it owes its development to Marowitz's view that there are no winners in *The Taming of the Shrew*. The modern lovers marry only when their relationship is doomed. 'What I wanted to say was . . . that no human relationship has the stamina to withstand long periods of intimate exposure,'[3] Marowitz explains, though only because that was the meaning he found buried in the play's conclusion. The final image of *The Shrew* is of a catatonic Kate framed by the modern couple smiling out to invisible photographers for a wedding picture.

Marowitz has admitted a description of his *Shrew* as Grand Guignol, but it is clearly possible to find a modern tragedy in this old comedy. In 1986, the Turkish director Yücel Erten presented it as a love tragedy, in which a Kate who has built a self-defensive wall around herself finds the wall shattered when she falls in love with Petruchio. Her subsequent humiliation on the journey back to Padua is a source, not of laughter, but of breakdown. She comes to the banquet with her arms swathed in a shawl, speaks her aria of submission and throws off the shawl to lay her hands on the floor. Only now, as she is about to die, do we see that she has slit her wrists.

Michael Bogdanov's Stratford production of 1978 began as startlingly as Erten's ended. With the audience almost all seated, there was one of those unseemly incidents with which the British seem especially ill-equipped to cope. A football hooligan had got into the auditorium, either ticketless or too drunk to find his seat. The poor usherette who was trying to deal with him suddenly found herself the centre of attention, and an inept one at that. No bloody woman was going to push him around. Uniformed constraint is provocation to a man like this, and he leaps onto the stage and starts destroying scenery. For a fair proportion of the audience, this looks like a 'real' crisis, and even those who recognize Jonathan Pryce are finding their metatheatrical sophistication put to the test. The auditorium is on the edge of panic, unsettled before it has had time to take possession. Later it will discover that the usherette is playing Kate and the hooligan doubling as Christopher Sly and Petruchio. Meanwhile, something very nasty either is happening or has just happened, and a degree of hostility between audience and play lingers. Bogdanov's aim was to pitch the text into the present tension, and the doubling of Sly and Petruchio was crucial to it. Pryce made a demonstrative exit as Sly when he heard the actors of Gremio and Hortensio protesting that Kate was too much for them, shortly to return as Petruchio on a gleaming motor bike, stage centre and phallocentric. Bogdanov viewed the play as

FIG. 75 Accounts rendered in a modern world: Michael Bogdanov's production of *The Taming of the Shrew*, Royal Shakespeare Theatre, 1978, with Jonathan Pryce as Petruchio and Paola Dionisotti as Katharine.

'a male wish-fulfilment dream of revenge upon women',[4] in which Petruchio, on Sly's behalf, turns the tables on the hostess/usherette. The real villain is an acquisitive society (Baptista with an adding-machine to calculate the assets of Bianca's suitors) governed by men who carve up first women and then each other. And yet, unobtrusively, as this modern-dress and overtly strident production proceeded, something much gentler was occurring. Through what I can only suppose was a slow fade of invisible acting, Paola Dionisotti's Kate, who had begun in sullen defiance of Petruchio, ended up compensating for his inadequacies. The final speech was an astonishing *tour de force*, spoken with absolute sincerity, but outfacing, in a variety of ways, all the diners at the green-baize card-table and us in the audience (fig. 75). It was a rare moment of Brechtian alienation on the English stage, as when Mother Courage says *earnestly*:

When you listen to the big wheels talk, they're making war for reasons of piety, in the name of everything that's fine and noble. But when you take another look, you see that they're not so dumb; they're making war for profit. If they weren't, the small fry like me wouldn't have anything to do with it.[5]

Bogdanov came to the conclusion, during his encounter with *The Taming of the Shrew*, that Shakespeare was a humanist who took on his own sexism. It is a melancholy footnote to this brief commentary on a production that merits more, that in 1994 his short-lived English Shakespeare Company became another victim of inadequate subsidy.

Michael Billington ended his *Guardian* review of Bogdanov's production by asking 'whether there is any reason to revive a play that seems totally offensive to our age and our society',[6] but the subsidized theatre has continued to be drawn to it. The radical experiments of the 1970s gave way, in the 1980s, to displays of directorial eccentricity, to which Bogdanov's production certainly contributed. Directors of subsidized Shakespeare are looked to for inspiration and, all too often, respond by manufacturing originality. But the taming of Kate poses an inexorable question in any modern production of *The Taming of the Shrew*. It is comparatively easy for the actress of

Kate to construct for herself a history of neglect. She has been replaced in her father's affection by a younger sister, and has concealed the hurt by donning a mask of shrewishness. Her love-story is then built on the release of her true self brought about by Petruchio's involvement with her. There is nothing in the play to encourage the actor of Petruchio to construct a parallel autobiography. If he falls in love with Kate, he must show it in by-play, since the spoken words deny it. In Barry Kyle's 1982 production at Stratford, Sinead Cusack and Alun Armstrong followed these lines. Billington was surprised to find the performance 'so loving, exuberant and large-spirited that it stifles much of the play's nastiness'.[7] Jonathan Miller's Stratford production five years later was altogether chillier. Once again it was a play about marriage, not love. Fiona Shaw found herself resenting Shakespeare's refusal to give Kate the soliloquy she yearns for, burdening her instead with the lame farce of the tailor's scene. She spoke the final speech very loudly, the only woman at a long table seating sixteen men, with a seventeenth standing behind it. This bleak display of gender pressure was something the Medieval Players, on tour in 1985, were determined to avoid. The casting of a man as Kate, their programme note promised, 'takes the play away from inappropriate modern reaction and lets us see the struggle as a game, not as a solemn treatise'. But this, of course, is only to replace one modern reaction with another, neither more nor less appropriate. Cross-gender casting in this determinedly jolly production was also applied to Bianca, Hortensio, Lucentio, and Tranio, but not to Petruchio—implicitly a comment on the gender of cruelty.

A staging of *The Taming of the Shrew* that labours to alleviate the harshness of Petruchio's project is, none the less, an intervention into the debate on the patriarchal subjugation of women. The outstanding production of the 1980s was Di Trevis's for the Royal Shakespeare Company on tour in 1985 (fig. 76). Here, as in Halle in 1967, the director framed the marriage plots with a vividly documented commentary on property and poverty. The first characters to enter along the traverse stage were the Victorian strolling

FIG. 76 The players and their wagon, pulled by 'Katharine' (Sian Thomas), who also carries her baby.
Di Trevis's *The Taming of the Shrew*, Royal Shakespeare Company regional tour, 1985.

players who would perform the comedy, a rags-and-tatters group, inured to privation. At the head of the procession, dragging a dilapidated and monstrously oversized property basket on wheels, was a young woman with a baby in her arms. It was a visual quotation from the Berliner Ensemble's *Mother Courage*, but with a social history of unmarried motherhood superimposed on it. The dirty banner that the players left at one end of the traverse announced 'THE TAMING OF THE SHREW—A KIND OF HISTORY'. That history, which included the desperate dependence of the acting troupe, was already in progress when the hostess propelled the drunken Sly down an aisle and onto the stage. There he cursed,

urinated, vomited, dropped a bit of rag over the vomit and fell asleep. This was a rag doll for the contemptuous practical jokers to clothe in the unlikely finery of white tails and a black top hat. He would watch the whole play with increasingly child-like wonder, usually from a couch at one end of the traverse, but intervening sometimes or trying to apply the love-lessons of the courtships to his 'wife'. The players themselves were shabbily costumed. Some items of the travelling wardrobe had evidently been lost: Kate and Bianca were reduced to performing in uncovered underskirts and bodices. The neediness of the players underlay the neediness of the characters in the play. They, like Sly, were playthings for the idle rich, and acting was both their fantasy and their bread and butter. The taming was in no way softened by Alfred Molina's Petruchio, but beneath the bullying there was a bond of shared adversity. Sian Thomas as Kate was always also the unmarried mother who had dragged the property basket, enduring the almost unbearable. At the end of Kate's final speech, Petruchio had to wipe away a tear: 'Why, there's a wench!' He picked up Kate's cap, placed it carefully on her head then on his own, and the two of them ran off arm-in-arm, returning to join the company in a bow. For Sly, caught up entirely in the fiction, the time was now ripe for him to take *his* wife, but her yielding move towards him was contemptuously transformed when she took off her wig and became a mocking page-boy. Michael Troughton held the miserable reality in the droop of Sly's body, and the lord reinforced it by tossing coins at his feet and following his page off. Some of the players returned to clear and clean the stage, ignoring Sly, but he had understood something from the play. To Sian Thomas, emptied into her 'real' poverty and carrying her baby, he offered one of the lord's coins.

A production as rich in resonances as this one is too easily reduced in posthumous commentary to sentimental socialism. Di Trevis had certainly set it, knowingly, before the creation of the welfare state to be performed during its destruction. I shall force a manifestly partial point by contrasting it with the only production of *The Taming of the Shrew* that I have seen in the 1990s. At the Northcott Theatre, Exeter, in 1993, John Durnin asked his designer to provide him with a film-studio to fill the theatre's big stage. The studio came equipped with its own bar, at which the barmaid refused to serve an alcoholic Sly. Knocked out by one of the actors, he was hoisted up to a viewing balcony. What followed was metatheatrical in a post-Fellini way, with actors commentating on their own decadence. There was clever play with studio equipment, much of it distracting. The choice of the play had been consciously provocative. Durnin had been attacked by a group of the university's students for what they felt to be the anti-Semitism of his previous annual Shakespeare, *The Merchant of Venice*, and he was ready to rile the feminists this time. In the event, though, the production was too soft at the centre and too tricksy on the surface to cause a stir.

I have tried, in this survey of selected productions of a single play, to convey something about the evolution of subsidized Shakespeare over four decades. It is undeniably regrettable and regrettably undeniable that the subsidized sector of the British theatre lost much of its confidence after 1979. The professional theatre was, by the early 1990s, expected to carry the major burden of governmental reductions in funding of the arts. One effect was to strengthen the hold over Shakespeare of the comparatively buoyant Royal Shakespeare Company. There was a growing tendency, endorsed by national critics, to take the RSC's Shakespeare as definitive. Regional repertory theatres rarely had the actors and never the budget to measure up, and their Shakespeare productions tended to lack a sense of occasion. The more innovative touring companies, like Shared Experience, Footsbarn, and Cheek by Jowl, more effectively developed a style. My concern, in the rest of this chapter, is to highlight specific achievements across the range of subsidized Shakespeare.

Hamlets for All

In 1965 the Victoria Theatre in Stoke-on-Trent was fairly newly converted from a cinema, and *As You Like It* probably its first Shakespeare. The theatre stood unimpressively amid shops and terraced houses, just before the Hartshill Road carried Stoke into Newcastle-under-Lyme. It was then Britain's only permanent theatre-in-the-round, and its local audience was largely composed of first-generation theatre-goers. Peter Cheeseman, the artistic director, liked his actors to stay in Stoke for a long time, to make it their home, and to become known in the community. The atmosphere front-of-house was homy, and the actors knew the audience liked them. This confidence affected performance, relaxing even when not strictly improving it. People were still enjoying the novelty of looking around the acting space at mirror images of themselves, and the proximity of the real and fictional worlds gave to this *As You Like It* an energizing intimacy. On first seeing Orlando in the Forest of Arden, perched between two banks of audience, Rosalind hailed him from between two other banks. I was close enough to Fiona Walker to be infected by her embarrassment at her tell-tale over-enthusiasm. She—Fiona Walker as well as Rosalind—had momentarily forgotten that she was pretending to be a man, and she needed our help in the deception. The 'scenery' was changed at the dimmer board: a mellowing of light from the harshness of Duke Frederick's court took us immediately into the Forest of Arden. It was easy to take pleasure in the company of the exiled Duke and his alfresco courtiers, above all because of Ben Kingsley's persuasive and moody singing in the role of a troubadour Amiens. One left the theatre feeling as if one had been at a party.

Much more celebrated in 1965 than Stoke's *As You Like It* was Stratford's *Hamlet*. R. A. Foakes has developed at some length an argument that *King Lear* has, since 1960, replaced *Hamlet* at the political centre of the Shakespeare canon:

> *King Lear* has come to seem richly significant in political terms, in a world in which old men have held on to and abused power, often in corrupt or arbitrary ways; in the same period *Hamlet* has lost much of its political relevance, as liberal intellectuals have steadily been marginalized in Britain and in the United States.[8]

Peter Hall's choice of David Warner to play Hamlet (fig. 77) was designed to enforce a modern sense of Cold War disempowerment and disaffection with politics. Foakes incorporates the production in his argument, noting that 'in the world of the H-bomb cynicism seemed the only stance; what possibility was there of commitment?'[9] A pin-striped court, dressed in approximate Tudor style, was supervised by an unrelentingly establishment Polonius. Tony Church told Stanley Wells that he had both Lord Burghley and Harold Macmillan in mind in planning his

impersonation. Warner's ganglingly unheroic Hamlet was always going to be outmanœuvred here. His performance was notoriously appealing to the student generation, for reasons which Wells pinpoints:

> Mr. Warner did much to emphasize Hamlet's nonconformity, his inner rebellion against the Establishment by which he was surrounded. This was a young man who made his own rules and did not mind appearing ridiculous or eccentric. He was making his own discoveries about life, and often enough he found it ridiculous.[10]

The student image was reinforced by the long scarf (discarded when the production was revived) which hung down to his ankles. By a significant historical coincidence, 1965 was also the year of David Halliwell's briefly popular play about student revolution, *Little Malcolm and his Struggle against the Eunuchs*. Both Halliwell and Peter Hall were accurately sensing the mood of the decade. Either might have used the other's work as a source of inspiration.

Fig. 77 Hamlet as rebellious student: David Warner in Peter Hall's production, Royal Shakespeare Theatre, 1965.

Peter Hall's entrepreneurial enthusiasms changed the face of subsidized Shakespeare during the ten years (1958–68) of his active involvement with the Royal Shakespeare Company. Both at Stratford and at the RSC's London base, the Aldwych, the plays became shows. Unsurprisingly, there was also a reaction against conspicuous expenditure: a reaction spearheaded all too briefly by Buzz Goodbody's communally sensitive work at the Other Place, an unadorned corrugated-iron shed a short walk from the Royal Shakespeare Theatre. Goodbody's 'Village Hall' *Hamlet* opened there in the spring of 1975 (fig. 78). Tickets cost 70p, and the production budget was comparably tiny. We were watching, within a stone's throw of the company's lavish headquarters, a meticulous and determinedly unspectacular 'fringe' performance. An end-stage, about 10 feet deep and backed by sliding paper screens, had been constructed at the opposite side of the room from its single access door. The audience shared, not only the room, but also this door with the actors. The Ghost vanished through it, Laertes battered on it, Fortinbras made his final, invasive entry through it—and it was our way out and in during the intervals. The play opened in darkness, broken by the torchlight of the nervous watch, picking each other out, and then the Ghost. The actors were behind us, among us, all round us. Whatever there was in this bare room became startlingly appropriate to the conduct of the play. This was a production that reinvestigated the *teatrum mundi* trope.

FIG. 78 Ben Kingsley as Hamlet and Bob Peck as the Grave-digger in Buzz Goodbody's production of *Hamlet*, The Other Place, 1975.

Buzz Goodbody's suicide during the first week of the run certainly coloured, probably deepened, the impact of the actors' progress towards feigned death. 'She was so young and clearly very talented,' Peter Hall noted in his diary. 'There seems to be a spirit of destructiveness in the air at the moment.'[11] It might, after all, have been a comment on Ophelia or Hamlet and Denmark. But the production needed no external impetus, since its internal logic was so intense. We were in the contemporary world, where political leaders make nation-shaking decisions and then come home to their families. George Baker's formidable Claudius, in an immaculately tailored blue suit with broad white stripes, knew that his wardrobe, as well as his policies, carried the Establishment's seal of approval. Every detail of costume was equally gestic, embodying both character and social status. Polonius followed, but did not rival, the fashion of the King; Reynaldo, in city pin-stripes, was the image of an ambitious civil servant whose aim was to replace soon those he flattered now; Laertes contradicted his student hair and beard with clothes his father might have chosen; Osric wore jodhpurs and Fortinbras combat gear. Buzz Goodbody had spent enough time in Arts Council meetings to know the sinking feeling that comes over a person urgent for change when he or she confronts a roomful of reasonable men in suits. And it was this dilemma that confronted Ben Kingsley's thinking Hamlet. It was a nice touch to give him, as his only ally, a north-country Horatio in frayed brown corduroys, loose overcoat, and long scarf. Theirs was a genuine friendship, sustaining at university but ineffectual at court, where a provincial scholarship-boy could be casually cold-shouldered. Kingsley's was the least histrionic Hamlet I have seen. The neat brown suit that replaced his mourning black was both in contrast and in keeping with the grimly proper court. He spoke fast (the rapidity of the whole production, uncluttered by added scenic business, permitted the presentation of an unusually full text by a company of only thirteen actors), but with precision, constantly testing the sound of his words against their meaning. The complexities of his project were laid open to the audience. My sense throughout was that Buzz Goodbody, against a directorial trend, had made the play available to the intelligence of the actors.

Footsbarn, a company which grew out of a Cornish commune in 1971, dispensed with a director altogether. Their 1980 *Hamlet* was their third Shakespeare, and the last before inadequate subsidy drove them into international migrancy. It was not so much a version of the play as an enacted response to it. Performed without an interval, it lasted less than two hours, and the text was not only heavily cut, but also, at times, replaced. But their approach was in no other ways comparable to Marowitz's. A Footsbarn production is not an analysis of deeper meaning but a celebration of theatricality. The actors are musicians, mimes, and acrobats, and the cultural world they inhabit is closer to circus than to theatre. *Hamlet* was staged in a tent to audiences that generally included a generous scattering of children. My own, of whom the oldest was 16 and the youngest 10, have vivid memories of it still. More mysterious than a pantomime, it contained similar invitations to hilarity and wonder, and depended almost equally on the vibrant contrast between the sophistication of the performers and the naïvety of the performance. The central playing-space was a high, raked rostrum, onto which the silent guards pole-vaulted. Later, the Ghost would rise at them from behind a curtain, to be held briefly on the end of a pole in a dangerous balancing act. The atmosphere was tense, and no one, certainly not Hamlet, was reliable. And, at any moment throughout the performance, folly might be unleashed. It was there when Polonius dispatched his bevy of spies, or when three grave-diggers, each to their infinite confusion called Derek, tried to battle their way to meaning something, or when the whole cast of nine tumbled on in the guise of the visiting players, dressed like circus clowns on a parade into the ring. Such violent contrasts between pain and laughter, carried off with physical panache, were not, in effect, crude, but challenging. Footsbarn, like Peter Brook, continue to search for a language of the theatre that is informed, but not cowed, by dramatic texts.

Dreams and Visions

Brook's 1970 production of *A Midsummer Night's Dream* at Stratford (fig. 79 and col. pl. 6) may have set a precedent for circus Shakespeare. I wrote at the time, 'More than anything I have ever seen, this production declared its confidence and delight in the art of performance,'[12] and the point still holds its meaning for me. Doubting the currency of symbols for fairy magic in the modern world, Brook proposed to substitute 'actions that a performer can execute that are quite breathtaking'[13] and opted for what he felt to be the pure theatricality of the circus and the acrobat. To establish a breathtaking convention of invisibility, John Kane as Puck mounted 6-foot stilts to harry Demetrius and Lysander. When the text required him to deliver the magic flower to Oberon, he swung down on a trapeze, spinning a plate on a wand. The plate did not become the flower, but the act of transferring it, still spinning, to Oberon's wand became the magic of the flower. This extraordinary production was set by Sally Jacobs in a white-walled box, not unlike a squash-court. A practical gallery offered a vantage-point for actors not engaged in a scene to look down at those who were, while providing sound effects and music. Ladders at the downstage end of the side walls gave access to and from the platform, but there was also access for the fairy characters from trapezes suspended from the flies and, for the Athenian mortals, through two upstage doors, narrower than those in De Witt's Swan but similarly sited. The trees of the wood were coiled-metal mobiles, suspended from the gallery by actors, that made eerie music as they twisted. Hermia was ensnared by them in the fierce vexation of her dream. Puck's yellow clown-suit and blue skull-cap reinforced the circus imagery, as did the red nose of Bottom's transformation. The artifice may have been elaborate, but the dominant impression was of rare simplicity and directness, nowhere more so than in the solemnity with which the

mechanicals approached the craft of acting. This was not knockabout farce. On the contrary, in their uncomplicated eagerness to perform, the mechanicals typified the attitude of the play's whole cast, who had just been directed by a conjuror.

For at least a decade, other productions of the play moved in the shadow of Brook's *Dream*. The doubling of Theseus/Oberon and Hippolyta/Titania became almost conventional. Braham Murray's employment of it, in his Manchester production for Theatre 69 (1970), followed too soon to avoid the accusation of mere derivativeness. By 1978, George Roman at Theatre Clwyd had reinvested it with meaning. Just as the fairies constructed Titania's love-bower at Oberon's orders, so the mechanicals prepared a wedding marquee under instruction from Theseus. Roman liked to involve aeronautical engineers from nearby Wrexham in the construction of his sets. He was interested, literally, in the *making* of theatre. Brook's quest may have been more spiritual, but he tried to admit nothing into performance for which he had not found a pretext. *A Midsummer Night's Dream*, he has written, 'touches lightly on the fundamental question of the transformations which may occur if certain things are better understood'.[14]

Better understanding is, of course, an elusive concept. When I was directing *Cymbeline* in Northern California in 1990, I found myself having to explain hierarchy, rather than taking it for granted that it was understood. Americans recognize power more readily than they recognize authority. In England, we have first to invest power with authority. The distinction is evident in Imogen's important early lines:

I something fear my father's wrath, but nothing—
Always reserved my holy duty—what
His rage can do on me.   (I. i. 87–9)

In the National Theatre's *Cymbeline*, Peter Hall instructed Geraldine James to respect the line-ending of 'what' as well as the natural flow of the syntax.[15] By an upward inflection, preceding what was never quite a pause, Innogen (as she was called in this production, after the text of Stanley Wells's and Gary Taylor's Oxford edition) could then suggest her determination

FIG. 79 Bottom's erotic triumph: Sara Kestelman and David Waller in Peter Brook's *A Midsummer Night's Dream*, Royal Shakespeare Theatre, 1970.

to find the right definition for her inner tumult. This *Cymbeline*, which opened to a three-sided audience in the National's smallest auditorium, the Cottesloe, in 1988, was a sinewy, unrelenting interpretation of the text. In their different ways, both Innogen and Posthumus progressed from immaturity through the bleakest of purgatories to purgation. Hall stressed the extremity of the play's contrasts, mirrored in Innogen's language, which oscillates between the controlled and the phantasmagoric. Cymbeline and Innogen shared a

family trait of impulsiveness. There was an important recognition that the wager on Innogen's chastity undermines Iachimo's misogyny whilst releasing Posthumus'. The part of Posthumus is not, of course, a grateful one. When Irving gave the play a rare Victorian outing, he elected to play Iachimo. Peter Woodward, in Hall's production, was humourless in the early scenes and disquietingly self-regarding in his purgatorial prison. It was not until late in the rehearsal period that Hall decided that he should have doubled

Posthumus with Cloten. The idea is a plausible one, despite the necessity of two exits as one character and immediate re-entry as another. There is some evidence that the Elizabethan stage relished such transformations when there was a point to be made by them. Hall's point would have been that Posthumus had to rid himself of Cloten-like aspects before he could be said to have merited Innogen. Theatrically, the doubling would certainly ease Innogen's task when she wakes beside the headless body of a man whom she believes to be Posthumus ('I know the shape of 's leg; this is his hand'), but who is, in fact, Cloten (fig. 80). There can be few more demanding scenes for an actress. Geraldine James played it with a sustained intimacy that made us almost voyeurs. Roger Warren reports that she considered it a kind of love scene.[16]

Cymbeline appeared in the Cottesloe as part of a season which also included *The Winter's Tale* and *The Tempest*. Such groupings often reveal networks of affinity, and the thematic links of the last plays are familiar territory. The climactic intervention of Jupiter in *Cymbeline* has either to be cut or enacted as fully as scenic invention and the production budget will allow. We think inevitably of the oracle whose message Leontes defies. Posthumus, as Hall was careful to expose, is almost as speedy as Leontes in his conversion of suspicion into diseased sexual obsession, but, unlike Leontes, he hears the god. Leontes has his purgatory ahead of him; Posthumus, in Hall's production, is already there. The end of the Cottesloe *Winter's Tale* was intentionally hesitant. Reconciliation remained provisional. It was not intended to be so in *Cymbeline*. Having forgiven Innogen, Posthumus could, at last, forgive himself. But Hall, mistakenly I think, was unwilling to allow the audience to express

its collusion with the plot through laughter in the play's notorious final scene. His keener perception was of a parallel between Innogen's self-loss in Wales and Hermione's sixteen-year death. It was almost as if we were being allowed a glimpse of the unwritten scenes of *The Winter's Tale*, with Pisanio playing Paulina to Innogen's Hermione, taking her through a first death to the stubborn hope of an afterlife.

This kind of illumination from play to play was only possible because the subsidized theatre could afford the luxury of playing three related Shakespearian dramas, including the box-office risk of *Cymbeline*, in the same repertory. By the 1990s the golden age of subsidized theatre in Britain was over. One effect is likely to be that there will be a gradual diminution of the Shakespearian canon to a core of 'safe' plays. The RSC has always had a box-office 'black list' of traditional losers such as *Titus Andronicus* and *Timon of Athens*; there is now emerging a 'grey list' of works, including *Cymbeline* and even *Coriolanus*, which the company cannot afford to risk playing on its main stage.

The trio of last plays at the National in the late 1980s marked the end of an era in another respect: they were the valedictory productions of Peter Hall, founder of the RSC and first director of the National in its vast, publicly funded three-house home on the South Bank. Moving with the times, Sir Peter turned in the 1990s to the private sector. But Hall has been a key figure in another respect, too: together with Peter Brook and John Barton, he so promoted the role of the director in British Shakespeare that we are now more likely to name a production after its director—the Deborah Warner *Titus*, for instance—than its leading player. That is the subject of the next chapter.

Facing: FIG. 80 Innogen with the body of Cloten: Geraldine James in Peter Hall's production of *Cymbeline*, National Theatre, 1988.

10
Directors' Shakespeare

ROBERT SMALLWOOD

A tempestuous noise of Thunder and Lightning heard: Enter a Ship-master, and a Boteswaine.

THUS begins the first play of the First Folio, the opening stage direction of *The Tempest* heralding a series of descriptive instructions highly unusual in their elaboration and possibly Shakespearian in their origin.[1] As the house lights go down to the sound of electronic music at the beginning of the production that occupies a place in the Royal Shakespeare Company's repertoire as this book goes to press, the lid of a theatrical property basket, placed in the centre of an otherwise bare stage, opens slowly. From the basket a blue-suited, blond-haired figure steps, with great deliberation, and walks, slowly, automaton-like, round the basket, carefully closes its lid, climbs onto it, and claps his hands. In response a ship's lantern is lowered from the flies to a point just above his head. Ariel (for so the blue-suited figure will later be identified) reaches up, takes hold of it, pauses a moment, then sets it swinging vigorously on its rope to and fro across the stage. As soon as it moves, we hear 'a tempestuous noise of Thunder and Lightning' and the Master and Boatswain make their appearance. We have been watching an example of directors' Shakespeare.

Sam Mendes's production of *The Tempest*, which opened at the Royal Shakespeare Theatre in Stratford-upon-Avon on 5 August 1993, is an appropriate point at

which to start this chapter not only because it is current at the time of writing. It is also a typical example of the kind of production that has dominated the professional Shakespearian stage in this country for the last three or four decades, the period with which this chapter is concerned. Intelligent and inventive, with a large-scale (and rather beautiful) set commissioned at considerable expense from a free-lance designer, Anthony Ward, who has had wide experience in large theatre spaces, operatic and dramatic, it offers an approach to the play that is likely to be of particular interest to those who already know *The Tempest*. Indeed, those who do not know it might be puzzled by the identity of the slow-moving figure who swings the ship's lantern; the wiser sort, of course, are invited to read back into the moment their awareness of Ariel's account to Prospero, in the second scene, of his creation of the tempest; they are also invited to remember what they might have read (or perhaps even written) of academic criticism of *The Tempest*'s self-conscious theatricality, for the sight of a flyman lowering a lantern and a property basket placed over a trapdoor deliberately draws attention to the idea of making theatre in the production's opening moments. By watching an actor make the tempest we are invited to think about actors making *The Tempest*, and thence, perhaps, to consider the further idea, pervasive in some critical thinking about the play, of the first of the Folio's list of 'The Principall Actors in all these Playes' (Shakespeare himself, of course) making, at the end of his career, the play that stands first in the 1623 volume.

The production, then, is not only going to present Shakespeare's play; it is also going to offer something of an interpretative essay upon it, showing its awareness of other critical essays, academic and theatrical. For most current professional productions of Shakespeare are not direct, unhampered encounters between actors and texts. 'Directors' Shakespeare' is a phenomenon deriving, indirectly but inevitably, from the great expansion of the academic Shakespeare industry over the last half-century and more: productions of the plays take their place in a general climate of critical thinking about Shakespeare and cater for audiences which include many who are well aware of the play and its recent critical and theatrical history and who thus provide a potentially awkward mixture with those who are coming to it for the first time.

Sam Mendes took a degree in English at the University of Cambridge. He is thus part of that tradition of directors, trained in English literary criticism, whose work has dominated recent Shakespeare production in Britain. I want to return at the end of this chapter to his production of *The Tempest*, partly because this was the first large-stage Shakespeare production by a young director whose work in smaller spaces had already been very successful, raising expectations that later editions of this book may need to chronicle. The Shakespeare director did not, of course, arise, Minerva-like, thirty years or so ago—with Peter Hall's reconstitution of the Shakespeare Memorial Theatre into the Royal Shakespeare Company, for example, important landmark though that was.[2] If by 'director' we mean the person who makes decisions when uncertainties arise in the rehearsal room, then it is difficult not to imagine the author of Shakespeare's plays as in some sense their first director. In fact, of course, the rehearsal room has not even been reached when the director is exercising what is perhaps the most significant aspect of his power, the casting of the play. And from the quartos of *Much Ado about Nothing* and

Romeo and Juliet, where actors' rather than characters' names occasionally appear in stage directions, we know that a certain amount of casting was going on in Shakespeare's head as he composed. His main exploration of a performance in preparation also shows Shakespeare perfectly well acquainted with what we might now call 'directing' a play, for in terms of taking charge of the rehearsal space (or endeavouring to do so) and, in particular, of controlling the casting (not without a struggle, but ultimately successfully) Peter Quince fulfils the main duties of a modern director in respect of the preparations for the performance of the tragical mirth of 'Pyramus and Thisbe'. Indeed, to take the matter a stage further back, Quince seems to have exercised the even more fundamental directorial prerogative of choosing the play to be performed.[3] If by 'directing' Shakespeare we mean choosing the text, casting the play, and deciding among options that emerge in the rehearsal room, then all the productions dealt with in this book are 'directors' Shakespeare' and the title of this chapter is meaningless.

As with so much in our recent understanding of Shakespeare one is helped to define the term more precisely by the work of the scholar whom this volume honours. In essays published in 1975 and 1976, Stanley Wells isolated some of the characteristics that distinguish the recent director of Shakespeare from his or her predecessors.[4] That crucial development of the late nineteenth and early twentieth centuries, the emergence of someone taking charge of the performance of a Shakespeare play who will not himself appear in it—William Poel, Harley Granville-Barker, the Duke of Saxe-Meiningen—is the beginning of the process. Their productions were obviously not part of the mainstream of commercial theatre: all their work was what we would now call 'subsidized', the result of wealth providing theatrical space and time for experiments which the box-office would not have been able to support. And it is not until the general acceptance of the principle of nationally subsidized theatre in this country in the 1960s (which the preceding chapter has dealt with) that the modern professional Shakespeare director becomes a reliably identifiable and more or less constant theatrical presence. Up to this period, in the years between the wars and just beyond, the director of a production of Shakespeare in the British theatre—who would, of course, have called himself the 'producer'—is likely to have been a theatre professional, educated, like Mr Vincent Crummles's pony, to the stage. As Wells points out, the two directors of the Stratford company immediately preceding the arrival of Peter Hall both went straight from school into theatrical careers. Since then, however, as Wells puts it, 'a degree in English seems in danger of becoming a required qualification for directing a Shakespeare play, at any rate at Stratford' ('The Academic and the Theatre', 6), and the list of men—John Barton, Peter Brook, Peter Hall, Terry Hands, Nicholas Hytner, Sam Mendes, Adrian Noble, Trevor Nunn—who, for the last three decades, have dominated the Stratford theatre is ample testimony to the truth, in part prophetic, of Wells's statement. Stratford is not, of course, the whole of British Shakespeare production—Jonathan Miller, for example, who has worked there only once, has directed many important productions at the National Theatre and elsewhere—but work there over the last thirty years or so provides a more than ample reservoir of examples of the phenomenon of 'directors' Shakespeare' during this period. In choosing examples for discussion I have made use of the two categories defined by Stanley Wells of 'open' and 'interpretative' productions. 'Open' productions concentrate on 'serving the play, interpreting it in so far as the text requires interpretative decisions, but allowing it to make its impact without nudging us into seeing significances beneath the surface', whereas 'interpretative' productions are 'selective', possibly 'esoteric', and often also 'challenging, unorthodox, disturbing' ('Directors' Shakespeare', 71–2, 77). In my selection of productions I have avoided some very obvious landmarks—John Barton's 'Wars of the Roses' in 1964, for example, or Peter Brook's *A Midsummer Night's Dream* in 1970—that have been widely discussed elsewhere (the latter in the preceding chapter of this book).

Not all recent Shakespeare directors have had degrees in English, of course, and exceptions even to the male hegemony can be found—Deborah Warner's productions of *Titus Andronicus* (1987) and *King John* (1988) at Stratford and *King Lear* at the National Theatre (1990) were major achievements by any standards—but the generalization made by Wells twenty years ago, that Shakespeare production in this country in the last third of the twentieth century has been in the hands of male graduates of university English departments, still largely holds true. The dominance of Cambridge as the source of most of the degrees is even more remarkable. Of the eight men listed above as dominating the work of the Royal Shakespeare Company over this period, five are Cambridge graduates, the more recent among them making Christopher McCullough's analysis of the 'Cambridge connection' of the Royal Shakespeare Company as a part of the Leavisite heritage (both Hall and Nunn were pupils of the late F. R. Leavis) seem—not inappropriately, given his critical stance—very much the product of the moment that produced it.[5] McCullough's essay is valuable, however, in raising critical issues deep within the concept of 'directors' Shakespeare'. 'The dominant concern of Shakespearean production over the last twenty-five years', he writes (p. 117), 'has been the effort by various directors to make their productions "relevant" through the process of seeing the poetic language of the plays as definitive of their entirety'—and he is clearly right to see this as a Leavisite enterprise, though with obvious Coleridgean antecedents. But a literary critical 'reading' of the text is, he goes on (p. 119), 'essentially an individualist practice' and this works 'antagonistically against the collectivist concept of theatre; theatre is not the product of an individual reading of the play, but the result of a collaborative effort in a continuous state of remaking'.

So fundamental a challenge, so baldly stated, to the idea of 'directors' (or director's) theatre'—and even the orthographical decision about where to place the apostrophe involves the question of individualism—raises issues that underlie the entire phase of British Shakespeare production that is my subject here. One reason for the emergence of directorial power in modern Shakespeare production, as Wells points out

('Directors' Shakespeare', 65–6), is purely pragmatic. There is now so much of a technical nature involved in putting on a play on a large professional stage (not just costumes and a probably highly mechanized set, but lighting of enormous sophistication and stage apparatus of great complexity) that it has proved convenient, if not essential, for one person to take responsibility for its co-ordination. But there are more basic factors at work than Wells allows, for this responsibility usually carries with it economic control in the most basic sense: we may talk about 'directors' Shakespeare' being threatened at times by 'designers' Shakespeare' or even by 'lighting designers' Shakespeare', but the fact remains that in almost all large-scale Shakespeare productions now and in recent years the director appoints a free-lance designer, lighting designer, composer, and any other specialists he or she may need; what is more, that ancient directorial right to 'cast the show' may very well involve the decision as to whether particular actors are in work or unemployed, for even at so apparently permanent a company as the RSC the longest actors' contracts are currently for sixty weeks (the period of rehearsal and performance of a Stratford season and the short annual visit to Newcastle upon Tyne that follows it). The directorial power of decision-making, then, in a profession where unemployment is chronic and on a massive scale, derives from the ultimate reality of giving or withholding work and wages. Artistic control is founded upon economic power.

It is against that ineluctable fact of life in most recent Shakespeare productions that McCullough's dialectic of 'individualist reading' and 'collaborative effort' has to be seen. Of course it is much less simple than this. The economic facts also dictate that the director, himself or herself almost certainly a free-lance temporary employee of the company, will have to leave the production as soon as it opens in order to find other work. The 'collaborative effort' of the acting company will then have collective control of the organic development of the production through the period of its life, which, in the case of a production at the RSC or the National Theatre, can frequently mean 100 or even 200 performances. That development will

be within the broad parameters of the director's 'individual reading' established by set, costume, and, above all, the chemistry of relationships created by casting, but will nevertheless often be very considerable. To encounter a mature production, of which the actors have taken comfortable control, in which they are all secure enough to experiment, adjust, and change, is to see directors' Shakespeare at its best. If the most important part of the director's job is to get the casting right, then surely the second most important part is to leave the chosen actors with a production in which they have space to grow and develop. The rehearsal process itself, which the popular concept always wishes to see as the area where tyrannical directorial power is wielded, comes a poor third.

Protests against the dominance of 'individual reading' allegedly inherent in directors' Shakespeare do not, of course, begin with cultural materialist criticism. Twenty years ago John Russell Brown published his plea to 'free Shakespeare' and envisaged a company of a dozen actors working, without a director, in what he saw as roughly Elizabethan conditions, with their own parts only and few group rehearsals; and the audience, freed from the usual passive state in which it watches the 'well-oiled machine' of most modern productions, would sit all around the stage in the same light as the actors, free to 'enter the enactment in imagination'.[6] There is a touch of 'back to Poel' about this, but it is clearly related to the search through the 1970s and 1980s for smaller, less formal spaces for Shakespeare performance than the picture-frame, design-orientated stages of established theatres, smaller spaces that might recreate the essential and elementary relationship between player and spectator that Shakespeare's plays were written to exploit. From simpler stages would follow the removal of those technical demands which had led to the need for someone to take directorial control, while much smaller production budgets would diminish the director's economic power. Small-space Shakespeare has been a potent force in the history of British Shakespeare performance over the last couple of decades and I shall return to a particular example of it later. But the extent to which it has modified the artistic dominance of the director is debatable. After a season with the RSC in 1984–5, Kenneth Branagh left to create the Renaissance Theatre Company and worked in studio spaces (at the Lyric, Hammersmith, Riverside Studios, and Birmingham Repertory Theatre) on productions of Shakespeare's plays directed by actors: *Romeo and Juliet* and *Twelfth Night* by himself, *Much Ado about Nothing* by Judi Dench (fig. 95), *As You Like It* by Geraldine McEwan, and *Hamlet* by Derek Jacobi. All of them were distinguished and interesting pieces of work, all of them had something of that actor-generated group energy that lies behind Russell Brown's vision, but all of them were very definitely 'directed', some falling rather more into Wells's 'open' category of production, some—Derek Jacobi's *Hamlet* in particular—into his 'interpretative' grouping.[7] For the most part, studio or 'chamber' Shakespeare in our period is as firmly associated with the names of major directors—Trevor Nunn with his *Macbeth*, *Othello*, and *Measure for Measure* at Stratford's Other Place, Peter Hall with the late plays at the National's Cottesloe Theatre, Declan Donnellan with his Cheek by Jowl touring productions—as is work on the larger scale.

How might one describe and characterize some of the achievements of 'directors' Shakespeare' over the last thirty years and more? Within a single chapter such a process must be highly selective while endeavouring to be reasonably representative. To divide productions into 'open' and 'interpretative' remains valid and useful, though clearly there are degrees of both. And even before the exercises of directorial power, artistic and economic, that I have been discussing, comes that earliest decision of all—which play to do and when. Is the motive behind that choice to *tell* the audience something new about a Shakespeare play or simply to *show* the play to them? The answer may partly be governed by whether or not the director thinks they know it already; and certainly the better-known plays, which means the plays that are financially safest at the box-office, have been the most subject to interpretative production. That is partly, of course, because their box-office potential means, even

in subsidized theatres (for subsidy in this country has never been at such a level as to take away from the principal Shakespeare companies the economic imperative of selling seats), that productions of them recur with greater frequency. Such repetition brings with it the built-in likelihood of idiosyncrasy of interpretation as the inevitable reaction to fear of sameness and monotony. Ironically, this situation has been exacerbated, at least for the Royal Shakespeare Company, by the arrival of the smaller auditoriums: since the opening of the Other Place (with less than 200 seats) in 1974, and of the Swan Theatre (430 seats) in 1986, the repertoire of the Royal Shakespeare Theatre itself has effectively been reduced from thirty-seven plays to a couple of dozen at the most, for no play of uncertain popular appeal, no box-office risk, is going to be tried in a 1,500-capacity theatre when there are spaces so much safer in which to present it.

Open vs. Interpretative Direction

All of which explains why my first example of 'open' directorial interpretation of a Shakespeare play, and one of the most remarkable achievements of modern British Shakespeare production, was of a rarely performed play in a small auditorium. Deborah Warner's production of *Titus Andronicus* opened at the Swan Theatre in Stratford in April 1987. A woman director, that extraordinary rarity in the world of post-war British Shakespeare production, Deborah Warner arrived at Stratford (without the standard requirement of the degree in English—her theatrical education had been through stage management) with a remarkable record of Shakespearian success with her own small-scale fringe company, Kick Theatre, bringing some of her actors with her. And she proceeded to flout the first rule of interpretative directors' Shakespeare by not cutting the text: perhaps for the first time every line of *Titus Andronicus* was to be given. This was in the sharpest contrast to the first directorial rehabilitation of the play, Peter Brook's in 1955, which cut nearly 700 lines. Brian Cox, who played the title-role, has written of what he calls the 'egalitarian' methods of Deborah Warner's rehearsal process.[8] Her rehearsals begin with thorough, painstaking readings and rereadings of the play, actors taking all and every part but their own. 'The process is extremely tiring', writes Cox (p. 177), 'as democracy can be, but effective, since it creates a responsibility within the ensemble towards the play as a totality and not just to the individual characters, with the result that a lot of the staging ideas come very quickly in rehearsal.' Nor were design ideas imposed on the company and announced at the first rehearsal, as economic and practical necessity—it takes at least as long to build the sets as the time allowed to rehearse

the play—so often dictates for scenically large-scale productions in big theatrical spaces. There was no composer appointed to the production, any music (and there was little beyond the notorious whistling of a certain 'merry tune' from *Snow White* as the company prepared the final banquet) being supplied by the actors. A comparatively unknown designer, Isabella Bywater, attended rehearsals; the set was simply the Swan Theatre itself (the auditorium as well as the stage) with a balcony for upper-level playing such as exhortations to the citizenry of Rome (a role fulfilled by the audience), a trapdoor for Mutius' grave or the pit in the hunting scene, and a rough wooden table for the Andronicus family's fly-disturbed meal and the final, astonishing banquet. Costumes flung together images from many periods. For his first unforgettable entry (fig. 81), sitting on a ladder carried

Fig. 81 *Titus Andronicus*, directed by Deborah Warner, RSC at the Swan Theatre, Stratford-upon-Avon, 1987: the first entrance of Titus (Brian Cox).

by his Gothic prisoners and leading Tamora on a chain like a captive beast, Titus wore a laurel wreath, Roman breastplate, and modern boots and trousers. Into an ordinary galvanized metal bucket, available from any ironmonger's, fell Titus' severed hand; like the *chef de cuisine* at a smart restaurant, Titus entered for the final showdown in tall white chef's hat and starched white overalls, leaping over the table in obsequious eagerness to welcome his victims; like grandpa on a bank-holiday Monday, he appeared to shoot his arrows in a string vest with a knotted handkerchief on his head, a dotty old man, seemingly harmless, as he quietly prepared his terrible vengeance. Such homely images, jostling against suggestions of the Roman and the medieval in randomly eclectic manner, had emerged organically from the rehearsal process, many of the costumes in fact coming from stock. Not that the look of the production was in the end anything other than precisely calculated. The sombre browns and buffs and oatmeals of the majority of the costumes contrasted with the crimson of Tamora's dress as empress or the stark white of imperial robes and banquet table-cloth for the final scene and with the grey clay which daubed Lavinia's stumps and had, one supposed, been used to staunch their bleeding. This, and the faintness of the suggestion of redness from her mouth, the severed heads and hand all discreetly bound in buff linen, led one for a long time to believe that, in this most notoriously bloody of plays, the use of stage blood was to be eschewed. And then Titus finally cut the throats of the loathsome Chiron and Demetrius and the audience's expectations, felt with such disturbing, shocking urgency, were at last fulfilled as the blood gushed into the great pastry bowl held between Lavinia's stumps. Peter Brook had had the sons killed off stage and had found a famously stylized method of presenting Lavinia's handlessness, with red and white ribbon streamers flowing from Vivien Leigh's lips and wrists at her entrance after the rape, an entrance accompanied by harp music that replaced nearly the whole of Marcus's speech of reaction. This elegant, even beautiful, and highly theatrical presentation of pain could not have been further from the bruised, groaning, mud-bedaubed figure of Sonia

Ritter's Lavinia appearing from her mutilation, to whom Donald Sumpter's Marcus spoke every line, every ingenious Euphuistic simile, of his speech of reaction. His hushed tones seemed a perfectly believable attempt to come to terms with the horror he was witnessing and the grief and shock he was feeling as he tried, again and again, to find a way of putting his reaction into words, coming round on the subject from different angles of his mind, all to no avail.

The aim of the production throughout was to hold the audience's attention firmly, unrelentingly, on the succession of horror, pain, and violence. We were permitted to laugh when the text allowed it—even at the self-sacrificing squabble among Titus, his brother, and his son about who should have the privilege of being the first to lose a hand to save Titus' captive sons—for the element of the ludicrous in human life, and suffering, which Cox emphasizes in his essay, was not shirked; but we were not allowed to escape or ever to stop believing, and even if we looked away from the horror, of Titus cutting off his hand with a cheese wire, perhaps, or breaking his daughter's neck like a chicken's, there was no escaping the sound of bones breaking. The exploitation of the space of the Swan Theatre (and subsequently that of the tiny white box of The Pit in London, to which it transferred) was part of the production's effect: exits and entrances were made through the auditorium and for any scene of public exhortation it was the audience who were the public. We were participants in the play's atrocities (particularly in the shock of realizing our gratification at the vengeance on the rapists), contaminated by its horrors, and the whole production became a study in the sources and consequences of violence at both a personal and a social level. For those who saw it it will never again be possible to dismiss *Titus Andronicus* as a minor example of its author's theatrical art.

To turn from Deborah Warner's *Titus Andronicus* of 1987 to John Barton's *Richard II* of 1973 is to move from an extreme example of 'open' directorial presentation to one of sharply idiosyncratic 'interpretative' direction. A much better-known play, being presented at the RSC's main auditorium, a major designer,

Timothy O'Brien, who had worked a good deal on the Stratford stage, a director not only with academic training but one who had formerly held an academic post at Cambridge and who was returning to the play after initial work on it for a touring version—the production had all the ingredients for full-scale, conceptualized directors' Shakespeare and delivered the finished article in as complete and polished a form as could be discovered in the British theatre in the period under review. 'When a director handles a play', wrote John Barton, 'he tries to focus on what seems to him most important in it. In doing so he is surely engaged in an act of critical interpretation analogous to that undertaken by the literary critic in his study . . . He tries to communicate what is implicit in the text as well as what lies on the surface.'[9] And what Barton found implicit in *Richard II* was the idea of 'the King's two bodies', as the programme note of that title by his wife Anne Barton, author of *Shakespeare and the Idea of the Play*, made clear. 'Probably never has the connection between the academic and theatrical Shakespeare establishments been closer', remarks Dennis Kennedy, and the production was a compelling, fascinating exposition, through a brilliant performance of the play, of certain critical theories

about it.[10] The stage was largely bare, but with long staircases or escalators on either side, reaching skywards, an immediate visualization of all the play's imagery of rising and falling—the power of Richard and Bolingbroke in the balance (III. iv. 83–9), the buckets in the well (IV. i. 180–8), Bolingbroke's rising 'thus nimbly by a true king's fall' (IV. i. 317) (fig. 82). Between the staircases a platform was usually stationary above, to provide an upper acting area, but could go up and down like a funicular rail-car, as when it carried Richard, resplendent in metallic golden robes, to the base court: 'Down, down I come like glistering Phaethon' (III. iii. 178).

That idea of rising and falling, of interchangeability, was encapsulated in the decision to have two actors, Richard Pasco and Ian Richardson, alternate the roles of Richard and Bolingbroke. To be aware of the full effect of this, of course, one needed to see the production both ways round; the alternative route to the information was by way of the souvenir programme with its critical extracts and essay. The real intention of the production—and this is a recurrent feature of severely interpretative directors' Shakespeare—was not to present the play as immediately and accessibly as possible for audiences coming to it afresh; it was to interest audiences who already knew it well in more conventional guises with a clearly argued, intellectually stimulating, individual critical reading of it.

It began with the entry of a figure resembling Shakespeare, followed by two columns of actors in rehearsal clothes, one led by Richard Pasco, the other by Ian Richardson. 'Shakespeare' then mounted a small dais, centre stage, upon which stood a scarecrow sort of figure, supporting the crown, a golden mask, the King's robe—the impedimenta of regal office. He took the crown and mask and presented them to the actor who was to wield royal power for the first section of the performance—to play Richard. There followed a ceremonial robing of the King as he assumed his role while the rest of the actors donned their costumes and wigs, preparing to perform the roles in which they too had been cast. The court bowed to Richard: 'Long live the King', 'May the King live for ever'; and, removing the ceremonial mask, the actor was ready to play the King: 'Old John of Gaunt, time-honoured Lancaster . . .' At the end of the play Bolingbroke received from Exton Richard's coffin, its dimensions incapable of containing a corpse that had not been dismembered, and to the sound of solemn music a vault opened and the coffin was placed in it. The dirge then gave way to coronation music, the figure of Shakespeare reappeared offering Bolingbroke the crown, the courtiers gathered round, the music reached a crescendo, and two courtiers were left standing on either side of the glittering figure of the King. They threw back their hoods and were revealed as Richard Pasco and Ian Richardson. The golden figure between them was empty, hollow, sham, the tailor's dummy scarecrow, and it wore a death-mask.

Between these two moments the production had energetically explored the ideas of the King as actor and of the role of monarch as an imposition by the hand of fate upon the man who tries to fill it. Richard's incompetence was in no sense blameworthy, for the terrible duty was not of his own seeking; as he fell from power Bolingbroke rose, willy-nilly, like the bucket in the well. Bolingbroke often seemed to be dominated by the Earl of Northumberland, a dark and menacing figure, sometimes wearing high buskins to give him greater physical presence, a kingmaker looming over the proceedings like some huge black crow. At the execution of Bushy and Green, Bolingbroke read out the charges against them with obvious distaste from a scroll which Northumberland had given him, just one of many adjustments that shielded Bolingbroke from culpability for the usurpation of the crown, presenting him as just as much the victim of historical forces as Richard. The process even included the provision of what Shakespeare has conspicuously failed to provide for Bolingbroke, a soliloquy: in v. iii lines taken from 2 Henry IV were adapted to present him in a mood of exhausted resignation to the fate that had befallen him and generalizing from it to the situation of all monarchs: 'Uneasy lies the head that wears a crown.' The culmination of this process came in the prison scene.

'If my word be sterling yet in England | Let it command a mirror hither straight,' Richard says in the deposition scene (IV. i. 263–4) and a large round mirror was brought to him. His smashing of it as he contemplated his face in it removed all the glass, leaving only the circular frame which Bolingbroke lowered slowly over Richard's head on the line 'The shadow of your sorrow hath destroyed | The shadow of your face' (ll. 291–2), halo becoming halter as he did so. Richard wore it as he was separated from his queen and it was still around his neck in the prison scene when the groom, in heavily hooded cloak, came to visit him. When Richard referred to being 'tired by jauncing Bolingbroke' (v. v. 94), the groom threw back his hood and there was Bolingbroke himself looking at him. Richard took the frame of the mirror from around his neck and held it up between them and they knelt in silence for several seconds before the groom/Bolingbroke's exit on 'What my tongue dares not, that my heart shall say' (l. 97) (fig. 83). Two kings, two victims of history, or of fate, two actors, both of whom have, during the course of the evening, had a

Facing: FIG 83 *Richard II*, Royal Shakespeare Theatre, 1973; Ian Richardson as Bolingbroke (hooded and disguised as a groom) and Richard Pasco as Richard confront each other in prison.

try at playing the royal role—and who will play it again tomorrow, though in the reverse order—knelt and gazed at each other through a mirror. Was it really Bolingbroke, or was Richard imagining it? Was it even just a case of an actor doubling parts, Bolingbroke and the groom? In a sense it did not matter, since the production had concerned itself from the start with the arbitrary way in which the royal role is cast and with the powerlessness of those who try to fill it. One was invited to contemplate two actors, each playing the king, each seeing the other as a reflection of himself, in a moment of silence, Shakespeare's text some little way below the surface: the moment crystallized many of the production's concerns and it exemplifies much that typifies the interpretative form of directors' Shakespeare.

Experiments and Epics

Between the extremes of Deborah Warner's *Titus Andronicus* and John Barton's *Richard II* the pendulum of director-dominated British Shakespeare production has swung for the last three decades and more. From time to time the cry that the plays should be 'allowed to speak for themselves' is heard—which usually means that they should be performed as the speaker remembers them being performed when he or she first started going to the theatre. It is, of course, a fatuous phrase, for a printed text is essentially non-vocal and the moment one gives it a voice by casting actors to speak its words the process of decision-making begins, even about so basic a question as the age of most of the characters in most of the plays. Sometimes one senses the director's choices rolling, as it seems, tank-like over things one thought precious in the play: Ian Judge's decision to have one actor for both Antipholuses and one actor for both Dromios in the 1990 Stratford *Comedy of Errors*, for example, thus

annihilating the romance of the play's conclusion, its anticipation of the endings of *Twelfth Night* and *Pericles* and *The Winter's Tale*, in mere puzzlement over the technique of solving the problem the director had created for himself. But against one's disgruntlement and indignation had to be set one's admiration for the brilliance of the actors in performing those doubles and the sheer delight of audiences at what they had been watching.

Doubling of parts to create a vehicle for actorly virtuosity is an example of what one might call the showman-director at work. Something rather more radical was to be seen in the Olivier auditorium of the National Theatre in 1992 when the French Canadian director Robert Lepage presented *A Midsummer Night's Dream* on a stage which the designer Michael Levine had converted into a large, mud-fringed pool, the balletic figure of Angela Laurier's Puck skittering crab-like across its surface to turn out—for this is to be a *night's* dream—a bare electric light-bulb to mark the beginning of the performance. The production provided an extraordinary theatrical experience, often visually astonishing, sometimes hauntingly beautiful as light was reflected off the stage's shimmering surface, sometimes bizarre and absurd as actors struggled in the glutinous mess. Vocally it was almost unrelievedly disappointing, a situation crystallized by the Puck of Angela Laurier, a circus artist and contortionist operating in what was for her a foreign language and basing a performance of remarkable verbal precariousness and great physical agility on the mistaken assumption that Puck refers to the marine crustacean rather than the fruit of the apple-tree when remembering himself in 'the very likeness of a roasted crab'. The primordial mud of its setting, the gamelan music that almost continuously accompanied its dialogue, the strange solemnity of the lovers in their metal bedstead being punted towards the disturbing and often distressing dreams of their sexual initiation, all these made a profound effect; the text did not, and one found oneself wishing, especially during the desperately unfunny performance of 'Pyramus and Thisbe', that the director had been more willing to use his blue pencil. Shakespeare 'offers a lot of permission to the actor, the translator, the director', remarks Lepage; 'you don't feel in a literal environment when working with him'.[11] That sense of 'permission' is the basis, obviously, of the interpretative freedom that makes possible directors' Shakespeare. Where interpretation ends and adaptation begins is a hazy (or, more pertinent to the present example perhaps, muddy) frontier, but by any standards Lepage was near it. 'The reason why a lot of people, and I include myself in this, are very caught by the image, is that we've lost faith in words' (*Platform Papers*, 3, p. 34). But all that survives of Shakespeare's *A Midsummer Night's Dream* is the words; the spectacle that took them as its starting-point in this production created a visual and musical entertainment alongside rather than through and upon them. The dominant member of the duo in this example of 'directors' Shakespeare' was not the dramatist.

Eight years earlier, in 1984, Peter Hall's production of *Coriolanus* had made a quite different kind of attempt to fill the great energy-absorbing space of the Olivier Theatre. Modern-dress Shakespeare on the professional English stage began with Barry Jackson and has been discussed in an earlier chapter. It remains a regular device in the directorial repertoire, sometimes in its pure form, sometimes in productions of deliberate chronological vagueness and eclecticism. Here Peter Hall was using it in the latter style, actors appearing in togas with modern sweaters and trousers visible beneath, or, in the case of Cominius, in Roman armour for the battle scenes and then in archetypal businessman's pin-stripes as the manœuvring to force Coriolanus into political power began. Coriolanus himself first appeared in the suavest of white suits straight from the latest fashion magazine, but with a Roman sword swung menacingly over his shoulder. For the fight scenes with Aufidius the period shifted to the studied timelessness of knotted jock-straps. The production stays in the memory for its acting—Irene Worth's cosily relentless Volumnia and Ian McKellen's Coriolanus (fig. 84), eccentric, disturbing, intelligent, ostentatious in its vocal and physical brilliance—but it is relevant to a chapter on directors' Shakespeare for its experiment in anachronism. The eclecticism of its costuming was part of its attempt to suggest the ease

with which the futile and destructive struggle of mindlessly opposed political forces can shift from ancient Rome to modern Britain, via Shakespeare's England and other points along the way. The sandpit arena of its set was peopled for the play's great mob scenes by embarrassed-looking National Theatre spectators dragooned (by political activists among the cast) from their stage-side seats to join half-heartedly in the scenes of political unrest. Was their lack of commitment and general sheepishness a comment, one wondered, on the pallor and inadequacy of political convictions in the 1980s, or were we to see the handbag- and briefcase-carrying 'demonstrators' as typical of their hapless predecessors down the centuries? The production was curiously successful in raising such questions and in its final image it brilliantly conveyed the fate of the politician who has himself become an anachronism. Responding to Aufidius' taunt of 'boy' with a whine of rage and resentment, Coriolanus flashed at the Volscian mob with the great sword which had carved his reputation. With shocking suddenness he was felled by the crack of rifle fire as a volley of shots from Aufidius' followers dropped him onto the steps of the arena in which he had flaunted his military skills and political ineptitudes, to roll dead onto the sand below.

If one considers the plays that audiences since the 1950s have been able to see regularly on the English stage compared with earlier generations of theatre-goers, it is perhaps with the history plays that directors' Shakespeare has achieved most. At regular intervals since 1951 Stratford audiences have been able to see the first and second tetralogies, or both, in sequence; and it was an assertion of the English Shakespeare Company's rising power that they were able, in 1986–7, to take productions of both tetralogies on a national tour. Each of Stratford's artistic directors has felt it to be part of the duties, and assertions, of office to encounter the great history cycles, starting with Anthony Quayle in 1951 in a version of the second tetralogy that stands as an early example of academic influence, for the productions owed much to the critical writing on the histories (then enjoying considerable influence) of E. M. W. Tillyard and John

Fig. 84 Ian McKellen as Caius Martius in Peter Hall's *Coriolanus*, National Theatre, 1984.

FIG. 85 The battle of St Albans in *The Plantagenets*, Royal Shakespeare Theatre, 1988.

Dover Wilson. The two-year project by John Barton and Peter Hall on both tetralogies, the first massively rewritten as *The Wars of the Roses* to produce two plays from the three parts of *Henry VI*, marked the Shakespeare quatercentenary in 1964. During the mid- to late 1970s Terry Hands slowly accumulated all eight plays, the three parts of *Henry VI* for once in full, in productions designed by Farrah and with Alan Howard performing all the kings except Henry IV (not easy if you are preparing for Henry V by playing Hal). The productions were never seen in sequence, though they were surely intended (and on the whole deserved) to be so—perhaps for the opening in 1982 of the RSC's new London theatre at the Barbican where instead we had Trevor Nunn, at the height of his reputation as an RSC director following the international success of *Nicholas Nickleby*, finding it necessary to mark the opening of the new building by making his only excursion during many years at the RSC into the

histories with the two parts of *Henry IV*. And it was exactly these plays that Adrian Noble chose to mark his début as Artistic Director of the company in 1991, having previously launched Kenneth Branagh at Stratford in *Henry V* in 1984 and reduced the first tetralogy to three plays in *The Plantagenets* (fig. 85) in 1988 (interestingly by a process of severe reduction and minimal rewriting, in sharp contrast to the much bolder willingness of John Barton in 1963 to write large quantities of mock-Shakespearian verse).[12] Clearly there is something in the large-scale, conceptualized, directors' theatre approach that has seemed appropriate to the great historical cycles, director and designer working together over a long period on a series of plays to create a coherent world within which the vicissitudes of the struggle for power may happen. Without directors' Shakespeare we should not, it seems incontestable, have seen so much of the histories as we have over this period.

Intimacy

Even as one identifies the epic sweep of productions of history cycles as typical of directors' Shakespeare, however, one recalls that some of its finest achievements over this period have been at the opposite end of the scale of bigness. It is difficult to pick one example of the dozens of revelatory Shakespeare productions in small spaces in the last few decades, but since the RSC's Other Place, the little studio up the road from the main theatre, has been so influential in the development of chamber Shakespeare, the production which, in the summer of 1991, reopened it after major rebuilding, Trevor Nunn's *Measure for Measure* (fig. 86), may perhaps stand as a representative. It was Nunn's third important Shakespeare production at the Other Place, following *Macbeth* (1976) and *Othello* (1988), and, like them, it took advantage of the spectator proximity of studio theatre by using many small properties to create its world. At the beginning, for example, the Duke, sitting on a couch—the production was set in the late

FIG. 86 An encounter in Freud's Vienna: *Measure for Measure*, directed by Trevor Nunn, The Other Place, 1990. David Haig as Angelo, Claire Skinner as Isabella.

nineteenth-century Vienna of Sigmund Freud—leafed through a series of newspaper cuttings which he had taken from a little green notebook; they would be identified later (in the scene in which he offered to Isabella the possibility of escape from her dilemma) as the account of Angelo's perfidy to Mariana. Here at the start, the Duke looking over them as he recited that odd little verse, possibly misplaced in Act III,[13] 'He who the sword of heaven will bear | Must be as holy as severe', they signalled the beginning of a psychological experiment on Angelo, whose appointment a few moments later as ducal deputy was received with astonishment by everyone, Escalus and Angelo above all. When Angelo predictably collapsed under the pressure placed upon him, his role as provider of human evidence for the Duke's psychological experiments was taken over by Isabella. By the end of the play the Duke, the middle-aged celibate contemplating marriage, seemed about to become the next subject of his own psychological curiosity.

Played out against the visually detailed world of Mistress Overdone's pavement café where plump women (Kate Keepdown would later turn out to be one of them) waited in poignant hopefulness for customers, and the prison, with its sordid slopping-out parade, its tired skivvy on her rounds with enamel mugs of tea (the Provost edged his kindly towards Claudio, but studio proximity allowed us to see his hands trembling too much to cope with it), the Freudian experiments first exposed David Haig's anxious, fussy, twitchy Angelo. The formal bureaucrat suddenly awakened to the overpowering strength of his own sexual feelings by the innocent naïveté of Isabella's touching him during her first appeal ('Go to *your* bosom'), he sat on that symbolic couch waiting for her return like some overgrown teenager waiting for his first date, anticipating the feel of her in his arms. His sexual approaches were clumsy, pathetic, a balding civil servant sidling along the couch to Claire Skinner's small, fair, schoolgirlish Isabella in her long black dress and little lace-up shoes. Her slowness in perceiving his intentions contrasted with the sudden ferocity and abhorrence of her rejection of them. 'Give me love', he whimpered; 'I will proclaim thee, Angelo', she

screamed, humiliating him and so goading him into a violence that had an appalling sense of the inevitable about it. Her little shoes kicked in the air as he forced himself upon her, the scene getting as horribly close to rape as perhaps it has ever done and thus again exploiting what here seemed the claustrophobic intimacy of small-space theatre.

Isabella, too, in this production, had her capacity for violence, her fists flying at Claudio as he begged her for life and pounding the table as the Duke deluded her with news of her brother's execution. The Duke's careful observation of these symptoms, not greatly surprised by them it seemed, continued the idea of psychological experimentation and case-study. Philip Madoc's Duke was endlessly curious about the motives and behaviour of those around him, the observer-physician gently guiding Isabella through the crises with which the story confronts her. Signs of his awakening affection for her were discernible, however, given the intimacy of the production. Did not his hand remain on her forehead an instant longer than was necessary for one of his friarly blessings and was not the comforting embrace at the news of her brother's death a little too warm? At the end, as the rest of Viennese society was pairing off, he risked the final experiment: 'What's mine is yours, and what is yours is mine'—and he held out his hand. The pause was even longer than the one Isabella had held a few minutes earlier as she considered whether or not to beg for Angelo's life; but there was no option for her, nowhere else to go. He waited, patiently, and in the physical intimacy of the studio space the focus was intense on that slender little hand as it trembled slightly and then, slowly, hesitantly, nervously came up to join his. They made a curious couple there at the end, the slim little girl and the middle-aged, bewhiskered, rather tubby physician whom she seemed to see rather as a father-figure than as a lover. Her earlier sexual fears had certainly not been cured and to allow one's thoughts to drift towards the idea of the consummation of this marriage was to contemplate another huge area of psychological upheaval.

Trevor Nunn's *Measure for Measure* was not at all interested in certain aspects of the play upon which modern criticism has sometimes concentrated—the nature of royal power, for example ('your grace, like power divine') and the possibility of reference to James I. It was firmly non-symbolic, always seeking naturalistic explanations for the behaviour of its characters. It did best what studio Shakespeare always does best: it offered to the audience a sense of immediacy and of recognition through its precise and detailed psychological observation of human beings in crisis.

Beginnings and Endings

The examples cited so far in this sketch of certain aspects of 'directors' Shakespeare' have offered little on the main group of comedies. Rather than offering a single representative production to redress the balance, however, let me look at two moments in the production of a play where directorial intentions may often be most clearly discerned: the beginning and the end—before Shakespeare started writing and after he stopped, leaving the director with a comparatively free hand. I choose examples of these theatrical versions of 'Once upon a time' and 'They all lived happily ever after' from two plays.

Folio (and Quarto) opening stage directions nearly always begin with the instruction 'Enter' followed by a list of characters usually in some discernibly hierarchical order. Strict adherence to what is printed would presumably mean a reasonably brisk parade onto the stage, or perhaps simultaneous manifestation through several doors, followed immediately by the first line of dialogue. Performances in the periods covered by most of the preceding chapters in this book substituted for this the immediately decisive action of raising the curtain. Modern directors have found much to exploit in the alluringly vague area between the house lights going down and the first word of

dialogue.[14] Three versions of *Much Ado about Nothing* will provide examples. 'Enter Leonato, Governor of Messina, Innogen his wife, Hero his daughter and Beatrice, his niece, with a messenger' says the Folio (and Quarto) direction. All three productions left out Innogen (a 'ghost' character who never speaks) and all three created a space between the appearance of the family and the arrival of the messenger, half a minute or so in which interpretative intentions were made clear and the production's manifesto declared.

On the Stratford main stage in 1988, in a modern-dress production by Di Trevis, the stage lights came up on Leonato's family lounging in the sunshine on the terrace of what was clearly their very expensive villa. They looked languid and listless, each isolated from the other, clearly rather irritable; and into this scene of bored wealth came the messenger in battle-dress. The image of a society that was rich, decadent, and selfish had been economically created with not a word spoken and was to colour our response to the rest of the play. In the preceding year Judi Dench's production for the Renaissance Theatre Company (fig. 95), set in the nineteenth century, had also presented Leonato's family sitting on a sunny terrace, but the relationships we saw were of co-operation and mutuality—Beatrice helping Leonato with a jigsaw puzzle, Margaret and Hero winding wool together—a community at peace with itself, in contented interdependence. One director wished the disintegrating events of the play to be unsurprising, almost what such a society deserved; the other made them seem a shocking intrusion into harmony, eliciting from us a response of pain and pity. In Bill Alexander's production, at Stratford in 1990, in splendid Renaissance costumes, the performance began with the somewhat incongruous spectacle of Beatrice and Leonato enjoying a little bout of rapier-fencing together, with Beatrice, in spite of the encumbrance of long, flowing skirts, winning rather easily. And then the messenger arrived and 'the play' began—except that it had really begun for the audience with this image of a woman defeating a man at what, in the period presented, was a man's game. 'O God, that I were a man!', Beatrice will say later, and here in this little directorial pre-play we were invited to think about the restrictions and frustrations imposed upon an intelligent woman in the play's patriarchal society. Here were three productions of *Much Ado about Nothing*, then, each postponing the entry of the messenger for a few seconds to create directorial space that would present a strong interpretative angle on the play.

'Exeunt' says the Folio (and the Quarto) text at the end of *The Merchant of Venice*: please, director, just get these seven principal players—and any attendants your budget has allowed you to afford (of late, in my observation, usually none)—off the stage. The method of removing them is up to the director, for the text offers absolutely nothing beyond the one word 'Exeunt'. And this single example is explanation enough of why a 'director', in one guise or another, will always be necessary, for someone has to make the decision. In making it, of course, it has to be borne in mind that six of the seven are three pairs of lovers (Portia and Bassanio, Nerissa and Gratiano, and Jessica and Lorenzo), at least one of whom, but by implication the others, are leaving to go to bed to consummate a marriage which took place in Act III but which was then left unconsummated because of urgent business in a Venetian court of law. The seventh person is Antonio, who opened the play speculating on the reasons for a state of sadness which has still not, at least textually, been explained. Earlier generations of 'producers', or of actor-managers (if they were not playing Shylock and had allowed the play to run beyond his Act IV exit), would have lowered a curtain on a final 'tableau'; and a modern director might, perhaps, similarly 'freeze' the scene before a final black-out. But a tableau or a freeze requires the placing of the actors in some series of relationships, so hardly avoids decision-making. The usual method nowadays is to obey the direction and get the actors off the stage. A simultaneous mass exit is of course possible (though I have never seen it); but since some of the participants in the exit are heading for the marriage bed such a suggestion of a group experience in the offing would not be as decision-evading as might at first seem to be the case. Every recent production in my experience has made firm conceptual choices here that bring to a

final point interpretative themes pursued through the play. Let us consider a selection of them.

The solution to the problem offered most commonly in recent productions is the one adopted by Terry Hands at Stratford in 1971. As the play ended the three pairs of lovers left the stage in turn, hand in hand, in their vivid and beautiful costumes, blues, whites, oranges. Portia and Bassanio moved off last and Antonio was left alone, pale and serious, in his black suit, his unanswered, undeclared love for Bassanio thwarted. Our last image was of him caught in a narrow spotlight in a solitariness that somehow recalled the loneliness of Shylock's exit at the end of the preceding scene. And as the lights went down a melancholy note on a horn was heard—the sound of the shofar that marks the end of the Day of Atonement for those who knew it, but for the majority of audiences, I suspect, just a sound in keeping with the seriousness of the moment. The production throughout had concerned itself with the isolation of Shylock and Antonio, and it pressed its point home at the close.

When John Barton directed the play in Edwardian costume at the Other Place in 1978 there was no such barrier to the gracious, easy friendship of Antonio and Bassanio, no suggestion of any connection between the elegant, easy-going Antonio of David Bradley and the shiny-suited, obsequious, nub-end-saving Shylock of Patrick Stewart. When the time came to get three pairs of lovers and Antonio off the stage, therefore, Gratiano and Nerissa and Lorenzo and Jessica made their exits first, leaving Portia, Bassanio, and Antonio on stage. To celebrate the legal victory (and the weddings), champagne had been served for the return to Belmont, and at the end Antonio refilled three glasses, drank a final toast to Portia and Bassanio, and walked briskly from the stage, leaving them to make their departure slowly, hand in hand, as the sound of the dawn chorus of birds began.

Neither of these productions may be accused of distorting the play, of not allowing it to 'speak for itself', for both had most meticulously observed all the information provided by the text—and in the process had found quite opposite meanings in the play's closing moments, and thence in the piece as a whole. At Stratford in 1984 John Caird, too, did what was required of him by the text when he took his seven actors off the stage, the two minor pairs of lovers first, then Portia taking Bassanio's arm and seeming about to turn upstage past an Antonio who had throughout been a dark, gloomy, unknowable presence. But as she passed him, in a moment of remorse, or compassion, something possessed her to take his arm too, and the three of them left together. As they did, and the lights went down, the thought popped alarmingly into one's head 'he'll be there for breakfast . . . And I bet he'll stay a month', the idea of 'love me, love my friend' that had pervaded the play thus brooding over its final moments. And still all the director had done was to take seven actors off the stage.

Bill Alexander likewise used the final 'Exeunt' to press home the concerns of his production of *The Merchant of Venice* at Stratford in 1987. The basic theme and motive of the production was the damage to human community inflicted by religious hatred: a Star of David and a Madonna and Child, crudely painted on the back wall of the set, were alternately lit according to which side was in the ascendancy; menacing figures lurked in the shadows when Antonio and Bassanio visited Shylock in the Ghetto and when Shylock ventured to the Rialto he was jostled and goaded by Salerio and Solanio; in the trial scene rival supporters bayed at each other across the court room and as Shylock prepared to cut the flesh the Christians intoned prayers in Latin and Shylock recited a Hebrew ritual, with Antonio tied to a spar of wood, arms akimbo (giving offence, the RSC's mailbag suggested, to members of both religious communities in the audience). When it came to the end of the play this idea of religious antagonism was pushed to the final black-out: in a scene of much extrovert heterosexual love-play between Portia and Bassanio (and Nerissa and Gratiano), clearly intended to humiliate Antonio and to press home the hopelessness of his overt homosexual love for Bassanio, one noticed that Lorenzo and Jessica were not indulging in the same enthusiastic preparations for bedtime. Their relationship, indeed, had clearly soured by the time

they arrived in Belmont in Act III, Jessica finding herself in a no man's land between her apostasy to the faith of her birth and the racial and religious prejudice she encountered as Lorenzo's wife. (Gratiano's 'cheer yond stranger' (III. ii. 237), for example, uttered with patronizing contempt, was met by a shrug of inactivity from Nerissa.) At the end, as the lovers rushed off to bed and Lorenzo drifted off after them, Jessica was left on stage with Antonio. She was looking around for something she had lost and suddenly one saw that Antonio had found it: it was the little cruciform necklace that Lorenzo had given her as a betrothal gift, symbol of her new (though more recently rather tarnished) love, or of her apostasy, as one cared to regard it. And as she, daughter of the head of the minority religious community, who seemed to be losing her commitment in a heterosexual love relationship, reached up for that necklace, hesitantly, not sure that she really wanted it any more, and Antonio, head of the majority religious community but the loser in a homosexual love relationship, withheld it, not sure whether he should give it to her; and as they stood, poised in a religious and sexual uncertainty that encapsulated much of what the production had been about, the lights went down.

'Now my charms are *all* o'erthrown', says Alec McCowen's Prospero in the 1993 RSC production of *The Tempest*, as he endeavours to come to terms with an extraordinary moment of directors' Shakespeare that, like these examples from *The Merchant of Venice*, follows the last words of dialogue. For Ariel has just spat in his eye (fig. 87). Let me end, then, where I began, with a current production by an increasingly prominent Shakespeare director, for Sam Mendes's version of *The Tempest* encapsulates many of the characteristics of the theatrical form we have been considering.

We left Ariel standing on a theatre property skip swinging a lantern to produce a storm. Twice during the scene he will stop the lantern to create silence for Gonzalo's longer speeches, a piece of self-aware theatricality that looks forward to much that follows; a little way into the storm we shall become aware of Prospero upstage and high up, surveying the scene as if from mid-air—the modern lighting-effects-man's equivalent of the Folio's instruction that, in a later scene, he should appear 'on the top'. Moments later, in a different lighting state, we shall see McCowen's Prospero climbing down a perfectly ordinary stage electrician's long step-ladder, the sort that used to be needed, in less mechanized days, for the hand-refocusing of theatre lamps. We shall see him often, later in the play, up in the sky, or up the step-ladder—a trick of the light will change it from the magical to the mundane—and on many occasions Prospero will himself wave a hand or click his fingers to produce a lighting change to mark his moving from the mortal world to the magic world of his spirit servant. An Ariel from a property basket and a Prospero up a stage electrician's ladder: the metatheatre of the play, an idea prominent in recent literary criticism of *The Tempest*, is clearly going to be explored in this particular example of directors' Shakespeare.

The motif continues through the production. When Prospero tells Miranda the story of his past, the persons he mentions step out one by one from behind an upstage screen, as if the stage-manager were taking a roll-call of the cast. When Caliban is required, Prospero brings on another stage skip, unlocks it, and out Caliban comes, snarling dangerously. The whole set, on closer inspection, has rather a 'backstage' look about it: Prospero's desk bears an odd resemblance to the assistant stage-manager's properties table and we are not at all surprised when the bunch of marigolds on it turns out to be a designer's scale model for the eight-foot sunflowers among which King Alonso's party will later wander. The floor looks like the bare planks of an undressed stage—which is precisely what

FIG. 87 Prospero spat upon by Ariel: Simon Russell Beale and Alec McCowen in Sam Mendes's production of *The Tempest*, Royal Shakespeare Theatre, 1993.

it is. The masque is presented as a Pollock's toy theatre, with actors pretending to be marionettes, or the figures on a music box, dancing with comic jerkiness—life pretending to be art pretending to be life. When Trinculo appears he is an old-fashioned, desperately *passé*, music-hall ventriloquist act, carrying a dummy replica of himself, with the same carroty hair, hideously check suit, and Little Titch boots. The two of them later finish up in the props basket with Stephano and Caliban, discarded stage bric-à-brac. But the sight of a professional entertainer with a puppet he thinks he controls, but which has a disconcerting way of taking over and speaking out of turn, is perhaps not unconnected with what is going on higher up the play's hierarchy. The idea comes to touching fruition in the final scene as Trinculo enters Prospero's magic circle lost and bewildered, without his doll but with his controlling finger and thumb still twitching away mechanically—a poignant reflection of the much grander puppet-master whom we shall shortly see, charms o'erthrown, an isolated old man whose efforts to change people, to create harmony and community, have met limited success and who now stands alone, close to tears, with only death to look forward to. But before we see that, there is one last use of the little character-presenting screen as Prospero knocks it down, its work done, to reveal Ferdinand and Miranda playing at chess; and one last appearance of the property basket, as he orders Caliban back into it with a textual change small in terms of orthography, rather larger in terms of significance: 'Go, sirrah, to *thy* cell', and the lock is snapped firmly shut as Caliban howls within. The rest of Prospero's cast of characters then line up for dismissal from the stage and file off into either wing, another slight textual adjustment thus leaving Prospero alone with the last of his puppets. The tension between Alec McCowen's Prospero and Simon Russell Beale's Ariel has been apparent throughout the production. Patient and meticulously obedient, Ariel has watched over virtually every scene in the play, stalking about the stage with a suppressed and silent hauteur that breaks surface in that initial quarrel and seethes in the various references to forthcoming freedom. 'Dost thou love me, master?', he asks (IV. i. 48) and watches, guardedly, standing there in his Malayan house-boy's blue uniform, as Prospero hesitates. 'No', he adds, flatly, just as Prospero replies, a touch impatiently (or is it even off-handedly?), 'Dearly, my delicate Ariel.' The master's casual, unquestioning, patronizing superiority, and the servant's strange mixture of the desire to be loved and the yearning to be free, elegantly pick up much that has been written in recent years on *The Tempest*'s exploration of colonialism and make Caliban's claim that his spirits all hate Prospero 'as rootedly as I' (III. ii. 96) perfectly plausible. At the close Ariel and Prospero, servant and master, are very close, face to face: 'Then to the elements | Be free, and fare thee well', says Prospero, kindly, but still patronizingly, and after a long, bitter stare Ariel spits in his face. The shock in the audience is palpable as every spectator tries to reassess the relationship in the light of this moment, to reread the text following this astonishing piece of theatrical deconstruction. As we do so, Ariel walks slowly towards the back of what has, all evening, seemed the blank curve of a brilliantly blue cyclorama. He grasps an unseen handle and in the evening's last splendid theatrical surprise opens what is suddenly revealed as a perfectly ordinary door, unnoticed until that moment in its background-matching blueness. Beyond it beckons a gleaming space of vivid white light. For a moment Ariel turns to look back, with that same still and haughty gaze, then disappears into the brightness; and Prospero is left alone to beg the audience's indulgence.

It is a challenging and disturbing reading of the relationship, defiant of nearly everything in the theatrical tradition of performing it, hugely controversial, of course, but providing what has surely always been the most valuable feature of 'directors' Shakespeare', a stimulus to think afresh about the play. And when Shakespeare productions cease to do that, the history that has been explored in this book will have come to an end.

II

A Career in Shakespeare

JUDI DENCH

MY first experience of Shakespeare was probably being taken to see my eldest brother, Peter, playing Macbeth at St Peter's School in York, when I was very little—6 or 7. I saw a production of Shaw's *Caesar and Cleopatra* with him playing Caesar and my second brother Jeffrey as Cleopatra, perhaps before the *Macbeth*. I also remember Peter playing Duncan, again when I was very young indeed, and I simply loved it. When I was at the Mount, a Quaker boarding-school, I was in *A Midsummer Night's Dream* and *Richard II*. *The Dream* was produced by Mrs McDonald, who had been an actress at the Old Vic under the name Joy Harvey. *Richard* was produced by a wonderful man called John Kay, a master at Bootham, the Quaker school for boys in York. He wanted someone to play the Queen, so I was allowed to do it—but, being a Quaker school, there had to be another Queen as well, so that one person didn't get too much of a good thing. A girl called Rachel Hartley and I took it in turns. It's difficult to say what the productions were like. I remember my first term at boarding-school I saw a really terrible production of *Julius Caesar* with all these big girls in bigger togas. That put me off the play and I've never been to see it since. I remember reading *As You Like It* round the class, about ten lines each—and that put me off that play too. I've never really wanted to do it, though I played Phebe at the Old Vic. Jeff used to learn reams of Shakespeare—just for pleasure, because he loved the sound of it—and that

made it very attractive to me, too. I think I caught all that from him.

The first professional play I saw was Ben Travers's farce *A Cuckoo in the Nest*, at a theatre in York. I've never seen the play since, but I can never forget that when a man appeared in long johns from a basket at the bottom of a bed I screamed. I laughed so much that my parents had to take me home because they thought I was going to make myself ill, but they let me go back the next night. I don't remember seeing any professional Shakespeare in York. I suppose the first was possibly Peggy Ashcroft as Cleopatra at Stratford in 1953. I also saw Marius Goring and Yvonne Mitchell in *The Taming of the Shrew* and Michael Redgrave as Lear in the same Stratford season, and Peggy as Imogen in 1957, and I saw a lot when I went up to drama school in London. It was that first visit to Stratford that made such a big impression on me: the excitement of going up there, even the smell of the inside of the theatre. Those were the days when I went up from school. We used to queue, and there was the excitement of wondering whether you'd be able to get a ticket.

I was most impressed by the way the plays were staged. At the time I saw Redgrave in *King Lear* I wanted to be a designer. It was directed by George Devine and the sets and costumes were by Robert Colqhoun. The Lear set was dominated by a huge saucer and a rock which was the throne, the cave, and everything else: it turned round completely (fig. 88). I had never seen scenery changes like that and I was enormously excited by it all. It convinced me, though, that I wasn't going to be that kind of designer, that I would never have that kind of imagination. I was in awe of Redgrave's Lear and Marius Goring's Fool, I had nothing to compare them with, and I sat there in intense excitement, an innocent spectator. I remember that my brothers were away, and I went with my parents. We sat on a bench on the far side of the river opposite the dressing-rooms during the matinée the next day, and saw everybody going up and down the stairs, and heard the performance on the tannoy. It must have gone very deep in me, because I can hear and see it now as though it was last week. I don't remember anything of *Antony and Cleopatra* except Peggy Ashcroft. I don't remember Antony or anybody else in it. I fell deeply in love with Marius Goring, playing Petruchio, and I remember seeing him come out of the stage door afterwards in a white shirt and grey flannel trousers to post a letter. The very first

time I played at Stratford was as Isabella to his Angelo in 1962, but it was a long time before I told him about watching him post that letter.

I started training as a designer, but I was accepted at Central, where Jeff had trained. I was 22 when I was chosen straight from drama school to play Ophelia at the Old Vic (fig. 89). That was my first professional engagement. I thought the production was wonderful, and it did get some very good notices, but although I myself got some good reviews when we opened in Liverpool, when we came to London I remember them as being frightful. One critic wrote a wonderful review out of town, then came and interviewed me—and wrote terrible things about me when we opened at the Old Vic. I never forgave him. But the production went well. The set was very dark, mostly black, and the costumes were Victorian—Ruritanian really—and stood out against the background. John Neville was

Facing: FIG. 89 John Neville and Judi Dench as Hamlet and Ophelia, in Michael Benthall's production, Old Vic, 1957.

FIG. 88 *King Lear*, directed by George Devine with designs by Robert Colqhoun, Shakespeare Memorial Theatre, 1953.

Hamlet, and Coral Browne was sensational as Gertrude. Her performance was one of the reasons I've always wanted to play the part, though I've never been able to play it properly. There's something in it that I can't catch at all, but she could; she made her a vain, beautiful woman, a bit silly, weak, and vulnerable. The director was Michael Benthall, a wonderful director who was never really appreciated.

Benthall came to the Vic when they were in dire financial difficulties, and decided he would do a 'five-year plan'—all the plays, with *Hamlet* done twice, once in the first year with Richard Burton and Claire Bloom, and again with John Neville in the final year of the cycle, when I arrived. When I went to the Vic we all wore dresses and high heels and the men would be in suits for the reading on the first day of rehearsing a play—it was the same in rep in those days. The democracy that we know now didn't exist. Everybody was called 'Miss Browne' or 'Mr Neville', and I was addressed as 'Miss Dench'. In the directing there was a lot of straightforward placing of people—'You come on here' and so on—which was the way it was then, but I seem to remember being given a great deal of freedom by Michael Benthall, and the most important thing he taught me about was *legato*. 'You mustn't just clip all your words off. You must just *use* some words.' He told us that vulnerability was the strongest asset you could have as an actor. For crowd noises and murmurs he would say, 'Just do your understudies', so you would hear a lot of good Shakespeare being muttered in the background. I don't remember verse speaking as such being mentioned. I had seen and admired Barbara Jefford at the Vic for years before I worked there, and I suppose I learned something from her marvellous innate sense of the verse.

Benthall was always very embarrassed about talking to you, and would go very pink and find it difficult to express himself—but eventually he would. He didn't talk about the deeper meaning of the play, but then you didn't expect that. You didn't do all the talking and the fluffy ball-throwing you sometimes get now because there were only three or four weeks before you opened cold to the press on the first night. I learned from Benthall and from everyone else around

me: I was helped enormously by the people in the company. When I was cast as Ophelia I wasn't supposed to tell anyone about it, and Benthall said, 'You must understand that in your first season you must walk on as well,' which is all I thought I was auditioning for. I played First Fairy in *A Midsummer Night's Dream*, in which Frankie Howerd played Bottom (hysterically funny, though he just made it up a lot of the time), Juliet in *Measure*, walked on in the *Henry VI* plays (I was one of the spirits conjured by Eleanor), and understudied Rosie Webster as Cordelia. Paul Rogers was Lear. When he made his first entrance there was a line-up of three women behind him: Barbara Leigh-Hunt holding an 8-foot sword, Adrienne Hill carrying a huge tree, and me with a gigantic smoking egg-cup. People used to laugh, because they could see that without any doubt we were the understudies for the three daughters.

I was Phebe in *As You Like It*, Maria in *Twelfth Night*, and the Princess in *Henry V*. Donald Houston was Henry at the Vic, and at the same time I played the part for television in the BBC 'Age of Kings' series, with different moves and cuts and with Robert Hardy as the King. When the company went to America I lost Ophelia, which was a blow. Shortly after we returned there was an invitation to Yugoslavia. I returned to Ophelia, for what turned out to be a hugely exciting tour, and played the part in Ljubljana, Zagreb, and Belgrade. After the tours there was *The Double Dealer*, in which Miles Malleson wore a wig on a wig on a wig: a full-bottomed wig over a bald cap over his own toupée.

I love the Old Vic as a theatre, which probably has a lot to do with its being the first theatre I played in but also because it feels so good, for acoustics and for reaching the audience. It was at the Vic that the idea of a 'company' was instilled in me. It's something I love being part of. Being a company you dispense with that awful embarrassed period you otherwise go through with every new play, of learning to laugh at yourself in front of other people, or letting them laugh at you and getting rid of your inhibitions. And once that feeling goes, you dare to do so many things. The company was 'led' by the principal actors. I'm convinced that if you are playing leading roles in a company it is your duty to make that work, to make your performance part of a whole. I have no time at all for squabbles within a company: the job is so difficult and it takes up too much energy to waste it that way.

All the Shakespeare I had done by the beginning of the 1960s was with Michael Benthall. He cast *Romeo and Juliet* for Franco Zeffirelli in 1960 when he was brought in to do the play. Benthall cast John Stride and Alec McCowen as Romeo and Mercutio and me as Juliet (fig. 90). He took us in to meet Zeffirelli, who just looked at us very searchingly and then said 'Yes, very good' to Benthall. I was sure the apple wasn't going to be given to me—it was going to be taken away and bitten by someone else—but I did get the part. It was thrilling to work with Zeffirelli. I remember it was said that there was incredible passion in the production. What he was most concerned to do was to get rid of 'English' passion and get a really

'Italian' feel. I remember the audience gasped when the curtain went up because it was all misty in this very real-looking Italian street and people were throwing out sheets to air: nothing as realistic had been seen for a very long time in Shakespeare. His English was fine, but he had no respect for the verse at all, and cut it appallingly, hacking at it, for which he was rightly criticized. He left the text to the actors, and it didn't survive at all well. Juliet is a part you long to play when you know a bit more about it technically, when you're in fact too old for it. In 1960 it hadn't been done by anyone as young as us, and had always been played by rather statuesque people who knew the business and could 'handle' the poetry. We weren't like that at all. When I directed a production in Regent's Park, in 1993, I cast the play very young, because I think Juliet should have no thought of marriage, and the precipitation towards tragedy is much more potent if Romeo and

Fig. 90 John Stride and Judi Dench as Romeo and Juliet in Franco Zeffirelli's production, Old Vic, 1960.

Juliet are like children. Unfortunately the actors were very untried, and I didn't feel that I was able to give them as much time as I should have done.

When I direct I suppose I want to pass on what I learned about speaking the verse from Peter Hall, Trevor Nunn, and John Barton. I've found too that a surprising number of younger actors have to be told that if you're not speaking, whether the scene is in verse or in prose, the battery inside you has to go on working—a lot of actors 'go soft' when they're not doing anything on stage. Young actors nowadays have a wonderful range of skills: they can sing, and play musical instruments, and dance. They often have to learn to project, to reach the back of the theatre with their voice. 'Style'—or 'company style'—in these things is the wrong word for the RSC in the 1960s. There was a move towards a concept of the company, working in a more democratic way, feeling as though each of you was contributing towards other people's performances as well as your own. Nobody's name was above the title in the billing. And the way of speaking was to make Shakespeare's language understood but still seem natural and—when it needed to be—colloquial. I had been lucky to work with Clifford Turner and Cicely Berry at Central, and then again with Cicely at Stratford, so that throughout my career there was a continuity in the approach to voice work.

One of the most successful productions I was in with the RSC was *Twelfth Night*, which John Barton directed in 1969. I like the play because of the melancholy, the degrees of love that everyone is in, sometimes with themselves, sometimes with someone else in disguise—and everyone with their idea of love. Olivia is in love with the idea of wearing black for her brother's death, and with the idea of loving a young boy who is not in fact a boy; Orsino's in love with his idea of Olivia, and with a young boy who he doesn't know is a girl; Viola loves Orsino but can't show it; Feste is presumably in love with Olivia; and Malvolio seems to be in love with Olivia too, as well as with himself. And then Maria is in love with Sir Toby. Shakespeare takes so many textures of that emotion, and gives it so many forms. The Old Vic production by

Michael Benthall in 1958 was very autumnal, set in a kind of bower, with russet and brown as the dominant colours. The production by John Barton at the RSC was set in a slatted wooden chamber, with a lot of greens, browns, and ochres in the costumes and lighting that came through the wooden slats. It was imbued with a kind of melancholy but didn't seem like a melancholy experience. Charles Thomas played Orsino when we opened (fig. 91). It was an inspired performance, and he looked like that miniature of Sir Walter Raleigh with curls and flowers in his hair— magical. To the devastation of the company, he died in Australia, just before we opened with the play. Richard Pasco took over, and gave a wonderful performance, but afterwards the play never seemed the same.

I suppose you could call that production 'Chekhovian', but I have to say that I enjoy being in Chekhov more than going to it. I'm always frightened that the production's going to be too 'Chekhovian' for its own good. We dwell too much on the melancholic side of the plays and not perhaps enough on the mercurial side to them, the ability to laugh and cry at once. I had a baptism of fire with Michel Saint-Denis when I first joined the RSC and was cast in his production of *The Cherry Orchard* at the Aldwych. He had seen a girl playing Anya at the Moscow Art Theatre, and was impressed by the way she came on stage laughing and crying by turns. He kept me in day after day doing this, but mine came out more crying than laughing; I felt totally beaten by him. Something of the quality of the two moods together was there in Patrick Wymark's performances as Shakespeare's clowns. He had a wonderfully merry face and a rotund figure but he was really melancholic, and that made him so good in those parts. You wouldn't have taken him for a melancholy or depressed man, though, and he was never depressing to others.

Twelfth Night was repeated at the Aldwych in 1970 and again in the 1971 season at Stratford. That was when I played Portia in *The Merchant of Venice*—and loathed it. I should never have done it. I don't think there's anything to redeem those people, I'm afraid. Everybody behaves appallingly, and there's nothing for

FIG. 91 Judi Dench as Viola and Charles Thomas as Orsino in *Twelfth Night*, directed by John Barton, Royal Shakespeare Theatre, 1969.

the *spirit* in the play—which is strange for Shakespeare. Even in *Macbeth* there is something of that: you feel 'that's quite right' when she dies and he gets killed. But at the end of *The Merchant of Venice* I couldn't care less about anybody. As for all that about the ring at the end, I could give Portia a good slap. I wouldn't ever even go to see it again. From my point of view the Stratford production was remarkable though for one of the worst 'corpses' I have ever done— breaking down in laughter uncontrollably. In the casket scene Michael Williams was standing in the

centre of the stage as Bassanio, about to make his choice. There was the wind band at the back of the stage, Peter Geddes as Gobbo, Polly James waiting to sing 'Tell me where is fancy bred', and my brother Jeff and Bernard Lloyd as monks. I was supposed to say

> I speak too long, 'tis but to peize the time,
> To eke it, and to draw it out in length,
> To stay you from election.

But I said 'erection'. The band just put down their instruments and walked off, as did the monks, leaving

Fig. 92 Judi Dench as Hermione in *The Winter's Tale*, directed by Trevor Nunn, Royal Shakespeare Theatre, 1969.

Polly James to sing on her own. I have never been in such a state, and the scene had only just started.

During that time with the RSC I doubled Hermione and Perdita in *The Winter's Tale*. When Trevor Nunn asked me to do Hermione, I said, 'Good grief, not mothers' parts already!' Then a few weeks later he said, 'How about Perdita as well?'—which I thought was only suggested because of what I had said at first, but I did accept. The double hadn't been done since Mary Anderson did it at the Lyceum in 1887 (figs 92 and 93).

It was a wonderfully exciting production, and when it came to Bohemia we all suddenly burst out into a wonderful hippy world. Not everybody liked it. I don't usually notice individual members of the audience, but I distinctly remember seeing Stanley Wells in the stalls on the first night. He had a beatific smile through the first half, but when we came to Bohemia he sat scowling. I loved Bohemia, because I felt quite different there, as though I were a totally different person. Playing both parts is very hard work, because you get no rest at all. Then you have to do the magic change to the statue. It's difficult for me to know

Fig. 93 Judi Dench as Perdita.

whether it looked all right from the front, but it did not
work for me. Even when it did work well, it left the
audience wondering how on earth it had happened,
instead of feeling the emotion of what was happening
between the characters. I didn't feel so much moved as
breathless, by the time I had swapped with the double
who played Perdita and rushed round to take the
statue's place in the perspex box at the back of the
stage, but I did feel as though I was another actress,
which is a very strange sensation.

Donald Sinden was Malvolio in the *Twelfth Night*,
and we later played in a revival of Dion Boucicault's
London Assurance, directed by Ronald Eyre. We worked
together again in 1976, when I was Regan in *King Lear*
(he played Lear) and Beatrice to his Benedick in a
production by John Barton, set in British India in the
nineteenth century (fig. 94). In *Much Ado* he worked in
a kind of Christmas pantomime style—if that sounds
disparaging it isn't meant to be. Peter Brook came to

see it and said it was one of the greatest performances
he had ever seen. Donald totally engaged the
audience, but I didn't know how to do that, so it must
have seemed a bit lopsided to some people, with me
playing one way and him another. I got better at it,
especially when we moved from Stratford to the
Aldwych in London, possibly because I could watch
him more closely in the more intimate theatre and see
how he worked the audience. One night someone in
the audience came in late and I heard him saying, 'Do
you know the story? Because if you don't . . .' There's a
touch of competition in playing opposite a
performance like that, which may work with Beatrice
and Benedick but perhaps isn't quite true to the
author's intention.

When I directed the play in 1988 the choice had a lot
more to do with the persuasive powers of Kenneth
Branagh than my own ambitions: the play, the cast,
and the job were all chosen for me. I was rehearsing

FIG. 94 Messina as British India: Judi Dench and Donald Sinden as Beatrice and Benedick in John
Barton's production of *Much Ado about Nothing*, Royal Shakespeare Theatre, 1976.

FIG. 95 Samantha Bond and Kenneth Branagh as Beatrice and Benedick in the final scene of *Much Ado about Nothing*, directed by Judi Dench for the Renaissance Theatre Company, 1988–9.

with Peter Hall for *Antony and Cleopatra* and he said, 'You must do it—go ahead and have a go at it.' With *Much Ado* I knew that I wanted the Hero and Claudio plot to be real and shocking. I knew that with Samantha Bond and Kenneth Branagh the Beatrice and Benedick part couldn't be the 'last summer' affair that I had played with Donald Sinden. I do think that when you direct it's wrong to go into work on a play with a strong concept that you have to impose on the actors. Actors are wonderfully inventive: when I directed *Much Ado* I knew that I wanted the play to be set in Italy, and that there should have been a war the men were coming back from, and Jenny Tiramani's designs gave this. The rest came from the actors creating a sense of place and mood and letting everyone in the audience feel it (fig. 95). I don't know what plays 'mean'—I just want them to be alive and

mean lots of things to lots of people. On the first morning of rehearsals for *Much Ado*, when I knew that I ought to tell the cast how I was going to approach the play, I found myself unable to talk about anything but tight white trousers and black leather boots! I couldn't stop myself. I wanted the men's world and the women's—which is also the household's—to be quite distinct. I had a chart of who was in which scene and what happened at what time of day: I have to have that for everything, because I'm an inveterate list-maker.

It's hard for me to tell what I think about the production. When I direct I can only tell from watching and listening, the way you would with a painting, seeing that some things should be darker, some lighter. It's like stepping back from a painting and saying, 'that needs to be brought out much more to emphasize that'—exactly the same process. In my

Much Ado there was a sound in the air, to create an atmosphere of mystery when the veiled women appeared. This wasn't planned from the beginning: at some point in the rehearsals I suddenly knew I wanted it. When I did *Romeo and Juliet* in Regent's Park I wanted a cry at the very end. At the beginning there was a sound like a sword being taken out of its sheath in slow motion, a harsh, silver, metallic sound. I wanted to arrest the audience's attention, as well as suggesting something to do with the state of the city. I wanted the play to end with all the characters ill at ease—a lot of blame attached to everyone, and not much forgiveness. I wanted something like the first sound but this time with terrible crying in it, though I couldn't get it right.

I don't consciously look forward to parts I might do in the future, but take them as they come. Peter Hall asked me about Cleopatra at a party at the end of the National Theatre season in 1982 when I had played Deborah in Pinter's *A Kind of Alaska* and Lady Bracknell. 'Sometime I would like you to play Cleopatra for me. We've got to find an Antony.' I didn't believe him, but he insisted he was serious about it. Then some time later Terry Hands and Trevor Nunn asked me if I would do it for the RSC. I was so flattered because I'd never dreamed I would play the part, so I said, 'Oh, wonderful—of course.' Then, later, I met Peter Hall again and said, 'You weren't ever serious about *Antony and Cleopatra*'—and he said, 'I was deadly serious. I'm looking at some Antonys now.' By this time I had been back with the RSC, doing *Mother Courage* and Granville-Barker's *Waste*. I asked to see Trevor and Terry, and confessed that I had already said 'yes' to both suggestions. It was very awkward, and took some sorting out.

When I did come to do it, with Peter, the rehearsals were twelve of the most exciting weeks I have ever had. Peter was on top form as a director, and Anthony Hopkins—who had just done a hundred performances of Howard Brenton's *Pravda* and was into a long run of *King Lear*, must have been exhausted but made a wonderful Antony. I felt that I learned such a lot from them both, and the first night was one of the happiest I can remember because we felt that we had done the

play to the best of our ability at that time. That's the most you hope to say of a first night: even if people hate it afterwards, you can at least say, 'It's the best we've done it so far.' That will never do for the next night because you have to do it better then.

I am sure part of it was surprise: my build isn't what anybody thinks of as Cleopatra—I am not tall, statuesque, and strikingly beautiful. I had to get over that hurdle first, but Alison Chitty's costumes helped enormously (fig. 96). Then there's energy. Peter Hall pointed out that after Antony's death she goes into overdrive, so you have to find a sort of 'fifth gear' for the final act. There are the rows with Antony, then the monument scene. This was a physical problem because we had an arch 20 feet high. Antony had to be hoisted up it and I had to come down from it, having decided to play the next part of the scene below. In the end, four days from opening, we decided I would be dropped into everybody's arms as they stood below to catch me. Then, after that, after a long scene coping with the aftermath of Antony's death, a live snake!

Tony Hopkins and I had established that we both like to change things, so that we would never be quite sure where the other was going to come on from. Peter Hall agreed that if we wanted we could have that freedom for the two of us. We moved the scenes in Cleopatra's court on the round stage of the Olivier in big circles; Peter said they should be like fish in a tank: 'Where one goes, they all go, and if it changes direction they follow.'

I played Gertrude at the National in 1989, in Richard Eyre's production of *Hamlet*. I've mentioned already that I don't think I have ever got her right. I didn't feel that I could ever have been Daniel Day-Lewis's mother—I had no problem with him, but just felt that the audience wouldn't believe in the relationship. I didn't feel that I looked right in the costumes or on the set, or that I had fulfilled either what in my mind's eye I saw I should do or what the director wanted. It wasn't his fault in any way. Gertrude doesn't say anything at times when you would think she would

FIG. 96 *Antony and Cleopatra*, National Theatre, 1987: Anthony Hopkins and Judi Dench.

do so, so you just have to make up your mind about her. That's true of any character in a play, but with her there are *vital* things left unsaid and unless you can express them in a way that fits in with the rest of the production it doesn't work. I think the performance stands or falls by that. When I did it for radio in 1992 I felt I was able to make more sense of it, and I could believe I was Kenneth Branagh's mother. But, apart from anything else, you don't have to make so many decisions about showing what isn't said when you're on radio.

I played Kenneth Branagh's mother again later the same year when we did *Coriolanus* at Chichester, but that's a very different relationship. It's a very difficult play, and we were in an extremely difficult space. I remember Ken and Iain Glen, who was Aufidius, alone in the middle of the vast thrust stage, still managing to bump into each other! Much of the production, which Tim Supple directed, worked well, and we had a very large, very disciplined crowd of 'extras', but not having seen it I only have the view from Volumnia, which consists of a number of fiendishly hard scenes. Some of it I never felt I got right. I'm sure something has been destroyed in her by the end. When she returns to Rome after persuading Coriolanus not to attack the city, she knows exactly what is going to happen—there's a death in her. She simply walks across the stage, without a hint of triumph. In a way she has sold out. She feels that what she does is right, but even when he says,

> But for your son—believe it, O! believe it—
> Most dangerously you have with him prevailed,
> If not most mortal to him,

she doesn't know the consequences. She realizes what they are later. Volumnia is quite capable of lying, earlier in the scene, when she tells Coriolanus, 'Thou hast never in thy life | Show'd thy dear mother any

courtesy.' It shows too in the scene where they are persuading him to go back to the people, 'mildly'. She resents not having him under her thumb. She is a very good ruler, who would have been totally ruthless, but it costs her at the end.

I suppose that if I could have a performance to see again, as though it was there 'on the mantelpiece' (as John Gielgud says) to pick up and look at and turn round in a way you never can while you're doing the part, it would have to be Cleopatra. But I'd want to remember the passion in *Romeo and Juliet*, even though I didn't get good notices when we opened. Over a period of time it came right, people stood up at the end: I know some kind of change took place, and I'd like to see how that grew or what happened to make the difference. I played Lady Macbeth in Trevor Nunn's simple and exciting studio production of *Macbeth* at the Other Place in 1976. When it was shown on television I thought that I had given a much better performance of Lady Macbeth on stage than the one I saw. One of the happiest times I've had was playing Titania in Peter Hall's stage production of the *Dream*, but I don't want to see the film we made of it again. In fact that's a play I have gone back to several times: Titania at school, First Fairy at the Vic in 1957 and Hermia there in 1960, Titania in 1962 at Stratford. In *Measure for Measure* I have played Juliet once and Isabella twice—at Nottingham and Stratford. You learn something all the time, and it's the process that's fascinating. With Volumnia there's the extraordinary shape of the part to make sense of; in *Hamlet* I wonder: 'What makes Gertrude behave like this? Does she know about Claudius?' In Cleopatra you have to find that fifth gear for the final act. The day I go into a play and don't have to learn anything or don't have a problem is the day I'll worry. I hope it never comes.

12

Shakespeare in Opposition: From the 1950s to the 1990s

RUSSELL JACKSON

Anger and After

BRITISH Shakespeare productions of the 1930s and 1940s for the most part made no bid to change the managerial and social structures of theatre. The performance might embody a director's or actor's view of the play or its roles, observe some version of what were understood to be the ways and means of the Elizabethan stage, and would by now be expected to achieve a specific aesthetic effect or mood. The best-regarded productions would achieve a degree of ensemble playing, but would acknowledge a hierarchy of rank among the players. They would be a contribution to what was acknowledged as a good cause: the enjoyment and better understanding of Shakespeare. The social purpose of the theatre could be defined as making this available to all at an affordable cost, like state-funded provision of national insurance, health care, housing, education, and the other elements of the 'Welfare State' which the postwar government was to implement. In the late 1940s the Olivier–Richardson–Burrell regime at the Old Vic and the revitalizing of Stratford seemed to promise that this would be secured. The feverish cultural activity on the home front that took place during the Second World War, and which the government subsidized initially through the Council for the Encouragement of Music and the Arts (CEMA)

and subsequently by way of the Arts Council, now appeared to be flourishing, although (as Peter Thomson's chapter reflects) the institutional foundations of subsidized theatre were not as secure as they might have seemed.

By the middle of the next decade, the outlook for the non-commercial theatre seemed less reassuring. In 1949 the Old Vic triumvirate had been replaced, in what looked like a *putsch*. Stratford, although promoted from its second-rank status by the energetic direction first of Barry Jackson and (after 1951) of Anthony Quayle, seemed by the mid-1950s to be without artistic policy beyond survival from season to season. Outside the theatre, in the country itself, idealism was at a discount, if the voice of a new generation of 'angry young men' was to be believed:

I suppose people of our generation aren't able to die for good causes any longer. We had all that done for us, in the 'thirties and 'forties, when we were still kids. There aren't any good, brave causes left. If the big bang does come, and we all get killed off, it won't be in aid of the old-fashioned, grand design. It'll just be for the Brave New-nothing-very-much-thank-you. About as pointless and inglorious as stepping in front of a bus.[1]

These lines, from John Osborne's *Look Back in Anger*, first performed in 1956, represent a new cynicism and

211

iconoclasm to which the British theatre of the mid-1950s was suddenly able to give voice. The immediate postwar period had a particular significance for the Left as one of utopian aspirations raised and defeated. After the break-up of the wartime coalition in 1945 the Labour government which succeeded it began to implement the basic legislation for the 'Welfare State' but simultaneously—with the impact of the economic consequences of the war—was obliged to inflict continuing hardship on the electorate. In the 'Age of Austerity', although national insurance and healthcare for all were designed to replace charity for 'the poor', the spirit of making do and mending was still called on, rationing persisted (until 1954 for some items) and belts remained tightened. In aid of what?

Britain still had to find the resources for a massive military effort: the Cold War against Russia had begun immediately after the defeat of the Nazis, and there were still obligations to maintain what was left of Britain's empire overseas. The long withdrawal from imperial power, which began in 1946, proved costly in terms both of finances and morale. The Festival of Britain, in 1951, conceived as a 'tonic for the nation', and the pageantry of the Coronation of Elizabeth II in 1953 might have been expected to foster a renewal of optimism. Economic conditions did indeed begin to improve in the early 1950s, and Britain began to experience the pleasures and temptations of the 'consumer society' to which the United States led the way, but by 1956 the power of appeals to a patriotic spirit was weakened by the failed (and to many, ignominious) attempt to retain control of the Suez Canal and the feeling that the old order had stubbornly refused to give way to new. For many the threat of destruction by nuclear warfare—the 'big bang' in Jimmy Porter's speech—summed up the senselessness of appeals to the spirit of British institutions. The demand to 'Ban the Bomb', articulated through the Campaign for Nuclear Disarmament (CND), focused anger against a raft of divisive, destructive, and reactionary forces: imperialist exploitation, the remoteness of 'high' politics and Cold War diplomacy, and above all the persistence of social class as the organizing principle of British life. At the same time

the crushing of revolts in East Germany and Hungary—the latter in 1956—provoked a crisis of conscience in the British Left. Good causes seemed to be in short supply from any of the established political sources. The new mass medium of television, revived in Britain after the war but not widely available until the mid-1950s (a second channel, commercially sponsored rather than state funded, began broadcasting in 1955), fuelled fears that the brave new world was being created at the behest of capital rather than in the interests of the people themselves. Television, more absorbing than radio and even less of a social, participatory activity than cinema-going, seemed to promise a new means of enslaving rather than freeing minds. Both left- and right-wing commentators were apprehensive about the possibility that the mass media would undermine 'traditional' values of true community and independent initiative. The live performing arts, in particular the theatre, had an even more powerful enemy than cinema or the radio to contend with.

The plays of the 'angry young men' of the mid-1950s represented a watershed in British drama and theatre: a notion reflected in the title of John Russell Taylor's influential 'Guide to the New British Drama', *Anger and After*, published in 1962. The social milieu, formal conventions, and traditional pieties of West End drama were under attack. Performances of Shakespeare could hardly escape the influence of the new ways of writing and the new interpretative techniques that they called for: redefined naturalism (in Pinter, Delaney, and Wesker, for example), the more insistently absurd plays of Beckett and Ionesco, and the example of Brecht and (in Britain) John Arden in recovering the vitality of old non-naturalistic forms to express commitment and foster debate.

Shakespearian performances express, with the institutions producing them, the social and political anxieties of a period, even when (as with much of the Shakespearian product on offer at any one time) they are not designed to express political commitment. In the mid-century decades the theatres were once again redefining themselves. The non-commercial theatrical institutions of the 1930s and 1940s were either revitalized or superseded by new organizations, methodologies, and definitions of the social purposes of performance. Theatre Workshop, based from 1953 at Stratford in East London, grew out of a left-wing activist touring company founded in the 1930s by Joan Littlewood and Ewan McColl. Its most successful productions included plays by Brendan Behan and Shelagh Delaney, and the satirical documentary *Oh, What a Lovely War!*, but the company also staged provocative versions of classic texts. The work of the English Stage Company at the Royal Court Theatre (*Look Back in Anger* was its first notable commercial success) also represented a new agenda for the theatre, not simply a change in the social attitudes expressed by the dramatists who wrote for it. The whole fabric of theatrical economics, which contrived to suppress activism in the name of 'quality', needed replacement. A special *bête noire* of the radicals was the powerful West End management of H. M. Tennent Ltd., and its managing director Hugh ('Binkie') Beaumont, whose tastes and attitudes were wholeheartedly those of the middle- and upper-class audiences he courted. The commercial theatre imposed limitations shared willingly, it seemed, by many repertory theatres and by the Old Vic and Shakespeare Memorial companies. It was not simply a matter of removing french-windowed drawing rooms and installing kitchen sinks. The questions to be answered were framed by Lindsay Anderson in 1957:

Is an alternative tradition possible? *What* ideas are the ones which will revitalize our theatre? Is there a new public that could be attracted to or reached by a progressive theatrical company? What do we mean when we talk about the relationship between theatre and life?[2]

These questions still preoccupy many theatre workers in Britain, and the history of British theatrical institutions since the 1950s is that of a series of attempts to find the answers and put them into practice. Many of the companies whose repertoire has included Shakespeare's plays have been dedicated to the pursuit of new forms of theatrical writing, redefinitions of the actor's and designer's work, and the social purposes of performance. In some cases political aims have

dominated the choice of repertoire, the way in which the company addresses its audiences and the interpretation of particular texts. Other companies make less specific reference to wider political issues or are professedly 'apolitical' or simply libertarian. In companies with explicit political agendas the performance of Shakespeare has often featured as an attack on what is seen as the harmful dominance of British culture either by the plays themselves or the attitudes that have become attached to them. In some cases the encounter between performance techniques and texts for which they had not been thought appropriate has been brought to the point where defining an authentic 'Shakespearian' style is considered hardly possible or desirable. The taking-apart of Shakespeare—or ideas of 'Shakespeare'—in a particular production often goes beyond the 'concepts' of a particular director, and is a matter of company aims and objectives. As will be apparent from Robert Smallwood's chapter on 'Directors' Shakespeare', interpretation led by the 'concept' of a director has found a home in the direct inheritors of the Old Vic and the Shakespeare Memorial Theatre—the National and the RSC. It is also the case that (as Peter Thomson shows) some of the production methods, aims, and personnel of the activist companies have often been accommodated in the 'nationals'.

Redressing Shakespeare

'Modern dress' has become such a commonplace of Shakespearian production that the kind of costuming and setting it challenges has been almost forgotten. 'Traditional' often indicates a vague sense of the Stratford or Old Vic stagings of the 1950s, rather than any vividly remembered experience of this supposedly authentic style. By this measure Romeo would wear tights and a short tunic, Lear would look like a William

Blake ancient, and the Romans would have stepped from the pages of a Latin primer. Perhaps the nearest approach to this kind of Shakespeare can be found in the productions of Glen Byam Shaw, whose *Macbeth* at Stratford in 1956 was remarkable more for its cast (Olivier and Vivien Leigh) than for the expression of any view of the play: it provided a serviceable, open staging with nothing to challenge any preconceptions about the play's historical setting or significance.[3] Such productions as this were the staple of Stratford, the Old Vic, and many repertory companies through the 1950s and early 1960s, but there was ample precedent for more disturbing approaches. The possibilities for redefining the plays by shifting their period setting had been explored in the Birmingham Repertory Theatre's modern-dress productions in the 1920s and by the work of Tyrone Guthrie and Theodore Komisarjevsky in Britain and Orson Welles in the USA. Guthrie's *Troilus and Cressida* at the Old Vic in 1955, for example, used an Edwardian setting to make the element of caricature more vivid: Pandarus (Paul Rogers) was 'an Edwardian epicene, lisping his lewdness above the toggery of a dandy bound for Ascot', Helen (Wendy Hiller) was 'a vapid Edwardian beauty playing a waltz at the piano' and the Trojan warlords were 'callow specimens of a privileged caste' in a minor Ruritanian state under Habsburg rule (fig. 97).[4] In the 1960s this revolutionary movement advanced on two fronts. In one strategy, the non-naturalistic methods of the Elizabethan theatre were revisited in the name of either Brechtian 'distancing' or existentialist *Angst*. The Berliner Ensemble's visit to London in 1956, with *The Caucasian Chalk Circle*, and the even stronger example of the production of Brecht's version of *Coriolanus* discussed in Chapter 7 (fig. 59) helped to define a new, sparser, and more socially engaged mode of staging and acting. In another, the social focus of the plays was sharpened and brought to bear on present-day issues, sometimes by moving the play to another period with all the paraphernalia of naturalism.

Facing: FIG. 97 Edwardian decadence in *Troilus and Cressida* at the Old Vic, 1955: Paul Rogers (Pandarus), Wendy Hiller (Helen), and Ronald Allen (Paris), leaning on piano .

A striking example of the first method in its Brechtian aspect was William Gaskill's *Macbeth* at the Royal Court in 1966, staged 'in a sandpaper box with one entrance at the back, a bare stage and continuous white light,' and garments that resembled primitive grey tracksuits (fig. 98).[5] The aim of the director was 'to see if the text would have its maximum potency in a naked space'.[6] Alec Guinness played the title role and—in a confrontational piece of casting—Simone Signoret was Lady Macbeth. Signoret's heavy French accent drew much of the ensuing critical hostility, but there was more at stake than a single casting decision. The furore encapsulated the issue of 'respect' for the dramatist and the contentious issue of the Royal Court's social and artistic mission. In any case before long the use of a plain setting, even light and 'neutral' costumes soon became a commonplace of Shakespeare at the major subsidized theatres and elsewhere: in 1969 the same designer, Christopher Morley, was responsible for a whole season of plays using such a box at Stratford. In 1966 Gaskill's refusal to glamorize the play or the hero fuelled the critics' hostility to what many thought a self-righteous sense of social mission at the theatre. By way of comparison, one might instance Michael Benthall's production of the play at Chichester Festival Theatre in the same year, which used a permanent set (a stepped stage with stairs on either side upstage leading to a level 'above') and stylized but 'historical' costumes, and featured performances of the leading parts that were no more than routine. It was, wrote Peter Roberts in *Plays and Players*, 'certainly no milestone in Shakespearian production', and it did not offer 'a searching reappraisal of the text', but it was a 'serviceable final contribution to the season that ought to ensure the viability of Chichester as a middle-brow festival venue'.[7] Nothing could be further from the aims of Gaskill, Morley, and the English Stage Company, but in fact the Chichester production was 'Elizabethan' in the architecture of its staging and of the theatre itself (a 'thrust' of the kind advocated by Guthrie and functioning at Stratford, Ontario, since 1953). The difference lay in the use to which the two directors put elements of the theatre for which the play had been written. Gaskill wished to scrutinize the heroic pretensions of the hero and the text, Benthall (a sensitive and forceful director in his own way) expressed more or less competently a received view of both, reassuring audiences where Gaskill needled them. The sense of exposure was common to Gaskill's work and to such subsequent reappraisals of the texts as Peter Brook's 1970 *Dream*.

The refusal to provide a heroic or decorative style, or to clothe the play in atmospheric lighting and scenery was especially evident in innovative stagings of the history plays. Some insisted on a grim, steel-and-stone version of the medieval world, such as that created by John Bury for the RSC's *Wars of the Roses* sequence in 1963. The designs for this production of three plays quarried by Peter Hall and John Barton

FIG. 98 Alec Guinness as Macbeth and Simone Signoret as Lady Macbeth, Royal Court Theatre, London, 1966.

from the three *Henry VI* plays and *Richard III* combined medieval costume shapes with encrusted, worn materials and showed the grim mechanism of power operating in a world defined by 'real' materials and dominated by the smoke of battle and the glint of blood. A throne and a council table represented the twin focuses of politics, and the casting of Peggy Ashcroft in the formidable role of Margaret presented a personal *tour de force* and established a link with a tradition of Shakespearian production on the British stage (fig. 99). The 'Middle Ages', as represented here, could hardly be further from the homely wooden platforms and graceful banners of such settings as that provided by Tanya Moiseiwitsch for the 1951 Stratford production of the second tetralogy. A vision of the medieval or Renaissance periods as damaged (if glamorous) goods was reflected in successive RSC productions of other plays, and (for example) in

Prospect Theatre Company's *Edward II* and *Richard II*, first seen together at the 1969 Edinburgh Festival.

More obviously confrontational were productions in which periods were mixed, aiming for another feature of Elizabethan theatre by combining modern dress and 'historical' elements. Theatre Workshop performed a conflation of both parts of *Henry IV* under Joan Littlewood's direction at the 1964 Edinburgh Festival. The stage was a bare rectangle, 45 feet long and 15 feet wide, and the basic costumes were modern, with armour and other 'historical' additions as necessary. Reviewers complained about this on technical grounds and reports suggest that the director was not always able to make all the play's episodes intelligible to all sides of the house (since Guthrie's *Ane Satyre of the Thrie Estatis* at the first festival in 1948, the Assembly Hall had usually been used for thrust stages). Littlewood was also attacked for her

FIG. 99 Queen Margaret (Peggy Ashcroft) dominates the council table: *The Wars of the Roses*, Royal Shakespeare Theatre, 1964.

alterations to the texts and the company's apparent failure to find an appropriate style for the language. Under the headline 'Scrambled Shakespeare', the drama critic of *The Times* complained that 'no coherent intention emerges beyond that of refusing to be overawed by the bard'. Littlewood responded to the poor notices by insisting that 'it is easier to attack the Royal Family than attempt to scrape off the patina of age and the dreary respect which stifles Elizabethan verse' (both may be easier in the 1990s than the mid-1960s) and by proclaiming her company's policy: to work 'without the assistance of smart direction, fancy dress, beards and greasepaint'.[8] A decade earlier, in 1955, she had even revived the previous season's *Richard II*, with Harry H. Corbett as the King, to demonstrate the contrast between the work of her fifteen actors and the forty-five currently employed at the Old Vic in Michael Benthall's production. Kenneth Tynan reviewed the two together, awarding the Old Vic a win on points on account of John Neville's 'clear diagrammatic outline for the definitive performance, as yet unseen' against Corbett's King, played 'in a frenzy of effeminacy'.[9] The combative spirit of Stratford East (imitated at repertory theatres up and down the country) was felt more strongly in the mid-1950s and early 1960s, when the 'decorative' and 'atmospheric' older style of production still dominated more respectable stages. The Brechtian combination of non-naturalistic staging and realistic situations, speech, and behaviour was given additional currency by the drama-documentaries presented by such companies as Peter Cheeseman's at the Victoria,

FIG. 100 Andrew Jarvis as Richard III in *The Wars of the Roses*, English Shakespeare Company, 1989.

Stoke-on-Trent. (The impact of that company's *As You Like It* is described by Peter Thomson in Chapter 9.)

By the 1980s, when Michael Bogdanov directed both tetralogies of history plays in eclectic designs and politically committed interpretations for the English Shakespeare Company, the old grandiloquence and fancy dress had largely disappeared. There was still a shock effect to be gained from a punkish Eastcheap (with Doll Tearsheet in fishnets and black leather), and the shift from chivalry to the computer age (fig. 100) was vividly reversed in *Richard III* when Gloucester and Richmond reverted to hand-to-hand combat with swords in full medieval armour. It was characteristic of Bogdanov to set up Richmond's concluding speech as a press conference, with the paraphernalia of broadcasting and journalism. For all their aggression, the ESC's productions of the history plays made shrewd use of old-fashioned *coups de théâtre*, vigorous and well-judged speaking of the text, and (with their sparse but somehow spectacular staging) a cultivation of the audience's feeling that they were collaborating in a difficult but exhilarating task. Comparison with productions of the history plays staged by the RSC during the same period, particularly Adrian Noble's cycle, *The Plantagenets* (1988), suggests that the abrasive, confrontational approach of the 1960s *Wars of the Roses* had been inherited by Bogdanov, while the 'national' company was moving to a less materialist approach. Noble's productions were dominated by symbolism, where Bogdanov's moved through a series of politically pointed episodes.[10]

An achievement of such enterprises as Gaskill's and Littlewood's—from which Bogdanov and others benefited—was not so much to habituate audiences to a particular performance style as to establish that the plays were open texts, liable to any kind of interpretative strategy. Before the launching of the ESC, Bogdanov's work had included artistic directorship of the Young Vic, a theatre adjacent to the Old Vic in London where (at first under the National's aegis) Frank Dunlop had established a company whose work attracted young audiences into the theatre and took productions and demonstrations and workshops out into the community. The very word 'community'

acquired great value in the minds of theatre companies and educators and the left-wing politicians in local government who supported them, especially as in the late 1970s and early 1980s the Thatcher government set about dismantling the Welfare State, reducing the autonomy of local government and setting aside the very notion of communality in the name of greater individual responsibility and freedom. Bogdanov's Young Vic work included the 'Action Man Trilogy' of three plays (*Richard III, Hamlet,* and *The Tempest*) which combined political analysis with shock effects of modernity. One actor described the Bogdanov style as 'modern dress, telephones, bicycles, combat dress, and general scorn of spectacle and magic'.[11] The choice of plays was in itself provocative, insisting that *Hamlet* and *The Tempest*, no less than *Richard III*, were 'about' power politics. In the event the late comedy fared least successfully: Prospero (Bill Wallis) sat at a café table in the middle of the stage with a bottle of wine and a cigar, and the events of the play seemed to unfold as if in his memory. One reviewer described the effect as that of 'an extended reverie, in which an ineffectual dreamer keeps building tenuous bridges to the future, only to see them collapse at the first tremor of a footfall'. Prospero was thus deprived of the authority customarily granted by his magic and status, and the ending was devoid of any sense that reconciliation had been achieved. The dissipation of the play's mystery and tension seemed disabling to a text already stretching the bounds of theatrical convention. 'One had been made privy to a peculiar dream,' wrote another critic, 'But there is more to *The Tempest* than can be contained within an after-dinner sleep.' In *Hamlet* (wrote one reviewer) 'most of the text [was] taken up by the personal, internal struggles of Hamlet, and to a lesser extent Ophelia, to come to terms with their society and the demands its politics make upon them,' and the prince was characterized as 'a high-minded and slightly pompous student'. The staging, on an octagonal platform surrounded by the audience, with few props and simple effects of sound and lighting, was designed to make the action of the plays clear.[12] These were in fact to be plays of 'action' and activist political theatre, and the title of the trilogy invoked the name of the military doll as an implicit challenge to romantic notions of the plays and their leading characters.

Performing the plays in this style might not in itself bring the Conservative government to its knees, but it soon became apparent in the work of other companies that there was a political significance in playing Shakespeare with non-naturalistic techniques and in unconventional spaces. Cheek by Jowl, the company started by Declan Donellan and Nick Ormerod in 1981, has rarely made the explicit political gestures familiar in Bogdanov's productions, but its vivid, economical story-telling has illustrated the politics of theatre itself by refusing to accept the 'star' system, performing in non-theatrical spaces, and showing a lively irreverence for the letter of the text that can usually be traced back to a close study of it. The company's Shakespeare productions have included an all-male *As You Like It* (fig. 101, discussed already by Jonathan Bate in the introduction to this volume), a *Twelfth Night* (1986) in which homosexuality was given a central role (Orsino really did fancy Cesario as a boy, Antonio was in love with Sebastian and at the end paired up with Feste), and a *Tempest* (1988) in which Prospero was a theatrical director with an identity crisis and Caliban was taught to sing a catch—'There's no such thing as Society'— that was a setting of words adapted from a pronouncement by Margaret Thatcher. The handbag-wielding Queen of Naples in this *Tempest* bore an uncanny resemblance to the Prime Minister herself.

Donellan was anxious to distance his company's work from conservative (or Conservative) notions of what was educational. *Macbeth* (1987) had a female porter whose repertoire included ribald comment on the state of the nation in the 1980s, and whose language owed more to the comedian Billy Connolly than the world of thanes: her first words were 'Fuck off!' The company decided to add a line to its publicity advising that the production was not considered suitable for audiences under the age of 16. Donellan commented: 'We have to protect ourselves. Shakespeare's not at all educational. He celebrates life in all its filth and dirt. I love to see the theatre full of young people, but as long as they come as a sort of

adult, sexy exercise.'[13] The relationship between Shakespeare in the theatre and education is a close and difficult one. A play's inclusion in the schools' examination syllabuses often leads repertory companies to produce it, but there is some apprehension that this restricts the choice of texts and the manner of presentation. (Moreover, Shakespeare's plays usually require large casts, with few parts for women.) On the credit side, such productions bring to the theatre an important element of that 'new public' sought by Lindsay Anderson and his successors.

There are other tactics than political engagement or artistic minimalism for attracting new audiences. At the Citizens' Theatre in Glasgow, Shakespeare has regularly been staged in stylish, flamboyant productions that cultivate a sense of scandal and confrontation: all-male productions of *Hamlet* and *Antony and Cleopatra*, a *Troilus and Cressida* that was 'transatlantic' and 'post-nuclear': 'Cressida was a nymph-starlet, Helen a dumb, blonde and spiteful film queen, Ulysses a gum-chewing egg-head, Achilles a vain pop idol using his pet, Patroclus, as a comforter' (fig. 102).[14] Such radical transpositions of well-known texts to 'inappropriate' settings have often fuelled the sense of excitement and danger, giving the Citizens' a reputation more valuable to them than the more obviously worthy *kudos* of other companies who mine the texts for 'relevance' to current social and political preoccupations. The company uses to the full its lavish Victorian proscenium-arch theatre, keeps seat prices low, and pursues energetically a policy which places overall theatrical effect above the verbal text. In the staging of 'classic' plays its peers are the state theatres of Europe rather than the RSC or the National in England (although the latter have not been slow to employ actors who have worked with the Citizens' and, on occasion, members of its artistic directorate).

Also disruptive of expectations, but not of customary ideas about performance practice and actor–audience relationships, the productions of

---

Facing: FIG. 101 Adrian Lester as Rosalind and Simon Coates as Celia in Cheek by Jowl's all-male *As You Like It*, 1995.

FIG. 102 On the beach: *Troilus and Cressida*, directed by Philip Prowse, Citizens' Theatre, Glasgow, 1972.

Jonathan Miller have characteristically resited the plays, for example by placing Shylock in a Venice of nineteenth-century capitalism, and setting *King Lear* (Nottingham, 1967) in the time of the Thirty Years War. For Miller, concerned with what he describes as the 'afterlife' of dramatic texts, the simplistic transposition of an Elizabethan text to a modern setting is too often 'a form of historical provincialism'.

He argues that 'We cannot act or see Shakespeare today as the Elizabethans and the author did but we can take into account that our perception is a modern one without rewriting the plays to make them contemporary.'[15] The late nineteenth-century setting of his National Theatre *Merchant of Venice* (1970) came from 'hearing certain speeches, in [his] mind's eye, delivered in a way that was incompatible with a sixteenth-century setting'.[16] Specifically, the removal of the 'trial' scene to a judge's chambers, with a green baize table and an atmosphere of sober legal dispute rather than public histrionics, made it possible for Portia's speech about mercy to be delivered 'as if having laboriously to explain what should have been self-evident to someone too stupid to understand. The dispute was too ugly to be argued out in public' (fig. 103).[17] At the same time, Miller was able to accommodate a performance of great virtuosity by Olivier and to underline points of interpretation with ideas that could only work given the chosen setting. Olivier's performance offered (according to one reviewer) 'the terrifying and exhilarating spectacle of a full-scale piece of heroic acting being given in an orderly, mercantile late-nineteenth-century setting'.[18]

Miller's *Merchant of Venice* offers a good example of the extra charge that can come to a Shakespeare text by this kind of shift in period whereby new responsibilities reveal themselves. Issues suddenly become problematic or incongruous, particularly attitudes expressed towards war, kingship, the employment of servants, and the treatment of women by men and foreigners by everyone. It is as though all the plays are now 'Problem Plays', in the sense of being problematic, if not in the stricter Shavian meaning of expounding problems. Unsurprisingly, the 'Problem Plays' identified in the early years of the century—*Measure for Measure, Troilus,* and *All's Well*—have enjoyed a new lease of life. It is hard to imagine that a production of *Measure for Measure* in the last three decades of the century would not regard the Duke's position as being as questionable as his deputy's, or would take entirely at face value his offer of marriage to Isabella. In this, as in other aspects of contemporary Shakespearian production, we can trace the effect of changing attitudes to issues of sex and gender. Ivor Brown's review of Guthrie's 1955 *Troilus* applauds Rosemary Harris's presentation of Cressida as 'a minx': 'Miss Harris was the prettiest villain indeed and abundantly supported the remark of Ulysses that "her wanton spirits look out at every joint

FIG. 103 A judge's chambers in nineteenth-century Venice: *The Merchant of Venice*, directed by Jonathan Miller, National Theatre, 1970.

and motive of her body." She was a bewitching and authentic "daughter of the game." '[19] Productions of the 1980s and 1990s have been less prepared to take Cressida at Ulysses' valuation, unless (as with the Glasgow Citizens' production referred to above) this was part of a wholesale devaluation of the dignity of Troy and Greece.

Decadence has occasionally been represented in productions of *Troilus* and *Measure for Measure* in such a way as to appeal to the preoccupations of the present and sharpen the sense of sexual ignominies and ethical contradictions in these and other texts. Prospect's 1973 *Pericles*, set entirely in a brothel was (wrote one reviewer) like reading the tale in 'a gorgeous, forbidden picturebook, part Dulac, part sleazy Grosz,' but in which 'real palpitating humans loving and losing each other' were visible from time to time as though through holes in its pages.[20]

New Accents, New Texts

Critics who object to new ways of staging and dressing the plays have often lamented a decline in standards of verse speaking. This has sometimes been conceived in social terms: the new actors did not have the *class* to play leading Shakespearian roles. A less class-orientated 'traditionalist' argument starts from the claim that we owe ourselves Shakespearian production done in as 'authentic' a style as possible, either because that style is a precious heritage to be maintained or (more interestingly) the 'authentic' Elizabethan technique can revitalize and widen the range of performing skills available. Much theatre practice and theory in the century has been devoted to such rediscoveries: the combination of research into skills and staging forms, communal living and unconventional theatre spaces has been inherited from such pioneers as Jacques Copeau and continues in the work of Peter Brook.

Since the mid-1950s, however, the 'Shakespearian' speaking voice has been radically redefined. In the early years of the century Shakespeare had been 'speeded up', and critics commented on the rapidity of speech in Granville-Barker's productions as a departure from a more orotund, self-consciously musical tradition. Musicality, even at the new, brisker tempos, remained a principal aim of verse-speaking well into the fifth decade of the century, with John Gielgud often cited as a leading exponent of the style. In the mid-1950s reviewers were already complaining that actors no longer seemed at home with verse: Ivor Brown's review of Guthrie's 1955 *Troilus*, quoted above, observes that young actors are reluctant to raise the pitch at the end of a line, for fear of being thought a 'ham'. By the 1960s, with the accumulated experience of extreme naturalism in acting (particularly the 'Method', Lee Strasberg's development of Stanislavski, exemplified by Marlon Brando) on film and television, actors were increasingly seeking an accommodation between blank verse and ordinary speech or simply ignoring the rhetorical patterning and metrics altogether.

A striking example, preserved on film, is Nicol Williamson's 'rasping, dentalised, round-shouldered lope of a performance' as Hamlet in the 1969 production by Tony Richardson (fig. 104). Staged (and filmed) at the Roundhouse, a converted engine-shed and one of the leading avant-garde venues of the time, this challenged convention in other respects, including the casting of a popular singer, Marianne Faithfull, as Ophelia. Charles Marowitz, a leading worrier at the heels of conventional or comfortable Shakespeare, found the production uninspiring but clearly could not resist the awful fascination of the new prince: 'For this Hamlet, the vow to revenge his father's death is a convenient excuse for venting an hostility which would have grasped at any pretext for unleashing itself.'[21] Williamson does not speak a 'standard' English, or express any easy nobility of mind. 'Who would fardels bear?' he asks, with a petulant contempt for the very idea that would do credit to Jimmy Porter. Michael Billington thought that the voice combined 'the slimy whine of Brumagem with the slightly

FIG. 104 Nicol Williamson as Hamlet, The Roundhouse, London, 1969.

pinched vowel-sounds of a puritanical Scottish lay-preacher,' but celebrated the new Hamlet's romanticism and the paradoxical combination of an instinct for death and destruction with an enthusiasm for life. This prince lacked 'irony, delicacy, gentleness' but 'match[ed] the play's questing feverishness with a bottled hysteria of its own'. Another reviewer insisted that Williamson knew how to 'phrase' the text: 'The vowels may be odd at times, the aitches absent, finer points may slip away as they would not be let fall (nor were) by Gielgud or Barrymore, but the stressing was always right, so that the force of the lines always came through.'[22]

Like David Warner's Hamlet in Peter Hall's 1965 Stratford production (discussed by Peter Thomson in Chapter 9), Williamson's was clearly one of the awkward squad, not self-evidently the expectancy and rose of a fair state. Warner's red scarf (in the first season of the Hall production) and his aggressively unregal behaviour may have been a sign that the 'Anger' of 1956 was moving towards the 'Events' of 1968. Both performances were simply too unprincely for many reviewers, but for some of the younger generation they showed that Hamlet could speak and feel with them.[23]

General notions of social behaviour as well as verse-speaking were felt to be at stake. Franco Zeffirelli's *Romeo and Juliet* (Old Vic, 1961) was agreed to achieve wonders of 'real' rather than 'decorative' activity. The young men of Verona lived and breathed in a world

Fig. 105 Passion in the streets: Franco Zeffirelli's *Romeo and Juliet*, Old Vic, 1960.

that had the urgency and roughness of urban Italy (if not of the New York to which *West Side Story* had transposed the play in 1957) (fig. 105). John Russell Brown identified the basic technique of speaking the text as naturalistic, 'unifying words and stage-business . . . making the actors' speech as lively and fluent as the physical action' so that 'the dialogue did not seem the effect of study and care, but the natural idiom of characters in particular situations'.[24] Zeffirelli (fresh from a triumphant *Cavalleria Rusticana* and *I Pagliacci* at Covent Garden) had directed the speaking with an ear for musical values of contrast and rhythmic variety, but at times the effect of the stage business seemed (in Brown's view) to break up and dissipate such longer speeches as Juliet's potion-taking monologue and Mercutio's Queen Mab speech. The director's main concern (as Judi Dench recalls in Chapter 11) was with immediacy of passion rather than the text. Alec McCowen was encouraged to play Mercutio as a wittily aggressive 'angry young man', so that (in the words of one reviewer) Benvolio became Cliff to his Jimmy Porter, and the Queen Mab speech became less of an aria than a fragmented series of inspirations, images sparked off from the young men he was addressing.[25] For some observers John Stride was simply too ordinary for Romeo: Laurence Kitchin diagnosed the presence of 'a vaguely international approach' (which he called 'proletarian Pop Shakespeare') in which the absence of a technique for heightened language was compensated for by making the dialogue serve 'as a commentary on physical action, groupings or personal feelings and the gist of it is all an audience needs to understand'. *The Times* resignedly admitted that, as Romeo and Juliet, John Stride and Judi Dench made 'their own cut-down poetry'.[26]

Although opponents of what is perceived as an 'RSC style' often cite pedantic verse-speaking as one of its undesirable features, the handling of Shakespeare's language has undergone an overhaul at the hands of that company's voice department since its early days. The company's work has been marked by the insistence of the voice teacher Cicely Berry, in particular, that feeling and sense should direct the musicality of the verse, and that its patterns should be lived through

rather than simply rendered as though they were a strict notation in a classical musical score.[27] In some quarters this is considered to have gone too far. Peter Hall, founder-director of the company but by then in charge of the National Theatre, described in his diary a performance of *King Lear* by the RSC on 18 June 1977:

Again there was this slow, over-emphatic, line-breaking delivery of the text. The actors are so busy telling us the ambiguities and the resonances that there is little or no sense of form. You cannot play Shakespeare without a sense of line. R.S.C. Shakespeare is getting slower and slower.[28]

In his productions at the National Theatre and, subsequently, for his own production company, Hall has sought to restore a stricter sense of the form of the verse, insisting that actors mark the end of a line and use the pentameter's rhythms and balances.

Little credit is given now to the notion that only a 'Received Pronunciation' (approximating to South-East English speech of the middle and upper classes) is appropriate for Shakespeare's non-plebeian characters, and that actors must disguise any regional accent. The typically English assumption that accent denotes class rather than simply geographical location is hard to defeat, although some direct assaults have been made on these prejudices, notably by Barrie Rutter's company, Northern Broadsides, whose work (including a vigorous *Richard III*) has celebrated the expressive qualities and sophistication of Northern speech. Productions of *A Midsummer Night's Dream* have often condescended to the mechanicals by giving them a rough 'working-class' speech contrasting with the polish of the other characters' voices; in 1994, Northern Broadsides did special justice to Bottom, Quince, and friends by having *everyone* speak in northern vernacular tones (fig. 106). More important, the company's policy insists on bringing the physical world of the plays close to that of an audience other than the university-educated middle classes. Productions are more likely now than in the 1970s or even 1980s to be cast across ethnic divisions either 'blind' (a black Banquo, among a lot of whiteish thanes, none of them attempting to sound like Scots) or with current preoccupations in mind (Romeo and

Juliet from different ethnic groups, for example). As with speech, theatre companies are increasingly anxious to dispel the assumption that only white people with 'standard' (that is, upper-class) accents can pass muster as Shakespeare's leading characters.

The texts of the plays have themselves been under review for some time, in many productions reversing the movement towards a 'full' text which marked the earlier reaction against the butchery required for Victorian and Edwardian scenic productions. Like stage speech, the texts have felt the effect of redefinitions of the theatre's basic structures—in this case, the institution of the individual playwright as an authority, and (less radically) of the nature of the dramatic text itself. Many directors feel free to shorten the plays by trimming what are considered obscurities, especially in comic dialogue, and the example cited above of the Porter in Cheek by Jowl's *Macbeth* represents a general readiness to tamper with what are considered incidental elements of the composition, the argument being that Shakespeare worked as a collaborator rather than a remote figure of authority, and that he would collaborate with our theatre were he able to do so. Sometimes a director has decided substantially to rewrite a play without wishing to forfeit the credit of producing work by Shakespeare, eliciting on occasion the kind of critical obloquy that attached itself to John Barton's 1975 RSC version of *King John*. More commonly, adaptation within what pass as 'conservative' productions has proceeded stealthily by cutting and transposing lines and words rather than adding new ones. For Franco Zeffirelli's *Much Ado* (National Theatre, 1965), set in a burlesque nineteenth-century Sicily, Robert Graves provided what amounted to paraphrases of lines thought difficult (a practice hallowed by Olivier's example in his 1948 film of *Hamlet*). Such adjustment might be seen as the ultimate expression of a desire to make Shakespeare 'our contemporary', a familiar, approachable writer, whose differences of expression and emphasis can be neutralized without fuss. Sometimes the desire to accommodate the texts to modern sensibilities produces such simple emendations as changing Benedick's declaration 'If I

do not love her, I am a Jew' (*Much Ado*, II. iii. 250–1) to 'If I do not love her, I am a villain'. More questionable is the removal of Portia's remark after the departure of the Prince of Morocco: 'Let all of his complexion choose me so.' Can audiences in the 1990s be expected to admire a heroine who lets slip such a racist sentiment, or should there be an appeal to the limited outlook of four centuries ago?

It has not been uncommon for directors to incorporate signals of their disapproval in a 'full' (or at least substantial) performance of a text. This amounts to the assertion not that the text agrees with the attitudes of *bien-pensant* audiences of the 1990s, but that any disposition they might have to take it to their bosoms is to be shunned. Among theories of directing, the notion that a valuable production takes issue with the text it starts from has an honoured place. For the most part, however, wholesale adaptation on the model of Brecht's *Coriolan* or Heiner Müller's *Macbeth* (1972) and *Hamlet Maschine* (1979) has been rare in the British theatre: most directors have tinkered piecemeal with the text, or cut and trimmed on grounds of time and comprehensibility, adding dumb shows and business to articulate their differences with what seem to be the text's messages. The Glasgow Citizens' company, anxious to move theatre away from fixation with text, seized on the 'Bad' Quarto of *Hamlet* as a contribution to the barrage of shock effects in a production which set the play in a mental hospital, with Claudius as one of the doctors.[29]

There has been one notable exception to this general (and relative) tendency to textual 'integrity'. The Shakespeare versions of Charles Marowitz, beginning with his 'collage' *Hamlet* in 1965, have been critiques of the plays' ideas and characters, achieved by wholesale cuts and transpositions, the adding of new material. The starting-point throughout has been Marowitz's impatience with what he sees as the pallid liberal co-opting of potentially revolutionary forces which are present in the plays' subtext. Hamlet is in his eyes 'a slob', whose ineffectual behaviour merits the contempt of the tyrant Claudius, all the other characters and the modern revolutionary alike. *The*

FIG. 106 The mechanicals in Northern Broadsides' *A Midsummer Night's Dream*, 1994.

Shrew (discussed by Peter Thomson in Chapter 9) showed the brutality of man's degradation of woman far more effectively than the original play, but it can be argued that the very process of adaptation reveals the extent to which the play deals with other matters than social and sexual domination. In *An Othello* a black Iago destroyed an Othello who had betrayed the cause of his fellow-blacks: 'the appropriation of one black man into the privileged suburbs of white society dismantles the revolutionary impetus of a thousand black renegades.'[30] The new material included a scene in which Desdemona was indeed enjoyed by the 'general camp' and a monologue in which Brabantio appeared as a bigoted Jewish father, angry that his daughter wants to marry a black. In the final scene Othello faltered as he was about to kill himself: the Duke held him down, Lodovico cut his throat, Desdemona (not really killed) rose up and 'the victorious whites [drew] together in smiling complicity'.

The plays which the critic Ruby Cohn has usefully dubbed 'Shakespeare Offshoots'—texts which parody, parallel, or owe their principal point of reference to Shakespeare's work—have had an influence on the reception of the originals on which they depend. Tom Stoppard's *Rosencrantz and Guildenstern are Dead* (1966) places Hamlet's schoolfriends in the centre of the stage, expresses the frustrations and absurdity of their existence, and allows the events of Shakespeare's play to unfold on the periphery of their experience. The assimilation of Hamlet's own world into a Theatre of the Absurd, typified by the soundless laughter with which David Warner's prince greeted the recognition 'that the rest is silence', is completed in Stoppard's comedy. Edward Bond's *Lear* (1972) articulates a bleak, cruel, and violent universe congruent with that of Peter Brook's Kott-inspired *King Lear* of 1962: it is the more effective, and more thoroughly political in its outlook, for being a text written alongside Shakespeare's rather than some sort of adaptation, but it can be argued that it has reinforced the tendency to nihilism in contemporary productions of the Elizabethan play.

New Causes

Since the 1960s and 1970s the methods and aims of earlier radicalisms have been reviewed. The shifting sands of subsidy, and the increasing demand that companies should find sponsorship and make money at the box-office, have led to a conflict of policies and artistic aims in much subsidized theatre. The fragmentations of 'post-modern' Shakespeare often spin the plays away from the thematic coherence and earnestness of purpose to which earlier activist theatres sought to attach their political programmes. Such productions of *Hamlet* as those of Ron Daniels with Mark Rylance as the pyjama-clad prince (RSC 1989) seem to suggest that the play is no longer susceptible of interpretation as a fable of resistance and social consciousness, and that paradoxically it has been returned to the world of alienation and personal *Angst* that characterized Existentialist work of the 1940s and 1950s and dominates Olivier's 1948 film. In the mid-1980s there was a movement to dethrone the director and reinstate an 'actors' theatre'. Focused in the book by Simon Callow, *Being an Actor* (1984) and the productions of Kenneth Branagh and David Parfitt's Renaissance Theatre Company, this was thought by some to herald a resurgence of actor-managers' theatre, and to those on the left its lack of a declared political agenda (beyond altering the power structure of the theatre itself) was suspect if not reactionary. In 1992 Renaissance staged its last Shakespearian production in a theatre—*Coriolanus* at Chichester with Branagh as Caius Martius and Judi Dench as a chilling Volumnia—and Branagh turned his attention to film-making. In the event, his film versions of Shakespeare, which had begun with *Henry V* in 1989, may have been more influential than the company's stage work.

At the turn of the century the two 'national' theatre companies in London and Stratford-upon-Avon were vying with each other in attempts to find financial security through the transfer of productions to the commercial sector. This occurred with some small-scale shows, but large-scale musicals were the big earners: the National's *Guys and Dolls* (1982) had been followed by others, including *Carousel* (1992), and for the RSC *Les Misérables* (originally staged at the Barbican theatre in 1985) continued to earn revenue internationally. It is arguable that audience expectations for spectacle, music, and emotional impact have carried over from such shows as these (and even grander spectacles like *The Phantom of the Opera*) to main-stage Shakespearian productions. Although some large-scale Shakespeare productions by both companies—notably Richard Eyre's 1990 *Richard III* at the National with Ian McKellen—had a long and influential career (in this case, touring internationally and then metamorphosing into a feature film), the tendency to prefer intimate spaces for Shakespeare persisted. After he left the RSC, bowing out with *Othello* at The Other Place, Trevor Nunn's most successful Shakespearian productions included *Timon of Athens* at the Young Vic (1991, with David Suchet as Timon). John Caird, a long-time collaborator of Nunn's at Stratford and elsewhere, directed *Hamlet* in the Lyttleton, the National's smaller theatre in 2000, with Simon Russell Beale in the title role. Richard Eyre's 'farewell' production as retiring director of the National was *King Lear* with Ian Holm, in the Cottesloe's studio space. Some of these productions were later followed by a transfer to larger spaces: in 2001 Caird's *Hamlet* was restaged in the arena-like Olivier. Others, like Nunn's RSC *Othello* and Eyre's *King Lear*, benefited from the intimacy of their original staging as the basis for television productions.

The National's South Bank stages and the RSC's Barbican (from which the company announced its withdrawal in 2001) were also the temporary venues for a handful of notable 'foreign' influences. Karin Beier's *Romeo and Juliet* (Barbican, 1996: from Düsseldorf) had uncompromisingly immature lovers in a world of mindless violence and egotistical and oppressive parenthood—the balcony scene was played with a delicious sense of dizzy risk-taking on two trapezes. The Canadian director Robert Lepage staged *A Midsummer Night's Dream* in a pool of water at the National in 1992, and the Young Vic was host to Peter Brook's elegantly pared-down Parisian production of *Hamlet* (with Adrian Lester in the title role) in 2001. In fact, though, it was difficult to find spaces and audiences for such productions outwith the framework of an established theatre or arts festival, and London was not as adventurously hospitable as Glasgow or even (in the case of Lepage) Nottingham. International cross-currents of the kind discussed in an earlier chapter by Inga-Stina Ewbank did not flow more forcefully for British audiences in the last decade of the century, and their effects were felt largely by those—mainly theatre professionals, critics, and academics—able to experience them abroad.

At Stratford, economics have demanded that the proscenium-arched main house, with its 1500 seats, should be the venue for the majority of the Shakespeare productions—and that most of these should be chosen from what has seemed an increasingly narrow range of popular scripts. A series of changes to the Royal Shakespeare Theatre itself, bringing the stage forward and placing renewed emphasis on voice and movement rather than scenic spectacle, have evinced a desire to 'reclaim' the large theatre for effective Shakespearian performance. A triumphant return to ensemble casting and a coherent production style across a group of plays was achieved in the two sequences of history plays that made up the 'This England' project in 2000–2001. In the first group, different teams of directors and designers in the Other Place, the Swan, and the main house staged *Richard II*, the two parts of *Henry IV*, and *Henry V* respectively. In the second group, the 'first tetralogy'—the three parts of *Henry VI* and *Richard III* were staged by one team (Michael Boyd and the designer Tom Piper) in one theatre—the Swan, with its neo-Elizabethan thrust reconfigured to make it a cruciform stage surrounded by audience seating. The vigour and coherence of the productions—particularly the second group—recalled the *Wars of the Roses* of the mid-1960s, with which the company had staked its claim. Unfortunately, even with the RSC's level of government funding, it seems

that *Henry VI / Richard III* sequence could not have been mounted without a co-production deal with the University of Michigan. The vision of a permanent (or even semi-permanent) ensemble conjured up by Peter Hall in the 1960s has proved unattainable in the bleaker climate of subsequent decades.

In the late 1990s the arrival after almost half a century of wearisome petition (and fund-raising) of a new and energetically 'authentic' venue altered the balance of power in Shakespearian playgoing in the capital. 'Shakespeare's Globe', the replica of the first Globe on a Bankside site adjacent to that of the original, was the brainchild of the American actor Sam Wanamaker, who died in 1993 but at least lived to see the construction under way. Since its first full season in 1997 it has been a source of lively debate if not always of critical satisfaction. Under the directorship of Mark Rylance (since 1996) the theatre acquired a reputation for innovation that has played well against what might be a quaint dullness of authenticity. Productions have not been uniformly in Elizabethan dress, and after early problematic attempts to encourage 'period' audience behaviour it has developed subtler ways of exploiting its unique open-air thrust stage surrounded immediately by groundlings and, beyond them, tiers of seated spectators. Rylance's performance as the queen in an all-male *Antony and Cleopatra* (1999) and that of Vanessa Redgrave as Prospero (2000) were received as bravely unconventional rather than wholly satisfying, but did at least reflect a desire to challenge assumptions, and Rylance's own performance as Hamlet (2000) was a worthy successor to his much-admired interpretation of the role at Stratford just over a decade earlier.

Within London, Shakespeare has figured occasionally in the repertoires of adventurous theatre companies such as the Almeida in Islington, whose twinned productions of *Richard II* and *Coriolanus* in 2000, with Joseph Fiennes in the title roles, opened at the reconditioned Gainsborough film studio in Shoreditch and subsequently toured to New York. One-off commercial ventures, such as a production of *A Midsummer Night's Dream* (2001) with the popular comic actress Dawn French as Bottom, have occasionally succeeded with the help of star names. Attempts to establish repertory companies including Shakespeare among other 'classic' scripts at the Old Vic under Jonathan Miller and at various theatres by Peter Hall have not been so successful. Elsewhere in the country, touring companies and regional repertory theatres have continued to play Shakespeare. Repertory theatres in the big cities strive to serve their local community, foster new writing, and stage adventurous productions of well-known plays. But this has to be reconciled with the demand that they balance the books with popular plays and school syllabus fare—including the occasional, reliable Shakespeare. For these companies, burdened with buildings and staff, it is often difficult to venture beyond 'safety' in choice of text and production values. Any renewal of the explosion of new buildings and

relatively generous funding embarked on under the Labour government of the early 1960s was beyond the means or political will of the 'New Labour' government elected in 1997. In 2000–2001 the Arts Council was able to fund the 'stabilisation' of the finances of many of its client theatres, but prospects for the ensuing seasons (or financial years, depending on one's point of approach) were not promising.

Nevertheless, it is possible to muster some optimism about the state of Shakespeare performance in Britain at the beginning of the new century. Audiences are more likely to be sitting (or standing) around a stage, than viewing it through a proscenium arch. Compared with their counterparts half a century earlier, they are less likely to hear the received upper-class accents of South-East England from the stage, to

Fig. 107 Hamlet (Mark Rylance) in Soliloquy at Shakespeare's Globe: Bankside, London 2000.

find the tragic heroes admirable, or to take the women at the value set on them by male characters. Today's audiences will have seen warriors who are suspect, fairies with unresolved sexual problems, and clowns who might have been conceived by Dostoevsky and trained by Beckett. They will probably expect to be shown the play's relevance to their own preoccupations, and its claims to be taken seriously may depend on their going home with a sceptical view of human happiness (if a comedy) or of the achievement of wisdom through suffering (if a tragedy). The production's physical resources may have rivalled those of an opera-house, or consisted of eight actors, two ladders, and six metal buckets. It is more probable now than fifty years ago that the company will have treated Shakespeare more as a collaborator than an authority, and that they want to help audiences find the means and arguments to change society for the better. On a good night, the audience may leave feeling that they have actively participated in something that engaged them directly, with a mind full of new arguments from old matter, and an appetite for more.

Notes

Introduction

1. Published in English in 1964, but Peter Brook read the chapter 'King Lear, or Endgame' in French prior to his 1962 production.
2. Peter Brook, *The Empty Space* (London, 1968, repr. Harmondsworth, 1972), 73–5.
3. *The Observer*, 11 Nov. 1962, repr. in Tynan's *A View of the English Stage 1944–63* (London, 1975), 343.
4. On this, and the likely date of the drawing (1604–15, not 1595, as is usually asserted), see my Arden edition of *Titus* (London, 1995), 38–43.
5. On Henslowe's documents and what may be learnt from them, see *Henslowe's Diary*, ed. R. A. Foakes and R. T. Rickert (Cambridge, 1961), *Documents of the Rose Playhouse*, ed. Carol Rutter (Manchester, 1984), and Neil Carson, *A Companion to Henslowe's Diary* (Cambridge, 1988).

1. Shakespeare's Elizabethan Stages

1. *The Elizabethan Stage*, 4 vols. (Oxford, 1923), ii. 526–7.
2. Glynne Wickham, *Early English Stages*, vol. ii, Part I (London, 1963), 204; G. E. Bentley, *The Jacobean and Caroline Stage*, 7 vols. (Oxford, 1941–68), vi. 249–50; Wickham, *Early English Stages*, vol. ii, Part II (London, 1972), 201.
3. See R. A. Foakes, 'The Image of the Swan Theatre', in *Spectacle & Image in Renaissance Europe*, Selected Papers of the 32nd Conference at the Centre d'Études Supérieures de la Renaissance de Tours, 29 June–8 July 1989, ed. André Lascombes (Leiden, 1993), 337–57 for a full discussion of the Swan theatre.
4. Andrew Gurr, Ronnie Mulryne, and Margaret Shewring, (eds.), *The Design of the Globe* (London: The International Globe Centre, 1993).

5. *Henslowe's Diary*, ed. R. A. Foakes and R. T. Rickert (Cambridge, 1961), 308.
6. For these measurements I have relied upon the account of their findings by Julian M. C. Bowsher and Simon Blatherwick, the archaeologists who worked on the site of the Rose for the Museum of London; see their essay, 'The Structure of the Rose', in Franklin J. Hildy (ed.), *New Issues in the Reconstruction of Shakespeare's Theatre* (New York, 1990), 63–4, 70.
7. *Henslowe's Diary*, 13, 308.
8. Thomas Middleton, *Father Hubburd's Tales; or, The Ant and the Nightingale* (1604), in *The Works of Thomas Middleton*, ed. A. H. Bullen, 8 vols. (London, 1885–6, repr. New York, 1964), viii. 93.
9. Middleton, *The Black Book* (1604), Bullen viii. 25; Thomas Dekker, *Satiromastix* (1602), *Dramatic Works*, ed. Fredson Bowers (4 vols., Cambridge 1953–70), i. 364, where Horace (Ben Jonson) reacts to the idea of being tossed in a blanket by stamping, and Tucca cries, 'dost stampe, mad Tamberlaine, dost stampe?'
10. *Discoveries*, ed. G. B. Harrison (London, 1923), 23. The casual remark by Muriel Bradbrook in *The Rise of the Common Player* (Cambridge, 1962), 196, that Alleyn referred to himself mockingly as 'the fustian king' in a family letter, has been repeated by Andrew Gurr in *The Shakespearean Stage 1574–1642* (3rd edn., Cambridge, 1992), 90, and by Michael Hattaway in *Elizabethan Popular Theatre* (London, 1982), 219. Alleyn wrote a joking letter addressed to his wife Joan, as from a boy actor, John Pyk, probably his apprentice, which ends with some rough verses, marked by spaces in the prose:

> Yet I swear to you by the faith of a fustian king
> never to retorne till fortune us bring

wt a Joyfull metyng to lovly london. I sesse
yor petty pretty pratlyng parlyng pyg…

The overt reference therefore is to Pyk or Pyg as the 'fustian king', but Joan would have recognized the handwriting as her husband's, and an element of self-mockery may have been intended. See *Henslowe's Diary*, 282.

11. Anonymous funeral elegy for Richard Burbage, 1619; cited in Andrew Gurr, *Playgoing in Shakespeare's London* (Cambridge, 1987), 233.

12. Joseph Hall, referring to 'the Turkish *Tamberlaine*', in *Virgidemiarum* (1597), Book I, Satire 3, cited in Gurr, *Playgoing*, 211; E.S., *The Discoverie of the Knights of the Poste* (1597), C2ᵛ, cited by Alexander Leggatt in *The Revels History of English Drama*, iii (London, 1975), 115. For illustrations of the impact of 'mighty' Tamburlaine on early readers and viewers, see Richard Levin, 'The Contemporary Perception of Marlowe's Tamburlaine', *Medieval and Renaissance Drama in England*, I (1982), 58–70.

13. *Henslowe's Diary*, 33.

14. *Dido Queen of Carthage*, thought to be Marlowe's earliest play, was probably written for boy actors to play; it was published, as by Marlowe and Thomas Nashe, in 1594. In Act II, Scene i, as edited by Roma Gill, *The Plays of Christopher Marlowe* (Oxford, 1971), Aeneas has a series of narrative speeches describing the fall of Troy.

15. Ulysses may also be Shakespeare's spokesman in his criticism of a 'strutting player whose conceit | Lies in his hamstring' (*Troilus and Cressida*, I. iii. 153), in a play written soon after *Hamlet*.

16. William Armstrong, 'Shakespeare and the Acting of Edward Alleyn', *Shakespeare Survey*, 7 (1954), 82–92; Andrew Gurr, 'Who Strutted and Bellowed?', *Shakespeare Survey*, 16 (1963), 95–102.

17. Gurr, 'Who Strutted and Bellowed?', 101.

18. The exact date is not known, but may coincide with his interest in buying the manor of Dulwich, negotiations for which began in 1605. See Chambers, *The Elizabethan Stage*, ii. 297–8.

19. Thomas Nashe, *Piers Penilesse* (1592), cited in Gurr, *Playgoing*, 209.

20. See Scott McMillin, '*The Book of Sir Thomas More*: Dates and Acting Companies', in *Shakespeare and Sir Thomas More: Essays on the Play and its Shakespearian Interest* (Cambridge, 1989), 57–76, esp. 62–4.

21. See Gurr, *Shakespearean Stage*, esp. 36–42.

22. See Hattaway, *Elizabethan Popular Theatre*, 196–7 for further commentary on the relation of Aaron to Tamburlaine here. James Shapiro, in *Rival Playwrights: Marlowe, Jonson, Shakespeare* (New York, 1991), 90, offers the most recent consideration of Marlowe's influence, but I believe he is mistaken to claim that Shakespeare

'generally avoids recalling Marlowe's style' during the early 1590s (p. 81); he sees the influence of *Tamburlaine* especially in *Henry V* (pp. 100–2).

23. See Douglas Bruster, *Drama and the Market in the Age of Shakespeare* (Cambridge, 1992); his first two chapters, pp. 1–28, detail the 'commercial basis' of the Elizabethan theatre.

24. Roslyn Lander Knutson, *The Repertory of Shakespeare's Company 1594–1613* (Fayetteville, Ark., 1991), 5.

25. See ibid. esp. 48–78.

26. Joseph Hall, *Virgidemiarum* (1597), II. i, Satire 3, cited in Gurr, *Playgoing*, 211.

27. John Marston, *Jack Drum's Entertainment* (1600), a private theatre play, Act v; cited in Gurr, *Playgoing*, 215.

28. Marston, *Sophonisba* (1606), in *Plays*, ed. H. Harvey Wood, 3 vols. (Edinburgh, 1934–9), ii. 44.

29. Gurr, *Shakespearean Stage*, 220.

30. An order for suppressing jigs at the end of plays; Middlesex general sessions of the peace, Oct. 1612, cited in Gurr, *Playgoing*, 225–6. The Fortune was not alone in staging jigs at this time, and they continued to be popular until much later, though the company at the Globe possibly ceased to offer them after 1600; see Gurr, *Playgoing*, 152, 236.

31. The term is used by Thomas Middleton in *A Mad World my Masters* (1608, as acted by the Children of Paul's), III. iii. 141, 'the hair about the hat is as good as a flag upo'th'pole at a common playhouse, to waft company'.

32. Thomas Middleton, *Father Hubburd's Tale* (1604), in *Works*, ed. Bullen, viii. 64; cited in Gurr, *Playgoing*, 218.

33. Sir John Davies, *Epigrammes* 17, 'In Cosmum' (?1593), cited in Gurr, *Playgoing*, 209.

34. The term is from Marston's *What You Will* (?1601), III. ii, in *Works*, ed. Harvey Wood, iii. 266; cited in Gurr, *Playgoing*, 216.

35. Thomas Dekker, *Satiromastix* (1601), in *Works*, i. 234.

36. *Amends for Ladies* (?1611), in *The Plays of Nathan Field*, ed. William Peery (Austin, Tex., 1950), 181, 'Faith, I have a great mind to see long-megg and the ship at the Fortune'; p. 234: 'she sweares all the Gentlewomen went to see a Play at the Fortune, and are not come in yet, and she believes they sup with the Players.

   Teare. Dam-me, we must kill all those rogues, we shall never keepe a whore honest for them.'

37. C1ʳ; cited in Gurr, *Playgoing*, 229.

38. 'I will confound her with complements drawne from the Plaies I see at the Fortune, and Red Bull, where I learne all the words I speake and understand not', says Trincalo in II. i, sig. C4ᵛ–D1ʳ. The play was staged at Trinity College, Cambridge, in 1614.

39. Alexander Gill, verses against Ben Jonson's *Magnetic Lady*; cited in Gurr, *Playgoing*, 239.

40. Shackerley Marmion, Prologue to *Holland's Leaguer* (1631), played at Salisbury Court; cited in Gurr, *Playgoing*, 239.

41. Hall, *Virgidemiarum* II, Book 1, Satire 3; cited in Gurr, *Playgoing*, 211.

42. Estimates vary; see Bruster, *Drama and the Market*, 19–22; Roger Finlay, *Population and Metropolis: The Demography of London 1580–1650* (Cambridge, 1981), 51; and E. A. Wrigley and R. S. Schofield, *The Population History of England 1541–1871: A Reconstruction* (Cambridge, 1989).

43. See Gurr, *Playgoing*, 57–8: 'women from every section of society went to plays'; also Richard Levin, 'Women in the Renaissance Theatre Audience', *Shakespeare Quarterly*, 40 (1989), 165–74.

44. The 'liberties' of London are described by Steven Mullaney in *The Place of the Stage: License, Play, and Power in Renaissance England* (Chicago, 1988), 21–5.

45. *Henslowe's Diary*, 308.

46. Gurr, *Shakespearean Stage*, 153.

47. *Henslowe's Diary*, 7.

48. Cited in Chambers, *Elizabethan Stage*, ii. 546. Glynne Wickham speculated about the purpose of the canopy at the Swan, and concluded that it could 'only serve one possible purpose—to protect something of value set below it on the rear half of the stage', and perhaps, in addition, to provide for a 'heavens'; see *Early English Stages*, ii. 304–5.

49. *Playgoing*, 36.

50. See III. iv. 122 ff.; 'Tucca... you, player, rogue, stalker, come back here: no respect to men of worship, you slave? What, you are proud, you rascall... you grow rich, doe you? and purchase, you two-penny teare-mouth? you have *fortune*, and the good yeere on your side, you stinkard?' Later in the same exchange, III. iv. 197 ff., Tucca says 'I hear, you'll bring me o'the stage... and you stage me... your mansions shall sweat for't, your tabernacles... your *Globes*, and your *Triumphs*.' The other reference is to IV. iv. This play was performed by a children's company, the Children of the Queen's Revels.

51. See Knutson, *Repertory*, esp. 36–7, 80–1.

52. John Orrell and Andrew Gurr, 'What the Rose Can Tell Us', *Antiquity*, 63 (1989), 428.

53. See R. A. Foakes, 'The Discovery of the Rose Theatre: Some Implications', *Shakespeare Survey*, 43 (1991), 147.

54. The phrase is from Thomas Middleton's *The Black Book* (1604), in *Works*, ed. Bullen, viii. 13; he refers to *Doctor Faustus*, so that the 'old theatre' points presumably to a time before 1593.

2. The King's Men and After

I am grateful to John Jowett and M. J. Kidnie for the help and information they have given in the writing of this chapter.

1. E. K. Chambers, 'Royal Patents for Players', *Malone Society Collections*, 1 (Oxford, 1907–11), 264.

2. Peter Thomson, *Shakespeare's Professional Career* (Cambridge, 1992), 162.

3. Chambers, 'Royal Patents for Players', 264.

4. The Shakespeare plays, as recorded in the Revels Account, were *The Moor of Venice* (1 Nov. 1604), *The Merry Wives of Windsor* (4 Nov.), *Measure for Measure* (26 Dec.), *The Play of Errors* (28 Dec.), and *Henry the Fifth* (7 Jan. 1605). Presumably they were all part of the 1604 Globe season.

5. E. K. Chambers, *William Shakespeare: A Study of Facts and Problems* (Oxford, 1930), ii. 332.

6. Philip Stubbes, *The Anatomie of Abuses* (London, 1583), sig. L8ʳ.

7. Virginia Mason Vaughan, 'Politics and Plagiarism: Othello in the Restoration', *Theatre History Studies*, 9 (1989), 7.

8. *1 Honest Whore*, IV. iii. 24, in *The Dramatic Works of Thomas Dekker*, ed. Fredson Bowers (Cambridge, 1953–61), ii. 80.

9. John Milton, *Complete Prose Works* (New Haven, Conn., 1953–82), i. 887.

10. William Shakespeare, *The Complete Works*, ed. Stanley Wells, Gary Taylor, John Jowett, and William Montgomery (Oxford, 1986), p. xlvi.

11. The play is quoted from Fredson Bowers's edition in *The Dramatic Works in the Beaumont and Fletcher Canon*, iv (Cambridge, 1979).

12. Baldwin Maxwell, *Studies in Beaumont, Fletcher, and Massinger* (Chapel Hill, NC, 1939), 44.

13. Samuel Rowlands, *A Whole Crew of Kind Gossips, All Met to be Merry* (London, 1609), sig. E1ʳ.

14. Chambers, *William Shakespeare*, ii. 337–41. Three of the plays he saw were by Shakespeare; the fourth was a *Richard II* which may have supplanted Shakespeare's in the repertory.

15. Geoffrey Tillotson, 'Othello and The Alchemist at Oxford in 1610', *Times Literary Supplement*, 20 July 1933, p. 494. Translation by Susan Brock.

16. John Webster, *The Works*, ed. F. L. Lucas (London, 1927), iv. 43.

17. *A Horrible Creuel and Bloudy Murther* (London, 1614), sigs. B2ᵛ–B3ʳ.

18. *Ben Jonson*, ed. C. H. Herford, Percy and Evelyn Simpson, 11 vols (Oxford, 1925–52), vi. 492.

19. Thomas Heywood, *Pleasant Dialogves and Dramma's* (London, 1637), sig. R4ʳ⁻ᵛ.

20. Maija Jansson Cole, 'A New Account of the Burning of the Globe', *Shakespeare Quarterly*, 32 (1981), 352.

21. Chambers, *The Elizabethan Stage*, ii. 420.

22. Ibid. 422, 423.

23. Ibid. 420.

24. Shakespeare treats the name as having three syllables, whereas Fletcher consistently gives it four.

25. C. C. Stopes, *Burbage and Shakespeare's Stage* (London, 1913), 117.

26. Gerald Eades Bentley, *The Jacobean and Caroline Stage* (Oxford, 1941–68), ii. 396–7.

27. Chambers, *The Elizabethan Stage*, ii. 309.

28. William Heminges, *The Fatal Contract* (London, 1653), sig. D4ʳ.

29. Namely *The Taming of the Shrew* (c.1631, 1633); *Richard III* (1633); *Love's Labours Lost* (c.1631); *A Midsummer Night's Dream* (1630); *Richard II* (1631); *1 Henry IV* (1625, ?1631, ?1638–9); *2 Henry IV* (c.1619–20); *The Merry Wives of Windsor* (?1635, 1638–9); *Julius Caesar* (1637, 1638–9); *Hamlet* (c.1619–20, 1637); *Twelfth Night* (1618, 1623); *The Moor of Venice* (1629, 1635, 1636); *Pericles* (1619, 1631); *The Winter's Tale* (1618, c.1619–20, 1624, 1634); *Cymbeline* (1634); *King Henry VIII* (1628); *The Two Noble Kinsmen* (c.1619–20, c.1625–6).

30. *Commons Journal*, ii. 747; *Lords Journal*, v. 335.

31. Vernon F. Snow and Anne Steele Young, *The Private Journals of the Long Parliament: 2 June to 17 September 1642* (New Haven, Conn., 1992), 330.

32. *A Deep Sigh Breath'd through the Lodgings at White-Hall, Deploring the Absence of the Court* (London, 1642), sig. A3ᵛ.

33. Alexander Brome (comp.), *Rump; or, An Exact Collection of the Choycest Poems and Songs Relating to the Late Times* (London, 1662), 33.

34. Chambers, *William Shakespeare*, ii. 348.

35. Stopes, *Burbage and Shakespeare's Stage*, 117.

36. Chambers, *William Shakespeare*, ii. 352.

37. Leslie Hotson, *The Commonwealth and Restoration Stage* (Cambridge, Mass., 1928), 19.

38. *Lords Journal*, v. 335.

39. Ibid. x. 41.

40. Bentley, *The Jacobean and Caroline Stage*, ii. 695.

41. *The Lord Henry Cromvvel's Speech in the Hovse* (London, 1659), 5.

42. Hotson, *The Commonwealth and Restoration Stage*, 400.

3. Improving on the Original: Actresses and Adaptations

1. BL Add. MS 19256, fo. 47; reproduced in David Thomas (ed.), *Theatre in Europe: A Documentary History: Restoration and Georgian England, 1660–1788* (Cambridge, 1989), 11–12.

2. All quotations from Pepys are from *The Diary of Samuel Pepys*, ed. Robert Latham and William Matthews (11 vols.; Berkeley, 1970–83).

3. Thomas Jordan, 'A Prologue to Introduce the First Woman that Came to Act on the Stage in the Tragedy, called the Moor of Venice', in *A Royal Arbor of Loyal Poesie* (London, 1664), 21.

4. Killigrew's original patent is in the possession of the Theatre Museum, Covent Garden. Reproduced in Thomas, *Theatre in Europe*, 16–18.

5. John Dryden, *Troilus and Cressida; or, Truth Found Too Late* (London, 1679), 'Preface'; Margaret Cavendish, *CCXI Sociable Letters, Written by the Thrice Noble, Illustrious, and Excellent Princess, the Lady Marchioness of Newcastle* (London, 1664), 244; John Dryden, *Of Dramatic Poesie: An Essay* (London, 1668), 48.

6. *The Tragedy of Hamlet, Prince of Denmark: As it is now Acted at his Highness the Duke of York's Theatre: By William Shakespeare* (London, 1676).

7. Sir William Davenant, John Dryden (and Thomas Shadwell, who provided the further operatic embellishments added to the original 1667 text in 1674), *The Tempest; or, The Enchanted Island* (London, 1674), 1, 5.

8. John Downes, *Roscius Anglicanus; or, An Historical Review of the Stage* (1708), ed. Judith Milhous and Robert Hume (London, 1987), 71–2.

9. [Sir William Davenant], *Macbeth, a Tragedy: With All the Alterations, Amendments, Additions, and New Songs* (London, 1674), 35–6.

10. Anthony Aston, *A Brief Supplement to Colley Cibber Esq. his Lives of the Famous Actors and Actresses* (1747); repr. in Colley Cibber, *An Apology for the Life of Mr Colley Cibber, Written by Himself* (1740), ed. R. W. Lowe, 2 vols. (London, 1889), ii. 299–300; Charles Gildon, *The Life of Mr. Thomas Betterton, the Late Eminent Tragedian* (London, 1710), 32, 102; Cibber, *Apology*, i. 109.

11. Cibber, *Apology*, i. 161–2.

12. These two Shakespearian sketches of the 1650s, along with a third (*Bottom the Weaver*) and a much larger number of such drolls abbreviated from the plays of Beaumont and Fletcher, were published in Francis Kirkman (ed.), *The Wits; or, Sport upon Sport* (2 pts., London, 1672–3).

13. Nahum Tate, *The History of King Lear* (London, 1681), 67.

14. Cibber, *Apology*, i. 103–4.

15. This famous piece of business remained mandatory until the late 18th cent. On Betterton's *Hamlet*, see esp. ibid. 100–2. 'When I acted the Ghost with Betterton,' remembered Barton Booth, 'instead of my awing him, he terrified me. But divinity hung round that man!'

16. See ibid. ii. 81–7.

17. *The Critical Works of John Dennis*, ed. Edward Niles Hooker, 2 vols. (Baltimore, 1939), i. 289–94.

18. Thomas Davies, *Dramatic Miscellanies*, 3 vols. (London, 1784), ii. 133. See also his *Memoirs of the Life of David*

Garrick Esq. (1780), ed. Stephen Jones, 2 vols. (London, 1808), i. 28.

19. Aphra Behn, 'Preface to *The Dutch Lover*', in *Works*, ed. Montague Summers [1915], 6 vols. (repr. New York, 1967), i. 224.

20. George Lillo, *Marina*, 'Epilogue', in *The Works of George Lillo; With some Account of his Life*, 2 vols. (London, 1775), ii. 127.

21. William Guthrie, *An Essay upon English Tragedy: With Remarks upon the Abbé de Blanc's Observations on the English Stage* (London, 1747), 10.

22. *The Works of Francis Beaumont and John Fletcher*, ed. Thomas Seward, 10 vols. (London, 1750), vol. i, 'Preface', pp. xv–xvi.

23. On the coexistence on this playbill of *As You Like It* and other attractions, see the letter on the subject published in the *Gentleman's Magazine*, Jan. 1741: 'I was surprised on my entering into the Pit to find it almost full, but was informed by my Friend, the House had been crowded ever since *Shakespeare's* play of *As you like it* had been acted and these Dancers had performed. I could not but reflect on the just Taste of the Public, which had received so fine a Piece with such universal Approbation. But then I knew not how to reconcile, that those polite Audiences, who gave judicious Applause to every beautiful Sentiment of *Shakespeare*, should at the same time be delighted with the Gesticulations and Capers of a Foreign Mimic.'

24. James T. Kirkman, *Memoirs of the Life of Charles Macklin, Esq.*, 2 vols. (London, 1799), i. 293–4; see also John Hill, *The Actor: A Treatise on the Art of Playing* (London, 1750), 250.

25. Charles Johnson, *Love in a Forest* (London, 1723), 'Prologue'.

26. Benjamin Victor, *The History of the Theatres of London and Dublin, from the Year 1760 to the Present Time* (London, 1771), 124–5.

27. Davies, *Memoirs of the Life of David Garrick Esq.*, ii. 186.

28. Hill, *The Actor*, 113–14.

4. The Age of Garrick

1. *The Letters of David Garrick*, ed. David M. Little and George M. Kahrl, 3 vols. (London, 1963), Letter 362 (ii. 463).

2. Ibid., Letter 69 (i. 119).

3. Quoted by George Winchester Stone, Jr., 'David Garrick's Significance in the History of Shakespeare Criticism', *Publications of the Modern Language Association of America*, 65 (1950), 187.

4. Ibid. 187–8.

5. *Westminster Magazine*, quoted Brian Vickers (ed.), *Shakespeare: The Critical Heritage*, 6 vols.; v: *1765–1774* (London, 1979), 483.

6. Quoted by Johanne M. Stochholm, *Garrick's Folly* (London, 1964), 9.

7. Quoted ibid. 11.

8. Quoted ibid. 79.

9. *Letters*, Letter 567 (ii. 675).

10. Ibid., Letter 28 (i. 43).

11. Ibid., Letter 93 (i. 152).

12. Ibid., iii. 1344.

13. Quoted Kalman A. Burnim, *David Garrick Director* (Pittsburgh, 1961), 136.

14. Quoted ibid. 131–2.

15. *The Dramatic Censor* (1770), i. 188.

16. *Letters*, Letter 178 (i. 256).

17. Quoted David Garrick, *The Plays*, ed. H. W. Pedicord and F. L. Bergmann, 7 vols. (Carbondale, Ill., 1980–2), iii. 422.

18. Quoted ibid. 428.

19. On this adaptation and Garrick's other work, see also Jean Marsden, *The Re-imagined Text: Shakespeare, Adaptation and Eighteenth-Century Literary Theory* (Lexington, Ky., 1995), ch. 3.

20. *Letters*, Letter 317 (i. 387).

21. Quoted George Winchester Stone, Jr., '*A Midsummer Night's Dream* in the Hands of Garrick and Colman', *Publications of the Modern Language Association of America*, 54 (1939), 474.

22. Quoted ibid. 479.

23. *Letters*, Letter 33 (i. 53).

24. *An Examen of the New Comedy Called 'The Suspicious Husband'* (London, 1747), 22.

25. Thomas Davies, *Dramatic Miscellanies*, 2 vols. (London, 1784), ii. 172.

26. Quoted by George Winchester Stone, Jr., 'Garrick's Production of *King Lear*: A Study in the Temper of the Eighteenth-Century Mind', *Studies in Philology*, 45 (1948), 93–4.

27. Quoted ibid. 95.

28. See J. D. Hainsworth, '*King Lear* and John Brown's *Athelstan*', *Shakespeare Quarterly*, 26 (1975), 471–7.

29. Quoted by Arthur John Harris, 'Garrick, Colman and *King Lear*: A reconsideration', *Shakespeare Quarterly*, 22 (1971), 61.

30. *Letters*, Letter 574 (ii. 682–3).

31. *An Examen*, 24.

32. Ibid. 22.

33. Ibid. 20.

34. Quoted by George Winchester Stone, Jr., and George M. Kahrl, *David Garrick: A Critical Biography* (Carbondale, Ill., 1979), 540.

35. *An Examen*, 18.

36. Davies, *Dramatic Miscellanies*, ii. 208.

37. Quoted Burnim, *David Garrick Director*, 145.

38. Davies, *Dramatic Miscellanies*, ii. 166.

39. Quoted by Arthur Murphy, *The Life of David Garrick* (London, 1801), i. 71.

40. Stephen Orgel, 'The Authentic Shakespeare', *Representations*, 21 (1988), 15.

41. Davies, *Dramatic Miscellanies*, ii. 73.

42. Quoted by George Winchester Stone, Jr., 'Garrick's Handling of *Macbeth*', *Studies in Philology* 38 (1941), 616.

43. Davies, *Dramatic Miscellanies*, ii. 73.

44. Jean Georges Noverre, *Letters on Dancing and Ballets*, trans. Cyril W. Beaumont (London, 1930), 84–5.

45. *Letters*, Letter 281 (i. 350).

46. Quoted Burnim, *David Garrick Director*, 107.

47. *Morning Chronicle*, 25 Oct. 1773.

48. William Cooke, *Memoirs of Charles Macklin, Comedian* (London, 1804), p. xxx.

49. Quoted Burnim, *David Garrick Director*, 121–2.

50. *Letters*, Letter 733 (ii. 846).

51. Ibid., Letter 93 (i. 152).

52. Cooke, *Memoirs of Macklin*, p. xxx.

53. Quoted by Denis Donoghue, 'Macklin's Shylock and Macbeth', *Studies: An Irish Quarterly Review*, 43 (1954), 428.

54. Ibid.

5. The Romantic Stage

1. *The Romantics on Shakespeare*, ed. Jonathan Bate (London, 1992), 123.

2. *Table Talk*, in *Romantics on Shakespeare*, 160.

3. Essay on the drama in the *London Magazine* (Jan. 1820), repr. in *The Complete Works of William Hazlitt*, ed. P. P. Howe, 21 vols. (London, 1930–4), xviii. 272.

4. Had Hazlitt begun reviewing a decade earlier, he would probably have named a fourth, G. F. Cooke, who, in his Richard III in particular, pioneered an energetically 'Romantic' acting style that was prototypical of Kean's.

5. William Robson, *The Old Playgoer* (1846), quoted in Dennis Bartholomeusz, *Macbeth and the Players* (Cambridge, 1969), 98.

6. Siddons, 'Remarks on the Character of Lady Macbeth', in *Romantics on Shakespeare*, 437.

7. G. J. Bell noted of her performance of the lines in III. ii, 'Things without all remedy | Should be without regard: what's done is done': 'Still her accents very plaintive. This is one of the passages in which her intense love of her husband animate[s] every word.... not contemptuous reproach, but deep sorrow and sympathy with his melancholy'—'Mrs Siddons as Lady Macbeth', in *The Nineteenth Century* (1878), repr. in *Papers Literary, Scientific, &c.* by Fleeming Jenkin, 2 vols. (London, 1887), i. 61–2.

8. Hazlitt, *Characters of Shakespear's Plays*, repr. in *Romantics on Shakespeare*, 426–7.

9. *A View of the English Stage*, repr. in Hazlitt's *Works*, v. 199.

10. Essay on O'Neill's premature retirement: *London Magazine* (Feb. 1820), repr. in Hazlitt's *Works*, xviii. 282–4.

11. On this distinction, see J. W. Donohue's excellent book, *Dramatic Character in the English Romantic Age* (Princeton, 1970).

12. Donohue's point: ibid. 222.

13. Details from the calendar of performances in John Genest, *Some Account of the English Stage, from the Restoration in 1660 to 1832*, 10 vols. (Bath, 1832).

14. Her introduction to the text of the play in vol. v of her *British Theatre* (London, 1808).

15. *Romantics on Shakespeare*, 282.

16. *Shakspeare's Coriolanus; or, The Roman Matron, A Historical Play, adapted to the stage, with additions from Thomson, by J. P. Kemble; and now first published as it is acted at The Theatre Royal in Covent Garden* (London, 1806), 59. The Kemble prompt-books have been reprinted in facsimile, edited by Charles H. Shattuck, 10 vols. (Charlottesville, Va., 1974).

17. *Shakspeare's Macbeth, A Tragedy, revised by J. P. Kemble; and now first published as it is acted at The Theatre Royal in Covent Garden* (London, 1803), 63–4.

18. Kemble, *Macbeth and King Richard the Third: An Essay, in Answer to Remarks on some of the Characters of Shakspeare* (London, 1817), 170–1.

19. *Times* review of première of Kean's *Macbeth*, 7 Nov. 1814.

20. *View of the English Stage*, *Works*, v. 207.

21. My account of the riots is heavily indebted to Marc Baer's definitive study, *Theatre and Disorder in Late Georgian London* (Oxford, 1992); see also Gillian Russell, 'Playing at Revolution: The Politics of the O.P. Riots of 1809', *Theatre Notebook*, 44 (1990), 16–26.

22. *Covent Garden Journal*, ed. J. J. Stockdale (London, 1810), 22, quoted, Baer, *Theatre and Disorder*, 27.

23. *Broad Hints at Retirement* (1809), quoted, Baer, *Theatre and Disorder*, 56.

24. Quoted from text in A. C. Sprague, 'A *Macbeth* of Few Words', in *Essays in Honor of C. A. Robertson:... All These To Teach*, ed. Robert A. Bryan *et al.* (Gainesville, Fla., 1965), 80–101.

25. All quotations from text in *Nineteenth-Century Shakespeare Burlesques*, ed. Stanley Wells, vol. i (London, 1977).

26. On this, see Joseph Donohue, *Theatre in the Age of Kean* (Oxford, 1975), 119–20. In the light of the patents' removal of *Lear* from the repertory during the years of the king's insanity, it is noteworthy that a burletta of *King Lear and his Three Daughters* played at the (ironically named) Royalty Theatre in 1812.

27. On this, see Richard Lansdown, *Byron's Historical Dramas* (Oxford, 1992), 20.

28. Quotations from *Morning Chronicle*, 27 Aug. and 14 Sept. 1814.

29. *Drury Lane Journal*, ed. Alfred L. Nelson and Gilbert B. Cross (London, 1974), 4.

30. *London Magazine* (Feb. 1820), in Hazlitt's *Works*, xviii. 283.

31. On this, see Jane Moody's groundbreaking thesis, 'Aspects of Cultural Politics in the Minor Theatres of Early Nineteenth-Century London' (Oxford D.Phil., 1993, revised version forthcoming from Cambridge University Press). I am grateful to Dr Moody for sharing her work with me and for comments on a draft of this chapter.

32. See Clive Barker, 'The Chartists, Theatre, Reform and Research', *Theatre Quarterly*, 1 (1971), 3–10.

33. *Wise Children* (London, 1991), 11.

6. Actor-Managers and the Spectacular

1. Thomas Carlyle, *Selected Writings*, ed. Alan Shelston (Harmondsworth, 1971), 84.

2. John Ruskin, *The Seven Lamps of Architecture* (Popular Edition, London, 1880; impression of 1906), 359.

3. William Morris, 'Gothic Architecture' (lecture of 1889; 1st pub. 1893), in Nonesuch Press edn., *William Morris: Stories in Prose, Stories in Verse, Shorter Poems, Lectures and Essays*, ed. G. D. H. Cole (London, 1934), 492.

4. Martin Meisel, *Realizations: Narrative, Pictorial and Theatrical Arts in Nineteenth-Century England* (Princeton, 1983), 4, 36.

5. On the theory and reception of history paintings, see Roy Strong, *And When Did You Last See Your Father? The Victorian Painter and British History* (London, 1978). The public life of one painting is examined by Jeremy Maas, *Holman Hunt and the Light of the World* (London, 1984).

6. J. W. Cole, *The Life and Theatrical Times of Charles Kean, F.S.A.*, 2 vols. (London, 1859), ii. 143. The general principles and practice of such productions are discussed by Michael R. Booth in ch. 2 of his *Victorian Spectacular Theatre: 1850–1910* (London, 1981).

7. *Illustrated London News*, quoted in G. C. D. Odell, *Shakespeare from Betterton to Irving*, 2 vols. (New York, 1920), ii. 347.

8. In Kean's production the Chorus appeared in muse-like garb, standing in a small temple. The effect was copied in an influential and popular production by Charles Calvert, the Manchester actor-manager. See Richard Foulkes, *The Calverts: Actors of Some Importance* (London, 1992), 55–75.

9. Prompt-book, Folger Shakespeare Library *RII*, 2 (Charles H. Shattuck, *The Shakespeare Promptbooks: A Descriptive Catalogue* (Urbana, Ill., 1965), 7).

10. Prompt-books of *Julius Caesar*, Folger Shakespeare Library *Jul. Caes.* 16 (Shattuck, *Promptbooks*, 13: Macready); *Jul. Caes.* 21 (Shattuck, *Promptbooks*, 16: Phelps).

11. The Meiningen Court Theatre Company's work is described by Simon Williams, *Shakespeare on the German Stage*, i: *1586–1914* (Cambridge, 1990), 161–71.

12. Phelps's production of *Timon* is described in Shirley S. Allen, *Samuel Phelps and Sadler's Wells Theatre* (Middletown, Conn., 1971), 243–4.

13. On dioramas see Meisel, *Realizations*, and Helmut and Alison Gernsheim, *L. J. M. Daguerre: The History of the Diorama and the Daguerrotype* (2nd edn., New York, 1968).

14. Henry Morley, *The Journal of a London Playgoer*, ed. Michael R. Booth (Leicester, 1974), 217.

15. Odell, *Shakespeare from Betterton to Irving*, ii. 214, quoting *John Bull*, 19 Mar. 1838.

16. In A. C. Sprague, *Shakespeare and the Actors: The Stage Business in his Plays, 1660–1905* (Cambridge, Mass., 1944), see 177 (Hamlet and the skull); 175–6 (the Grave-digger's waistcoats); 197–200 (Othello 'collaring' Iago); and 5–6 (the 'kitchen scene' in *Twelfth Night*).

17. John McGrath, *A Good Night Out: Popular Theatre: Audience, Class and Form* (London, 1981). On Shakespeare burlesques and travesties, see Stanley Wells (ed.), *Shakespeare Burlesques*, 5 vols. (London, 1978).

18. Alan Hughes, *Henry Irving, Shakespearean* (Cambridge, 1981), 232.

19. Arthur Symons, *Plays, Acting and Music: A Book of Theory* (London, 1909), 49, 50.

20. Hughes, *Henry Irving*, 101.

21. The dress (now in the Ellen Terry Memorial Museum at Smallhythe, Kent) is described by Alice Comyns Carr, *Reminiscences* (London, 1925), 111–12. Wilde's remark is quoted by W. Graham Robertson, *Time Was* (London, 1931), 151.

22. Hughes, *Henry Irving*, 109; reviews in the *Stage*, 4 Jan. 1889, and the *Era*, 5 Jan. 1889. On the conclusion of the banquet scene in Victorian performances, see Sprague, *Shakespeare and the Actors*, 264–5.

23. On William Poel, see Cary Mazer, *Shakespeare Refashioned: Elizabethan Plays on Edwardian Stages* (Ann Arbor, 1981) and Robert Speaight, *William Poel and the Elizabethan Revival* (London, 1954).

24. On Granville-Barker's Shakespeare productions, see Dennis Kennedy, *Granville Barker and the Dream of Theatre* (Cambridge, 1985) and Christine Dymkovski, *Harley Granville Barker: A Preface to Modern Theatre* (Washington, 1986).

25. Folger Shakespeare Library, *Temp*, 15 (Shattuck, *Promptbooks*, 39).

7. European Cross-Currents: Ibsen and Brecht

1. See Peter Hall's Introduction to John Barton and Peter Hall, *The Wars of the Roses* (London, 1970). The production actually opened in 1963 but found its

definitive form in the 1964 season. See also Michael Billington, *Peggy Ashcroft* (London, 1988), 201.

2. Ronald Hayman, *British Theatre since 1955: A Reassessment* (Oxford, 1979), 7.

3. See the excellent bibliographies appended to each chapter in Dirk Delabastita and Lieven D'Hulst (eds.), *European Shakespeares: Translating Shakespeare in the Romantic Age* (Amsterdam, 1993).

4. Georg Brandes, *William Shakespeare*, 3 vols. (Copenhagen, 1895–6), quoted from Eng. trans. by William Archer *et al.* (London, 1899), 689.

5. Oswald LeWinter (ed.), *Shakespeare in Europe* (Harmondsworth, 1963), 17.

6. *Henrik Ibsens Samlede Verker*, ed. Francis Bull, Halvdan Koht, and Didrik Arup Seip, 21 vols. (Oslo, 1928–57), i. 120. Throughout this chapter, translations from non-English texts are my own, unless otherwise indicated.

7. Cited from P. M. Mitchell, *A History of Danish Literature* (Copenhagen, 1957), 112.

8. Paul Botten Hansen, in *Samfundsbladet*, 13 Apr. 1850. Quoted from Karl Haugholt, 'Samtidens kritikk av Ibsens *Catilina*', *Edda*, 52 (1952), 77.

9. Henrik Ibsen, letter written from Dresden, 24 June 1852. Translation by James McFarlane, *The Oxford Ibsen*, 8 vols. (London, 1960–77), i. 638.

10. See Robert Prölss, 'Shakespeare-Aufführungen in Dresden vom 20. Oct. 1816 bis Ende 1860', *Jahrbuch der deutschen Shakespeare-Gesellschaft*, 15 (1880), 173–210.

11. See Robert Prölss, *Geschichte des Hoftheaters zu Dresden: von seinen Anfangen bis zum Jahre 1862* (Dresden, 1878), and Egon Frohberg, *Die Entwicklung des Schauspiels am Dresdner Hoftheater zur Zeit Eduard Devrients* (Munich, 1926).

12. Cited from Simon Williams, *Shakespeare on the German Stage: 1586–1914* (Cambridge, 1990), 183.

13. Julius Bab, *Die Devrients: Geschichte einer deutschen Theaterfamilie* (Berlin, 1932), 211. On the Devrients, see also Heinrich Hubert Houben, *Emil Devrient: sein Leben, sein Wirken, sein Nachlass* (Frankfurt, 1903); Friedrich Kummer, *Dresden und seine Theaterwelt* (Dresden, 1938); and Herbert Füldner, 'Eduard Devrient und das Dresdner Hoftheater' (1921; unpublished dissertation in Leipzig University Library).

14. Bab, *Die Devrients*, 142.

15. Kummer, *Dresden und seine Theaterwelt*, 141.

16. Henry Morley, *The Journal of a London Playgoer* (London, 1866), 40. See also Barry Duncan, *The St. James's Theatre* (London, 1964), 90.

17. Rolf Kabel (ed.), *Eduard Devrient, Aus seinen Tagebüchern: Berlin–Dresden 1836–1852* (Weimar, 1964), 598.

18. Clement Scott, *Some Notable Hamlets of the Present Time* (London, 1900), 43–4 and 51.

19. See Alfred v. Würzbach, *Bogumil Dawison* (*Zeitgenossen*, 1st ser., no. 11) (Vienna, 1871). Also Peter Kollek, *Bogumil Dawison* (*Die Schaubühne*, vol. 70) (Kastellaun, 1978); and Prölss, *Geschichte*, 570 ff.

20. Eduard Devrient, *Tagebücher*, 594–5.

21. Ludwig Speidel, *Schriften*, 4 vols. (Berlin, 1910–11), iv (*Schauspieler*), 2.

22. Sille Beyer, *Livet i Skoven* (Life in the Forest) (Copenhagen, 1850); George Sand, *Comme il vous plaira*, in *Œuvres complètes de George Sand: Théâtre*, iv (Paris, 1877), 111–209.

23. Cited from reviews of *Life in the Forest* in Birgitte Gad, *Sille Beyers bearbejdelse av William Shakespeares lystspil* (Copenhagen, 1974).

24. Charles Dickens, letter of 22 Apr. 1856, quoted in Edgar Johnson, *Charles Dickens: His Tragedy and Triumph*, 2 vols. (London, 1953), ii. 860.

25. See the helpful notes on the genesis, execution, and eventual abandonment of Brecht's *Coriolanus* project in *Bertolt Brecht, Stücke*, ed. Werner Hecht, Jan Knopf, Werner Mittenzwei, and Klaus-Detlef Müller, vol. ix (Frankfurt am Main, 1991).

26. *Theaterarbeit* (1952), cited from John Willett, *Brecht on Theatre* (London, 1964), 229.

27. 'Sollten wir nicht die Aesthetik liquidieren?' (1927), cited from Willett, *Brecht on Theatre*, 20.

28. From Brecht's comments on his 1924 production of Marlowe's *Edward II*, cited from John Rouse, *Brecht and the West German Theatre: The Practice and Politics of Interpretation* (Ann Arbor, 1989), 16.

29. See the useful bibliography in Darko Suvin, *To Brecht and Beyond* (Brighton, 1984), 204–7.

30. Rouse, *Brecht and the West German Theatre*, 99.

31. See *Stücke*, ix. 344.

32. R. W. Leonhardt, 'Können wir den Shakespeare ändern?', in *Die Zeit*, 2 Oct. 1964, cited from Rouse, *Brecht and the West German Theatre*, 100.

33. See Kristina Bedford, *'Coriolanus' at the National* (London, 1992).

8. From the Old Vic to Gielgud and Olivier

1. P. P. Howe, *The Repertory Theatre: A Record and a Criticism* (London, 1910), 25–6.

2. H. Granville-Barker in George Rowell and Anthony Jackson, *The Repertory Movement* (Cambridge, 1984), 23, 16.

3. Hugh Hunt, *The Abbey: Ireland's National Theatre 1904–79* (London, 1979), 19.

4. St John Ervine in Rex Pogson, *Miss Horniman and the Gaiety Theatre, Manchester* (London, 1952), p. vi.

5. George Rowell, *The Old Vic Theatre: A History* (Cambridge, 1993), 94.

6. Donald Spoto, *Laurence Olivier: A Life* (London, 1992), 50.

7. *The Times*, 24 Apr. 1923.

8. Claire Cochrane, *Shakespeare at the Birmingham Repertory Theatre 1913–1929* (London, 1993), 102.

9. Sally Beauman, *The Royal Shakespeare Company: A History of Ten Decades* (Oxford, 1982), 86.

10. Anthony Holden, *Olivier* (London, 1988), 54.

11. Norman Marshall, *The Producer and the Play* (London, 1957), 175.

12. *New Statesman*, 11 Feb. 1928.

13. *Birmingham Daily Post*, 25 Feb. 1929.

14. Garry O'Connor, *Ralph Richardson: An Actor's Life* (London, 1982), 51–2.

15. Michael Billington, *Peggy Ashcroft 1907–1991* (London, 1991), 40.

16. James Agate, *Brief Chronicles* (London, 1943), 259.

17. James Agate, *More First Nights* (London, 1937), 82.

18. Trewin in Holden, *Olivier*, 103.

19. Olivier, ibid. 109.

20. Agate, *More First Nights*, 184.

21. St John Ervine in Spoto, *Laurence Olivier*, 118.

22. J. C. Trewin, Jessica Tandy, and W. A. Darlington in Holden, *Olivier*, 110.

23. Agate, *Brief Chronicles*, 214.

24. John Gielgud, *Memoirs*, quoted in Holden, *Olivier*, 115.

25. Olivier in Hal Burton, *Great Acting* (London, 1967), 17.

26. Jill L. Levenson, *Shakespeare in Performance: Romeo and Juliet* (Manchester, 1987), 51.

27. *New Statesman and Nation*, 1 Jan. 1938.

28. *Daily Telegraph*, 28 Dec. 1937.

29. Kenneth Tynan, *He that Plays the King* (London, 1950), 40.

30. Ronald Harwood, *Sir Donald Wolfit: His Life and Work in the Unfashionable Theatre* (London, 1971), 166, 153.

31. Susan Brock and Marian Pringle, *The Shakespeare Memorial Theatre: 1919–1945* (Cambridge, 1984), 12.

32. Beauman, *The Royal Shakespeare Company*, 120.

33. Anthony Quayle, *A Time to Speak* (London, 1990), 316.

34. Richard David, 'Drams of Eale', *Shakespeare Survey*, 10 (1957), 126.

35. Alan C. Dessen, *Titus Andronicus* (Manchester, 1989), 18.

36. J. C. Trewin, *Peter Brook: A Biography* (London, 1971), 84.

37. Robert Tanitch, *Olivier* (London, 1985), 70.

38. Alec Guinness, *Blessings in Disguise* (London, 1985), 71.

39. Billington, *Peggy Ashcroft*, 89.

9. Shakespeare and the Public Purse

1. Kenneth Tynan, *Observer*, 26 June 1960.

2. Charles Marowitz, *The Marowitz Shakespeare* (London, 1978), 24.

3. Ibid. 17.

4. John Elsom (ed.), *Is Shakespeare Still our Contemporary?* (London, 1989), 69.

5. *Mother Courage and her Children*, sc. iii, trans. Ralph Manheim, in Bertolt Brecht, *Collected Plays*, v (New York, 1972), 156.

6. Billington, *Guardian*, 6 May 1978.

7. Ibid. 14 Oct. 1982.

8. R. A. Foakes, *Hamlet versus Lear: Cultural Politics and Shakespeare's Art* (Cambridge, 1993), 6.

9. Ibid. 39.

10. Stanley Wells, *Royal Shakespeare. Four Major Productions at Stratford-upon-Avon* (Manchester, 1977), 34.

11. *Peter Hall's Diaries*, ed. John Goodwin (London, 1983), 158.

12. Peter Thomson, *Shakespeare Survey*, 24 (1971), 126.

13. Quoted by John Barber in *Daily Telegraph*, 14 Sept. 1970.

14. Peter Brook, *The Shifting Point* (London, 1988), 101.

15. See Roger Warren, *Staging Shakespeare's Late Plays* (Oxford, 1990), 28.

16. Ibid. 69.

10. Directors' Shakespeare

1. Stephen Orgel, in the most recent edition of *The Tempest* (Oxford, 1987), endorses Greg's statement that 'there can be no doubt that these directions are fundamentally the author's', though as printed in the Folio he believes they also record memories of the play in performance.

2. See Sally Beauman, *The Royal Shakespeare Company: A History of Ten Decades* (Oxford, 1982), 236–65.

3. Ralph Berry's interviews with several recently prominent Shakespeare directors (*On Directing Shakespeare: Interviews with Contemporary Directors* (2nd edn., London, 1989)) stress again and again the significance of choosing the play, and the appropriate moment at which to direct it. Several recent productions of *A Midsummer Night's Dream* have taken the matter of Quince's directorship rather further by implying that he has not only chosen, but also written, 'Pyramus and Thisbe'.

4. Stanley Wells, 'The Academic and the Theatre', in Joseph G. Price (ed.), *The Triple Bond: Plays, Mainly Shakespearian, in Performance* (University Park, Pa., 1975), 3–19; and 'Directors' Shakespeare', *Shakespeare Jahrbuch* (West), 113 (1976), 64–78.

5. Christopher J. McCullough, 'The Cambridge Connection: Towards a Materialist Theatre Practice', in Graham Holderness (ed.), *The Shakespeare Myth* (Manchester, 1988), 112–21.

6. John Russell Brown, *Free Shakespeare* (London, 1974), 83–90.

7. It may or may not be a coincidence that of the four directors only Derek Jacobi had been through a university English department—yet again the one at Cambridge.

8. Brian Cox, 'Titus Andronicus', in Russell Jackson and Robert Smallwood (eds.), *Players of Shakespeare, 3* (Cambridge, 1993), 177.

9. John Barton and Peter Hall, *The Wars of the Roses* (London, 1970), p. xxv.

10. Dennis Kennedy, *Looking at Shakespeare: A Visual History of Twentieth-Century Performance* (Cambridge, 1993), 241–2. For other accounts of John Barton's *Richard II* see James Stredder, 'John Barton's Production of *Richard II* at Stratford-upon-Avon', *Shakespeare Jahrbuch* (West), 113 (1976), 23–42; Stanley Wells, *Royal Shakespeare: Four Major Productions at Stratford-upon-Avon* (Manchester, 1977), 65–80; and Liisa Hakola, *In One Person Many People: The Image of the King in Three R.S.C. Productions of 'Richard II'* (Helsinki, 1988), 50–92.

11. 'Robert Lepage in Discussion with Richard Eyre, 19 November 1992', *Platform Papers*, 3, Royal National Theatre (London, 1992), 29.

12. The original plan for rewriting in *The Plantagenets* was much more radical. It is discussed by Ralph Fiennes in his essay on his performance of the role of Henry VI in Jackson and Smallwood, *Players of Shakespeare, 3*, 99–113.

13. The somewhat unanchored state of this soliloquy at the end of III. i is discussed by the Oxford editors, though with no suggestion, of course, that it might drift so far as to achieve the status of a prologue. (See Stanley Wells and Gary Taylor, *William Shakespeare: A Textual Companion* (Oxford, 1987), 468.)

14. I have discussed this topic at greater length in '"Beginners, Please"; or, First Start your Play', *Shakespeare Jahrbuch*, 130 (1993), 72–84.

12. Shakespeare in Opposition: From the 1950s to the 1990s

1. John Osborne, *Look Back in Anger* (London, 1957), 84–5.

2. Lindsay Anderson, 'Vital Theatre?' (*Encore*, Nov. 1957), in Charles Marowitz, Tom Milne, and Owen Hale (eds.), *The Encore Reader: A Chronicle of the New Drama* (London, 1965), 46–7.

3. On Byam Shaw's *Macbeth* see Michael Mullin (ed.), *'Macbeth' on the Stage: An Annotated Facsimile of Glen Byam Shaw's 1955 Promptbook* (Columbia, SC, 1976) and Dennis Bartholmeusz, *'Macbeth' and the Players* (Cambridge, 1969), ch. 12.

4. Ivor Brown, *Theatre, 1955–6* (London, 1956), 66–7.

5. On the Royal Court *Macbeth*: Philip Roberts, *The Royal Court Theatre, 1956–72* (London, 1986), 51–7; William Gaskill, *A Sense of Direction: Life at the Royal Court* (London, 1988) 76–81.

6. Gaskill, *A Sense of Direction*, 84.

7. *Plays and Players* (July 1973), 67.

8. Howard Goorney, *The Theatre Workshop Story* (London, 1981), 130; review, 'Scrambled Shakespeare', in *The Times*, 18 Aug. 1964.

9. Kenneth Tynan, *Curtains* (London, 1961), 88–9.

10. The principal source of information on the ESC is a book by its joint directors: Michael Bogdanov and Michael Pennington, *The English Shakespeare Company: The Story of 'The Wars of the Roses' 1986–1989* (London, 1990). (The *Richard II–Henry V* cycle was first seen in 1986). *The Plantagenets* was performed by the RSC in 1988–9. For a comparative review see Lois Potter, 'Recycling the Early Histories: "The Wars of the Roses" and "the Plantagenets"', *Shakespeare Survey*, 43 (1991), 171–81.

11. Bill Wallis, 'Whose Young Vic?', *Theatre Quarterly*, 9/34 (1979), 1–16.

12. Reviews of *The Tempest*: Michael Billington, *Guardian*, 29 Nov. 1978; Francis King, *Sunday Telegraph*, 3 Dec. 1978. Review of *Hamlet*: Colin Ludlow, 'Action Man Trilogy', *Plays and Players*, (Feb. 1979), 30–2.

13. Nick Ormerod in *Plays International* (Nov. 1988): quoted by Simon Reade, *Cheek by Jowl: Ten Years of Celebration* (Bath, 1991), 71. Comparable work has been done by other small-scale companies, notably Shared Experience (*Cymbeline*, 1981) and Kick Theatre Company (*King Lear*, *Measure for Measure*, and *The Tempest*). See Mike Alfreds and Clive Barker, 'Shared Experience: From Science Fiction to Shakespeare', *Theatre Quarterly*, 10/39 (1981), 12–22; Debbie Wolfe, 'Alive and Kicking' (article and interview with Kick's founder and director Deborah Warner), *Drama*, 4 (1985), 11–13.

14. Cordelia Oliver, 'Scotland', *Plays and Players* (July 1973), 67. For a review of the company's work, see Michael Coveney, *The Citz: 21 Years of the Glasgow Citizens' Theatre* (London, 1991).

15. Jonathan Miller, *Subsequent Performances* (London, 1986), 119.

16. Ibid. 107. The production is discussed by James C. Bulman in ch. 4 of his *Shakespeare in Performance: 'The Merchant of Venice'* (Manchester, 1991).

17. Miller, *Subsequent Performances*, 107.

18. Michael Billington, *The Modern Actor* (London, 1973), 83.

19. Ivor Brown, *Theatre, 1955–6*, 67.

20. Cordelia Oliver, 'Edinburgh 1', *Plays and Players* (Oct. 1973), 64–5. See also W. Stephen Gilbert, 'Prospect for the Future', in the same issue, pp. 24–7.

21. Charles Marowitz, *Confessions of a Counterfeit Critic* (London, 1973), 150–1.

22. Billington, *The Modern Actor*, 83; Philip Hope-Wallace, review of *Hamlet* in the *Manchester Guardian*, 18 Feb. 1969.

23. On Hall's production, see Stanley Wells, *Royal Shakespeare: Four Major Productions at Stratford-upon-Avon* (Manchester, 1977), ch. 2.

24. John Russell Brown, *Shakespeare's Plays in Performance* (Harmondsworth, 1969), 184.

25. 'Cliff to his Jimmy Porter…', *Observer*, 9 Oct. 1960, quoted by Jill L. Levenson, *Shakespeare in Performance: 'Romeo and Juliet'* (Manchester, 1987), 97–8.

26. Laurence Kitchin, *Drama in the Sixties: Form and Interpretation* (London, 1966), 161; *Plays and Players* (Nov. 1960), quoted by Levenson, *Shakespeare in Performance*, 97.

27. See Cicely Berry, *The Actor and his Text* (London, 1977).

28. John Goodwin (ed.), *Peter Hall's Diaries: The Story of a Dramatic Battle* (London, 1983), 302.

29. Coveney, *The Citz*, 161–2.

30. On *An Othello*: John Burgess, 'Charles Marowitz Directs *An Othello*', *Theatre Quarterly*, 2/8 (1972), 68–77. Marowitz's Shakespeare texts are among the plays examined in Ruby Cohn's *Modern Shakespeare Offshoots* (Princeton, 1976).

Further Reading

General

Dennis Bartholmeusz, *'Macbeth' and the Players* (Cambridge, 1969).

—— *The Winter's Tale in Performance in England and America, 1611–1976* (Cambridge, 1982).

John Gross, *Shylock* (London, 1992).

Tori Haring-Smith, *From Farce to Metadrama: A Stage History of 'The Taming of the Shrew', 1593–1983* (London, 1985).

Wilhelm Hortmann, *Shakespeare on the German Stage. The Twentieth Century* (Cambridge, 1998).

Margaret Lamb, *'Antony and Cleopatra' on the English Stage* (London, 1980).

Toby Lelyveld, *Shylock on the Stage* (London, 1961).

Raymond Mander and Joe Mitchenson, *Hamlet through the Ages: A Pictorial Record from 1709* (2nd edn., London, 1955).

W. Moelwyn Merchant, *Shakespeare and the Artist* (London, 1959).

John Mills, *'Hamlet' on Stage. The Great tradition* (Westport, Conn., and London, 1985).

Allardyce Nicoll, *A History of the English Drama 1600–1900*, 6 vols. (Cambridge, 1952–9).

George C. D. Odell, *Shakespeare from Betterton to Irving*, 2 vols. (New York, 1920).

Plays in Performance: editions recording details from productions: *King Lear*, ed. Jacqueline Bratton (Bristol, 1987); *Othello*, ed. Julie Hankey (Bristol, 1987); *Richard III*, ed. Julie Hankey (London, 1981).

Marvin Rosenberg, *The Masks of Othello* (Berkeley, 1961).

—— *The Masks of King Lear* (Berkeley, 1972).

—— *The Masks of Macbeth* (Berkeley, 1978).

—— *The Masks of Hamlet* (Newark, Del., 1992).

Gāmini Salgādo (ed.), *Eyewitnesses of Shakespeare: First Hand Accounts of Performances, 1590–1890* (London, 1975).

Shakespeare in Performance: studies of individual plays (Manchester, in progress); titles so far published include Roger Warren, *Cymbeline* (1989), James C. Bulman, *The Merchant of Venice* (1991), Jill L. Levenson, *Romeo and Juliet* (1987), Alan C. Dessen, *Titus Andronicus* (1989).

John Ripley, *'Julius Caesar' on Stage in England and America, 1599–1973* (Cambride, 1980).

—— *'Coriolanus' on Stage in England and America* (Madison, NJ, 1998).

Shakespeare in Production (continues the series *Plays in Performance*, under the general editorship of J. S. Bratton and Julie Hankey, published by Cambridge University Press.) So far published: *Hamlet* (Robert Hapgood), *A Misummer Night's Dream* (Trevor Griffiths), *Much Ado about Nothing* (John F. Cox), *The Tempest* (Christine Dymkowski).

Charles H. Shattuck, *The Shakespeare Promptbooks: A Descriptive Catalogue* (Urbana, Ill., 1965).

—— *Shakespeare on the American Stage*, 2 vols. (London, 1976–87).

Robert Speaight, *Shakespeare on the Stage* (London, 1973).

Sprague, A. C., *Shakespeare and the Actors: The Stage Business in his Plays, 1660–1905* (Cambridge, Mass., 1944).

—— *Shakespearian Players and Performances* (Cambridge, Mass., 1955).

—— *Shakespeare's Histories: Plays for the Stage* (London, 1964).

Alden T. Vaughan and Virginia Mason Vaughan, *Shakespeare's Caliban. A Cultural History* (Cambridge, 1991).

Virginia Mason Vaughan, *'Othello', a Contextual History* (Cambridge, 1995).

Stanley Wells (ed.), *Shakespeare in the Theatre. An Anthology of Criticism* (Oxford, 1997).

Gary J. Williams, *Our Moonlight Revels. A Misummer Night's Dream in the Theatre* (Iowa City, 1994).

Shakespeare's own time to the Restoration

Leeds Barroll, *Politics, Plague, and Shakespeare's Theatre: The Stuart Years* (Ithaca, 1991).

Gerald Eades Bentley, *The Jacobean and Caroline Stage*, 7 vols. (Oxford, 1941–68).

—— *The Profession of Player in Shakespeare's Time, 1590–1642* (Princeton, 1984).

M. C. Bradbrook, *The Rise of the Common Player* (Cambridge, 1962).

Douglas Bruster, *Drama and the Market in the Age of Shakespeare* (Cambridge, 1992).

Neil Carson, *A Companion to Henslowe's Diary* (Cambridge, 1988).

E. K. Chambers, *The Elizabethan Stage*, 4 vols. (Oxford, 1923).

—— *William Shakespeare: A Study of Facts and Problems*, 2 vols. (Oxford, 1930).

John D. Cox and David Scott Kastan (eds.), *A New History of Early English Drama* (New York, 1997).

Alan C. Dessen, *Elizabethan Stage Conventions and Modern Interpreters* (Cambridge, 1984).

Richard Dutton, *Mastering the Revels: The Regulation and Censorship of English Renaissance Drama* (London, 1991).

R. A. Foakes, *Illustrations of the English Stage 1580–1642* (London, 1985).

—— and R. T. Rickert (ed.), *Henslowe's Diary* (Cambridge, 1961).

Andrew Gurr, *Playgoing in Shakespeare's London* (Cambridge, 1987).

—— *The Shakespearean Stage, 1574–1642* (3rd edn., Cambridge, 1992).

—— *The Shakespearean Playing Companies* (Oxford, 1998).

—— and Mariko Ichikawa, *Staging in Shakespeare's Theatre* (Oxford, 2000).

Michael Hattaway, *Elizabethan Popular Theatre* (London, 1982).

T. J. King, *Shakespearean Staging, 1599–1642* (Cambridge, Mass., 1971).

Roslyn Lander Knutson, *The Repertory of Shakespeare's Company* (Fayetteville, Ark., 1991).

Steven Mullaney, *The Place of the Stage: License, Play, and Power in Renaissance England* (Chicago, 1988).

John Orrell, *The Quest for Shakespeare's Globe* (Cambridge, 1983).

Carol Rutter (ed.), *Documents of the Rose Playhouse* (Manchester, 1984; revised ed., 1999).

Ann Pasternak Slater, *Shakespeare the Director* (Brighton, 1982).

Keith Sturgess, *Jacobean Private Theatre* (London, 1987).

Gary Taylor and John Jowett, *Shakespeare Reshaped, 1606–1623* (Oxford, 1993).

Peter Thomson, *Shakespeare's Theatre* (London, 1983).

—— *Shakespeare's Professional Career* (Cambridge, 1992).

Glynne Wickham, Hubert Berry, and William Ingram (eds.), *Theatre in Europe: A Documentary History. English Professional Theatre, 1530–1660* (Cambridge, 2000)

The Restoration and eighteenth century

Emmett L. Avery *et al.*, *The London Stage, 1660–1800*, 5 pts. in 11 vols. (Carbondale, Ill., 1960–8).

Kalman A. Burnim, *David Garrick, Director* (Pittsburgh, 1961; repr. Carbondale, Ill., 1973).

Sandra Clark (ed.), *Shakespeare Made Fit. Restoration Adpations of Shakespeare* (London, 1997).

Christian Deelman, *The Great Shakespeare Jubilee* (London, 1964).

Michael Dobson, *The Making of the National Poet: Shakespeare, Adaptation, and Authorship, 1660–1769* (Oxford, 1992).

David Garrick, *Letters*, ed. D. M. Little and G. M. Kahrl, 3 vols. (London, 1963).

Philip H. Highfill, K. A. Burnim, and E. A. Langhans, *A Biographical Dictionary of Actors, Actresses, Musicians, Dancers, Managers and other Stage Personnel in London, 1660–1800*, 12 vols. (Carbondale, Ill., 1973–91).

Charles Beecher Hogan, *Shakespeare in the Theatre: 1701–1800*, 2 vols. (Oxford, 1952–7).

Peter Holland, *The Ornament of Action: Text and Performance in Restoration Comedy* (Cambridge, 1979).

Leslie Hotson, *The Commonwealth and Restoration Stage* (Cambridge, Mass., 1928).

Elizabeth Howe, *The First English Actresses: Women and Drama, 1660–1700* (Cambridge, 1992).

Ian McIntyre, *Garrick* (London: Viking, 1999).

Jean Marsden, *The Re-Imagined Text: Shakespeare Adaptation and Eighteenth–century Literary Theory* (Lexington, Ky., 1995).

Judith Milhous, *Thomas Betterton and the Management of Lincoln's Inn Fields, 1695–1708* (Carbondale, Ill., 1979).

Allardyce Nicoll, *The Garrick Stage: Theatres and Audience in the Eighteenth Century* (Manchester, 1980).

H. W. Pedicord and F. L. Bergmann (eds.), *The Plays of David Garrick*, vols. iii–iv, *Garrick's Adaptations of Shakespeare* (Carbondale, Ill., 1981).

Cecil Price, *Theatre in the Age of Garrick* (London, 1973).

Gunnar Sorelius, *'The Giant Race Before the Flood': Pre-Restoration Drama on the Stage and in the Criticism of the Restoration* (Uppsala, 1966).

Christopher Spencer (ed.), *Davenant's Macbeth from the Yale Manuscript* (New Haven, 1961).

—— *Five Restoration Adaptations of Shakespeare* (Urbana, Ill., 1965).

George Winchester Stone, Jr., and George M. Kahrl, *David Garrick: A Critical Biography* (Carbondale, Ill., 1979).

David Thomas (ed.), *Theatre in Europe: A Documentary History: Restoration and Georgian England, 1660–1788* (Cambridge, 1989).

John Harold Wilson, *All the King's Ladies: Actresses of the Restoration* (Chicago, 1958).

The Romantic, Victorian, and Edwardian periods

Shirley S. Allen, *Samuel Phelps and Sadler's Wells Theatre* (Middletown, Conn., 1971).

Herschel Baker, *John Philip Kemble: The Actor in his Theatre* (Cambridge, Mass., 1942).

Jonathan Bate, *Shakespearean Constitutions: Politics, Theatre, Criticism 1730–1830* (Oxford, 1989).

—— (ed.), *The Romantics on Shakespeare* (London, 1992).

Michael M. Booth, *Victorian Spectacular Theatre, 1850–1910* (London, 1981).

Carole Jones Carlisle, *Helen Faucit: Fire and Ice on the Victorian Stage* (London, 2000).

Harold Child, *The Shakespearean Productions of John Philip Kemble* (London, 1935).

J. W. Cole, *The Life and Theatrical Times of Charles Kean, F.S.A.*, 2 vols. (London, 1859).

Joseph W. Donohue, Jr., *Dramatic Character in the English Romantic Age* (Princeton, 1970).

—— *Theatre in the Age of Kean* (Oxford, 1975).

Alan S. Downer, *The Eminent Tragedian: William Charles Macready* (Cambridge, Mass., 1966).

Christine Dymkovski, *Harley Granville-Barker: A Preface to Modern Theatre* (Washington, 1986).

Theodor Fontane, *Shakespeare in the London Theatre 1855–58*, translated with an introduction and notes by Russell Jackson (London, 1999).

Richard Foulkes (ed.), *Shakespeare and the Victorian Stage* (Cambridge, 1986).

William Hazlitt, *A View of the English Stage* (London, 1818); repr. in vol. v of his *Complete Works*, ed. P. P. Howe (London, 1930–4).

H. N. Hillebrand, *Edmund Kean* (New York, 1933).

Alan Hughes, *Henry Irving, Shakespearean* (Cambridge, 1981).

Leigh Hunt, *Dramatic Criticism, 1808–1831*, ed. L. H. and C. W. Houtchens (New York, 1949).

Dennis Kennedy, *Granville-Barker and the Dream of Theatre* (Cambridge, 1985).

George Henry Lewes, *On Actors and the Art of Acting* (London, 1875).

William Charles Macready, *Reminiscences, and Selections from his Diaries and Letters*, ed. Sir Frederick Pollock, 2 vols. (London, 1875).

Roger Manvell, *Sarah Siddons: Portrait of an Actress* (London, 1970).

Cary Mazer, *Shakespeare Refashioned: Elizabethan Plays on Edwardian Stages* (Ann Arbor, 1981).

Henry Morley, *The Journal of a London Playgoer*, ed. Michael R. Booth (Leicester, 1974).

Richard W. Schoch, *Shakespeare's Victorian Stage. Performing History in the Theatre of Charles Kean* (Cambridge, 1998).

George Bernard Shaw, *On Shakespeare*, ed. Edwin Wilson (Harmondsworth, 1969).

Robert Speaight, *William Poel and the Elizabethan Revival* (London, 1954).

Stanley Wells (ed.), *Nineteenth-Century Shakespeare Burlesques*, 5 vols. (London, 1977–8).

Since 1914

John Barton, *Playing Shakespeare* (London, 1984).

—— and Peter Hall, *The Wars of the Roses* (London, 1970).

Cicely Berry, *The Actor and his Text* (London, 1987).

Ralph Berry, *On Directing Shakespeare: Interviews with Contemporary Directors* (2nd edn., London, 1989).

Michael Billington, *Peggy Ashcroft 1907–1991* (London, 1991).

Michael Bogdanov and Michael Pennington, *The English Shakespeare Company: The Story of 'The Wars of the Roses' 1986–1989* (London, 1990).

Susan Brock and Marian J. Pringle, *The Shakespeare Memorial Theatre, 1919–1945* (Cambridge, 1984).

Philip Brockbank, Russell Jackson, Robert Smallwood (eds.), *Players of Shakespeare*, 4 vols. (Cambridge, 1985–1998).

Jonathan Carole, *Gielgud. A Theatrical Life* (London, 2000).

Peter Brook, *The Empty Space* (London, 1968, repr. Harmondsworth, 1972).

—— *The Shifting Point* (London, 1988).

John Russell Brown, *Shakespeare's Plays in Performance* (London, 1966).

—— *Free Shakespeare* (London, 1974).

Claire Cochrane, *Shakespeare and the Birmingham Repertory Theatre 1913–1929* (London, 1993).

Gordon Crosse, *Shakespearean Playgoing, 1890–1952* (London, 1953).

Richard David, *Shakespeare in the Theatre* (Cambridge, 1978).

Anthony Holden, *Olivier* (London, 1988).

Graham Holderness (ed.), *The Shakespeare Myth* (Manchester, 1988).

Peter Holland, *English Shakespeares: Shakespeare on the English Stage in the 1990s* (Cambridge, 1997).

Dennis Kennedy, *Looking at Shakespeare: A Visual History of Twentieth-Century Performance* (Cambridge, 1993).

Jonathan Miller, *Subsequent Performances* (London, 1986).

George Rowell, *The Old Vic Theatre: A History* (Cambridge, 1993).

Carol Rutter *et al.*, *Clamorous Voices* (London, 1988).

David Selbourne, *The Making of A Midsummer Night's Dream: An Eyewitness Account of Peter Brook's Production from First Rehearsal to First Night* (London, 1982).

Shakespeare Quarterly: annual reviews of productions (in progress, since 1950).

Shakespeare Survey: annual accounts of Shakespeare on stage in London and Stratford-upon-Avon (in progress, since 1948).

Robert Shaughhessy, *Representing Shakespeare. England, History and the RSC* (Hemel Hepstead, 1994).

Antony Sher, *The Year of the King* (London, 1985).

Donald Spoto, *Laurence Olivier: A Life* (London, 1992).

J. L. Styan, *The Shakespeare Revolution: Criticism and Performance in the Twentieth Century* (Cambridge, 1977).

J. C. Trewin, *Shakespeare on the English Stage, 1900–1964* (London, 1964).

Kenneth Tynan, *A View of the English Stage 1944–63* (London, 1975).

Roger Warren, *Staging Shakespeare's Late Plays* (Oxford, 1990).

Stanley Wells, *Royal Shakespeare: Four Major Productions at Stratford-upon-Avon* (Manchester, 1977).

Index